Library of
Davidson College

SELF-FULFILLING PROPHECIES
READERSHIP AND AUTHORITY
IN THE FIRST
ROMAN DE LA ROSE

SELF-FULFILLING PROPHECIES

READERSHIP AND AUTHORITY IN THE FIRST *ROMAN DE LA ROSE*

DAVID F. HULT

Department of French
The Johns Hopkins University

CAMBRIDGE UNIVERSITY PRESS

Cambridge
London   New York   New Rochelle
Melbourne   Sydney

Published by the Press Syndicate of the University of Cambridge
The Pitt Building, Trumpington Street, Cambridge CB2 1RP
32 East 57th Street, New York, NY 10022, USA
10 Stamford Road, Oakleigh, Melbourne 3166, Australia

© Cambridge University Press 1986

First published 1986

Printed in the United States of America

Library of Congress Cataloging in Publication Data
Hult, David F., 1952–
Self-fulfilling prophecies.
Includes index.
1. Guillaume, de Lorris, fl. 1230. Roman de la Rose.
I. Title.
PQ1529.H85   1986   841'.1   85-16649

British Library Cataloguing in Publication Data
Hult, David F.
Self-fulfilling prophecies : readership and
authority in the first Roman de la rose.
1. Roman de la rose
I. Title
841'.03'09   PQ1528

ISBN 0 521 32014 3

For El and Florence

Contents

List of illustrations	*page* ix
Acknowledgments	xi
Note on texts and translations	xiv

HORS TEXTE   1

ONE
THE SPECTRAL AUTHOR

Jean de Meun and the authorship of the *Roman de la Rose*	10
The medieval author	25
The literary work in the Middle Ages	64
Medieval text/modern reader	93

TWO
THE NARRATION OF ALLEGORY

Allegory and incompletion	105
The prologue: dreams and their significance	114
The prologue: the authority of writing	127
Autobiographical prophecy: gates of horn or gates of ivory?	137
The allegory of incompletion	160
An allegory of love	175

THREE
LYRIC AND ROMANCE

The genres of courtly literature	186
The lyric *Rose*	208
Corpus Dominæ	250

FOUR
NARCISSUS AND THE ALLEGORICAL FOUNTAIN

Narcissus, Echo, and the Rose	263
Allegorical fountain or fountain of allegory?	283
Reversed perspectives	291

POSTSCRIPT	301
Name and title index	317
Topical index	320

List of illustrations

1. Author at his desk. British Library Ms. 20. A. XVII, Fol. 35v°. Reprinted by permission of the British Library. page 79
2. Author at his desk. Cambridge University Library Ms. Gg 4.6, Fol. 30r°. Reprinted by permission of the Syndics of Cambridge University Library. 80
3. Guillaume de Lorris and Jean de Meun at desks writing. British Library Ms. Stowe 947, Fol. 30v°. Reprinted by permission of the British Library. 81
4. Author at his desk. Bibliothèque Nationale Ms. Fr. 19153, Fol. 31r°. Phot. Bibl. nat. Paris. 82
5. Author at his desk. British Library Ms. Harley 4425, Fol. 127r°. Reprinted by permission of the British Library. 83
6. Scribes at work. Bibliothèque Nationale Ms. Fr. 25526, Fol. 77v°. Phot. Bibl. nat. Paris. 84
7. Author at his desk. Beinecke Rare Book and Manuscript Library, Yale University, Ms. 418, Fol. 151. 85
8. Author at his desk. Bodleian Library, Oxford University, Ms. E. Museo 65, Fol. 30v°. 85
9. Guillaume de Lorris passing book to Jean de Meun. Bibliothèque Nationale Ms. Fr. 1569, Fol. 68v°. Phot. Bibl. nat. Paris. 86
10. Author reading text to a crowd; Lover in bed, Dangier standing to one side. Bibliothèque Nationale Ms. Fr. 1569, Fol. 1r°. Phot. Bibl. nat. Paris. 87
11. Author at his desk. Bibliothèque Nationale Ms. Fr. 1569, Fol 28r°. Phot. Bibl. nat. Paris. 88

Qui aquestz digz estiers enten,
si mielhs hi dis, non lo·n repren,
quar s'a trops sens una razos,
mout m'es mieller quan quecx es bos.
(anonymous *devinalh*)

Canchon, va t'ent [. . .]
(Richard de Fournival, XIII, 33)

Acknowledgments

The writing and rewriting of this book go back many years and I have, accordingly, incurred many debts. Some important sections of Chapter Two have been taken from my 1977 Cornell University dissertation, but the book as a whole took shape as a separate project and was largely written between January 1980 and July 1982. The greater portion of Chapter Four appeared as "The Allegorical Fountain: Narcissus in the *Roman de la Rose*," *Romanic Review,* Vol. 72, No. 2 (March 1981), 125–48. I am grateful to the Trustees of Columbia University for granting me permission to reprint much of this article. A section of Chapter One was translated into French and published under the title "Gui de Mori, lecteur médiéval," *Incidences* (Université d'Ottawa), Nouvelle série, Vol. V, No. 1 (Jan.–April 1981), 53–70. My warm thanks to Yvan Lepage for asking me to contribute to this issue.

It is a great pleasure to thank a handful of teachers and fellow students who many years ago helped guide my formation as a medievalist and a literary critic: Joe Duggan, Josué Harari, Phil Lewis, Giuseppe Mazzotta, Manfred Sandmann, David Savran, Pete Wetherbee, and Carol Zuses. Several friends and colleagues at Yale provided encouragement, support, and well-needed criticism through the most difficult periods of writing: Elizabeth Archibald, John Boswell, Gérard Defaux, Shoshana Felman, Ann Higgins, Chuck Porter, Fred Robinson, and Jim Schultz. Ralph Sarkonak goaded me through the project in more ways than one. A special debt of gratitude and friendship is due Claire Nouvet for an exciting, and I hope ongoing, dialogue. I thank Paul Zumthor for inviting a young medievalist to present some evolving ideas on the *Roman de la Rose* at the Seventh Annual Colloquium of the Medieval Institute of the Université de Montréal in April 1980.

Howard Bloch and Michel Zink were generous enough to read large portions of the manuscript and offer welcome commentary. The final shape of the manuscript has benefited greatly from the comments of Wilda Anderson, Sylvia Huot, and an anonymous

ACKNOWLEDGMENTS

reader for the Press, whose abundant and insightful criticisms were heeded with as much critical acumen as I could muster. Physical preparation of the manuscript was facilitated by Anna Clarke and Kitty Letsch.

In final place, I must express my thanks and appreciation to Alice Colby-Hall, who has been with the project since its inception. Although certainly skeptical of many of my ideas, she has always listened patiently and with an open mind; her uncommon good sense has served as an important example, steering me away from many a philological pitfall.

Of the many personal friends I would like to mention, I single out Aldo, Pat, Kathy, and Ron, whose very special ties keep me on the right track. Thanks to Jed E. Rose for his unwitting help with the title.

I would like to acknowledge the assistance of the Humanities Council at Yale for grants under the Griswold fund, which enabled me to travel to several European libraries and to have the manuscript typed. A fellowship from the American Council of Learned Societies allowed me the free time in which to complete my writing. I am grateful to the staffs of the following libraries for granting me access to manuscript materials: Bibliothèque Nationale (Paris), Bibliothèque Municipale de Dijon, Bibliothèque Municipale d'Arras, Bibliothèque Municipale de Tournai (Belgium), Royal Library of Copenhagen, British Library (London), Bodleian Library (Oxford), Cambridge University Library, Fitzwilliam Museum (Cambridge), Biblioteca marciana (Venice), Vatican Library (Rome), Beinecke Rare Book Library (New Haven), and the Pierpont Morgan Library (New York). A special thanks to the courteous and helpful staff of the Institut de Recherche et d'Histoire des Textes in Paris for allowing me to take advantage of their card catalogues, microfilm resources, and library.

I would be ungrateful indeed were I not to mention three scholars whose works have been of central importance and without whose intellectual guidance the present study could not be: Paul Zumthor, Roger Dragonetti, and Hans Robert Jauss. In lieu of specific references that could, and should, extend to nearly every page of this essay, I here refer to the quite distinct ways in which they have influenced my thinking: Zumthor, for his careful erudition and his opening up of the Middle Ages to modern theoretical methodologies and modes of thought; Dragonetti, for his brilliant sensitivity to poetic language and metaphorical imagery; and Jauss, for his theoretical work on the intricacies of literary reception and tradition.

Two books that came to my attention only after the bulk of writing had been completed, or in the lengthy space thereafter, deserve mention. Maxwell Luria provides a good introduction to the *Rose* and critical problems surrounding the text intended for English-speaking audiences (with an excellent bibliography) in his *Reader's Guide to the Roman de la Rose* (Hamden, CT, 1982); and Jean Dufournet has recently edited a volume of essays on Guillaume de Lorris, the very appearance of which attests to the uniquely modern possibilities of the text's reception which I attempt to account for in the present essay: *Etudes sur le Roman de la Rose*, Collection Unichamp, 4 (Paris, 1984) (Contributions by Jean Batany, Emmanuèle Baumgartner, Eric Hicks, Georgette Kamenetz, Jean-Charles Payen and Armand Strubel).

Note on texts and translations

The edition of the *Roman de la Rose* used throughout is that prepared by Félix Lecoy for the Classiques Français du Moyen Age series, Volumes 92, 95, and 98 (Paris, 1965–70). References by line number are included in the text. Occasional reference to the discussions and variant readings of the formerly authoritative edition by Ernest Langlois (SATF, 5 Vols. [Paris, 1914–24]) is marked in the notes.

For the convenience of readers whose knowledge of Old French is limited or nonexistent, I have used Charles Dahlberg's mostly reliable and quite literal translation of the *Rose* (Princeton, 1971) as a basis for the English equivalents. Page references to this translation are provided in the text. There are occasional unacknowledged divergences between his translations and those included herein; they are in large measure due to three factors: textual differences between Lecoy and Langlois, the latter of which served as the basis for Dahlberg's translation; frequent license in Dahlberg's rendering of Old French verb tenses (see Chapter Two, Note 53); and special syntactic clarification required at certain moments of my exposition.

Italics for emphasis in the Old French passages and in the translations is mine, and I am responsible for all other translations of Old French and Latin, except where noted.

The quotations of the poet Richard de Fournival, which serve as a guide through every step of this study, are taken from the excellent and much needed new edition of his lyric works by Yvan G. Lepage, Publications médiévales de l'Université d'Ottawa, No. 7 (Ottawa, 1981).

Hors texte

τιμῶσα δὲ ἡ γραφὴ τὴν ἀλήθειαν καὶ δρόσου τι λείβει ἀπὸ τῶν ἀνθέων, οἷς καὶ μέλιττα ἐφιζάνει τις, οὐκ οἶδα εἴτ' ἐξαπατηθεῖσα ὑπὸ τῆς γραφῆς, εἴτε ἡμᾶς ἐξηπατῆσθαι χρὴ εἶναι αὐτήν. ἀλλ' ἔυιω.

The painting has such regard for realism that it even shows drops of dew dripping from the flowers and a bee settling on the flowers – whether a real bee has been deceived by the painted flowers or whether we are to be deceived into thinking that a painted bee is real, I do not know. But let that pass.
(Philostratus the Elder, *Eikones [Imagines]*, ed. and trans. Arthur Fairbanks, Loeb Classical Library [London, 1931], pp. 88–91)

The bee views the flower and we contemplate the bee viewing the flower. Presumably the flower is a painted image, but what about the bee? Where can one draw the line of representation? How do we know whether the bee belongs *in* the artistic frame or *outside* of it? This is not a simple question of *trompe l'oeil,* where the beholder cannot distinguish reality from illusion; Philostratus's intriguing description superimposes a further degree of illusionism, intercalating a second subjectivity whose own perception, whose own reality, we cannot be perfectly certain about. One solution would of course consist in the extension of one's hand, touching the painted bee or chasing the real bee, either of which would provide an assurance as to the artistic integrity of the painted surface. Such verification, however, is clearly not at issue: "Let that pass," declares Philostratus. A portion of the aesthetic experience that he has undertaken to describe with such care involves that unknowing speculation which follows upon an irreducible visual or verbal enigma.

That this detail forms a part of Philostratus's description of a painting of Narcissus is certainly not accidental, the latter being the mythological character par excellence who exemplifies the coincidence between visual illusion and inner speculation. As far as the fascinated query of the spectator (in this case, both Narcissus and ourselves) is concerned, Philostratus states quite clearly that the reflected image in the water cannot hear our questions and will provide no clues: "We must interpret the painting for ourselves." The illusion that works of art "give" us meaning is thereby dashed to the ground. At least four figures become caught in a web of self-enclosed aesthetic entrancement: the bee before the flower; Narcissus before his image; the beholder before the painting; and of course ourselves, as readers, before Philostratus's exercise in verbal rhetoric. A complex layering of subjectivities evokes the broader question of fictional involvement — the delimitation of any artistic work vis-à-vis its observer, the differentiation of a created, fictional interior from a creative, author-itative exterior. As Borges might add, in a further complication of Philostratus's ingenious enigma of fictional participation and penetration, we ourselves looking at Philostratus looking at the bee looking at the flower are conceivably the object of some other beholder, part of some grander figurative scheme.

Philostratus's description of an illusionistic theme which certainly had a long history in Greek aesthetic speculation is as subtle as it is seductive. His own attempt to translate visual painting into a rhetoric of description whose desired effect would be that of surpassing the primary visual medium offers an interesting comment on the limits (both the conceptual limitations and the physical boundaries) of representation. Whether the actual paintings he purports to describe ever in fact existed has occasioned considerable critical debate. An answer to the question is probably not even relevant since, as a large part of the above quotation suggests, we need not perceive or intuit the borderline between reality and imitation, be they contiguous as in Philostratus's painting, or extant at two successive moments in the form of model and copy. His refusal to mention actual painters in the *Imagines* lends support to this view, implying that his enterprise involves the "creation" of visual paintings by mere verbal allusion. In this way, the imitation of reality succeeds through the simplest and most unassailable technique of realistic representation — an insistence on the truth. Indeed, perhaps the greatest *trompe l'oeil* effect is the verbal insistence "This is true; this happened," which in fact "says" nothing but yet proves a sense of reality more than any visual portrayal ever could.

But Philostratus's query is not simply an arcane bit of rhetorical sophistry; rather it becomes one facet of a broader theme of aesthetic perception according to which, first, fictional barriers sometimes float more than we would like them to, and, second, a layering of superimposed subjectivities risks assuming the central focus of visual fascination. Aristotle (*Poetics*, Chapter IV [1448 b 5–17]) discussed the penchant for imitative activities (*mimèsis*) as a constitutive part of human behavior. We might, after Aristotle and with the added remarks of Philostratus, coin the term *homo mimeticus*, which would refer to man's pleasure in the creative process and, more specifically, to his fascination with the borderline of fictional works, be it realized as a mask, a painted surface, a mirror reflection or a verbal echo. Given this crucial aspect of man's aesthetic pleasure, it is probably unwise to expect all works of art to offer an evocation of some "reality" at the expense of their own illusionistic means; it would be equally neglectful to assert that art was in some way flatly equivalent to such illusionism. My point is, however, that aesthetic appreciations of whatever kind are neither ingenuous nor are they universally valid. The phrase that I have chosen for my title, "Self-Fulfilling Prophecies," is borrowed from the domain of psychology and describes that mechanism by which an individual "makes" supposedly unrelated events happen merely by wishing or expecting it to be so — especially when the outcome is one that the individual does not consciously desire. I would extend this expression beyond the realm of human comportment and submit that it functions as a general aesthetic principle, by which we know or feel something because we already "know" it, meaning that perception and knowledge are never innocent, "objective" faculties, but rather a function of the store of experiences that we have already accumulated. Furthermore, as Philostratus's verbal image strongly suggests, the inability to separate one's own visual impression from a total aesthetic effect (or the disinterest in attempting to do so) places illusionism squarely within the subjective critical eye. There is a kind of perverse fatality that leads artists and critics alike to strikingly foreseeable types of expression. It is this basic, interlocking conjunction of subjective experience with a kind of hermeneutic predestiny that serves as a recurring motif in the study that follows.

The Self-Fulfilling Prophecy of interpretation, predicated upon cultural and ideological presuppositions, is not uncommon in current literary discussions. However, the shape our fictions take (either through philological textual apparatus, canon formation, or genre determination) is usually relegated to another domain, as the objective side of our discipline. I would suggest, contrariwise, that this supposedly objective domain is itself subject to interpretive preconceptions but that they are kept carefully hidden in a modern culture that delineates and protects author and text alike. The early Middle Ages knows no such rigid classification, or at least deals with its classifications in a different way, and so offers an interesting proving ground for those deeply ingrained notions that we are hesitant to call into question (or incapable of doing so).

The thirteenth-century *Roman de la Rose* is one of the most significant literary contributions of the entire Middle Ages. From its extensive manuscript attestations, one can infer that it was the most widely read vernacular poem after the *Divine Comedy;* it is, moreover, the only major poem in the French tradition to have commanded a continuous readership from the Middle Ages to the present day (compare Marc-René Jung, "Der Rosenroman in der Kritik seit dem 18. Jahrhundert," *Romanische Forschungen,* 78 [1966], 203–52). It also has the distinction of being a composite work – text and continuation – by two separate authors, Guillaume de Lorris and Jean de Meun. The critical tradition has always taken cognizance of this fact and yet only rarely has it dealt with any of its implications, either with regard to the interpretation of the work itself (works themselves) or to its (their) inclusion in the literary canon – two pursuits that, as suggested by the quotation of Philostratus, are not quite so separate as one might think. If the relationship between art object and beholder is always a complex one, then this is all the more true when hundreds of years separate a work from its audience. One must take account not only of linguistic and semantic changes, but also of broad cultural shifts arising within the literary domain itself.

The study that follows started out as a simple reading of the poem attributed to Guillaume de Lorris, the first *Roman de la Rose*. It became immediately apparent, however, that this "simple" undertaking was complicated by a number of historical factors related to the nature of the poem's composition and, more importantly, by its reception through the intervening centuries. The influence of tradition can be nefarious when its dictates extend to the irresponsible partition, dismemberment, or even obliteration of a text in the name of philological accuracy; successive generations of readers accept these findings, thus consecrated by literary histories, and assume that it could be no other way. In such cases, rather than an accretion of learned commentary, as was the patristic philological ideal, the situation turns to one of palimpsest, where the original is rubbed out and covered over by writing of a different sort. Is this "writing," we may ask, an integral part of the textual reality or a function of the artistic illusion?

For specific reasons that will be treated more fully in Chapter One, Guillaume de Lorris's *Rose* has always been accepted as a fragmentary, unfinished work, obligingly completed four decades later by the verbose and erudite Jean de Meun. From the time of Jean, the composite has invariably been viewed as *one* poem with a more or less single poetic vision. Even those critics who consider that Guillaume and Jean are ideologically and artistically opposed do not go very far with Guillaume, acting on the assumption that his poem was never completed as he intended. A small handful of critics have timidly suggested that Guillaume's *Rose* might be complete as it stands, but for lack of a clear methodological or historical justification, the "suggestion" has not gone much further: Perhaps first in line, Edmond Faral proposed that the taking of the castle might destroy the poem's delicacy ("Le *Roman de la Rose* et la pensée française au XIIIe siècle," *Revue des deux mondes,* 35 [1926], 430–57); Rita Lejeune ("A propos de la structure du *Roman de la Rose* de Guillaume de Lorris," in *Etudes . . . Félix Lecoy* [Paris, 1973], 315–48), and Daniel Poirion (*Le Roman de la Rose* [Paris, 1973],

p. 60) have both reiterated the appropriateness of such a possibility without considering any of the implications, either with regard to literary history or poetic interpretation. How indeed does one offer an interpretation of a fragment?

My working hypothesis in this study is as follows: I would like to propose that Guillaume's poem is a finished work, insofar as it can be seen to form an artistic whole consistent with stylistic and narrative standards of judgment as well as with medieval poetic traditions. A corollary to this view is the assertion that the philological "misreading" of Guillaume's text has resulted primarily from the perpetuation of Jean de Meun's reading and interpretation of his predecessor's text — in sum, a straightforward example of critical myopia. The reader should therefore not expect any reference to Jean de Meun outside of my preliminary chapter, and only minimal attention to those critical works that assume the two parts of the poem to be of one cloth; the absence of Paré and Gunn (whose work is seminal in this regard), and to a lesser extent Robertson and Fleming, should thus be attributed to a calculated omission on my part. A brief word about my own critical methodology: As is perhaps already clear — and will become increasingly so in the following pages — my study is greatly concerned with problems stemming from the *Rose*'s reception in the Middle Ages as well as by modern readers. In this regard, I have been primarily influenced by the work of Hans Robert Jauss, who has dealt widely and authoritatively with the transhistorical coordinates of textual reception as a central issue in the domain of hermeneutics. An increasingly broad corpus of critical works has been developing in the United States and Europe over the last fifteen years, commonly known under the rubric "reader-response criticism," and is well represented in two recent anthologies edited by Susan Suleiman and Inge Crosman (*The Reader in the Text* [Princeton, 1980]) and Jane P. Tompkins (*Reader-Response Criticism* [Baltimore, 1980]); they cover an extremely diverse cross-section of interests extending from psychological analyses of the actual reading process to theoretical questions of reader competence (involving the positing of an "ideal reader," "superreader," and so forth). Of the authors included therein, probably Stanley Fish treats problems most closely related to my own, but his formulations have been of little direct influence.

HORS TEXTE

Caveat lector: The following study is *not* an application of "reader-response" criticism to the *Rose*.

⁓

The most basic modern literary assumptions involve a rigid conceptual construct gravitating around the notions of authorship, intentionality, and literary reception – a construct that is not always sensitive to the differences that are operative in a remote culture such as that of the Middle Ages. The traditions of literary history can serve as a significant guidepost, but they can also blind us to factors that do not enter into more strict modern visions of textuality, inasmuch as they assume a minimum of material change from one context to the next. Chapter One of our study, "The Spectral Author," serves an introductory function, insofar as it attempts to investigate potential medieval views toward authorship and the relationship between writers of poems and their material production, a process that involved many more steps than we would like to think. The immediate purpose of this investigation is to construct a methodological basis for the study of Guillaume de Lorris, toward which it inevitably leads – a justification, in other words, for our separate treatment of the first *Roman de la Rose* as a discrete poem. The question of authorship refers us to the aesthetic and methodological quandary of where to place the frame. The further one penetrates into the inscrutable world of medieval poetic practice, frequently involving indistinguishable strokes of author, scribe, and continuator, the more one comes to realize that the reader's choice itself serves to place the frame in some cases. No such choice can be totally ingenuous, involving as it does preconceptions (literary, historical, ideological, poetic) which, tautologically, dictate their own result. First Self-Fulfilling Prophecy.

The second chapter, "The Narration of Allegory," studies the Narrator's acknowledged use of his poem as a poetic prophecy of sexual fulfillment through an investigation of the complicated grammatical and narrative structuring of the work; it discovers, further, that the text itself functions as an instrument of seduction destined to procure that same fulfillment. Two antagonistic tendencies, which I term "prophecy" and "autobiography," work at cross-purposes and eventually dissolve into a solitary voice of unrequited love-longing. The third chapter, "Lyric and Romance," elaborates the same tension through an investigation of Guillaume's most immediate literary influences, specifically the courtly genres of the lyric and the romance. By means of his continually shifting allegorical framework – the personified, and therefore fragmented, evocation of human behavior – Guillaume effects a fusion and, ultimately, a con-fusion between the two generic constructs. The final return to the voice of the lyric poet, abandoning the obfuscation created by the rhetorical mode of personification, substantiates the fundamental ineffability of human relations, their resistance to generalization or codification of any kind. Through both of these analyses, we are called upon to observe a Self-Fulfilling Prophecy at another level, the inadvertent return to a humble position of request and unrequited longing – a failure that is, ultimately, part and parcel of Guillaume's poetic construct.

Once one understands that Guillaume's poem works as a text of seduction, one that attempts to elicit an appropriate response from its reader, then one can see that seduction works on (at least) two levels. The most obvious is, of course, the seduction of the Lady, but the other, no less significant, is the seduction of the reader, the call to contemplate, to perpetuate, and possibly to continue the poetic journey. The unfinished ending, the jagged edge, can be seen as part of a sophisticated rhetorical strategy calculated to oblige a continuation. The outward-turning structure of reception is already internalized in the work, most notably through the central figure of Narcissus, which serves as the focus of our fourth chapter, "Narcissus and the Allegorical Fountain." Our methodological queries on medieval authorship and textuality in Chapter One find their poetic reason in an internalized strategy of question and answer, text and response. The outward-turning aesthetic vision, the final Self-Fulfilling Prophecy, is the endlessly circular path of creation and reception, the very essence of poetic tradition. Like the painting of Philostratus, Guillaume has created an elaborate *trompe l'oeil* situation, a layering of subjectivities that we would like to touch in order to verify, but that we unfortunately cannot, due to the nature of the object. Guillaume's *trompe l'oeil is* the unfinished edge that itself becomes a part of what is from another point of view a completed masterpiece.

There is thus a way in which Guillaume's poem calls for the continuation of Jean de Meun. We should not be surprised, therefore, that generations of readers have frequently admired the artistry of Guillaume while feeling the need to include Jean's lengthy appendage. Guillaume's *Rose* is a poetic jewel, and as with other objects of pure beauty, it calls for stupefied admiration. There is something significant about the historical fact that Guillaume's poem could not survive without a continuation, that is, without some response which in some way reduces or violates its fragile beauty. The question of response is equally characteristic of the paradoxical nature of the critical discourse, which necessarily speaks *about* beauty, but which can never be beauty itself.

The relation between Jean and Guillaume offers a layering of subjectivities at least as complex as Philostratus's image of the bee and the flower: the reader reading Jean reading Guillaume dreaming of a rose quest. But whereas, for Philostratus, verification was within arm's reach, we can never touch the surface of this far-off literary creation. Where to draw the line of fiction? Perhaps, ideally, we should be able to echo Philostratus's luxuriant "let it pass," but for the moment our task is a more basic and reductive one: We must attempt to discover, through the overgrown jungle of a long critical tradition, the contours of this complicated literary palimpsest and perhaps we will resurface with a lost masterpiece once again ready for the contemplation of a more supernal critical vision.

ONE

The spectral author

> Je mais cis sons n'ert oïs
> se ma dame ne l'otroie,
> C'onques riens ne dis ne ne fis
> Qui sans son congié soit mais canté.
> (Richard de Fournival, X, 57–60)

> L'impression est aux manuscrits ce que le théâtre est aux femmes, elle met en lumière les beautés et les défauts; elle tue aussi bien qu'elle fait vivre [. . .]. (Balzac, *Illusions perdues*)

JEAN DE MEUN AND THE AUTHORSHIP OF THE *ROMAN DE LA ROSE*

After several thousand lines of rhymed octosyllabic couplets that recount an involved allegorical/didactic tale, the patient reader of the *Roman de la Rose* comes across a most peculiar and fascinating discussion of the poem's authorship.[1] Amor, the seemingly all-powerful god of love, has finally decided to participate actively in the Lover's protracted quest to gain access to his beloved rose. In the course of delivering a rallying speech to his assembled barons, Amor calls the attention of listener and reader alike to the identity of the utterly helpless, *heretofore unnamed* Lover:

> Vez ci Guillaume de Lorriz,
> cui Jalousie, sa contraire,
> fet tant d'angoisse et de deul traire
> qu'il est en perill de morir.   (10496–9)

(Here is Guillaume de Lorris, whose opponent, Jealousy, brings him so much anguish and sorrow that he is in danger of dying. [p. 187])

According to Amor, however, considerably more is at stake than the simple seizure of Jalousie's castle: One facet of Guillaume's duty, part and parcel of the feudal oath that he has

---

[1] For an excellent general introduction to problems of interpretation in the *Roman de la Rose*, see Daniel Poirion, *Le Roman de la Rose* (Paris, 1973).

pledged and reconfirmed to Amor, will consist in his later creation of a romance based on the dream experience — in fact the very romance we are in the process of reading:

> Et plus oncor me doit servir,
> car por ma grace deservir
> doit il conmancier le romant
> ou seront mis tuit mi conmant.   (10517–20)
>
> (He should serve me still more, for, to merit my grace, he is to begin the romance in which all my commandments will be set down. [p. 187])

What appears at first sight to be a rather straightforward example of literary self-consciousness reveals further complications as we discover that Guillaume will not live to finish his poem.[2] In fact, the final six lines of Guillaume's allegedly fragmentary poem are at this point dutifully quoted by Amor:

> ... jusque la le *fornira*
> ou il a Bel Acueill *dira,*
>   ...
> "Mout *sui* durement esmaiez
> que *entroubliez* ne m'*aiez,*
> si en *ai* deul et desconfort,
> ja mes n'*iert* riens qui me *confort*
> se je *per* vostre bienveillance,
> car je n'*ai* mes ailleurs fiance."   (10521–30)
>
> (He *will finish* it up to the point where he *will say* to Fair Welcoming ... "I *am* terribly afraid that you *may have forgotten* me, and I *am* in sorrow and pain. If I *lose* your good will, there *will* never *be* any comfort for me, since I *have* no confidence elsewhere." [p. 187])

Now, insofar as we are dealing here with an explicit quotation, demarcated by the verb "dira" on line 10522, as well as a general

---

2 The self-conscious pose of the literary artist, clearly a *topos* already in classical times, becomes a hallmark of romance and lyric composition after the twelfth century. The reader is referred to the important catalogue by Ulrich Mölk, *Französische Literarästhetik des 12. und 13. Jahrhunderts: Prologe-Exkurse-Epiloge,* Sammlung Romanischer Ubungstexte, 54 (Tubingen, 1969). E. R. Curtius studies the wider development of this *topos* from classical times in his *European Literature and the Latin Middle Ages,* trans. Willard R. Trask (New York, 1953), pp. 305–32, 468–73, 476–7 and 485–6.

shift from future to present tense, we should expect to find these lines (10525–30) repeated elsewhere in the poem, either later (prospectively) or earlier (retrospectively).³ While a prospective quotation would seem the most likely in view of Amor's decidedly prophetic stance – the larger part of his discourse is framed in the future tense – the quotation, in point of fact, proves to be retrospective. A bit of detective work, or a very good memory, tells us that lines 10525–30, quoted above, repeat verbatim a previous part of the poem, lines 4023–8. Not only does Amor prophesy the future death of the author of the poem that we are reading, while standing *in front of* that author's fictional persona, but he also articulates the paradox of the reader having proceeded farther than the alleged end of the Poet's fragmented work. Any reader of fiction, even if his own activity is situated after the historical death of an author, implicitly assumes, nonetheless, that he is following or retracing the author's purported writing of the fiction. He posits, in other words, a fictional authorial voice (not to be confused with that of the Narrator) that in a sense "speaks" the text.⁴ He assumes that, for want of a notation to the contrary, *some* living individual had to write the poem and bring it to a conclusion. Amor's paradox serves to pull the rug out from under the reader, thereby dislocating his typical expectations, by telling him that whatever he is reading, it is not a product of the unified voice that he has assumed all along. Moreover, as a fictional strategy, the perplexing revelation incites the reader, at present exceedingly involved in the story's development, to emit a quizzical response: Who, he ought to ask himself, wrote the text that is being read at line 10534 (a text which idiosyncratically permits itself to stress its own otherness through the very act of quotation), along with the preceding 6,500 lines if, as has been asserted, Guillaume de Lorris discontinued writing at line 4028?

---

3 One early editor of the *Roman de la Rose*, Lenglet du Fresnoy (and not a few medieval scribes), assumed that the quotation was *simultaneous*. In other words, he situated the death of Guillaume de Lorris, and therefore the breaking off of his poetic fragment, at the moment of Amor's eulogistic speech.

4 Wayne Booth, *The Rhetoric of Fiction* (Chicago, 1961), esp. pp. 70–7 (the "implied author"); Lucien Dällenbach (*Le Récit spéculaire* [Paris, 1977], pp. 100–1) has recently suggested replacing the term "auteur implicite" by the depersonalized "instance productrice."

Happily, Amor wastes no time in alleviating the reader's pangs of curiosity:

> Puis vendra Johans Chopinel,
> au cuer jolif, au cors inel,
> qui nestra seur Laire a Meün,
> . . .
> Cist avra le romanz si chier
> qu'il le voudra tout parfenir,
> se tens et leus l'en peut venir,
> car quant Guillaumes cessera,
> Jehans le continuera,
> enprés sa mort, que je ne mante,
> anz trespassez plus de .XL.   (10535–7, 10554–60)

(Then will come Jean Chopinel with gay heart and lively body. He will be born at Meung-sur-Loire; . . . He will be so fond of the romance that he will want to finish it right to the end, if time and place can be found. For when Guillaume shall cease, more than forty years after his death – may I not lie – Jean will continue it. . . [pp. 187–8])

More than forty years after the death of Guillaume prophesied above, another writer named "Johans Chopinel . . . [de] Meün" will come to continue ("continuera") and end ("parfenir") the romance. Amor, with his accustomed precision, includes a parallel quotation (10565–6), again introduced by the verb "dira," which specifies the two first lines of Jean's alleged continuation.[5] These lines do indeed repeat lines 4029–30, those that earlier in the poem immediately follow the final words attributed to Guillaume. To summarize the somewhat complicated narrative situation at

---

5   Jehans le continuera . . .
    et dira por la mescheance,
    par poor de desesperance
    qu'il n'ait de Bel Acueill perdue
    la bienvoillance avant eüe:
    "Et si l'ai je perdue, espoir,
    a poi que ne m'en desespoir,"
    et toutes les autres paroles . . .   (10558–67)

(Jean will continue it . . . and through the despairing fear that he may have lost the good will that Fair Welcoming had shown him before, he will say, "And perhaps I have lost it. At least I do not despair of it." And he will set down all the other speeches. [p. 188])

ONE: THE SPECTRAL AUTHOR

the point of Amor's authorial digression, the text being read is actually a secondary one, that of the continuator Jean de Meun, and it situates its own beginning at a point of rupture hitherto unmarked and/or unnoticed within the narrative movement of the poem. Amor seemingly steps outside of the fictional space, replacing even the Narrator in the hierarchy of narrative authority through his omniscient evaluation of the poem's very conditions of existence. Lest the maintenance of the quasi-autobiographical "I" narration in Jean de Meun's continuation lead us astray, we should keep in mind that while the author has changed, the Lover-persona has not — that is, Jean de Meun maintains the "I" narrational voice, not in order to tell his own story, but that of someone else. The heretofore unsuspecting reader must certainly readjust his perception of the poem following upon this unorthodox example of romance composition.

༄

The preceding brief analysis constitutes an attempt to investigate the authorial designations in the *Roman de la Rose* as they are revealed through the verse lines of the poem. The text artfully circumscribes its own authorial and temporal situation, delaying the revelation of such information until a relatively late moment in the story, at a point where the reader can only react with surprise and wonderment. The utility of such a reading is underscored by its ability to suggest certain paradoxical motivations behind the apparently neutral task of authorial naming while, at the same time, involving the reader in a reevaluation of his own fictional expectations. The possibility of such a reading, it should be added, proves to be purely hypothetical, given what the modern forewarned reader knows about the *Rose* text and its authorship. For instance, any of the modern critical editions of the poem reveal the authorial situation through its very title: "*Le Roman de la Rose* par Guillaume de Lorris et Jean de Meun." Whether or not we can be sure that this refers to successive authorship and not to a collaborative effort, it is virtually impossible for the modern reader to read the *Rose* text without such an advance warning. This is not simply a modern imposition, however. In an analogous manner, the large majority of the extant *Rose* manuscripts abstract the authorial information from inside the poem, committing it to the exterior in the form of rubrics naming the two authors, illuminated miniatures portraying them or, as is often the case, a physical division marking the rupture between the two parts of the poem.[6] Inasmuch as the text is clearly manipulating the authorial information, carefully measuring the moment of revelation, such scribal or editorial annotations have an effect on the reader analogous to that of a murder mystery on the first page of which a previous reader has penciled in the name of the killer: While the reader's enjoyment might not be lost, the narrative surprise certainly is. Unfortunately this historical development in the text's reception, dating back to the earliest manuscript copies, induces the reader to overlook the possibility that authorship for the *Rose* might pose a textual, as well as a historical, problem.

The presumed relationship between the two authors that can be pieced together from the passages detailed above is as follows: in the early thirteenth century Guillaume de Lorris undertook the creation of an allegorical poem which he named the *Roman de la Rose,* but died before he could finish it. It should be noted, however, that in view of the absence of any topical references, his poetic fragment in itself offers virtually no dating information, a situation compounded by our inability to find any independent evidence of a writer named Guillaume de Lorris.[7] In sharp contrast,

---

6 See the many examples given by Langlois in his invaluable (though incomplete) catalogue: *Les Manuscrits du Roman de la Rose: Description et classement,* Travaux et Mémoires de l'Université de Lille, Nouvelle Série: Droit-Lettres, 7 (Lille, 1910) (hereinafter referred to as Langlois I). The reader is also referred to our own discussion of the relationship between the manuscript illuminations and the text of the *Rose,* pp. 74–89.

7 Symptomatic of the attempt to circumvent this frustrating state of affairs is the recent article by Rita Lejeune, "Propos sur l'identification de Guillaume de Lorris, auteur du *Roman de la Rose,*" *Marche Romane,* 7 (1976), 5–17. Her article is divided into two distinct parts, the first of which accepts without question the existence of Guillaume de Lorris-author, and the second of which pursues a historical investigation of the seigneurial house of Lorris-en-Gâtinais. Conclusion: Nothing in the association between authorial naming and historical personages is certain *but,* "on aurait plus de torts encore si l'on supprimait d'un trait de plume, sans les prendre en considération, tant de coïncidences" (p. 17). The attempt to verify the historical existence of Guillaume de Lorris is, in fact, a building up of "coïncidences," which eventually tell us nothing of the work itself. Curiously, Lejeune leaves out an interesting attempt by a nineteenth-century historian to deal with the problem both historically *and* textually: Félix Guillon, *Etude historique et biographique sur Guillaume de Lorris, auteur du Roman de la Rose, d'après documents*

ONE: THE SPECTRAL AUTHOR

Jean de Meun, who "more than forty years later" completed the poem, is a comparatively well-documented medieval author, having left to posterity a half dozen other works and translations.[8] Moreover, certain historical accounts included in his continuation allow us to date it in the period between 1269 and 1278.[9] In accordance with the forty-year interval between the writing of the two poems, as stipulated by Amor, Guillaume must have undertaken his work somewhere between 1225 and 1235.

By means of this schematization of the biographical facts surrounding the *Rose* authorship, which results almost exclusively from a treatment of Amor's discourse as a fully historical account, we have assembled the principal events leading up to the conception and writing of the poem's two unequal halves. The historical weight accorded to these facts is, however, discredited to a considerable extent by two distinctive features to which we have alluded above: the blatant tactics of deferral that suspend the reader's knowledge of these facts; and the unorthodox expression of these facts by the fictional character Amor, who, in a paradoxical move, proffers information of which the Author/Lover figure is apparently unaware. The entire incident, in fact, articulates a studied contrast between the unquestioned fictionality of the narrative frame (no one believes that Amor, his garden, and the barons *actually* existed) and the inherent historicity attendant upon information concerning authorship, regardless of the context in which it is found (there is, by the same token, no doubt that Guillaume de

---

inédits et révision critique des textes des auteurs (Orléans, 1881). The ostensible object of Guillon's monograph is to prove that Guillaume was *not* from Lorris-en-Gâtinais, but rather Loury-aux-Bois, also in the Loiret. Unlike Lejeune, however, he attempts to locate an authorial signature within the text, in the form of a heraldic *blason* incorporated into the description of Deduit, who is interpreted as a figure for Guillaume. The fundamental circularity of Guillon's enterprise becomes most evident when, after taking certain liberties with the literal meaning of the text, he defends his reading by asserting, "Nous lui attribuons cette dernière couleur parce que c'est G. de Lory qui écrit, et que ce blason est celui des Sires de Lory" (*Etude historique*, p. 79). Two lines later, this altered description becomes the principal proof of Guillaume's identity: "Cette description nous permet donc d'établir l'origine de Guillaume de Lory."

8 For a convenient listing of the works attributable to Jean de Meun, as well as the principal biographical facts, see Félix Lecoy's introduction to his edition of the *Roman de la Rose*, pp. v–x.

9 It is uncertain how much time Jean de Meun might have taken to compose his 17,000 line continuation; but based upon his account of Charles d'Anjou, Manfred, and Conradin (lines 6601–710), it must have been undertaken in late 1268 at the earliest. Cf. ibid., pp. vii–viii.

Lorris and Jean de Meun can be considered historical personages). Our automatic acceptance of both appraisals, historical and fictional, proves somewhat curious in view of the fact that neither one is directly sanctioned by the text, except to the extent that a traditionally solid boundary line has been overstepped.

But to perceive even in this marginal way the arbitrariness of our critical judgment is the first step in a larger questioning of the epistemological status of history and fiction as types of linguistic discourse.[10] Indeed, it can be argued that fiction is opposed to history not because its events are false (never happened) but because it places into question, through a variety of signals, the referential basis of linguistic representation, which we take to be the major component of historical "realism" in the broadest sense. However much an Aristotelian foundation of modern critical theory has led us to believe in historical and fictional writing as two *inherently* different types of discourse, it should here be stressed than *any* written text is susceptible of treatment as historical or fictional depending upon the context into which it is fitted. They are both judgments passed by the reader upon a text's capacity to refer to the real world, frequently based on claims made by the text. Given that the status of history is granted to a text that recounts events purported to have taken place, and the status of fiction to one whose events either *have not* taken place or *could not* take place, we are no longer obliged (or even entitled) to make such a distinction when material referentiality is no longer at issue.[11]

What is merely a theoretical problem in a modern context takes on considerably more urgency when applied to a literary corpus such as that of the vernacular writings in the Middle Ages, where traditional claims on reality are for the most part scarcely distinguishable from those of contemporary fictions.[12] One can no more speak of texts that are totally historical in character than one can

---

10 Cf. Paul Veyne, *Comment on écrit l'histoire*, Collection "Points" (Paris, 1979 [1971]); and Michel de Certeau, *L'Ecriture de l'histoire* (Paris, 1975).
11 Because he does not adequately differentiate between the status of events (as having, or not having, happened) and the quality of language as a form of imitation, Aristotle ends up providing conflicting statements with regard to the nature of historical writing (*Poetics*, esp. chs. 9, 24, and 25).
12 Cf. Paul Zumthor, "Roman et histoire: aux sources d'un univers narratif," in *Langue, texte, énigme* (Paris, 1975), pp. 237–48.

eliminate the claim to representational fidelity from most apparently fictional works.[13] Many works will call for both types of evaluation. Works portraying Charlemagne, for example, encompass a rich variety of viewpoints as regards the historical nature of their account. A historical reading of the *Chanson de Roland* would only delve into questions of whether the events described actually occurred, which characters "really" existed, and so forth.[14] Such a reading is indeed possible but it scarcely scratches the surface of the text's complexities. While the reader of medieval poetry must take care to use supporting documents in order to evaluate a text's historicity (much as he would do his best to ascertain its literal meaning), the fictional possibilities should not be overlooked.

Amor's discussion of authorship, as we have seen, presents a similar problem. Only, in this case, the critical reaction has not been nearly so nuanced. Few readers have asked, for instance, what sorts of fictional strategies might be at work in the playful revelation voiced by the god of love. Again, we must remember that using truth or falsehood as a judgmental frame is not relevant when it comes to evaluating fiction; to return to the example of the defaced murder mystery, whereas the annotator might well be correct in his revelation of the culprit, he totally destroys the fiction's *raison d'être,* its engaging hold on the reader, which is based precisely on the reader's *not knowing* what will happen until the proper moment. We encounter a more substantial difficulty in the *Roman de la Rose,* inasmuch as we have never been accustomed to treating authorship in other than a historical manner. It is indeed possible that, historically speaking, Jean de Meun took up another author's (Guillaume de Lorris's) unfinished poem, eventually de-

---

13 Ibid., "Historiographie ni roman n'avaient pour fonction de prouver une vérité, mais de la créer: ils comportaient, du moins à l'origine, une connotation générale commune, celle même que R. Barthes définissait 'c'est arrivé'" (p. 245). The treatment of King Arthur from Geoffrey of Monmouth through Wace and up to Chrétien provides an example of the fluid margins between professedly historical and romance (fictional) traditions.

14 Research on the *Roland's* evenemential prehistory has served as a point of departure (and occasionally as an end in itself) for many a study of this famous poetic monument. For an interesting attempt to use aspects of the poem's historicity in order to infer the conditions of its own creation, see Ramón Menéndez Pidal, *La Chanson de Roland et la tradition épique des Francs,* 2nd ed. rev. with René Louis, tr. I.-M. Cluzel (Paris, 1960), esp. pp. 181–330.

ciding to include this information within his continuation as a grand and somewhat playful gesture of artistic self-consciousness. And yet, had Jean intended the authorial discussion purely as a means of communicating information about his own writing of the poem and its initial creation, why would he not have done so in a more direct, less perplexing manner? Why would he choose to develop the elaborate narrative paradox of Guillaume's death and Amor's amusing prophecy aimed at the future victim? Although such questions cannot be said to invalidate the historical interpretation of Amor's speech, they do suggest its inadequacy to explain all but the most superficial of the text's particularities.

At this point in the discussion, a possible fictional reading of Amor's account could be proposed. Let us suppose that a certain Jean de Meun was the author of the entire work and decided to introduce the authorial excursus as an element of his global fictional scheme.[15] In other words, let us imagine that the notion of two parts and two successive authors might itself be construed as a fiction. The artistic importance of the scene is indeed highlighted by its material centrality, occurring as it does in the precise center of the poem.[16] Once possessed of the substantial clue that authorship and writing might provide a thematic key to the interpretation of the entire *Roman de la Rose*, the reader would find plausible explanations for a number of the more obscure passages in the poem. The figure of the first author would thus be elevated to the status of a metaphor, much as we find other authors used metaphorically in the same passage (Tibullus, Catullus, Ovid, and so forth). Moreover, the theme of literary succession would find its textual analogue in Jean de Meun's widespread use of quotation and translation. In terms of the poem's tonality, Jean's attempt to bait the reader with a literary hoax of the highest caliber would certainly accord with his extended use of irony and parodic undercutting at nearly every moment in the poem.

Our discussion of the figure Amor and the relevance of his

---

15 As, for example, recently suggested by Roger Dragonetti, "Pygmalion ou les pièges de la fiction dans le *Roman de la Rose*," in *Orbis Mediaevalis: Mélanges de langue et de littérature médiévales offerts à Reto Raduolf Bezzola à l'occasion de son quatre-vingtième anniversaire*, ed. George Güntert, Marc-René Jung, Kurt Ringger (Bern, 1978), pp. 89–111.

16 This has been pointed out by Daniel Poirion, *Roman de la Rose*, p. 3. In the Lecoy edition, the passage covers lines 10465–648, out of a total of 21,750 lines.

authorial discussion to a reading of the entire *Roman de la Rose* could at this point be developed and form the logical starting point for an entire study of Jean de Meun's poem. Such is not the purpose of the present book, however, which purports to investigate the nature of Guillaume de Lorris as an author and the unity of the text ascribed to him. The seductiveness of the fictional reading outlined above might make us wonder, indeed, whether or not Guillaume de Lorris ever did exist or whether even the attempt to speak of a "first" poetic fragment, left unfinished, is at all feasible. Can one justify a historical reading of Amor's text? As stated above, the independent prior existence of a writer named Guillaume de Lorris proves absolutely unverifiable. Now, such a circumstance is not unusual in cases of twelfth- and thirteenth-century vernacular authorship; the understandably famous names of Chrétien de Troyes, Marie de France, and Béroul correspond to no historical existence that we can ascertain. But they do differ in one crucial respect from the naming of Guillaume de Lorris: Chrétien, Marie, and Béroul all name themselves *within* their poems, establishing an inner frame of reference.[17]

It seems, moreover, extremely improbable that the name "Guillaume de Lorris" was ever associated with the *Roman de la Rose* before Jean de Meun's continuation was attached to the poem, a

---

[17] While this inner naming of the author, usually in the third person, could simply be meant for the oral recitation of these works by a performer, it is probably attributable to the author him(her-)self inasmuch as it is associated with prologue material or even inserted in the text itself:

> "Por ce dit Crestiiens de Troies. . . ." (*Erec et Enide*, line 9)
> (For this reason Chrétien de Troyes says. . .)
> "Del Chevalier de la Charrete
> Comance Crestiiens son livre" (*Le Chevalier de la Charrete*, lines 24–5)
> (Chrétien begins his book about the Knight of the Cart)
> "Crestiiens seme et fet semance
> D'un romanz que il ancomance." (*Le Conte du Graal*, lines 7–8)
> (Chrétien is sowing the seed of the romance that he is now beginning)
> "N'en sevent mie bien l'estoire,
> Berox l'a mex en sen memoire" (*Tristan*, lines 1268–9)
> ([Those storytellers] don't know the story well at all; Béroul remembers it better)
> "Marie ai num, si sui de France" (*Esope*, Epilogus, line 4)
> (My name is Marie and I am from France)

Texts quoted from Ulrich Mölk, *Französische Literarästhetik* (note 2, above).

fact that lends little support to an exclusively historical understanding of the purported first author. This biographical hypothesis—and we must insist that it can be considered no more than a hypothesis—would presuppose the unlikely possibility that, from among hundreds of readers and scribes, Jean de Meun alone had access to Guillaume's identity or thought to make something of it. Or perhaps Jean found a unique manuscript examplar, now lost, and decided to delete the authorial attribution contained therein, incorporating it into a later portion of his own text. In attempting to chart the events lying behind the creation of the poem, it is obvious that numerous hypotheses can be advanced; but the one stated above, according to which the entire *Rose* is one poem of single authorship, would be the most attractive were it not for two manuscripts that prove conclusively that the fragment that Jean de Meun attributed to Guillaume existed autonomously prior to the writing of the continuation.

Of the more than 250 manuscripts containing all or part of the *Roman de la Rose*, spanning the period from the late thirteenth to the late fifteenth centuries, one and only one bears no trace of Jean's continuation: B.N. f. fr. 12786, ascribed by Langlois to the late thirteenth or early fourteenth century.[18] The manuscript, relatively early, contains a large number of poems and lays, including a series of courtly and allegorical pieces (for example, *Le Roman de la Poire;* the prose redaction of the *Bestiaire d'Amours* of Richard de Fournival) along with the *Roman de la Rose*.[19] The *Rose*

---

18 Langois I, pp. 49–52.
19 In this, it is quite typical of the earliest manuscripts containing the *Rose*, which tend to associate it with courtly/chivalric texts, over and against the later mss. which either place it on its own or with the *Testament* and *Codicile* of Jean de Meun. One of the Turin manuscripts (University Library L. III. 22) likewise associates the *Rose* with the *Bestiaire d'Amours,* while Dijon 526 contains a veritable anthology of courtly didactic works on love, including several attributed to Richard de Fournival (*Li Commens d'Amours, La Puissance d'Amours, Li Bestiaires d'Amours*). Still other early manuscripts of the *Rose* contain *Le Jeu de Robin et Marion* (B.N. f. fr. 1569; late thirteenth/early fourteenth century), *La Chastelaine de Vergi* (Brussels, Royal Library 9574–5; early fourteenth century), and a miscellany of short poems and *dits* (B.N. f. fr. 378; late thirteenth century). Cf. Langlois I, pp. 2–212. Pierre-Yves Badel discusses the increasingly frequent association between the *Rose* and moral/didactic works of a religious nature in manuscripts after the mid-fourteenth century in his invaluable study, *Le Roman de la Rose au XIVe siècle: Etude de la réception de l'oeuvre* (Geneva, 1980), pp. 63–6. However, by virtue of the fact that he groups together all thirteenth- and early fourteenth-century manuscripts in his discussion he tends to undervalue the likelihood that thirteenth-century manuscript compilers identified the *Roman de la Rose* more exclusively with courtly, and not religious, didacticism, as exemplified by the

text appears as few modern (or later medieval) readers have ever imagined it: The fragment normally attributed to Guillaume de Lorris (lines 1–4028, ed. Lecoy), *pace* Amor, is followed by seventy-six lines that bring the poem to a conclusion. The latter section, found in six other manuscripts and normally termed the "anonymous conclusion," has been considered without exception since the time of Langlois as a small-scale attempt on the part of a first continuator to end the poem left incomplete by Guillaume.[20] Langlois attempts to secure our agreement by stating – misleadingly, I might add – that the conclusion "fut d'abord ajoutée au poème inachevé de G. de Lorris."[21] Even if such were to have been the case, it could not be proven by the present manuscript, the scribe of which copies the text smoothly and unhesitatingly through to the end of the "anonymous conclusion." Consistent with our hypothesis that Jean de Meun invented the attribution to Guillaume de Lorris, *no* author's name is provided in this manuscript. Indeed, were this manuscript example the only version of the poem to have survived, we would undoubtedly consider the *Roman de la Rose* to be an anonymous, completed work.

A second manuscript pertinent to the present discussion, B.N. f. fr. 1573 (late thirteenth century), contains Guillaume's fragment (without the "anonymous conclusion") copied by one scribal hand, followed by Jean de Meun's continuation in another, markedly different, hand.[22] The last line of Guillaume's text, "car je n'ai mes ailleurs fiance," falls in column c of folio 34, the rest of which is left blank. Jean's continuation starts on the next folio, belonging to a new quire, the present number 35. According to Langlois, this manuscript offers precious evidence of what must have been the most common mode of promulgation of Jean de

---

popular works of Richard de Fournival. In a forthcoming book based upon her 1982 Princeton dissertation, Sylvia Huot analyzes techniques and strategies of vernacular manuscript compilation practices from the thirteenth through the fourteenth centuries and demonstrates convincingly the importance of scribal interpretation in the constitution and ordering of anthology manuscripts.

20 A full transcription of the anonymous conclusion is to be found in the notes to Langlois's edition of the *Roman de la Rose*, vol. 2, pp. 330–3. The first six lines are unique to this manuscript, while the final couplet, found in all the others, is here lacking.

21 Langlois I, p. 50. In the context of Langlois's discussion, we assume that he is describing facts made apparent by the manuscript's appearance, which turns out not to be true.

22 Ibid., pp. 29–32.

Meun's continuation: It was added on to existing manuscript copies of Guillaume's unfinished text.[23] He goes on to infer that Guillaume's poem attained a certain popularity and circulated widely for decades on its own.[24] Considering, however, that only two out of the 250-plus extant manuscripts attest to the prior existence of Guillaume's poem, such a suggestion seems barely defensible. Lecoy's hypothesis, that Guillaume's poem was never widely circulated before being coupled with Jean's continuation, perhaps attaining a distribution on the scale of Chrétien's less successful romances, provides a more convincing explanation of the manuscript legacy.[25] It is certain that the vital interest expressed by fourteenth- and fifteenth-century audiences, who were after all responsible for nearly all of the manuscripts that have come down to us, focused primarily on the long doctrinal essays composed by the continuator and *not* on its courtly pretext.[26] Whatever the truth might be about the respective popularity of Guillaume and Jean, this manuscript provides evidence independent of that adduced by Amor to the effect that the first part of the poem was never continued past line 4028. B.N. f. fr. 1573 modifies somewhat the information to be inferred from B.N. f. fr. 12786, by sustaining the probability that the "anonymous conclusion" was indeed a continuation grafted to a first poem and not an integral part which was later suppressed. Neither manuscript, in the context of the first part of the poem, presents an authorial designation of any kind.

Curiously enough, then, while the manuscript tradition as it has survived justifies our separation of the *Rose* fragment from the totality as a separate work, it offers no support for the commonly

---

23 Ibid., pp. 30–1, 235.
24 Ibid., p. 235: "Le poème de Guillaume de Lorris, avant que Jean de Meun lui eût donné une suite, était déjà très lu; les copies s'en étaient donc multipliées." One of the few verifiable examples of poetic influence exercised by Guillaume's poem before it received the continuation of Jean is to be found in the *Roman de la Poire*. See Langlois's edition of the *Rose*, vol. l, pp. 6–8. For later "admirers" of Guillaume, to the possible exclusion of Jean, see Badel, *Roman de la Rose*, pp. 151–8.
25 Lecoy, ed., *Rose,* vol. I, pp. xxxvi–vii: "Il semble bien . . . que le poème de Guillaume n'a été sauvé que grâce à la continuation de Jean." This evaluation, it should be stressed, is based upon *relative* numbers of manuscripts and thus can claim no absolute validity with respect to the *Rose* readership.
26 Poirion, *Roman de la Rose*, pp. 98–144; Badel, *Roman de la Rose.*

accepted authorial attribution. In other words, the above-mentioned manuscripts prove (as much as anything can be proven from such evidence) that in all likelihood the first 4,028 lines of the *Roman de la Rose* (ed. Lecoy) had an independent and prior existence as an autonomous text, previous to the addition of Jean de Meun's continuation at a later date. Amor's assertion about the unfinished state of the text, as well as his delineation of the terminating lines, would appear to be confirmed as to their historical accuracy. None of the manuscript evidence, however, lends any support to the assertion that a certain Guillaume de Lorris wrote the text. In the latter case, it is Amor's word against that of the manuscript tradition, intratextual (fictional) versus extratextual (historical) evidence. The normally interrelated questions of textual definition and authorial attribution would not seem to find an equally satisfying solution in Amor's explanation.

Far from constituting a simple statement destined to enter the annals of literary history, Amor's provocative (and provoking) assertion undercuts the most commonly accepted of fictional expectations. The normally systematic relationship between author, narrator, and fictional hero is thereafter irremediably disrupted. In view of our inability either to verify or to reject by independent channels all of the information offered to us concerning the poem's authorship, we are forced to question the unhesitating acceptance of such information. The two major points adduced by Amor and which have always gained acceptance are the following: That Guillaume de Lorris, the first author, started the *Rose;* and that his poem was left unfinished. The former assertion, as has been shown, can scarcely be trusted. In terms of our previous discussion, its historical validity (the truth-value of its referent) must be placed into doubt for lack of supporting evidence. More importantly, however, it suggests a difficulty in the very conception of authorship and authorial naming in the Middle Ages. In what way can we consider authorial naming significant in a preprint culture and should we always expect the author to name himself from within his text? Did the author-figure stand in the same relationship to his text as in modern times? Should authorship always be treated in a historical manner? Is the situation described by Amor at all typical?

As for the second point made by Amor — the poem's fragmentary status — we do find an independent corroboration. And yet it might be asked whether a poem's "fragmentary" nature constitutes sure evidence of its being incomplete, unfinished. In other words, how do we decide upon such crucial critical concepts as textual unity and poetic closure? Can these concepts differ in a culture based on a manuscript circulation of texts? How will the authorial uncertainty affect our method of constituting the text?

These complications arise from the fact that Amor's speech is squarely implicated in another fictional system, that superimposed upon the first one by Jean de Meun. The conceptual and theoretical problems that we face are direct tributaries of the medieval literary aesthetic, wherein fiction and history resist a categorization as antithetical concepts. The problem of the delimitation of the fictional space lies, in fact, at the heart of the controversy. A strictly literal or historical interpretation of Amor's discourse risks falsifying a considerably more elaborate system of literary signification (in the case of Jean de Meun) as well as disguising certain characteristics of a poem written by another author. However, does our abandonment thereof, and along with it our sure denomination of the text's relation to reality, risk an even greater loss of understanding? At this point, it would perhaps be helpful to take a glimpse at medieval notions of authorship and textualization before attempting a further discussion of Amor's puzzling interlude and its textual application. It is hoped that through such a study we may become sensitized to certain conceptual categories that we apply to the study of literature, and take steps to adjust them for use in a cultural and literary context far removed from our own.

THE MEDIEVAL AUTHOR

To investigate medieval literary creation in all of its complexity, even restricting one's vision to the material aspects of the production of texts and their diffusion, would far exceed the bounds of the present study. We can only hope in the present limited space to indicate certain parameters of the question, as a way of suggesting that the purported authorial situation of a poet bears to a great extent upon the substance and quality of the finished product, not to mention the manner in which we interpret it.

The social being of the medieval vernacular poet was totally devoid of the complex of legalistic and proprietary factors which have served to characterize and circumscribe authors of the Western world since the eighteenth century.[27] The contemporary author not only "owns" his texts and all rights to their inviolable integrity, but he earns money from their free flow in the economic exchange of goods. The roots of this development are obviously far-reaching and connected to the most basic tenets of modern capitalistic society, but to a great extent they can be explained by the availability of the mass-produced book as a relatively low-cost commodity, a situation made possible by the invention and widespread implementation of the printing press.[28]

Indeed, one of the commonplaces of medieval studies suggests that the advent of the printing press, as the primary transformer of documentary preservation and diffusion in the Western world,

---

27 England (1709) and France (1793) led the way in Europe through their legislation of copyright laws, which will only become generalized in the nineteenth century. Up until the time of these legal sanctions, authors sold their works to printers but, in so doing, risked losing their own as well as their descendants' personal ownership rights to the works in question. Additionally, copyright laws protected publishers from piracy, which had become a rampant problem as early as the seventeenth century. Cf. Lucien Febvre and Henri-Jean Martin, *L'Apparition du livre* (Paris, 1971 [1958]), pp. 233–42; and S. H. Steinberg, *Five Hundred Years of Printing*, 3rd ed. (Harmondsworth, Sussex, England, 1979 [1955]), pp. 298–302.

28 From the beginning, printing was seen as a way of commercially exploiting the written word: "Tout, dans la typographie, la fabrication, la mise en vente, indique que leur principal souci fut le rendement commercial," Robert Escarpit, *La Révolution du livre* (Paris, 1965), p. 20. While stressing in this work the sociological aspects of books as a commercial product, Escarpit does conclude that in the long run the sale of books cannot be considered equivalent to that of other products. The mercantile interest in book producing undergoes a gradual shift from the fifteenth century, when the operation was almost totally centered around and motivated by the printer, to the eighteenth century when, with newly entrenched authors' rights and privileges, the commercial enterprise is shared by author, printer, binder, and bookseller. Febvre and Martin (*L'Apparition,* p. 242) even assert that the "métier d'auteur" in the modern sense was not established until this relatively late development. Elizabeth L. Eisenstein (*The Printing Press as an Agent of Change,* 2 vols. in 1 [Cambridge, 1980]) concurs, while nuancing the view by stressing the mutual influence of traditional habits and new developments: "Partly because copyists, after all, never paid those whose works they copied, partly because new books were a small portion of the early book-trade, and partly because divisions of literary labor remained blurred, the author retained a quasi-amateur status until the eighteenth century." (p. 154). Cf. Steinberg, *Five Hundred Years,* pp. 15–116; Febvre and Martin, *L'Apparition,* pp. 39–164; and Rudolf Hirsch, *Printing, Selling and Reading: 1450–1550,* 2nd printing (Wiesbaden, 1974).

marks the end of the Middle Ages and the beginning of the modern era. Not only did the printing press profoundly alter the material appearance and multiplication of copies, but also the writer's relationship to his text.[29] First of all, the printing press codifies, solidifies, and regularizes the written version of a work as no purely manuscript tradition could. Whereas errors or faults are easily rectified on the basis of a single copy, once a text has "gone to press" and been reproduced in 100 or 100,000 copies, the idea of making widespread changes no longer remains practicable. Moreover, barring unforeseen circumstances, printed copies of a single pressing will be uniform, virtually identical; manuscript copies by practical inevitability demonstrate a variance at all levels.[30] It is perhaps the paradoxical combination of the depersonalization resulting from the increased distance between author and text, and the greater assurance of textual integrity made possible by the printing press, which, along with the above-mentioned economic factors, has had the most important role in defining the modern authorial figure.

While many studies of medieval literary works acknowledge the transition from a pre-printing to a printing culture, rarely do they readjust the attendant notion of authorship. Furthermore, the resultant binary division only partially explains the situation. Numerous recent studies have demonstrated a third distinct mode of circulation of literary texts in the Middle Ages: oral composition

---

29 Cf. Eisenstein, *Printing Press*, pp. 43–159. It should be stressed that the perceptual change from individual, handwritten texts to mechanically reproduced ones, which now seems so obvious, was not immediate. In fact, the first books attempted for the most part to imitate the appearance of manuscripts, through their use of typography, disposition of lines on the page, use of illustrations (which were on occasion colored in, or "illuminated," after the woodcut was printed), use of colophons, and so on. A feature such as the title page, which we consider constitutive of the printed book, was a later development. Even the number of copies of incunabla was vastly limited compared to what is presently the case; many books in the first few decades after Gutenberg were probably printed in no more than 100–150 copies. Cf. Febvre and Martin, *L'Apparition*, pp. 307–15. Moreover, during at least the first fifty years after the invention of printing, manuscript circulation of texts remained common, some even being copied from printed books (see Cora Lutz, "Manuscripts Copied from Printed Books," in *Essays on Manuscripts and Rare Books* [Hamden, CT, 1975], pp. 129–39).

30 Cf. Eugène Vinaver, "Principles of Textual Emendation," in *Studies in French Language and Medieval Literature, presented to Mildred K. Pope, by Pupils, Colleagues and Friends* (Manchester, 1939), pp. 351–69. Modern notions of error and verification, or strict grammaticality, simply do not function in the same way for manuscript texts.

and diffusion.[31] Often associated with pre-printing societies, orality is nonetheless to be distinguished from handwriting, both as a creative medium and as a means of communication. Inasmuch as the well-documented bilingualism of medieval Europe situated itself on the dividing line between oral and nonoral usage — that is, between the use of the vernacular languages and use of Latin — the true point of transition from an oral to a nonoral (or written) culture is to be situated at the moment when the vernaculars were first transcribed.[32] This "moment," of course, represents a period of several centuries, given that the very first vernacular writing occurs in the ninth century in France, while the vernacular was probably not widely viewed as a serious or versatile written language before the beginning of the thirteenth century.[33]

It is for this reason that, when investigating vernacular literature of the twelfth and thirteenth centuries, well before its establishment as a codified literary medium, the reader must take care to preserve the distinction between vernacular and Latin literary usage.[34] Poetic expression in Latin was not the same as in the

31 Cf. Jean Rychner, *La Chanson de geste: Essai sur l'art épique des jongleurs* (Geneva, 1955); Paul Zumthor, *Introduction à la poésie orale* (Paris, 1983) (general, with bibliography) and *La Poésie et la voix dans la civilisation médiévale* (Paris, 1984). The work of Walter J. Ong on the broader aesthetic implications of the oral vs. written word is most instructive: see especially *Interfaces of the Word: Studies in the Evolution of Consciousness and Culture* (Ithaca, NY, 1977), and *Orality and Literacy: The Technologizing of the Word* (London/New York, 1982).
32 Cf. H. J. Chaytor, *From Script to Print* (Cambridge, 1945) as well as my article "Vers la société de l'écriture: Le Roman de la Rose," *Poétique* 50 (1982), 155–72.
33 Cf. Paul Zumthor, *Histoire littéraire de la France médiévale (VIe–XIVe siecles)* (Paris, 1954), pp. 33–4; 129–30; and especially 233–5. "La langue latine perd, en l'espace d'une génération, la plupart de ses positions littéraires. Elle est encore porteuse d'une littérature abondante, mais de caractère de plus en plus exclusivement spéculatif.... On peut dire que, dès 1230–40, le latin n'est plus, en France, qu'un instrument scolaire (théologique, scientifique, juridique) et liturgique" (p. 233).
34 For Zumthor, it is in fact the vernacular's growing capacity to be exploited as a sophisticated rhetorical medium that offers some explanation for its eventual replacement of Latin. Cf. *Histoire*, p. 129: "Ces langues [the vernacular tongues] ont une plasticité et une richesse formelles supérieures, à bien des égards, au latin. Leur faiblesse relative, par rapport à celui-ci (sans doute compensée par le geste et la voix, dans les genres déclamés) réside dans leur syntaxe, inhabile à rendre toujours exactement les articulations de la pensée: d'où leur inaptitude, avant le XIIIe ou le XIVe s., à se prêter aux jeux les plus raffinés de la rhétorique." Zumthor will expand and nuance these observations in his later *Essai de poétique médiévale* (Paris, 1972): "Les procédés qui, en français, paraissent provenir de la pratique latine comportent souvent un réajustement, soit aux tendances propres de la langue vulgaire, soit à des besoins thématiques particuliers. Des distorsions se sont produites, dont résulte la plupart du temps *une quasi-impossibilité de déterminer la part réelle de la rhétorique classique dans tel usage de la poésie romane*" (p. 53; emphasis mine).

vernacular and certainly did not share the same conceptual or affective structures. The type of bilingualism under question certainly served to separate and fragment social groups rather than to unite them in a common cause.

From the evidence that has sifted down to us, the first creators of narrative in the vernacular language were the poets who translated hagiographical accounts and who sang the *chansons de geste*.[35] The latter, traditional stories of the Frankish kings and their vassals, have occupied the center of medieval authorship debates since their rediscovery in the nineteenth century. The basic question revolves around whether these epics, in the form that has come down to us, were composed after several layerings of creative interventions (traditionalism) or by the efforts of one creative individual (individualism).[36] The additional question arises as to whether the texts in our possession were first written down (thus representing a written "version" which transforms the supposed oral substratum) or produced orally (and thus a faithful transcription of the oral performance).[37] While the debate will almost certainly never find a sure resolution, owing to the inexistence of the type of evidence that would be required as proof (aural recordings, for example), it is nonetheless evident that a large part of the controversy stems from our incapacity to stretch our vocabulary to fit the needs of the situation. Even most "individualists" will

---

35 Cf. Cesare Segre, "Il 'Boeci,' i poemetti agiografici e le origine della forma epica" and "Dai poemetti agiografici alle 'Chansons de Geste': L'Insegnamento della tradizione," both in his *La Tradizione della "Chanson de Roland"* (Milan, 1974), pp. 14–62 and 80–93, respectively.
36 Pierre Le Gentil gives a summary of this specific aspect of the debate in his *La Chanson de Roland*, 2nd ed. rev. (Paris, 1967), pp. 31–4. For a more detailed expression of the two principal positions – traditionalist ("Il n'y a jamais eu de Turoldus, compositeur unique de la *Chanson de Roland*") and individualist ("Tout le mérite revient à Turold") – by their most forceful recent exponents, see Pidal, *Chanson de Roland*, pp. 451–5, and Maurice Delbouille, "La Chanson de geste et le livre," in *La Technique littéraire des chansons de geste* (Paris, 1959), pp. 295–407. Through an extension of the related problems of authorship and originality to other medieval literary genres, Le Gentil attempts to mediate between the two extreme positions in his "Réflexions sur la création littéraire au Moyen Age," in *Chanson de geste und höfischer Roman* (Heidelberg, 1963), pp. 9–20.
37 Cf. Delbouille, "Chanson de geste." These are only the simplest of the possibilities. Additionally one can imagine any number of hypothetical reworkings, both at the stage of oral and of written commitment of the text. Madeleine Tyssens discusses this in the context of specific manuscript variants in her "Le Style oral et les ateliers de copistes" in *Mélanges de linguistique romane et de philologie médiévale offerts à M. Maurice Delbouille* (Gembloux, 1964), II, 659–75.

agree, for example, that the *chansons de geste* contain what is generally referred to as an "oral" stylistic and contextual base; their primary misgiving results from their reluctance to deny single authorship to an acknowledged masterpiece such as the *Chanson de Roland*. They are, of course, making a narrow equation between single authorship, literary excellence, and written composition. If we cannot speak of a distinct author, ask the individualists, how can we account for the *Roland's* greatness? In the same way, the otherwise indisputable presence and role of the *jongleur* as manipulator/adaptor of stories totally eludes our single-minded approach to authorship.[38]

One would expect the situation to become somewhat less complicated as we enter the domain of the romance, a genre that so designates itself from the middle of the twelfth century and that does not display in any significant proportion the above-mentioned oral characteristics.[39] Indeed, on the surface, the romance text seems unequivocally to originate in the work of a single author.[40] In point of fact, however, the romance creative scheme seems no less convoluted than that of the scheme of the *chansons de geste*. We know, for instance, surprisingly little about the "mechanics" of romance composition, much less than we have been able to surmise about oral composition. We often assume that the writer of romances sat down and composed his text as does a modern author, and yet other factors call into question such a characterization. The creator of romance almost certainly aimed at a listening, and not a reading, public.[41] Most romances through the thirteenth century, it is assumed, would have been read aloud

---

38 For a complete and detailed account of the *jongleur*'s role in literary composition of the Middle Ages, see the important study by Edmond Faral, *Les Jongleurs en France au moyen âge* (Paris, 1910).

39 Zumthor, *Histoire*, pp. 149–50. In his study of the formulaic qualities of several *chansons de geste*, Joseph J. Duggan demonstrates the unformulaic qualities of contemporary romances (*The Song Of Roland: Formulaic Style and Poetic Craft* [Berkeley, 1973], esp. pp. 16–30).

40 Signs of this are the relative fixity of the romance texts among different manuscripts, along with the frequent inclusion of an authorial name. On the romance author's self-designation see Pierre Gallais, "Recherches sur la mentalité des romanciers français du moyen âge," *CCM* 7 (1964), 479–93, and *CCM* 13 (1970), 333–47; and Michel Zink, "Une Mutation de la conscience littéraire: Le language romanesque à travers des exemples français du XIIe siècle," *CCM* 24 (1981), 3–27.

41 Ruth Crosby, "Oral Delivery in the Middle Ages," *Speculum*, 11 (1936), 88–110; and Gallais, "Recherches," *CCM* (1964), 483–7.

to an audience. Are the early romances that have come down to us transcriptions of some kind, either of a public or private recitation? Did the poet actually put quill to parchment (or stylus to wax)? Was he or she always literate?[42] What is meant by translation in the case of romance poets?[43] In a society where illiteracy was widespread (that is, where the ability to *speak* a language is separate from the ability to *read* or *write* it), and additionally where the language employed was not even directly associated with writing, none of these questions finds a conclusive answer.[44] The precise material instance of creation through the thirteenth century totally escapes our view. And yet it is specifically with the romance tradition that the image of the vernacular author becomes solidified. An important subject of research, which I can only touch upon briefly in the present space, would question possible generic influences upon anonymity or its converse, authorial naming.[45] Whereas the *chansons de geste* and the branches of the *Roman de Renart* are characteristically anonymous, the prevailing tendency after the third quarter of the twelfth century is for writers of verse romances to name themselves in a prologue or epilogue. Works of short fiction, the *lais* and *fabliaux,* show little regularity as far as authorial attribution is concerned. Lyric poets rarely name themselves within their works, but the poems themselves are usually included under authorial rubrics in the *chansonnier* manu-

---

42 Cf. Franz H. Bäuml, "Varieties and Consequences of Medieval Literacy and Illiteracy," *Speculum,* 55, no. 2 (1980), 237–65. For a recent account of the philosophical, theological and legal implications of the growth of literacy after the eleventh century, see Brian Stock, *The Implications of Literacy: Written Language and Models of Interpretation in the Eleventh and Twelfth Centuries* (Princeton, 1983).

43 One of the *topoi* of romance composition in the vernacular asserts that the work is translated from Latin (except in the case of Marie de France, who in her *Lais* opts for orally recounted Celtic tales, since everyone else is translating from Latin). Significantly, the word *roman* in the twelfth century suggested both a literary genre *and* the vernacular tongue, *metre en roman* meaning simultaneously "translate into the vernacular" and "turn into a romance." Cf. Zink, "Mutation," pp. 10–11.

44 While it remains a mystery why or how the earliest vernacular works came to be written down in the first place, some speculation can be made. For the *Séquence de Sainte Eulalie,* cf. our article (note 32, above), pp. 155–63.

45 From this point of view, the author's "presence" would seem to be genre-conditioned. Cf. Rainer Warning, "Moi lyrique et société chez les troubadours," in *Archéologie du signe,* ed. Lucie Brind'Amour and Eugene Vance, Papers in Mediaeval Studies 3 (Toronto, 1983), pp. 63–100 (esp. 63–75); and "Formen narrativer Identitätskonstitution im höfischen Roman," in *Grundriss der romanischen Literaturen des Mittelalters,* vol. 4, tome 1 (Heidelberg, 1978), pp. 25–59.

scripts.[46] One striking example of a thirteenth-century work with a thematically pertinent anonymity is the *Prose Lancelot*, which develops the fictional account of its own transcription and perpetuation.[47] After the mid-thirteenth century, and for some time thereafter, rhetorical play with the author's name (as in Rutebeuf and Colin Muset) will become a common practice. These various cases have been mentioned not so much in order to determine where we should and should not expect to find authors naming themselves, but rather to suggest that before the mid-thirteenth century such designations cannot be taken for granted and thus anonymity must be reconsidered according to various literary criteria: *topoi* of group presentation and oral production in the case of the *chansons de geste;* a fictional need for secrecy in the case of the lyric *chanson;* pretensions to a universalizing quasi-religious fiction, as is the case for the greatly expanded prose Grail legends.

As with the creators of the *chansons de geste,* the question of originality has frequently come to the fore in discussions of romance composition. Can we speak of "originality" when treating poets who based themselves on known stories (priding themselves, in fact, on their established nature), writing in the context of a tremendous stock of rhetorical, topical, and formulaic devices? While some critics have answered in the negative, one might ask why there are constant protestations of *nouveauté* in the romance tradition, or what Chrétien de Troyes means when he distinguishes between the *sens* and *conjointure* of a poem.[48] It seems likely that some sort of innovation was envisaged but one perhaps aimed more at matters of technique than of content, which seems to constitute the major criterion of originality in modern literary discussions. Can we, in short, consider medieval authorship in the same light as we would its modern counterpart, given the distinct

---

46 The prestige granted to authorial designations and portraits in some of the illuminated *chansonniers* could be compared with the *vidas* and *razos* (fictionalized prose narratives recounting the poet's life) found in thirteenth- and fourteenth-century troubadour manuscripts.

47 On the simulacra of authority in the *Prose Lancelot*, see Alexandre Leupin, *Le Graal et la littérature* (Lausanne, 1982).

48 See the important discussion by Douglas Kelly in his *Sens and Conjointure in the "Chevalier de la Charrette"* (The Hague/Paris, 1966), pp. 31–97.

notions of originality and subject matter that characterize the latter construct?

The directness of a poet's relation to his audience and his patron, which we can infer from the almost certain destination of his work through the middle of the thirteenth century — oral recitation —, meant that his role vis-à-vis his material diminished accordingly, perhaps on the order of an important director for the theater or, better yet, of a ballet choreographer who prepares and commits to paper a "new" version of an older, already-known vehicle. Just as the meaning of the word "director" has changed in the last hundred years as his centrality to the mounting of new productions along with his reinterpretation of familiar works have become more and more pronounced, so the notion of authorship has evolved radically for a host of reasons since the Middle Ages. The principles of evaluation that are a direct tributary of the authorial construct must be confronted anew.[49]

Finally, in terms of the medieval poet's posterity, the mode of transmission particular to a pre-printing society certainly alters the aspect of the finished work and what we find great security in calling the "authorial hand." Another figure who remained at the center of the literary chain for at least 200 years but who is rarely mentioned in literary discussions is that of the scribe.[50] The scribe's duty was that of copying already existing written works so that they could be circulated and receive a wider audience. Before the fourteenth century, we have little or no evidence of a ver-

---

49 As an example of a comparable alteration in literary habits that affected the nature of the literary output, D. A. Russell (*Criticism in Antiquity* [Berkeley, 1981], pp. 34–51) suggests that a shift in the primacy of the spoken word toward that of the written word, which took place in ancient Greece from the fifth to the third century B.C., explains the falling off in the Hellenistic period of those works highly dependent upon performance and music (tragedy, comedy, lyric).

50 One exception, however, is the scribe Guiot, whose purported reworkings of the texts of Chrétien have inspired a number of studies: See the introduction by Mario Roques to his edition of *Erec et Enide*, CFMA 80 (Paris, 1952), pp. xxxvii–li, as well as his article, "Le Manuscrit 794 de la Bibliothèque Nationale et le scribe Guiot," *Romania*, 73 (1952), 177–99; I. Frank, "Le Manuscrit de Guiot entre Chrétien de Troyes et Wolfram von Eschenbach," *Annales Universitatis Saraviensis (Philosophie-Lettres)*, Université de la Sarre, I, no. 2 (1952), 169–83; B. Woledge, "Un Scribe champenois devant un texte normand: Guiot copiste de Wace," in *Mélanges . . . Frappier* (Paris, 1970), II, pp. 1139–54; and T. B. W. Reid, "Chrétien de Troyes et le scribe Guiot," *Medium Aevum*, 45 (1976), 1–19.

nacular author who had anything to do with book publication.⁵¹ More importantly for our purposes, the scribe is in many cases not simply the transmitter of a text but also its interpreter. Manuscripts of the *Roman de la Rose,* for example, often contain scriptorial "commentary," not only in the form of rubrics and glosses that render explicit certain allusions in the text (such as the authorial attributions, as we saw above) but also in the form of illuminated miniatures.⁵²

Any study of the scribe by modern medievalists has been almost exclusively carried out by textual editors, as a way of eliminating contaminations that the scribe would have introduced into the text that was being copied.⁵³ Those who have taken to commenting on the texts of the Middle Ages have usually preferred to accept the modern edition as a preliminary *datum,* leaving unproblematized the role of the scribe. Insofar as his work corresponds in the most narrowly reproductive sense to the modern function of the printing press he is viewed, accordingly, as a passive, virtually invisible figure. And yet, to eliminate the scribe from our consideration would obscure an important facet of medieval literary production.

One fascinating figure in the manuscript history of the *Roman de la Rose* is called Gui de Mori, a cleric who lived in the late thirteenth century and who undertook a "new" version of the poem, recopying it as it came to him while effecting deletions and additions that he deemed appropriate.⁵⁴ As the following passage from Gui's prologue clearly demonstrates, his immediate purpose was to supplement (and not to supplant) the *Rose* text as a means

---

51 Sarah Jane Williams, "An Author's Role in Fourteenth Century Book Production: Guillaume de Machaut's 'Livre ou je met toutes mes choses'," *Romania,* 90 (1969), 433–54; and, by the same author, "Machaut's Self-Awareness as Author and Producer," in *Machaut's World: Science and Art in the Fourteenth Century,* ed. Madeleine Pelner Cosman and Bruce Chandler (New York, 1978), pp. 189–97.

52 For a description of the division of labor in the making of the medieval book, the reader is referred to David Diringer, *The Hand-Produced Book* (New York, 1953), esp. pp. 205–23, and our discussion of the authorial portraits, pp. 74–89.

53 See the article by Vinaver (note 30, above). The authors of a recent book on the procedures for editing Old French texts continue to minimize the pertinence of the scribe's presence: Alfred Foulet and Mary Blakely Speer, *On Editing Old French Texts* (Lawrence, KS, 1979), p. 44: "But he [the modern editor] must interfere still further to correct the scribe's errors."

54 The two major articles on Gui de Mori are: Ernest Langlois, "Gui de Mori et *Le Roman de la Rose,*" *Bibliothèque de l'Ecole des Chartes,* 68 (1907), 249–71 (hereinafter designated as Langlois II); and Marc-René Jung, "Gui de Mori et Guillaume de Lorris," *Vox Romanica,* 27 (1968), 106–37.

of making it more accessible, and therefore more enjoyable, to future readers:[55]

> Mais sauf ce ke ja empiree
> Ne sera par moi ne quassee
> L'ententions ne la mataire,
> Tant i vaurai je dou mien faire
> C'aucune cose en osterai,
> Aucune cose i meterai,
> Si en sera *plus entendables*
> Et a oïr *plus delitables*.

(However, having taken care that the [work's] intended meaning and subject matter will neither be worsened nor destroyed by me, I will add so much of my own composition to it, taking out some things and putting in others, that it will be more accessible and more enjoyable to listen to.)

While Gui expresses a clear desire to maintain the intended meaning ("entention") and subject matter ("mataire") of the text that he received, he also sees no contradiction in his plan to excise parts of the original text and interpolate passages of his own composition ("dou mien"). Now, the studies of Langlois and Jung, as important as they are for their publication of extracts from Gui's reworkings, limit themselves to discussions of the doctrinal changes effected by Gui's reinterpretation; they hardly touch upon the implications of Gui's unique undertaking for our understanding of reading, writing, and authorship in the Middle Ages. In the following pages we will consider Gui's precious comments on his own method as well as on his relationship to his illustrious predecessors.

We should perhaps begin with a few words about the manuscripts in which Gui's redactions have survived. Of the half-dozen manuscripts that bear witness to Gui de Mori's editorial talents, two are distinctly older and more complete than the others: *Ter* (which belonged at one time to the abbé de Tersan); and *Tou* (which is presently located at the Municipal Library in Tournai).[56]

---

[55] Langlois II, p. 261.
[56] I am following the commonly accepted shorthand introduced by Langlois to designate the various manuscripts. The version of Gui's reworking that appears in ms. *He* (Royal Library of Copenhagen, ms. Gl. Kgl. S. 2061 4º) – also of the fourteenth century – bears little relevance to the present discussion (cf. the remarks of Jung, "Gui de Mori").

The curious fortune of *Ter* merits a brief discussion: Consulted and copied by M. Méon, the first modern editor of the *Rose*, around the first decade of the nineteenth century, the manuscript was lost after 1814, only to reappear a century later, in 1910.[57] According to Jung, it disappeared from its depository in Maihingen in 1934, and, as far as we know, its present location or condition remains unknown.[58] Since Langlois seems not to have had the opportunity to consult this manuscript, the only information which we have as to its contents is limited to the few passages transcribed by Méon more than a century and a half ago.[59] The fragility of manuscript attestations in the modern age should make us all the more conscious of the mass of *lacunae* that have certainly resulted over the seven centuries since Jean de Meun. The loss of *Ter* is especially frustrating because it contained a passage of central importance for our present discussion. Following is the text of that passage, situated between the two parts attributed to Guillaume de Lorris and Jean de Meun, and whose reconstruction is based on the transcriptions of Méon and Langlois:[60]

> C'est li songe que j'ai songiet.   [last line of the
> Enssi fine li Rommans maistre Guille de Loris,   "anonymous conclusion"]
> comment il mena ses amours à fin.   [rubric]
>   En l'an del Incarnation
>   Jhesu-Crist, par dupplication

The references for the other manuscripts, all copied in the fifteenth century, that contain passages from Gui's reworking can be found in Jung's article, note 4, pp. 106–7. For a description of the illustrations contained in *Tou*, along with some reproductions, cf. L. Fourez, "Le Roman de la Rose de la Bibliothèque de Tournai," *Scriptorium*, 1 (1946/7), 213–39.

57 Langlois suggests that the prince of Ottingen-Wallerstein bought the manuscript from the abbé de Tersan in 1814, soon after Méon consulted it. Whatever was the exact year of the manuscript's transferral, *Ter* was not listed in the sale catalogue issued at the death of the abbé de Tersan in 1819. Cf. Langlois I, p. 164.

58 Still another manuscript, *Rou*, several passages of which were transcribed by Rouard ("D'un Manuscrit inconnu du *Roman de la Rose*," *Bulletin du Bibliophile* [1860], 976–87), has to my knowledge not been identified since that time. Cf. Langlois I, pp. 207–9.

59 One passage transcribed by Méon is included in the preface of his edition of the *Rose* (Paris, 1814), vol. I, pp. ix–x. Our access to other passages from *Ter* is made possible thanks to Langlois's transcriptions taken from Méon's manuscript copy of his edition; these passages are included in Langlois II.

60 We quote the passage in verse from Méon's edition, vol. I, pp. ix–x, while the prose sections are taken from Langlois II, pp. 250–1. I have indicated in the margin the identification of each section.

>   de VI^c, de V et XL,   [verse interpolation
>   le jeudi devant ce c'on cante   of Gui de Mori]
>   *Resurrexi,* fu terminés
>   Chis livres, et ainssi finés
>   Com maistre Guillaume le fine,
>   Si com je suppose et devine,
>   Car plus n'en ai millieu [sic]
>   En livre qu'aie encore leu.
>   Si ai en maint lieu moult ostées
>   De paroles et adjoustées
>   C'on puet bien veir et savoir.
>   Et se de mon nom veult avoir
>   Aucuns aucune cognoissance,
>   Ne l'en ferai or demonstrance
>   Autrement fors que par mos teus,
>   C'on entre par moi es osteus.
>   De plus or ne descouverroie
>   Moi, ne mon sournom ne vorroie
>   Rimer ne par apiert retraire:
>   Chi veil me nel [*sic: lire* nef] à rive traire.

                                  [prose
                               interpolation
                             of Gui de Mori]

Après ce que je Guis devant dis enc [*lire:* euc] ce premier livre aussi fait comme chi deseseure [*sic*] est contenu, vint antre mes mains li livres maistres Jehan de Meun, ouquel j'ai adjousté et osté si comme j'avoie fait en l'autre, et ai chest livre deviset en cincq parties. En la premiere partie, qui est li quarte de tout le Rommant, sont contenu li dit de Raison, et commence où Belacueil est encore en prison, et oste le fin du Rommant maistre Guillaume, por ce qu'il se vantoit closement que s'amie estoit à lui venue. Si se tient maistres Jehans de Meun, par qui est signifiés li amans si comme desesperance [*sic*] de chou que leurs fais estoit apercheüs; et pour ce qu'il s'estoit d'amors complains et l'avoit comparé à fortune pour sa muableté, pour che enquiert il qu'est Amors et qui est fortune. Et nuls ne l'en puet si bien dire le verité comme Raisons. Et pour avoir la continuation des dis maistres Jehan as autres, nous recommencerons à la complainte de l'amant qui dit ainssi:

ONE: THE SPECTRAL AUTHOR

Hé Bel-acueil bien sai de voir [repetition of the
. . . . 12 last lines of
Car ge n'ai mes aillors fiance. Guillaume de Lorris's
incomplete text]

Chi commenche li livres maistre Jehan de Meun sur le Rommant de la Rose, qui est li quarte partie de ce livre. [rubric]

Et si l'oi-ge perdu espoir, etc. [first line of Jean de Meun's continuation]

([poem]   This is the dream that I dreamed.
[prose]   Thus ends the Romance of Master Guillaume de Lorris, [telling] how he brought his love to an end.
[poem]   In the year of Jesus Christ's Incarnation, by duplication of 645, on the Thursday before *Resurrexi* is sung [i.e., Holy Thursday], this book was brought to completion and ended in the way that Guillaume ends it, or so I assume it to be so, for I have not read any more of it in any book I have read up to this point. And I have excised many words and added some in a number of places, just as it can be seen and ascertained. And if anyone wishes to have some information concerning my name, I will not now reveal it to him in any other way than by the following words: for it is through me that one enters one's lodging. I would not now unveil myself any more than this, nor would I place into rhyme, or openly provide, my surname: here I wish to bring my boat to shore.
[prose]   After I, the aforementioned Gui, had made this first book as it is contained above, the book of Master Jean de Meun came into my hands; I made insertions and deletions to it just as I had done with the other one, and I divided this book into 5 parts. In the first part, which is the fourth of the entire Romance, are contained the sayings of Reason and it begins at the point where Bel Acueil is still in prison, and it/he eliminates the end of Mas-

ter Guillaume's Romance, because of the fact that he was secretly boasting that his *amie* had come over to him. Here stands Jean de Meun, through whom is symbolized (*signifiés*) the lover who seemed to be in despair over the fact that their relationship had been discovered. And since he had lamented over Amor and had compared him to Fortune because of his changeableness he inquires what Love (Amor) is and who is Fortune. And no one can explain the truth to him so well as Reason. And in order to have the continuation comprising the writings of Master Jean [which were added] to the others, we will begin again at the lament of the Lover, who speaks thus:

[poem] Ah! Fair Welcoming, I know in truth . . . since I have no ties of faith elsewhere.

[prose] Here begins the book of Master Jean de Meun on the Romance of the Rose, which is the 4th part of this book.

[poem] And perhaps I have lost it . . .)

This informative passage provides valuable information concerning the editorial history of the *Rose* along with precious comments on the activity of the medieval scribe. Gui de Mori seems initially to have known the *Rose* poem as the first part, completed by the "anonymous conclusion," presumably as the text is copied in B.N. f. fr. 12786. Moreover, Gui accepted this continuation as having been written by Guillaume de Lorris; that is, he believed that the two parts (which he does not, in fact, distinguish as such) formed a *single poetic unit* by one author.[61] Only at a later time did Jean's continuation "come into his hands," thus prompting him to perform the same editorial tasks on it, while fusing together what he now perceived as two separate parts. Nonetheless, Gui pursues his conviction of the integrity and completion of Guillaume's text to such an extent that he accuses Jean de Meun of the "crime" of literary dismemberment: ". . . oste le fin du Rommant maistre Guillaume, por ce qu'il se vantoit closement que s'amie

---

[61] Cf. above, note 21. Rouard, "D'un Manuscrit," believed that he had in *Rou* the complete poem of Guillaume de Lorris.

estoit à lui venue."⁶² (". . . he eliminates the end of Master Guillaume's Romance, because of the fact that he was secretly boasting that his *amie* had come over to him.") Gui interprets Jean's assertions of the incompleteness of the first *Roman de la Rose* as a mere pretext, an excuse for his own continuation.

Gui measures his temporal coordinates with surprising care. He dates his work at 1290 ("par dupplication/de VI^c, de V et XL") and, in a second move (this time, only in the prose section), he tells us that Jean de Meun's continuation was made available to him only after he had completed his first "draft": "Après ce que je Guis . . . euc ce premier livre . . . fait . . . , vint antre mes mains li livres maistres Jehan de Meun." ("After I, Gui, had made this first book, Master Jean de Meun's book came into my hands.") While confirming Amor's tale of two successive authors, this statement lends support to the traditional dating of Jean de Meun's poem (around 1275). It would also indicate that the "takeover" of Jean's continuation was rapid and definitive.

The corresponding interpolated passage in *Tou*, while appearing quite similar in many respects, contains some variations of considerable importance. First, the concluding verse line in *Ter*, "Chi veil ma nef à rive traire," a typical scribal closing formula, is replaced in *Tou* by five lines that introduce Jean de Meun and his continuation (which in *Ter* were only mentioned in the prose section):⁶³

> A maistre Jehan me voel traire
> de Meun, ki a autrement
> Fait fin sur ce commencement,
> Et voel chi escrire ses dis
> Selonc les singnes deseurdis.

(I wish to pass over to master Jean de Meun, who constructed another sort of ending upon this beginning, and here I wish to write down his sayings according to the above-mentioned signs.)

Everything concerning the prior existence of Guillaume's solitary text is deleted in the prose that follows. Finally, in the introductory

---

62 To be sure, the subject of this sentence is ambiguous (either Jean de Meun or the continuation itself "removed" the ending ["oste le fin"]). The corresponding passage from *Tou*, however, quoted below, removes the ambiguity.
63 Langlois II, p. 254.

rubric, the name of Gui de Mori appears after that of Guillaume de Lorris: "Chi fine li oevre maistre Guillaume. Et dans Guis de Mori dist apriès ensy. XXIX."[64] ("Here ends the work of Master Guillaume. And Lord Gui de Mori spoke afterwards thus. XXIX.") We find in *Tou* a shift in orientation that tends simultaneously to obliterate all traces of the chronological development of Gui de Mori's commentary (some layers of which remain in *Ter*) and to legitimize his creative role. Basing themselves on this change in orientation, Jung and Langlois agree that *Ter* was written before *Tou*;[65] indeed, a manuscript that traces the steps in the commentary's development almost as it is taking place (we see clearly the state of the commentary *before* the discovery of Jean's continuation, as well as the story of the discovery) logically precedes one that makes no mention thereof. Jung develops this observation a bit further by suggesting that, while *Ter* represents Gui's first edition, *Tou* provides an example of a later systematization that attempts to correct and regularize the text, "une sorte d'édition critique."[66] It remains to be seen whether Jung's supposition of two editions overseen by Gui is at all plausible in the medieval context.

The conception of *Tou* as an innovative reworking is also reflected in the insertion of an eighty-eight-line prologue, totally lacking in *Ter*. In this prologue, Gui describes a system of diacritical signs that he intends to place in the margins of the manuscript; their function will be to mark and classify his textual alterations. I will at this point recall briefly Gui's system, which has been studied at some length in the articles by Jung and Langlois. The textual revisions are predicated upon four distinct operations: (1) the omission of one or several verse lines (marked by "une petite vergiele," a horizontal line); (2) an addition ("une estoilete," an asterisk); (3) a change in form that retains the original meaning ("l'estoilete avoec la vergiele"); and (4) a "subtraction reprise" (".II. roses escriptes"). In accordance with the manuscript relationships he posits, Jung suggests that the latter sign refers to previously deleted passages that were restored in a later, revised

---

64 Ibid. The number "XXIX" refers to a chapter-like division that Gui applied to the entire text. Accordingly, Gui's interpolated passage, itself designated with a number, is fitted into the totality of the text as he organized it.
65 Langlois II, p. 263 and Jung, "Gui de Mori," pp. 107–10.
66 Jung, "Gui de Mori," p. 110.

edition.[67] Throughout, Gui demonstrates a remarkable and singular interest in his reader, desirous that the latter be constantly aware of the divergences between the original text and the edited version. At the very least, his systematic editorial policy foreshadows the type of attention to texts and variants that will be found a century later in the first Humanist textual editors.[68] Gui nonetheless feels no compunction in interpreting obscure passages according to his own moral categories and, moreover, he leaves himself open to an infinite number of future textual variants, all of which will depend on the viewpoint of each new reader:[69]

> Et voel ke cist signe escrit soient
> Si ke li liseour les voient,
> Pour ce que s'a aucuns ne plaist
> Çou ke j'avrai mis ou soustrait
> Par les margieles desus dittes,
> Entre tes .ii. roses escriptes,
> Qui feront ausci com devise
> De la subtraction reprise,
> Auques tost, s'il i voet pener,
> Pora le risme ramener

(And I want these signs to be written down in such a way that the readers will see them; this is so that if someone doesn't like what I have inserted or excised as indicated by the abovementioned marginal notations, he will rather rapidly, if he is willing to work at it, be able to put back the original text between two inscribed roses, which will thus act as a marker for deletions which have been put back in [*subtraction reprise*])

Gui's textual alterations are at times considerable, occasionally affecting several hundred lines. His strictly borderline position

---

67 Ibid., p. 111.
68 Cf. L. D. Reynolds and N. G. Wilson, *Scribes and Scholars: A Guide to the Transmission of Greek and Latin Literature,* 2nd ed. rev. (Oxford, 1974), pp. 108–29 and Bibliographical Notes, pp. 234–8.
69 Langlois II, pp. 261–2. Jung, "Gui de Mori," p. 111, offers a different punctuation for this difficult passage, which, in my opinion, needlessly alters the meaning. Specifically, Jung omits the comma after "dittes" and places "s'a aucuns ne plaist/Çou ke j'avrai mis ou soustrait" within parentheses. Insofar as "Par les margieles dessus dites" refers to the three previous diacritical marks and the reader's perception of them, while "Entre tes .ii. roses escriptes" designates the future reader's textual emendations (thus complementing "Pora le risme ramener"), the comma placed between them provides an appropriate syntactic division. Jung's punctuation confuses the two "moments."

leads us to ask whether he should be considered a scribe or an author. His entire undertaking, that of presenting someone else's text, along with his frequent acknowledgments to "celui ou ciaus ki ont rismé le roumans" ("the person or persons who put the romance into rhyme"), would seem to classify him as a scribe; on the other hand, several indications in the prologue would speak for a consideration of him as an author. Indeed, the very fact of writing a prologue replete with rhetorical formulae and authorial commonplaces elevates the lowly redactor to a commanding position. The very first lines echo a maxim undoubtedly suggested by the beginning of Richard de Fournival's *Bestiaire d'Amours:* "Toute discrete creature/Desire asavoir par nature"[70] ("Every single creature wishes by nature to have knowledge"). While the inclusion of a proverb in a poem's *exordium* was a well-known and widely used rhetorical technique in the Middle Ages, it is tempting to see in the "creature" seeking "asavoir" – that is, wishing to distinguish or improve himself in some way – the plight of a redactor adding a prologue on top of ("sur") a romance which was already a recognized text of authority.

In the course of the prologue, Gui appears to be attempting an appropriation of the work's subject as well as its structuring principle. Not only does he introduce the subject of *his* poem, "C'est Amours" ("It is Love"), but he also recounts his own personal inspiration by Amor, the God of Love:[71]

> Et pour çou que jou trés m'enfance
> Me sui penés du maintenir
> Amours, ne me puis plus tenir
> Que ne face sa volenté.

(And because I have taken pains to uphold Amor since my childhood, I can no longer keep from fulfilling his desire.)

He has been requested to write an inspirational work, he adds:

> Et cil ki sont de no couvent
> M'ont requis et proié souvent

---

70 *Li Bestiaires d'Amours di Maistre Richart de Fornival e li Response du Bestiaire*, ed. Cesare Segre (Milan, 1957), p. 3: "Toutes gens desirent par nature a savoir." This proverb, translated from Aristotle's *Metaphysics,* was quite popular as an opening *sententia* in vernacular works.
71 Langlois II, p. 260.

> C'un petit m'entente aploiasce
> A ce c'aucun dit retrouvaisce
> D'Amours et de ses dous conmans
> Qui peuist estre as vrais amans
> Au lire consolations
> De lors grans tribulations.

(Those who are of our order have often asked, and even begged, me to use my skill [*entente*] to compose some poem about Amor and his sweet commandments, which might, when read, console true lovers for their great tribulations.)

Then, by a movement of modesty striking in this context, Gui decides that he could do nothing better than take up an already written poem, exemplary in its genre, *Le Roman de la Rose:*

> Si ai mout grant piece pensé,
> Tant k'il m'est venu en pensé
> Ke en nul sens je ne peuisse,
> Com bien ke m'entente i meïsse,
> Nul si biel dit d'Amours trouver
> Com cil fist cui sens esprover
> Poons par les dis de le Rose.

(And so I thought for a great while, until it occurred to me that, however much I might concentrate on it, I could never in any way compose such a beautiful poem about Amor as did he whose talent we can witness in the writings of the Rose.)

If his pose is subservient, his rhetoric is triumphant; here and elsewhere, his discourse overflows with terms borrowed from authorial topics: *entent, entention, mataire, trouver, metre paine.*[72] Indeed, Gui's desire to appropriate authority in a rhetorical fashion should remind us that the expression of humility was itself a classical and medieval authorial commonplace.[73]

While Gui's reverential attitude toward his predecessors and their illustrious text easily explains the scribal adoration of them

---

72 Cf. Kelly, *Sens,* pp. 31–85 and Gallais, "Recherches," *CCM,* 13 (1970), 338–44.
73 This *topos* undergoes a number of extremely subtle variations in the works of Chrétien de Troyes, especially at those moments when the author undertakes a description of some difficulty: Cf. *Le Chevalier au lion,* ed. Mario Roques, CFMA 89 (Paris, 1960), lines 2161–5 and *Erec et Enide,* ed. Mario Roques, CFMA 80 (Paris, 1952), lines 6640–50. For a wider view of the application of this *topos,* see Curtius, *European Literature,* pp. 407–13.

in later manuscripts, it is also easy to see how he himself could be enshrined along with them.[74] Gui treats his source in much the same way as romance writers are accustomed to in their dealings with Latin materials: The original serves initially as an authoritative pre-text, but ultimately as an excuse for one's own creative efforts.[75] Even authorial succession within the vernacular tradition is not without precedent; let us not forget Huon de Méry's remarks concerning *his* forebears, Chrétien de Troyes and Raoul de Houdenc:[76]

> Joliveté semont et point
> Mon cuer de dire aucun bel dit;
> Mes n'ai de quoi; car tot est dit,
> Fors ce qui de novel avient. . . .
> Pour ce que mors est Crestïens
> de Troies, cil qui tant ot pris
> De trover, ai hardement pris
> De mot a mot meitre en escrit
> Le tournoiement Antecrit
>
> I meint dex Hugon de Meri,
> Qui a grant peine a fet cest livre,
> Car n'osoit pas prendre a delivre
> Le bel françois a son talent,
> Car cil qui troverent avant
> En ont coilli tote l'eslite,
> Pour c'est ceste oevre meins eslite
> Et plus fu fort a achever.
>   Molt mis grant peine a eschiver

---

74 From the earliest manuscripts that have come down to us, Guillaume de Lorris and Jean de Meun are referred to in rubrics as *aucteur* or *maistre,* both terms of reverence (cf. for example, mss. B.N. f. fr. 378 and 1559 – both dating from the end of the thirteenth century). Another sign of this view is the portrayal of the author at work in many of the poem's illuminations. The illuminator of *Tou* even chose to portray an author at his desk inside the large illuminated "T" which begins the prologue – undoubtedly a portrait of Gui de Mori. This page is reproduced in Alfred Kuhn, *Die Illustration des Rosenromans,* Jahrbuch der Kunsthistorischen Sammlungen des Allerhöchsten Kaiserhauses, Band XXXI, Heft I (Vienna/Leipzig, 1913–14), p. 23.
75 To take only one of many examples, one might mention Chrétien's reference to his source, "un des livres de l'aumaire/Mon seignor saint Pere a Biauvez" (*Cligés,* ed. A Micha, CFMA 84 [Paris, 1957], lines 20–1) ("one of the books from the library of my Lord Saint Peter at Beauvais").
76 *Li Tornoiemenz Antecrit,* ed. Georg Wimmer (Marburg, 1888), lines 6–9, 22–6, 3526–37.

> Les diz Raol et Crestïen,
> C'onques bouche de crestïen
> Ne dist si bien com il disoient.

> (Gayety requests and incites my heart to recount some beautiful poem: But I don't have the means, for everything has been said, except what comes from novelty.... Since Chrétien de Troyes, who was so praised for his poetic creation, is dead, I have been so bold as to write down, word by word, the Tournament of Antechrist.
>   ...
> May God lead Huon de Méri there [to Paradise]; he took great pains to compose this book, for he did not dare to use the fair French language as freely as he desired, since those who wrote before him picked all the choicest morsels of it. That is why this work is less perfect and was harder to finish.
>   I took a lot of trouble to sidestep the poems of Raoul [de Houdenc] and Chrétien, for never did the mouth of any Christian speak as well as they.)

Huon de Méry's statements and those of Gui de Mori present numerous similarities: the exterior agent ("Joliveté semont" ["Gayety requests"]; "Amors m'en a amounesté" ["Love advised me to do it"]); importance of the heart; personal powerlessness ("mes n'ai de quoi" ["but I don't have the means"]; "en nul sens je ne peuisse" ["in no way could I do it"]); the idea of novelty. The striking difference in the two authors' responses to the question of novelty is, however, revealing. For Huon, in spite of the fact that "tot est dit" ("all has been said"), there is hope: "Fors ce qui de novel avient" ("Except for that which arises from novelty"). He repeats a similar contradictory thought at the end of his poem by establishing the comparison between the use of language and the harvesting of grain: Chrétien de Troyes and Raoul de Houdenc "en ont coilli tote l'eslite" ("picked the choicest morsels of it"). The solution, of course, is to say something else (as it were, glean what was left after the reapers passed through the field): "eschiver les diz Raol et Crestïen" ("sidestep the poems of Raoul and Chrétien"). But this is only theoretically the case, for Huon's narration has as its starting point the magic fountain of Brocéliande – the very fountain textualized so marvelously by Chrétien in his *Yvain*. Thus, Huon's story and inspiration ("pensé"), which he terms "novel" ("fresh, new"), is generated by the author's personal insertion in another author's fictional world.

Gui de Mori's approach to the theme of novelty is quite different:[77]

> Pour ce ne voel en *noeve cose*
> Trover maintenant metre paine,
> Maismement c'au jor d'ui se paine
> Cascuns de trover *noviaus dis,*
> S'est aucune fois enlaidis
> Ly mieudres pour le mains vaillant,
> C'on dit: De *noviel* tout plaisant.
> Pour ce ne m'en voel entremetre.

(This is why I don't at present wish to put a lot of effort into composing *something new,* especially since everyone today tries to compose *new poems,* and sometimes excellence is demeaned for the sake of something less good. For as they say: Everyone likes something *new.* That's why I don't want to get involved in it.)

What can he be suggesting but that these "new" poems such as that of Huon supplant the "classics," relegating them to a position of obscurity? This difference in perspective between our two authors is borne out by the difference in their products: an original, though partially derivative, narrative account, on the one hand, and a greatly revised textual edition, on the other. Nonetheless, the similarity in their expressed concerns and a shared authorial rhetoric suggest their conformity to a particular tradition of writing which occupies a continuum lying somewhere between scribal subservience and literary independence. The *rapprochement* is not meant to minimize their differences but, instead, to highlight their common ground.

Another element typical of romance composition, as we saw above, is the author's explicit naming of himself.[78] Gui does not mention his own name in the prologue, but presents later, in the

---

[77] Langlois II, pp. 260–1.
[78] Many scribes do indeed name themselves, but usually in passages restricted to prose or occupying a maximum of two lines. For an extremely useful catalogue, the reader is referred to *Colophons de manuscrits occidentaux des origines au XVIe siècle,* par les Bénédictins de Bouveret (Suisse), Spicilegii Friburgensis Subsidia, 2–5 (Fribourg, 1965–76). Four volumes out of seven have appeared.

midst of the previously cited passage interpolated between the two parts of the poem, an enigmatic version thereof:

> Et se de mon nom veult avoir
> Aucuns aucune cognoissance,
> Ne l'en ferai or demonstrance
> Autrement fors que par mos teus,
> C'on entre par moi es osteus.

> (And if anyone wishes to have some information concerning my name, I will not now reveal it to him in any other way than by the following words: for it is through me that one enters one's lodging.)

A satisfactory answer to Gui's riddle has never been found. According to Méon, for instance, the copyist was probably named La Porte ("on entre par moi es osteus").[79] Langlois understandably doubted this solution, but his own suggestion, that the word *perron* understood should designate the scribe's family name, is equally unlikely.[80] The solution to this enigma, it seems to me, can be found in a word used in the very text of the *Rose* and which describes the portal through which the Lover gains entry into the garden: "*gui*chet" (522). Gui himself was obviously not impressed by the subtlety of this maneuver, quite common at the time, inasmuch as he states quite matter-of-factly, not two sentences later: "Après ce que je Guis devant dis . . . " ("After I, the aforementioned Gui . . . "). This answer to Gui's riddle appears even more likely when we consider that through this clever strategem our scribe/author's name becomes for the Lover, and at the same time for the reader, the gateway to the allegorical world of Deduit's garden.

This game of poetic substitution accelerates at the moment of Amor's authorial excursus. Gui inserts at this point a passage of his own creation which, while borrowing a series of expressions from Jean de Meun's text, clearly establishes the former in the lineage of the successive authors; suddenly, Amor's prophecies announce the arrival of Gui de Mori: "uns autres vendra;" "Assés tenra bien mes conmans;" "Et vaura as amans aprendre;" "Sour

---

79 Méon, *Rose*, I, p. x.
80 Langlois II, p. 255.

tous roumans il amera/Ce roumans, et l'amendera."⁸¹ ("Another one will come;" "Quite well will he keep to my commandments;" "And he will wish to teach lovers;" "Above all romances he will love this one and will improve upon it.") If Jean established the principle of a secondary author/continuator who functions on an equal footing with the first author, Gui de Mori wishes to fix himself in a tertiary position, as a charter member, albeit a modest one, of the authorial "club":⁸²

> On ora de lui mention
> En l'an de l'incarnation
> Mil et II^c et quatrevins
> Et dis, desci en sui devins.
> Guis de Moiri avra a non,
> Mais il n'ert pas de tel regnon
> Com cis Jehans ne chil Guillaumes.

(One will hear talk of him in 1290 A.D. I know of this by divination. He will be called Gui de Mori but he will not be of such renown as Jean or Guillaume.)

The precedent, established by Jean and elaborated by Gui, prepares the way for a potentially infinite chain of future continuator/editors who will successively renew the fiction and replace the previous controlling subjects.

Gui's final move, again foreshadowed by Jean de Meun, consists in the total insertion of the author into the romance fiction, the very fictionalization of his own persona. In the case of the *Rose* fiction, this process takes the form of a fundamental allegorization, marking the return to the original basis of Guillaume's account:⁸³

> Mais Fortune li [Gui] ert contraire
> Lonc tamps, et si vil le tenra
> C'a paines a honnour venra.

---

81 Ibid, pp. 255–6. Cf., in the text of Jean de Meun, "Puis *vendra* Johan Chopinel" (10535); "ou seront mis tuit mi *conmant*" (10520); "Puis *vodra* si la chose *espondre*" (10573); "Cist *avra* li romanz si chier/qu'il le *vodra* tout parfenir" (10554–5).
82 Langlois II, p. 256.
83 Ibid., pp. 256–7.

>   Malebouce et sa compaignie
>   Li feront mainte vilonnie.
>
> (But Fortune will for a long time serve him adversely, and will consider him so low that he will have difficulty attaining honor. Male Bouche [Evil Tongue] and his company will deal him many a low blow.)

While echoing the personal experience recounted in the prologue — Gui as Amor's servant — this passage disassembles the narrative's fictional barriers. Characters ostensibly removed from reality and contained inside the fiction (Fortune and Male Bouche) take part in the author/continuator's story and vice versa. Considering that Jean de Meun performs precisely the same reversal on Guillaume de Lorris, who in turn predicated his account on the intimate and interchangeable relationship established between lover and writer at the outset, we might here be approaching an understanding of the fascination exercised by the *Rose* fiction on its succession of readers.

In view of this phenomenon of the successive fictionalized authors, certain assertions made by Gui concerning Jean de Meun should not at all appear surprising. First, in the manuscript — now lost — described by Rouard (*Rou*), Gui states, "Et premierement, s'ensuit le traittie que il [Jean de Meun] rima en demantiers que belacueil estoit en prison....."[84] ("And first there follows the treatise that he [Jean de Meun] rhymed while Bel Acueil was in prison"). Very clearly, Jean and his activity (writing the text) are situated at the same conceptual level as the fictional account, the tale of Bel Acueil's doleful plight. The lack of syntactic rigor attributable to Gui's expression — due perhaps to a real lack of linguistic precision or, on the other hand, to a determined reinterpretation of external reality — forces the barriers separating author and story to blur to such an extent that their mutual distinctiveness is erased. The following variant from *Tou* provides an even more striking example of this device: "Si ke maistres Jehans le reprent chi si com Belacuel est en prison. Et se complaint *com amans* devant le castiel, *el lieu de* maistre Guillaume."[85] ("And Master Jean takes it up here just as Bel Acueil is in prison. And he

---

84 Rouard, "D'un Manuscrit," 986.
85 Langlois II, p. 255.

voices his plaint *as the lover* before the castle, *in place of* Master Guillaume.") In this instance, Jean has unequivocally become the Lover, replaced Guillaume, and quite literally stationed himself outside the castle. This interpretation is especially surprising in view of the fact that in Jean de Meun's writing of the fiction, the Lover continues to be identified with the former author, Guillaume de Lorris, while the new narrator occupies an exterior position. An echo of the same interpretation occurs in the prose from *Ter*, cited above: "Si se tient maistres Jehans de Meun, *par qui est signifiés* li amans si comme desesperance [*sic*] de chou que leurs fais estoit apercheüs" ("There thus stands Master Jean de Meun, by whom is symbolized the lover, in despair over the discovery of their situation.") Supported by the past participle *signifiés* (signified, symbolized), an allegorical explanation is being proffered, and one whose key is to be found in the circumstances of the poem's very creation. Jean's suppression of Guillaume de Lorris's original ending is justified, accordingly, by moral and not aesthetic imperatives: "Et por coi il commence la, je croi que ce soit por ce ke maistres Guillaumes vint trop tost a fin et ke il se vante closement que s'amie vint a lui."[86] ("And the reason why he begins there, I believe it is because Guillaume came too quickly to the end and was secretly boasting that his *amie* came to his side.") Gui's reinterpretation of the conventional roles of writer and reader offers support for his own unorthodox departure from the limited role of scribe/compiler.

The alternating use of verse and prose offers an additional textual symptom of the inherent duplicity of Gui's position. The different types of information conveyed in the verse and the prose suggest a certain repulsion between the two basic modes of discourse. For instance the verse section is distinguished by a temporal specificity (dating) lacking in the prose. Gui de Mori, as we have seen, refuses to name himself in the verse portion of his connecting passage, while he freely reveals his identity in the prose. He even says, "mon sournom ne vorroie/rimer ne par apiert [variant from *Tou:* rime] retraire." ("I would rather not put my name into rhyme or openly reveal it.") If we accept the temporal

---

[86] Ibid. Cf. *Rou:* "et pour ce qui luy sembla que maistre Guillaume de Lorris mettoit un peu de ventence en ce qu'il venoit si toust a fin d'avoir sa mie a son talant pour ce fist-il ce traictie plus long...."

succession in the writing of the two manuscripts, *Ter* and *Tou*, we notice that the verse section undergoes considerably less change than the prose. Indeed, in the second redaction (*Tou*), the mention of Jean de Meun enters the verse section, constituting the only substantial addition. The relatively static nature of verse should come as no surprise, given that it constituted the essence of poetic language – prose, less stable and certainly of lesser importance next to a verse text, was habitually reserved for scribes. The reworkings of Gui de Mori, consisting of prose sections along with lengthy verse passages, thereby reflect his midway position, marking a struggle between scribal passivity and authorial aggressivity.[87]

[87] This midway position explains Gui's last line which belongs to an authorial, as well as to a scribal, *topos:* "Chi veil ma nef a rive traire." Cf. *Colophons*, no. 262:

> Sicut nautes desiderat portum videre
> Ita scriptor desiderat librum complere.

(Just as the sailor wishes to see the port so does the scribe [*scriptor*] wish to complete his book.)

quoted by Fred C. Robinson, "Old English Literature in its Most Immediate Context," in *Old English Literature in Context: Ten Essays*, ed. J. Niles (Bury St. Edmonds, 1980), p. 13; as well as the more spiritual formula:

> Sicut desiderat navigator ad ripam venire
> Si desiderat Scriptor Maganarius ad regnum dei venire.
> (*Colophons*, no. 12892).

(Just as the navigator wishes to come to shore, so the scribe Maganarius wishes to come to the kingdom of God.)

Examples in Old French, both from the first half of the thirteenth century, include Jean Renart, *Le Lai de l'Ombre* (ed. Félix Lecoy, CFMA 104 [Paris, 1979]):

> Mout par me torne a grant delit
> . . .
> une aventure a metre en rime.
> L'en dit, qui bien nage et bien rime,
> qui de haute mer vient a rive,
> qui a port de bien dire arrive,
> plus l'en proisent et roi et conte. (42–9)

(It gives me very great delight . . . to commit an adventure to rhyme. It is said that if someone swims and rhymes (*rime*) well, and makes it to shore from the high sea, arriving at the port of good speech [or through his good speech], then kings and counts consider him all the more worthy for it.)

which was certainly copied by Gerbert de Montreuil in his *Roman de la Violette* (ed. Douglas Labaree Buffum, SATF [Paris, 1928]):

> Gyrbers de Mosteruel define
> De la Violete son conte,

Jung expresses surprise that the hypothetical edited version of Gui's first redaction, as found in the Tournai manuscript, incorporates the anonymous conclusion.[88] He is implying, of course, that the replacement of one continuation, or ending, by another should entail the total eradication of the former. Not so, according to what Gui tells us. Unlike his modern counterpart, Gui sees no contradiction or difficulty in the possibility of multiple continuations. Even though he considers the anonymous conclusion to be Guillaume's own (and thus "definitive" in our eyes) there is no hesitation in presenting an alternative. Gui mentions "le Romant Maistre Jehan de Meun" ("The Romance of Master Jean de Meun") but also "la fin que Maistre Jehans de Meung a fait a ce romans."[89] ("The end which Master Jean de Meun made for this romance"). It is not clear whether there exists only one *roman,* or several entities conceivable as such, for the scribe. We might add that a distinct difference is expressed by Gui concerning the two words *roman* and *livre.* Whereas *roman* seems to designate a work in the abstract sense ("li Rommans maistre Guille de Loris"), *livre* refers specifically to the material volume that results from the scribe's work.[90] Gui would never talk about his own *roman* al-

> N'en velt plus faire lonc aconte,
> Tant a rimé k'il est a rive. (6634–7).
>
> (Gerbert de Montreuil ends his tale of the Violette, and doesn't wish to go on any longer; so much has he rhymed [*rimé;* or possibly *ramé,* "rowed"] that he has come to shore.)

In both cases, as Lecoy suggests in his notes (pp. 43–4), a play on words is undoubtedly intended between *rimer* and *ramer.* For the universal use of this *topos* in a variety of authors, cf. Curtius, *European Literature,* pp. 128–30.

88 Jung, "Gui de Mori," p. 110: "il est remarquable que Gui de Mori ait conservé la fin apocryphe dans *Tou,* et qu'il l'ait manifestement corrigée d'après un modèle qui nous est inconnu." Jung's remark covers two distinct points: that the end should have been included in the reworking (after the addition of Jean de Meun's continuation) *and* that *Tou* contains an inner contradiction (an interpolation within the text of *Tou* refers to a version of the anonymous conclusion which is not the one included therein).

89 Both are from *Rou;* cf. Rouard, "D'un Manuscrit," 984–6. It might be suggested that these two distinct ways of expressing the work of Jean de Meun in some way negotiate the delicate midway point between author and scribe, between object of creation (the *roman* once it has come into existence) and the effort (*faire*) of the artisan.

90 Cf. Gallais, "Recherches," CCM, 13 (1970), 334–7. This perhaps overly subtle distinction between *livre* and *roman,* which is perfectly maintained in *Ter,* certainly left some medieval readers bewildered. Not only does the scribe of *Tou* replace in the interpolated verse portion "fu terminés/Chis *livre*" and "En *livre* qu'aie encore leu" with "fu terminés/Cis *roumans*" and "En *roumans* que j'aie leü" (cf. Langlois II, p. 254), but in the adjacent prose passages he eliminates every instance of the word *livre,* replacing it with *oevre.*

though he does discuss his *livre:* "Après ce que je Guis devant dis euc ce premier livre fait;" "fu terminés chis livres;" "vint antre mes mains li livres maistres Jehan de Meun."

I would like to discuss one final point that concerns Gui de Mori's relationship to Guillaume de Lorris. The only piece of evidence that invalidates the supposition that the name of Guillaume was first made known through Jean de Meun's continuation is the small rubric placed immediately after Guillaume's poem in *Ter:* "Enssi fine li Rommans maistre Guille de Loris, comment il mena ses amours a fin." ("Thus ends the Romance of Master Guillaume de Lorris, telling how he brought his love to completion.") Langlois understood very well the question that this rubric poses to our evaluative judgment: Did Gui de Mori indeed know the name "Guillaume de Lorris" and its attachment to the first part of the *Roman de la Rose* before reading Jean's continuation, as a purely linear reading of the passage would indicate (and which, moreover, seems doubtful in view of the absence of any independent corroboration)? Or was the name of Guillaume interpolated only afterwards? Langlois finally avoids both questions.[91] In order to take this particular manuscript as proof of Gui's independent knowledge of Guillaume de Lorris, we must assume, as do both Langlois and Jung, that *Ter* was Gui's working copy and that, moreover, the two parts must have been copied at different times. While the latter assumption rests upon no evidence at all, the former seems to be contradicted by the mechanics of manuscript transmission. Given that each new manuscript copy incorporated a series of changes, one cannot expect or count on a rigorous consistency within a particular copy. One must, in fact, expect the contrary. A consideration of the differences between *Tou* and *Ter,* along with Gui's editorial systematization, demonstrates the way in which manuscripts develop through accretion of potentially disparate elements: In each new copy, words are added, deleted, and disfigured — much of the time without our being able to discriminate among successive layerings.[92] The complica-

---

91 Langlois II, pp. 258–9.
92 We might mention in passing the problem of dating Gui de Mori's work. The date of 1290 is twice given in the text: in the interpolated passage found between the two parts of the poem ("par dupplication/de VI^c et V et XL") and in the passage quoted above, in the midst of the authorial discussion ("Mil et II^c et quatrevins/et dis"). Now, *Tou* is also given a later date (1330) by the scribe who copied that particular manuscript: "Escris fu

tions develop in such a way that a *discontinuous* reading can become necessary, a normally clear and straightforward *linear* reading having become impractical.

Taking the passage at hand as an example of this manner of reading, we note first that Gui declares quite openly that he has *already completed* his version of Jean de Meun's continuation ("j'ai adjousté et osté si comme j'avoie fait en l'autre") ("I added and excised just as I had done with the other"), a fact which suggests that the present manuscript (*Ter*) is at least a second copy of the edited version. *Ter,* in other words, is certainly not an autograph copy, being already at a second remove from the hypothetical combined manuscript of Gui (as imagined by Jung and Langlois). As such, the copying of *Ter* would have followed the discovery of Jean's continuation and the name of Guillaume contained therein. Nothing would have been more natural than for the scribe copying *Ter* to insert the statement of Guillaume's identity as a rubric. This "reading" is supported by the fact that the verse section that announces Guillaume's name forms an autonomous syntactic and metrical unit that could easily be excised from the rest with no changes whatsoever. Moreover, when Gui mentions the author(s) of the poem in his prologue (*Tou*), no names are provided ("celui ou ceus ki ont rismé/Le roumans") ("the one, or ones, who rhymed the romance"); the scribe would be more resistant to changing the verse lines of the poem, as would be required in this case. Lest we be disturbed by the contradictions that inhere in the successive and indiscriminate layerings of textual revisions, we should keep in mind the medieval reader's relative lack of concern for such now sacrosanct notions as consistency and continuity. The additive nature of the manuscript textual compilation takes little account of blatant discontinuities and, as we have seen, multiple endings for a single poem.

---

l'an mil et .CCC./et . XXX. [...]." Given that the latter scrupulously maintains Gui's own dating *within* the text through a sort of overdetermined localization, one should not be surprised by other, more purely textual, consequences of this aesthetic based on the accretion of once disparate elements.

ONE: THE SPECTRAL AUTHOR

Although such a lengthy discussion of a figure so minor as Gui de Mori might seem superfluous, he serves to point up two crucial aspects in our evaluation of the *Roman de la Rose* and the authorial quandary elicited by Jean de Meun. First of all, Gui provides a splendid illustration of the earliest reception of the *Rose* text by its readers. In this manner Gui, considerably less enigmatic than Jean de Meun, furnishes the modern reader with a background against which he can interpret more surely the historical and literary role played by Jean de Meun as a reader and author in his own right. Moreover, we can see the sorts of misunderstandings to which medieval texts fall victim at the hands of later readers, with the ensuing perpetuation of those misunderstandings.

Indeed, precious few medieval readers of the *Roman de la Rose* make any mention of the authors and those who do inevitably focus their praise upon Jean de Meun, who subsumed the poem under his own doctrinal program and, more importantly, managed to complete the work.[93] Typical of this trend is the following statement made by the anonymous fourteenth-century author of the *Echecs d'amour*:[94]

> . . . le mieulx en traitte
> Et le plus gracieusement [est]
> Chilz qui fist le commencement
> du joly *Rommant de la Rose* . . .
> Mais sur tous nottable oevre fist
> Chilz qui cest bel *Rommant* parfist
> Ou il declaire apprez comment
> Chilz amoureux finablement
> Cueilla le bouton gracieux
> Qui tant estoit delicieux,
> Et l'ot a sa voulenté plaine,
> Comment que ce fust a grant paine,
> Si com chilz livrez le devise,
> Qui tant est de soubtil devise
> Et tant est plain de grant mistere
> Qu'oncquez mais de ceste matere

---

[93] Badel, *Roman de la Rose*, pp. 135–65.
[94] Quoted from ibid., p. 271.

> Ne fu nulz plus biaulx livrez fais
> Ne plus complez ne plus parfais.

(The best and most gracious in execution [of those who have told of delightful gardens] is the one who did the beginning of the pretty *Romance of the Rose*... But above all others he who finished [*parfist*] this beautiful *Romance* created a noteworthy work; afterwards in it he declares how the lover finally picked the gracious rosebud, which was so delightful, and fulfilled his every wish with it – however difficult the process might have been – as described in this book which is of such an artful design and so full of great mystery that never since has there been any more beautiful, more accomplished or more complete book on this subject.)

However, as though in response to the current opinion expressed above, there is one medieval reader of the *Rose* who makes an astonishingly original statement in defense of the poem's first author:[95]

> Cy fait fin li premier aucteur,
> Qui de moult hault entendement
> Ce livre fist premierement.
> Bien part que fut saichant docteur:
> A lui donc comme inventeur
> Premier, a part et en commun,
> Je veulx que soit donné honneur,
> Non pas a maistre Jehan de Mehun,
> Combien certes que ung chascun
> Y doit avoir honneur et los;
> Car pour tant, se je loe l'un,
> De loange l'autre ne exclos.
> Certainement bien dire l'os
> Que ne congnois homme mortel,
> Nul n'en excepte, tous en forclos,
> Qui sceust perfaire ung oeuvre tel
> Comme cestui, qui est tant bel
> qu'on jugeroit estre tout un,
> Ja soit que trouve bien nouvel
> L'escript de maistre Jehan de Mehun.

---

95 Langlois I, pp. 58–9.

(Here ends the first author, who out of very great understanding made this book initially. He really seems to have been a knowledgeable scholar. I want him — and not Master Jean de Meun — to be accorded honor, on his own and in collaboration, as the first inventor, even though each one certainly deserves to have honor and praise. This certainly follows, for if I praise one of them I do not exclude the other one from praise. I daresay, I am absolutely certain that I do not know any mortal man — and here I make no exceptions, all are excluded from this pronouncement — who would know how to end such a work as this one, which is so beautiful that one would judge it to be totally unified/complete, however much one might find Jean de Meun's writing to be most innovative.)

This statement is signed by a certain "Philibertus" and is to be found in the lower margin of a fourteenth century *Rose* manuscript, B.N. Ms. fr. 24389, Fol. 27v°, at the point where Guillaume de Lorris's poem ends. On this page there is also to be found an authorial portrait. Fleming interprets this passage to mean simply that Philibertus wants us not to forget Guillaume de Lorris in the face of the entire poem's overwhelming unity.[96] I would take exception to Fleming's hasty reading of the passage. Philibertus is not simply "coyly" referring to Guillaume as the *premier aucteur,* but he is specifically desirous of reducing the attention normally paid to Jean de Meun ("non pas a maistre Jehan"). The crux of the matter resides in our interpretation of the word *oeuvre:* Is Philibertus using this word to refer to Guillaume's work, which ends on this very page, or to the entire poem with two parts? Philibertus's initial point seems to be that because of the particular nature of the rapport between the two authors, each of them necessarily receives a measure of praise through the reception of the work: "if I praise one of them I do not exclude the other one from praise." Far from leaving the question of praise at that, Philibertus goes on to specify the nature of his appreciation: "I daresay, I am absolutely certain that I do not know *any* mortal man — and here I make no exceptions, all are excluded from this pronouncement — who would know how to end [*perfaire*] such a work [*oeuvre*] as this one, which is so beautiful that one

---

[96] John V. Fleming, *The Roman de la Rose: A Study in Allegory and Iconography* (Princeton, 1969), pp. 104–5.

would judge it to be totally unified/complete [*un*], *however much* one might find Jean de Meun's writing to be most innovative [*nouvel*]." Fleming automatically assumes that the "oeuvre . . . tout un" refers to the two parts of the poem unified. There seem to be three strong reasons, however, for interpreting the *oeuvre* exclusively as that of Guillaume. First, Philibertus's marked desire to praise Guillaume separately seems to be thwarted by the impossibility of excluding the other author from praise; his repetition of the idea of exclusion ("exclos . . . forclos") accentuates this preoccupation. Second, his outright statement that no mortal man could *perfaire* the *oeuvre* suggests that he is speaking of an ostensibly unfinished work (thus, Guillaume's poem) and that Jean, being mortal, was not up to completing it adequately. We recall that *parfaire* is the word most commonly used in rubrics to describe Jean de Meun's poetic activity. The third piece of evidence is Philibertus's use of a concessive clause (introduced by "Ja soit que") in order to express the contrast between the *oeuvre*'s unity ("qui est tant bel") and the hypothetical compliments that might extend to Jean's *escript* ("bien nouvel"). It seems likely that Philibertus is reacting against common opinion in this marginal notation, praising Guillaume's unfinished poem as beautiful and, by some stretch of the critical imagination, complete. If it is taken together with the remarks of Gui de Mori, we can detect certain evidence for a different medieval reading of the *Rose,* one that could separate the authorial attributions in the face of an overwhelming cult that had developed around the author-figure of Jean de Meun.

In addition to what Gui de Mori tells us about one type of reception of the *Rose* in the late thirteenth century, his work underscores the insuperable distance that lies between our perceptions of literary creation and distribution and the most common medieval notions. The conceptual differences are certainly not without their inner effect on the composition of literary works themselves. If, as we are suggesting, any medieval author was also, in part, a scribe and, conversely, that scribes exercised a creative and manipulative power over their materials, then the strict dividing line that we are accustomed to drawing between the unique, active creator and the several passive forms of literary distribution proves totally misleading. To be sure, Gui's "philological" attitude toward his predecessor's text is surprisingly modern (in the sense outlined above), but what it suggests is that he is a transitional figure whose profoundly "medieval" conception of textuality has already undergone an alteration, however slight, in the direction of conservation and historical fidelity (which will become widespread only at the time of the Italian Renaissance).

The fundamental question of authorship and its relationship to interpretation points our discussion in two distinct directions. Authorship viewed as a strictly historical phenomenon calls into question, first, the status and self-conception of the medieval literary artist in the early Middle Ages. On the one hand, the position of a writer in a quasi-oral, pre-printing society is largely unknown, and perhaps ultimately incomprehensible, to the modern reader. The paucity of documentation that we have concerning the specific nature of writing, literary patronage, and contemporary appreciations of medieval romance is certainly compounded by the profound difference in outlook and perception attendant upon the use of a language that is not predominantly written. Moreover, a public either illiterate or unaccustomed to the profusion of printed pages common to the modern library would have received such literary works with a totally different understanding and appreciation.[97]

A second historical difficulty more specifically related to the production of the literary artifact results from the medieval writer's reduced responsibility toward his task and the incumbent sharing of duties which constituted the making of a medieval manuscript. The "work" of Gui de Mori provides an example, admittedly exaggerated, of the place of the scribe in the transmission of the medieval literary text. The candid view he takes of his procedures does permit us to expand considerably the overly simplified "writer-reader" characterization of the literary chain by positing a series of possible intermediary figures: the passive scribe (simple copyist); the active scribe (or editor); the compiler;[98] the continuator; the miniaturist/illuminator; the poet (self-proclaimed

---

97 Cf. Chaytor, *From Script*, pp. 5–47; Ong, *Orality*, pp. 31–77.
98 Cf. M. B. Parkes, "The Influence of the Concepts of *Ordinatio* and *Compilatio* on the Development of the Book," in *Medieval Learning and Literature: Essays presented to Richard William Hunt*, ed. J. J. G. Alexander and M. T. Gibson (Oxford, 1976), pp. 115–41; and Alastair J. Minnis, "Late-Medieval Discussions of *Compilatio* and the Rôle of the *Compilator*," *Beiträge zur Geschichte der Deutschen Sprache und Literatur* 101 (1979), 385–421.

or anonymous); and, perhaps finally, God, who, in the theological view taken of writing in the Middle Ages, was the ultimate responsible.[99] Such an abstract philosophical conception of authorship certainly contributed to the view of writing as a symbolic gesture and to the resultant elimination of the boundary between the "internal" fictional account and the "external" circumstances of its creation.

The latter observation is substantiated by the early medieval use of the word *auctor,* a term that otherwise provides little help for our investigation of vernacular authorship. Ostensibly, the word refers quite specifically to a group of Latin writers, mostly the important Church fathers, whose writings served as a support for later theological speculation.[100] The *auctores,* taken together, con-

---

[99] In the introduction to his commentary on the first book of Peter Lombard's *Sententiae,* St. Bonaventure discusses the complicated philosophical question of whether the human writer of a doctrinal work can properly be called its author (*auctor*) when God is the ultimate source of its doctrine (*doctor*). Having decided that Peter Lombard *can* be called the author, insofar as he, and not God, wrote with his own finger and spent his own effort ("multo labore et sudore"), Bonaventure presents the following scheme of gradations:

> quod quadruplex est modus faciendi librum. Aliquis enim scribit aliena, nihil addendo vel mutando; et iste mere dicitur *scriptor.* Aliquis scribit aliena, addendo, sed non de suo; et iste *compilator* dicitur. Aliquis scribit et aliena et sua, sed aliena tamquam principalia, et sua tamquam annexa ad evidentiam; et iste dicitur *commentator,* non auctor. Aliquis scribit et sua et aliena, sed sua tanquam principalia, aliena tamquam annexa ad confirmationem; et talis debet dici *auctor.* (The way of making a book is fourfold. For one man writes down others' works, adding or changing nothing, and he is simply to be called a scribe [*scriptor*]. Another writes others' works, adding material, but not of his own confection; and he is called a compiler [*compilator*]. Another writes both the works of others and his own, but in such a way that the works of others are in principal place, and his own are added for the purpose of clarification; and he is called a commentator [*commentator*], not an author [*auctor*]. Another writes both his own works and those of others, but in such a way that his own are in principal place and the others are added for the sake of confirmation; and such a man should be called an author [*auctor*].

Saint Bonaventure, *Commentarius in primum librum sententiarum Petri Lombardi,* in *Opera Omnia,* Vol. 1 (Quarracchi, 1882), pp. 14–15. Cf. Eisenstein, *Printing Press,* pp. 121–2; and Minnis, "Late Medieval," pp. 415–16. On the spiritual use of the book as metaphor, see Curtius's chapter entitled, "The Book as Symbol," op. cit., pp. 302–47; and the fascinating article by Dom Jean Leclercq, "Aspects spirituels de la symbolique du livre au XIIe siècle," in *L'Homme devant Dieu: Mélanges de Lubac* (Paris, 1963–4), pp. 64–72.

[100] Cf. Marie-Dominique Chenu, "Auctor, actor, autor," *Bulletin de Cange – Archivium Latinitatis Medii Aevi,* 3 (1927), 81–6, as well as his expanded study, "Authentica et Magistralia," in *La Théologie au douzième siècle* (Paris, 1957), pp. 351–65. See also Curtius, *European Literature,* pp. 48–61, 260–4, 465–7.

stituted the basic corpus of works used for educational purposes. As M.-D. Chenu has demonstrated, its derivative *auctoritas* was eventually emptied of any ideas of human agency, coming to refer directly to the texts themselves.[101] At the same time, the word *auctor* came to be confused with another word of related meaning, *actor,* which recuperated the primitive meaning of human agency.[102] Given this significant semantic development, the fictionalization of the creative figure in medieval poetry should come as no surprise.[103]

The second direction in which the authorship questions lead us is backwards, to our own interpretive methodology. If there exists such a difference between the conception of literary creation in the Middle Ages and that of the modern world, then we should perhaps make an attempt to modify our received notions in order to accommodate them to a foreign system. Pursuing this idea even further, Michel Foucault has brilliantly demonstrated the extent to which the modern use of the word *author* is immersed in a complex of social and political ideologies.[104] Deconstructing the superficial biographical definition of the word, according to which the author, occupying an exterior space, desires to communicate or express an individual intention, Foucault lays open the consid-

---

101 Chenu, "Authentica," pp. 354-5: "*auctoritas.* . . signifie d'abord la qualité en vertu de laquelle un homme. . .est digne de crédit, de considération, de créance. Par métonymie, l'*auctoritas* désigne ensuite la personne même possédant cette qualité, puis bientôt, par transposition du sujet humain à son acte extérieur, l'écrit . . . . par une nouvelle métonymie, le texte lui-même est directement appelé *auctoritas*, et non plus seulement qualifié comme ayant autorité. Une autorité, c'est le texte même qu'on invoque."

102 *Auctor* from the Latin verb *augere,* "to increase," means most literally "he that brings about the existence of any objects, or promotes the increase or prosperity of it, whether he first originates it, or by his efforts gives greater permanence or continuance to it" (Charlton Lewis and Charles Short, *A Latin Dictionary* [Oxford, 1879]); an *actor,* from the verb *agere,* "to move or act," is, properly speaking, "one who drives or moves anything [. . .] a doer or performer."

103 In addition to the terms *maistre* and *auctor/actor,* many rubricated *Rose* manuscripts designate the narrator in the dream account as *amant*. Owing to the complexity of narrative levels toward the end of Guillaume de Lorris's poem (q.v., below, Chapter Two), the terms *amant* and *auctor/actor* are frequently interchanged in an arbitrary fashion. For a discussion of one example out of many, see my "Closed Quotations: The Speaking Voice in the *Roman de la Rose,*" *Yale French Studies* 67 (1984), esp. pp. 260-1.

104 "Qu'est-ce qu'un auteur?" *Bulletin de la Société francaise de Philosophie,* 22 février 1969, pp. 77-95 (English translation in Michel Foucault, *Language, Counter-Memory, Practice: Selected Essays and Interviews,* trans. Donald F. Bouchard and Sherry Simon [Ithaca, NY, 1977], pp. 113-38).

erable classificatory and eventually repressive powers of the term. An important component of Foucault's argument is the eradication of what might be called the "natural origin" of authorship, the idea that the living, breathing human being so designated provides an absolute point of departure for the text; in fact, the authorial proper name does not designate in the same way as other proper names, which unambiguously refer to the exterior existence of particular individuals: "le nom d'auteur ne va pas comme le nom propre de l'intérieur d'un discours à l'individu réel et extérieur qui l'a produit, mais [. . .] il court, en quelque sorte, à la limite des textes, [. . .] il les découpe [. . .] il en suit les arêtes, [. . .] il en manifeste le mode d'être ou, du moins, [. . .] il le caractérise."[105] The authorial name, in other words, alludes to an exteriority without ever relinquishing its fundamental textual determination. A later statement demonstrates most efficiently the absolute circularity and unidentifiable origin of authorial denomination: "En effet, c'est bien en tant qu'il est texte de l'auteur et de cet auteur-ci que le texte a valeur instauratrice, et c'est pour cela, parce qu'il est texte de cet auteur, qu'il faut revenir vers lui."[106] Foucault's final ambiguity, the uncertain referent of the pronoun *lui* (text or author?), highlights the critical revisionary impetus that perforce works in two directions; the discovery of a new work by a particular author transforms the vision we have of the author's *oeuvre* and consequently of the author's intentions, while the very cohesiveness of this construct determines a work's potential entry into the established canon.

Thus the formalist critical ideal of considering a text solely as a decodable message immune to biographical determinations is itself an illusion. Even if the author as a figure remains unmentioned, such concepts as "poetic originality," "individual expression," and, most importantly, "unity" cling to our most basic judgmental reflexes. Whereas the example of Gui de Mori demonstrates that the first two need not be eliminated from our critical vocabulary, but at least employed with specific qualifications, the latter concept has yet to be investigated. One's decisions about poetic unity, perhaps the only interpretive notion we might call universally ap-

---

105 Ibid., p. 83 (English trans., p. 123).
106 Ibid., p. 93 (English trans., p. 136).

plicable, are indeed intimately connected to attitudes toward authorship. To speak of a poetic unit is to posit an individual intentionality, even in cases where no outside substantiation is available. And the status of a figure such as Gui de Mori (not to mention Guillaume de Lorris or Jean de Meun) is contingent upon our being able to delineate textual units and separate their attribution.

None of these remarks would be necessary were authorial attribution and textual delineation always as consistent as they are in the modern world of printed texts, where the author's name usually occupies a privileged place and the separation between discrete works is scrupulously maintained. But the relative ease of attribution induces us to forget not only the subjective operations involved in our manipulation of categories destined to delimit the literary work, but also the significant fact that the situation has not always been the same. By contrast, the documentary remains that grant us access to the medieval tradition force us to reconsider our accustomed position. Even leaving aside momentarily the difficulty of acquiring authorial information, as we discussed in our previous section, we find that the very presentation of the text in its material form is a cause for concern. If the advent of printing has caused a perceptual effect in terms of the author, its influence on textual permanence, regularity and closure has certainly altered the literary work in its most basic material presentation. Furthermore, the economic restraints to which we alluded above place limitations on the flow of information, restricting the very nature of textual borrowing and quotation, the incessant borrowings and citations which were a hallmark of pre-Renaissance literary and speculative writing. As a consequence, and insofar as legal views of property and plagiarism do not enter into the definition of a work, the medieval perception of what constituted a literary work differed considerably from our own. In the following pages, I would like to discuss a number of ways in which the medieval written tradition in France dictated the transmission and presentation of the vernacular literary work.

THE LITERARY WORK IN THE MIDDLE AGES

It is well known, and has been dealt with quite extensively, that on the microscopic level of words, phrases, spelling, and syntax, variations among different manuscript examples of one same work abound.[107] The task of the textual editor has been that of attempting to sort through problems that occur when trying to establish a textual model out of the profusion of variants. Some variants can be termed "errors" – words or expressions that occur nowhere else, or whose obvious meaning clashes with the context – while others simply propose a different, equally satisfactory meaning. Given that the medieval French language, especially before the late thirteenth century, did not benefit from any imposed standardization and, indeed, was composed of a variety of distinct dialects, we should not be surprised that writer/scribes demonstrate a cavalier attitude toward spellings, conjugations, case endings, and the like. To call such variants "cavalier" or "careless," in fact, is to devalue the period's sense of its own language – disavowing to a great extent the vernacular's resistance to Latin domination – in favor of a modern ideal of standardization and mass communication.

The dividing line between outright errors and perfectly satisfactory readings, understandably vague, places a good deal of authority on the shoulders of the modern editor. He must decide what to allow and what to eliminate. One example of the sorts of difficulties that can arise (of which there are limitless examples in medieval French literature) occurs in the episode of the crystals in the fountain, an important scene in Guillaume de Lorris's poem. Briefly, the Lover/Narrator looks into the fountain and sees on the bottom two crystals. In a number of manuscripts, a short passage immediately following speaks explicitly of *one* crystal only, to return later to a plural usage. One's initial impulse is to regularize the entire episode, making it all plural or all singular, since it is highly unlikely that the number of crystals would have changed. Such was Langlois's editorial solution.[108] Lecoy presents the contradiction in his text, but declares in a note that the manuscript

---

[107] For a general discussion of this state of affairs with regard to texts in Old French, see Foulet and Speer, *On Editing*. While the editor of any such text must negotiate the dual problem of microscopic textual variation inherent to a manuscript tradition *and* the practical need for a single text, few have treated the problem so thoroughly or so openly as Alexandre Micha in his illuminating study, *La Tradition manuscrite de Chrétien de Troyes* (Paris, 1939).

[108] Cf. the edition of Langlois, vol. 2, pp. 80–1.

tradition is corrupt.[109] I have attempted to demonstrate elsewhere that the transference from two crystals to a single one presents a physical parallel to the two types of perception that are being highlighted in the poem.[110] The change is, in fact, an exceedingly subtle way for Guillaume to extend his discussion of Narcissus to the situation of the Lover. It is quite likely that scribes, who often attempted to understand and, if need be, alter that which they were copying, already "regularized" the seeming contradiction much in the manner of modern editors.

In addition to the myriad of careless mistakes which go hand in hand with manuscript transcription, a number of variants result from intentional alterations. As is well known, a scribe copying a work written in a dialect different from his own, would adjust the spellings and declensions to fit his own system. Of course this transformation would usually not be based on a regular model, so a variety of anomalies and rhythmic peculiarities result.[111] The example of the crystals offers another cause for widespread variances: scribal misunderstandings. Still another type of transformation characteristic of the fourteenth and fifteenth centuries, results from the modernization or translation of a language that was becoming too archaic to be readily understood. The *Roman de la Rose*, for example, was modernized in a verse redaction and even turned into a prose work in the fifteenth century.[112] In fact, the trend toward modernization of old texts, rather than the faithful reproduction of an original, remained the prevailing attitude through the early eighteenth century.[113]

---

[109] Lecoy, ed., *Rose*, vol. 1, p. 275: "qu'il y ait eu 'deux pierres de cristal au fond de la fontaine' (1535–36), cela ne fait pas de doute. Il n'en est pas moins vrai que les vers 1541–1568 posent à l'éditeur un problème pratiquement insoluble, aucun des manuscrits jusqu'ici consultés n'ayant une leçon cohérente, sauf quelques-uns de ceux qui ont adopté en principe le singulier pour la tirade (comme c'est le cas du nôtre). Ce singulier peut, à la rigueur, se défendre, si l'on y voit le singulier d'un nom de matière (cf. cependant 1603)."

[110] Cf. "The Allegorical Fountain: Narcissus in the *Roman de la Rose*," *Romanic Review*, LXXII, no. 2 (March 1981), 125–48; and Chapter Four, below."

[111] Cf. Woledge, "Un Scribe champenois."

[112] There were, it appears, two prose versions of the *Rose*, one anonymous and the other attributed to Jean Molinet. Cf. *Le Roman de la Rose, dans la version attribuée à Clément Marot*, ed. Silvio F. Baridon (Milan, 1954–7), I, 15; and Langlois's edition of the *Rose*, vol. I, pp. 32–5.

[113] The sixteenth and seventeenth centuries contented themselves with the modernized version dating from the end of the fifteenth century. Symptomatic of a change in outlook toward the Middle Ages as of the late seventeenth century, Pierre Desmaiseaux

The fluidity of texts on the microscopic level is, of course, a central characteristic of the oral transmission of texts that carried over to the first written transcriptions of vernacular texts. When we have more than one manuscript version of an earlier *chanson de geste*, the differences can be enormous. The several distinct versions of the *Chanson de Roland*, for instance, attest to the dynamic possibilities of textual variation.[114] The differences displayed are so dramatic, however, that it is left open to question whether we should call them merely variants of the same work, or different poems in their own right. Commenting on a tradition more closely related to that of the written text, that of the lyric *chanson*, Paul Zumthor has developed the concept of the *mouvance des textes*, which as an aesthetic appreciation goes far in explaining the characteristic strophic and lexical variations of the genre.[115]

In speaking of the many varieties of manipulation that medieval texts underwent once they entered a certain performative or scribal circulation, we must not forget that in the broadest sense reading for the Middle Ages was an activity, a *practice*. Nothing would have been more foreign to medieval readers than the sort of passive consumption of texts that characterizes the modern literary appetite. We have already discussed the reasons for such a situation, but might ask ourselves here about its consequences. Insofar as the reader (and *not* listener) was in most cases a scribe, one of the major purposes would have been undoubtedly a recopying of the work. The work of reading, in other words, was intimately connected with the function of reproducing, of promulgating. Even for those whose goal was purely entertainment, it seems that the most common manner of "reading" vernacular texts

writes, "Ils [the composers of the modernized version] ont cru rendre l'ouvrage meilleur, et ils n'ont fait que le gâter. On ne reconnaît plus dans ces exemplaires retouchés, l'état où était notre langue dans le treizième siècle" (quoted in Marc-René Jung, "Der Rosenroman in der Kritik seit dem 18. Jahrhundert," *Romanische Forschungen*, 78 [1966], 207). Such a desire to return to manuscript sources will lead to the first "modern" edition of the *Rose*, that of Lenglet-Dufresnoy published in 1735.

114 Raoul Mortier, ed., *Les Textes de la Chanson de Roland*, 10 vols. (Paris, 1940–9).
115 Zumthor, *Essai*, p. 507: "mouvance: 'le caractère de l'oeuvre qui, comme telle, avant l'âge du livre, ressort d'une quasi-abstraction, les textes concrets qui la réalisent présentent, par le jeu des variantes et remaniements, comme une incessante vibration et une instabilité fondamentale'." While for Zumthor this definition applies theoretically to all medieval texts, its most immediate affinity is with those texts which were orally composed and promulgated, i.e., the lyric and the epic songs.

would have been oral, that is, a private or public reading aloud.[116] In this sense, reading coincided with performance or acting, thus marking a return to a pseudo-oral framework.

Nor was the activity of the scribe simply mechanical. As we saw above, the scribe often varied the text he was copying, either in view of his own comprehension or that of his eventual reader. For an audience that did not particularly care about the definitive nature of a work, or who could accept the mention of "authority" as a proper substantiation, part of the activity of reading was a perpetuating or recreating of the work in one's own style. The individual's imposition of an idiosyncratic ordering or meaning upon already existing materials, undoubtedly the two activities which Chrétien de Troyes refers to as *conjointure* and *sens*, extends to the scribe as well as the poet.

If medievalists have been coming to grips with the question of textual variation and "tampering" on the microscopic level, very little work has been done on the macroscopic level, namely, placement and alteration of entire episodes. Perhaps the fullest debate of this kind has revolved around the acceptability of the "Baligant" episode in the Oxford version of the *Chanson de Roland*. Most early participants in the controversy based their judgment on aesthetic grounds – whether or not the episode fit into the entire poetic scheme;[117] more recently, attempts have been made to evaluate the episode according to quantifiable criteria.[118] Whatever

---

116 The word *lire* in Old French is certainly to be translated "to read out loud." Cf. Crosby, "Oral Delivery," and Chaytor, *From Script*, esp. pp. 5–21. The texts assembled by the latter would seem to indicate that while silent reading and copying of texts was a monastic ideal, few medieval readers would have been capable of understanding the text before their eyes without in some way evoking the auditory correlative of the written word. On the performative aspects of reading, see Zumthor, *Essai*, pp. 37–44.

117 Pidal's analysis betrays the impossibility of divorcing a perception of structure from frankly aesthetic judgements. On the one hand, p. 121, he insists that the two are separate: While "Baligant est une addition évidente," "il n'y a pas de règle en matière de goûts." On the other, he uses purely aesthetic judgements in order to prove "Baligant"'s obvious eccentricity. "L'épisode est mal ajusté" (123); "Le début de l'épisode est très maladroit" (123); the idea of following Roland's superior "moral vengeance" with the outright material vengeance of Charlemagne is an "exemple positif de mauvais goût" (125); and finally "L'épisode de Baligant tend à transformer la tragique épopée de Roland en un roman 'moralisateur,' au goût des esprits les plus candides" (126).

118 Cf. the *mise au point* by Duggan, *Song of Roland*, pp. 63–104, who concludes that while the question of the literary value of the "Baligant" episode is purely a matter of taste, a formulaic analysis demonstrates that the episode was a part of the song's

the various opinions might conclude, we have for the moment two undeniable facts: (1) the Oxford manuscript, a unique exemplar, contains the "Baligant" episode well-integrated into its structure; (2) no one has ever doubted that any of the other versions of the *Roland,* even those lacking the "Baligant" episode, comes close to matching the beauty and the artistic strengths of the Oxford text. Given this, the literary critic should perhaps attempt to evaluate the text which he has rather than postulate an archaic hypothetical version. First of all, nothing has ever proven that the "oldest is best"; second, such an activity, far from investigating the literary or the aesthetic, remains squarely in the field of history.

I would now like to discuss a few models of medieval texts displaying a resistance to the fixed, closed nature that we have found characteristic of the modern printed edition. The *Roman de la Rose* presents a particularly complicated example of a very common literary modality in the thirteenth century: the continuation. The most outstanding example of this period, a veritable mine for continuators, is provided by Chrétien de Troyes's *Conte du Graal.* The fascinating situation as it has come down to us in several manuscripts is that of a manifestly unfinished work, ending in mid-sentence, continued by no fewer than four other writers.[119] The First Continuation, so-called because of its anonymity, is not really a continuation at all, inasmuch as it does not pick up all the narrative threads left dangling by Chrétien; although it pursues the narrative of Gauvain's adventures, it never comes back to Perceval. Moreover, another character is introduced, Carados, whose adventures occupy over 5,000 lines in the long version of the continuation. Only in the Second Continuation, by another continuator, are the adventures of Perceval taken up once more. I might add that the "technique" of a series of adventures, seemingly unrelated, was already a feature of Chrétien's *Conte du Graal*

---

tradition for some period of time ("the poem's two major divisions must have passed, as a unity, through the same style-creating process or, in the terminology of oral-formulaic studies, must have been elaborated in the same tradition of singers" [p. 101]).

[119] William Roach, ed., *The Continuations of the Old French Perceval of Chrétien de Troyes,* 5 Vols. (Philadelphia, 1949–83). For a somewhat more detailed discussion of the relationship among the several continuations, see Roach's "Les Continuations du Conte du Graal," in *Les Romans du Graal aux XIIe et XIIIe siècles* (Paris, 1956), pp. 107–18.

(as well as of his earlier romances), leading some critics to suspect that his part of the romance ended even earlier.[120] Inasmuch as the Gauvain adventures are considered by many as digressive and therefore less artistic, they are not to be attributed to our author. The "Baligant" reasoning reappears.

The two final continuators, Gerbert de Montreuil and Manessier, apparently unaware of each other, take up the story after the unfinished Second Continuation, but are found together in one manuscript, as if the one followed the other.[121] The prevailing theory suggests that, originally, both had endings but that the original ending of Gerbert's continuation was suppressed in order to fit it in between the Second Continuation and that of Manessier. Guillaume de Lorris's *Rose* and Chrétien's *Conte du Graal* resemble each other not only because they are unfinished, or suspended, narratives, but also because they both tell of a quest – and a rather mysterious one, at that. The response elicited by these two otherwise quite different poems is undoubtedly not coincidental. Where the quest for a particular goal was one of the major frameworks for romance composition, this goal could be, and was, deferred indefinitely. For the romance writer, and reader, definitive closure meant the end of the fictive participation as well as the end of the reading experience. Indeed, the prevailing penchant for indefinite, open-ended texts, which we witness in another form in the widespread use of quotation, is here translated on the fictive level as the invitation extended by the writer of romance to his projected reader/participant. The creation and perpetuation of fictional worlds, perhaps the major task of medieval romance writers, encompassed both his activity and that of his reader.

In Huon de Méry's *Tornoiement d'Antecrist* we have seen the example of an author who, all the while situating himself in the authoritative shadow of his predecessors Chrétien de Troyes and

---

120 See particularly Leo Pollmann, *Chrétien de Troyes und der Conte del Graal*, Beiheft CX zur *Zeitschrift für romanische Philologie* (Tubingen, 1965).

121 The continuation of Gerbert is found in two manuscripts, B.N. f. fr. 12576 (*A*) and B.N. nouv. acq. fr. 6614 (*B*). Whereas *A* contains all the continuations, Gerbert's text of some 17,000 lines beginning and ending with the same lines from the end of the Second Continuation, followed by the continuation of Manessier (which therefore starts at the same point as Gerbert), *B* is cut off in the middle of Gerbert. Manessier's continuation is found in other manuscripts where there is no trace of Gerbert. Cf. Mary Williams (first two volumes) and Marguerite Oswald (vol. III), eds., Gerbert de Montreuil, *La Continuation de Perceval*, CFMA 28, 50, and 101 (Paris, 1922–75).

Raoul de Houdenc, relives the fiction of the former author (as generated by the fountain of Brocéliande) and recasts it in the narrative terms (first-person allegorical voyage) of the latter.[122] Another type of fictional creation/continuation which more closely reflects persistent tendencies of the long-standing debate tradition in medieval poetry is exemplified by Richard de Fournival's popular *Bestiaire d'Amours*. Richard's imaginative work weaves well-known bestiary figures around a first-person love plaint addressed to the Narrator's Lady. As a fictional strategy, it can be compared to earlier narrative constructs such as are found in Renaut de Beaujeu's *Le Bel Inconnu,* and the anonymous romances *Partonopeu de Blois* and *Joufroi de Poitiers*.[123] In each case, the narrator solicits a favorable response from his lady upon receipt of the document. The documentary status of Richard's work is very much in evidence, for it is, as the narrator tells us, his last in a series of written attempts to sway his lady; he terms it his *arrière-ban,* a last call to arms that will marshal all the rhetorical forces at his disposal. It is perhaps not surprising that four of the seventeen extant manuscripts include an adjunct text, a *Response au Bestiaire,* which constitutes the Lady's negative reply, a detailed refutation of the terms of Richard's argument. Whether or not the *Response* was originally conceived along with the *Bestiaire* — that is, whether or not it can be attributed to the authorial hand of Richard de Fournival — it does provide an integral component to the type of rhetorical exercise latent in the *arrière-ban*. An intriguing complement to this initial situation arises from the fact that three manuscripts contain an "apocryphal" continuation to the *Bestiaire* and one includes two additional responses.[124] One of the manuscripts with the continuation added on to the *Bestiaire* is outfitted with an anonymous prologue that, comparable to a troubadour *vida,* attempts to provide a biographical sketch of the author/narrator based largely upon material culled from within

---

122 Cf. Hans Robert Jauss, "La Transformation de la forme allégorique entre 1180 et 1240: d'Alain de Lille à Guillaume de Lorris," in *L'Humanisme médiéval dans les littératures romanes du XIIe au XIVe siècle,* ed. Anthime Fourrier (Paris, 1964), pp. 107–46.
123 Cf. John L. Grigsby, "The Narrator in *Partonopeu de Blois, le Bel Inconnu,* and *Joufroi de Poitiers,*" *Romance Philology* vol. 21, no. 4 (May 1968), 536–43.
124 *Li Bestiaires d'Amours,* ed. Segre, pp. lviii–lxiv, cxxxi. I am grateful to Sylvia Huot for bringing this information to my attention.

the work.[125] There is perhaps no better example of the active scribal expansion of fictional texts based upon the principles of limitless debate than in the manuscript tradition of the *Bestiaire d'Amours*.

We might take as another example of fictional ordering in the Middle Ages, equally characteristic of the thirteenth century, the trend toward manuscript collections of once separate stories. The most prominent of these collections would be the Renart stories, or the large cyclical collections of a particular *chanson de geste* hero.[126] Historically speaking, it is clear that the discrete works making up each collection reflect a creation at different times and by different writers. Although we may speak of single authorship in the case of the Renart stories, in that they were probably written by clerics, their relationship to a previous oral tradition is not clear.[127] The uncertainty is heightened by the anonymity of a number of the branches. At a given time, the once-distinct branches were gathered and copied together in large collective manuscripts. Given that the separate branches have virtually only survived in collected form, the notion of separate promulgation is in fact only a hypothesis.[128] The question arises as to whether we should treat the branches separately, or as a collective effort: Should we speak of *Le Roman de Renart* (as if each branch were a chapter) or *Les Romans de Renart?* Either choice is possible depending upon the definition which we give of textual unity or

125 Ibid., pp. lviii–lix. Portions of this prologue are quoted below, Chapter 3, p. 205 (note 47).
126 For the *chanson de geste,* see particularly Madeleine Tyssens, *Le Geste de Guillaume d'Orange dans les manuscrits cycliques* (Paris, 1967); for the Renart cycle see the excellent introduction by Robert Bossaut, *Le Roman de Renard* (Paris, 1967) along with the more detailed remarks accompanying the edition by Mario Roques of which six volumes have appeared, CFMA 78, 79, 81, 85, 88, 90 (Paris, 1948–).
127 After considering the various theories concerning a possible folkloric origin for the *Renart* tales as they have come down to us, Bossuat concludes in a polemical summary aimed primarily at L. Sudre, p. 87: "Chaque poète a travaillé pour son compte, en exploitant selon son tempérament une matière à succès dont il pensait tirer profit. Son oeuvre est le résultat d'un effort conscient qui exclut toute intervention de ce génie populaire qui n'a jamais été défini clairement, mais qui a longtemps servi à masquer nos ignorances." After this rather firm, categorical statement, however, Bossuat does stop to wonder whether the Latin sources of some of the branches might not have been influenced by some common oral source.
128 The large majority of extant *Renart* branches are contained within collected manuscripts, which were probably undertaken as early as the late twelfth century (and thus very soon after the earliest of the dated branches). Cf. Roques, *Le Roman de Renart (Première Branche),* CFMA 78, pp. iii–ix.

completeness. How might our treatment compare with a reading of Marie de France's *Lais* or Boccaccio's *Decamerone,* both of which are collections of once-separate stories, but which have been assumed under a single author's creation? In the case of the *Renart,* might the scribe/compiler's effort to bring together the disparate stories not be viewed as comparable to that of Marie de France?

The cyclical *chanson de geste* manuscripts bring up a related yet distinct perceptual problem. Here the question of authorship at the level of writing is already problematized, in view of the certain yet unknowable layers of oral creation and elaboration that we have already discussed. The scribe/compiler could have shown a creative impulse in his first copying of the epic songs, a role that has been much debated in the case of the *Roland*.[129] Moreover, it is clear that the compiler of the Guillaume cycle worked toward a systematization of the materials made available to him, presenting the "historical" spectrum of the hero's career through the piecing together of works spanning as many as two centuries.[130] Conceptually speaking, do we evaluate the epics of the Guillaume cycle on the basis of each distinct work's postulated oral creation, its written version, or on the level of the global organization and synthesis effected by the compiler?

The preceding questions have been posed more for polemical purposes than any other. The "answer" is of course that there is no single unequivocal response. There exists no *one* exclusive way of dealing with any of the textual groupings we have discussed in this chapter. The real point is that the moment of discovering or evaluating textual unity is not inherent in any text, but rather it results from the formative vision of the reader/critic. The reader defines, and always has defined, the object of his research according to specific criteria that it is his obligation to render explicit before proceeding to his study. The definition will naturally be

---

129 Tyssens, *Geste,* and J. Wathelet-Willem, "Encore et toujours l'origine des chansons de geste," in *Proceedings of the Fifth International Conference of the Société Rencesvals* (University of Salford, 1977), pp. 5–21. Transcription and compilation would seem to have been closely associated in this corpus: Whereas there are some twenty separable poems contained in the cyclical *Guillaume* and *Aymeri* manuscripts, only three of them appear in noncyclical manuscripts. Moreover, the *Chanson de Guillaume,* extant in only one manuscript, is not incorporated *tel quel* into the larger cycles.
130 See the conclusions of Tyssens, *Geste,* pp. 431 ff. and especially 450–8.

based on the idea that he makes of unity. As can be witnessed by our faltering attempts in this section, our idea of unity *inevitably* turns back to rest upon notions of authorship and intentionality that we had thought we could keep separate. At each step of our investigation, from continued works to collected ones, our delimitation of textual unities has been accompanied by authorial differentiations representing specific levels of intentionality. The recourse to authorial designation would seem to satisfy a fundamental need to anthropomorphize the literary object. Taking the *Renart* as an example, we can treat it at the level of the discrete branch, postulating an oral, written, or perhaps collaborative creation, or we can evaluate the collection as a whole, in which case we either speak of the compiler's unifying efforts or perhaps a "collective intentionality" indicated by the unity of the matter. The choice of an authorial designation is assuredly not innocent, for it in turn reflects back on our interpretation of the work itself. All these possibilities are latent in the text, but we must keep in mind that our eventual choice will directly influence our seemingly separate interpretation.

Let us now turn back to the *Rose* text. One of the principal ways in which the *Rose* is partitioned within the manuscript is by means of the illustrations and, most especially, by the inclusion of an authorial portrait, a motif that has garnered virtually no attention either with respect to its iconographic or to its literary significance.[131] Kuhn is primarily interested in showing the cliché value of the *Rose* illustrations, their foundation in religious stereotypes, and so the short shrift which he gives the authorial portraits once he has determined that they are simply imitations of the well-known iconographic tradition of the Evangelists' portraits is not surprising.[132] The authorial portraits nearly all look alike, says Kuhn, and in spite of their manuscript attribution, one must not make the mistake of confusing them with *true* authorial portraits. Their contemporaries certainly did not. The portraits in fourteenth-century manuscripts were reminiscences solely of classical

---

[131] The major works available dealing with aspects of the *Rose* illustrations are those of Alfred Kuhn (*Illustration;* note 74, above) and John V. Fleming (*The Roman de la Rose: A Study in Allegory and Iconography;* note 96, above); a comprehensive iconographic catalogue of the *Rose* manuscripts is sorely needed.
[132] Kuhn, *Illustration,* p. 57.

authors or of the Evangelists. Kuhn's assertions betray a number of naïve assumptions and, as we shall see, are astonishingly misinformed. While he asserts that the portraits are often found twice or three times within a given manuscript, I have encountered only a couple of manuscripts in which two portraits are included.[133] Furthermore, the portraits do *not* all look alike, nor do they describe precisely the same scene. It is somewhat contrived to assume that the medieval readers did not "believe" the portraits were meant to identify the authors, since they are nearly all assigned such an attribution and, as far as I know, there is not a single manuscript indication to the contrary. Kuhn's most pernicious critical assumption is that, since we have precedents for the portraits in other traditions, their use in the *Rose* manuscripts can only be an uninspired imitation. To be sure, one should not expect anything like a verisimilar portrait painted after a living model, but that does not mean that the theme of authorship within the *Rose* text is not being exploited in some way *through* the illustrations. One could even go so far as to suggest an ironic overturning of what had been strictly a theological iconographic motif. In any event, Kuhn has made an outrageous confusion between artistic stylization and manuscript attribution, which must, at least initially, be taken at face value. Would Kuhn have denied that the portraits of Narcissus at the fountain were meant to portray that mythological figure? That the "Lover" was meant to be the Lover? As we noticed in the above discussion of authorship, there is a frequent resistance to the fictional (literary or artistic) treatment of the author figure.

Fleming, while generally critical of Kuhn's study, nonetheless accepts this judgment in a rather blithe fashion.[134] The superficial discussion of this topic is in all respects consistent with Fleming's approach, which manifestly avoids the persistent traits of the manuscript tradition in order to concentrate on eccentric iconographic treatments at variance with what is to be found in the text of the poem. What results is a certain disdain for the manuscript tradition as a whole, certain manuscripts that represent an

---

133 Namely, the Pierpont Morgan Library (New York), ms. 948, and B.N. f. fr. 1569, which contains three portraits (Cf. Figures 9, 10, and 11). There are certainly other examples to be found, but these are in the minority.
134 Fleming, *Roman de la Rose*, p. 105.

idiosyncratic religious interpretation (for example, Valencia 387) being granted an undue privilege. In comparing several different manuscript representations of the opening scenes of the poem, Fleming makes it clear that, paradoxically, those illustrations striking closest to the text are the least interesting by way of explaining the poem's "significant content."[135] The reader quickly understands that the real point behind Fleming's study is to interpret the iconography of a series of doctrinally oriented manuscripts, far and away a minority (and, for the most part, not the oldest manuscripts), and that his pretense to say anything directly about the poetic text itself is illusory. As for the question that interests us here, Fleming has absolutely no use for the theme of dual authorship, characterizing it as a modern "diagnosis of schizophrenia"[136] – as though Jean de Meun had never written on the subject. The secular theme would of course have a devastating effect on his own religious convictions, inasmuch as it signals an interest in the poem as a human and not divine creation, supporting in some positive manner the vanity of writing.

Both Kuhn and Fleming pursue the illustrations in the narrow context of the iconographic cliché, paying little or no attention to the organization of the manuscripts, the placement of the miniatures, or the iconographic programming – that is, their relation to the poetic text. It is, to be sure, important to note that the authorial portrait was a highly conventional religious motif, but our recognition that such a motif would not be found in *Rose* manuscripts were it not a theme in the secular poem is equally fundamental. Either one decides that *no* icon has any meaning because it is conventional, or one treats them all as an artistic attempt at representation.

In discussing the question of artistic intentionality in the medieval manuscript, some measure of caution is called for. First, it is clear that the creation of the medieval book involved a division of labor, and that the textual scribe was only one out of a sequence of artisans. The illustrator and the scribe had distinct roles, as did the

---

135 Ibid., p. 22: "But the action represented is still quite close to the text, and its value as a gloss is limited. Like Erasmus, we must seek those glosses which depart most of all from the letter."
136 Ibid., p. 104. He also asserts, p. 105, that the portraits "neither reveal an incipient cult of literary personality nor a concern with the problem of the poem's dual authorship."

rubricator. However, at some point in the conception of the manuscript someone decided whether or not illustrations would be included, how large and numerous they should be, which motifs would be included, and where they would be placed. Initially, the parchment was lined, and the text written with spaces left for the miniatures. We have a number of manuscripts in which the marginal notes identifying the subject of the illustration destined to fill the blank have not been erased. Presumably the illustrator *and* the *rubricator* would take their lead from these preliminary indications. This ordering of the labor is clear from several surviving manuscripts containing blanks where miniatures were to be executed but for some reason were not. One can, at the global level of the manuscript project, speak of some sort of guiding direction which articulates text and illustration.

In a perusal of nearly one hundred illuminated *Rose* manuscripts, I have been able to locate some forty miniatures portraying one or another of the authors. It seems to have been one of the most popular iconographic motifs, rivaled only by the initial portrait of the Lover sleeping, the series of courtly vices on the garden wall, and Narcissus at the fountain. It might be added that while certain episodes of Jean de Meun's continuation were extremely popular as illustrations (The Wheel of Fortune, Faus Semblant and Male Bouche, Pygmalion), the density of illustrations devoted to Guillaume's poem is nearly always much higher. There are even manuscripts (for example, B.N. Ms. fr. 378) in which Guillaume's poem is illustrated in the usual fashion, while no illustrations at all were planned for Jean de Meun's section. In the following lines, I will attempt to describe the variety of authorial portraits to be found in *Rose* manuscripts and their place in the context provided by the poem.

The most typical placement of the portrait is between the two parts of the poem, and it usually shows a figure seated at a desk with a book open before him, either writing in the book or simply looking at it. In most cases it is not certain whether the figure in the portrait is supposed to be Guillaume de Lorris or Jean de Meun. The rubric usually calls attention to the fact of the text's continuation rather than to the identity of the portrait, using the simple formula "Ci commence maistre Jehan de Meun" or the equally common "Ci commence le roumans maistre Iehan de

Meun et le parfist iusqu'a la fin." In a relatively small number of cases a more elaborate rubric mentions the fact of Guillaume de Lorris's incompletion, as in the following example from B.N. Ms. fr. 378:[137]

> Ci endroit fina maistre Guillaume de Lorris cest roumanz, que plus n'en fist, Ou pour ce qu'il ne vost, Ou pour ce qu'il ne pot. Et pour ce que la matiere embelissoit a plusors, il plot a maistre Jean Chopinel de Meun a parfaire le livre et a ensivre la matiere. Et commence en tele maniere comme vous porroiz oïr ci après.
>
> (Right here Master Guillaume de Lorris ended this romance, for he wrote no more than this, either because he did not wish to do so, or because he was not able. And because the subject matter was pleasing to many, Master Jean Chopinel de Meun was glad to complete [*parfaire*] the book and follow through with the subject matter. And it begins in such a way as you will be able to hear right after this.)

There is frequent confusion as to the precise identification of Guillaume. In some manuscripts he is identified as Guillaume de Saint-Amour (B.N. Ms. fr. 1569; Bibliothèque Mazarine 3873; Falaise, Bibliothèque Municipale 37) and two manuscripts twist around the information so that Guillaume de Lorris finished the poem at the request of Guillaume de Saint-Amor, who had begun it (Lyon, Palais des Arts 23; Turin, University Library L. III. 28). One scribe humorously misunderstood Jean de Meun's authorial passage, which includes Amor's lament over the death of Tibullus: "Ci fenist Guillaumes Tibullus et commens maistre Jehans de Meun" (Oxford, Bodleian Library, Ms. Astor A12, fol. 89r°). I have come across only one rubric that actually points to the illuminated portrait and not to the text: "Vesci mestre Jehan de Meun ou il siet en sa chaiere et fet son livre" (Paris, Bibliothèque Sainte-Geneviève, Ms. 1126, fol. 29r°). It is likely that the portraits attempt to represent the continuator, that person who carries on the task of writing, but any notion of precise attribution or verisimilar portraiture is foreign to the aesthetic context.

In many instances, as we have said, the person seated at the desk is manipulating the instruments of the scribe (Figs. 1, 2, 3). Is this

---

[137] Langlois I, p. 8.

Figure 1. Author at his desk. British Library Ms. 20. A. XVII, Fol. 35v°. Reprinted by permission of the British Library.

the author writing his own text or the scribe copying the work? It is rare that two books are shown open, as if the one were being copied from the other (Fig. 4). Moreover we know that medieval books were probably first transcribed on large parchment leaves and only later folded and bound into volumes. It is interesting, therefore, that the large majority of these portraits show the figure writing in a book *already bound* and not on folio leaves (as in Figs. 1, 2, 4, and 5). The marginal figures of Fig. 6 without a doubt

ONE: THE SPECTRAL AUTHOR

Figure 2. Author at his desk. Cambridge University Library Ms. Gg 4.6, Fol. 30r°. Reprinted by permission of the Syndics of Cambridge University Library.

portray scribes, with their completed sheets hung on horizontal poles beside them. It might be suggested that to show the figure writing in a book is a way of giving a visual, figurative, and fundamentally unrealistic image of the authorial imaginative faculty; scribes produce sheets and authors produce books. In conjunction with this observation, whereas the author's most common setting is within a room in the later, more elaborate manuscripts (Figs. 4, 5, and 7) or in an ill-defined space with a figured background in the earlier ones (Figs. 1, 3, and 8), some show the author in a "natural" setting, before a tree, almost as if his text were a linguistic transcription of a visual perception – again, a figurative portrayal of authorial imagination (Fig. 2).

Figure 3. Guillaume de Lorris and Jean de Meun at desks writing. British Library Ms. Stowe 947, Fol. 30v°. Reprinted by permission of the British Library.

The other significant variation in the authorial portrait depicts not a writer but more likely a reader seated at a desk with an open and completed book (Figs. 7 and 8). In some the finger is pointed at the text (Fig. 8), perhaps as a reading guide and perhaps as an admonishing or instructive act, much as one finds in some manuscripts marginal fingers pointing at specific lines – fulfilling an underscoring function equivalent to the scribal NOTA. Both the scribal and the contemplative author will be found on occasion

Figure 4. Author at his desk. Bibliothèque Nationale Ms. Fr. 19153, Fol. 311ʳ°. Phot. Bibl. nat. Paris.

with a variety of books placed on a reading stand (Figs. 4 and 8), on or in the desk (Figs. 5 and 7), or strewn on the floor (Fig. 7).

In most cases the figure is portrayed as a monk, in robes and tonsured. The figure is almost always alone (see, however, Fol. 1 of Oxford, Bodleian Library, Ms. Douce 195, fol. 1, reproduced in

Figure 5. Author at his desk. British Library Ms. Harley 4425, Fol. 127r°. Reprinted by permission of the British Library.

Kuhn, facing p. 50). The author's attitude admits of a wide variety of emotions, from a pixy-like glare (Fig. 1), to serene contemplation (Fig. 4), to a nearly coquettish sense of intrusion (Fig. 5), to gentle distraction (Fig. 8), to near horror at the printed page (Fig. 7). A few examples, by far the least frequent, make a fascinating attempt to vary the basic motif, by inscribing the theme of authorial succession into the portrait itself. One such attempt, which also happens to come from one of the oldest known illustrated manuscripts of the *Rose* (Fig. 9), shows one author handing a book to another – a visual translation of the fact of continuation. In this unique example, moreover, the figure at the left handing over the book has a raised finger accompanied by a pronounced stare, as if in some way dictating the later progression of the romance according to his wishes. A second, quite distinct, way of

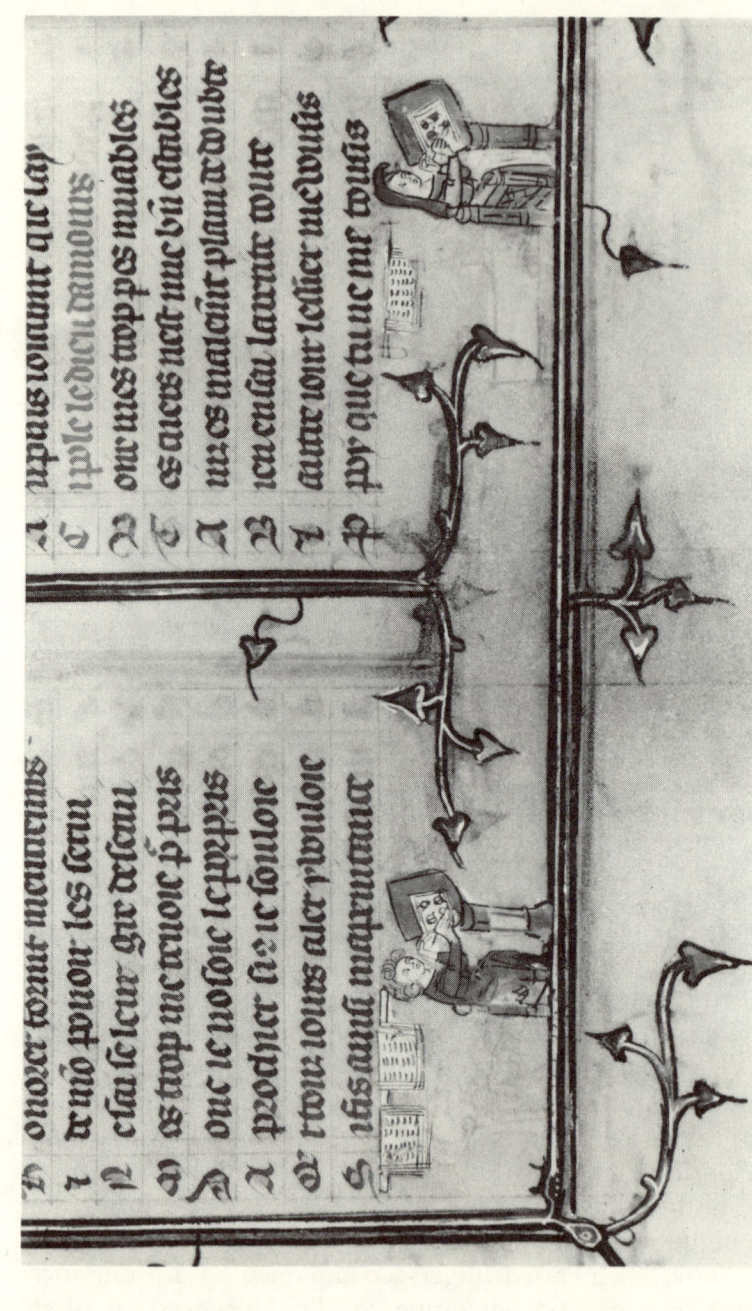

Figure 6. Scribes at work. Bibliothèque Nationale Ms. Fr. 25526, Fol. 77v°. Phot. Bibl. nat. Paris.

Figure 7. Author at his desk. Beinecke Rare Book and Manuscript Library, Yale University, Ms. 418, Fol. 151.

Figure 8. Author at his desk. Bodleian Library, Oxford University, Ms. E. Museo 65, Fol. 30v°.

Figure 9. Guillaume de Lorris passing book to Jean de Meun. Bibliothèque Nationale Ms. Fr. 1569, Fol. 68v°. Phot. Bibl. nat. Paris.

handling the theme of authorial succession involves showing two author/scribes side-by-side copying different manuscripts (Fig. 3). The figure on the left has nearly completed his leaf while the one on the right has only begun, perhaps an additional allusion to the fact of interruption and continuation, closure and openness.

The use of the authorial portraits, above and beyond their thematic inclusion in the iconographic program, certainly extended to the demarcation of the textual division. Indeed, the authorial portrait is most often found at the end of Guillaume's section, following the line "car je n'ai mes aillors fiance" (4028). This is the case for Figures 1, 2, 3, 4, and 8. Other locations were possible, however. The bulk of the remaining manuscripts containing this portrait situate it at the moment of Amor's discourse, when he announces the death of Guillaume (Figs. 7 and 9). While placement at this point seems to make the portrait much more of a mimetic representation (in Amor's speech, Jean de Meun's birth and *writing* of

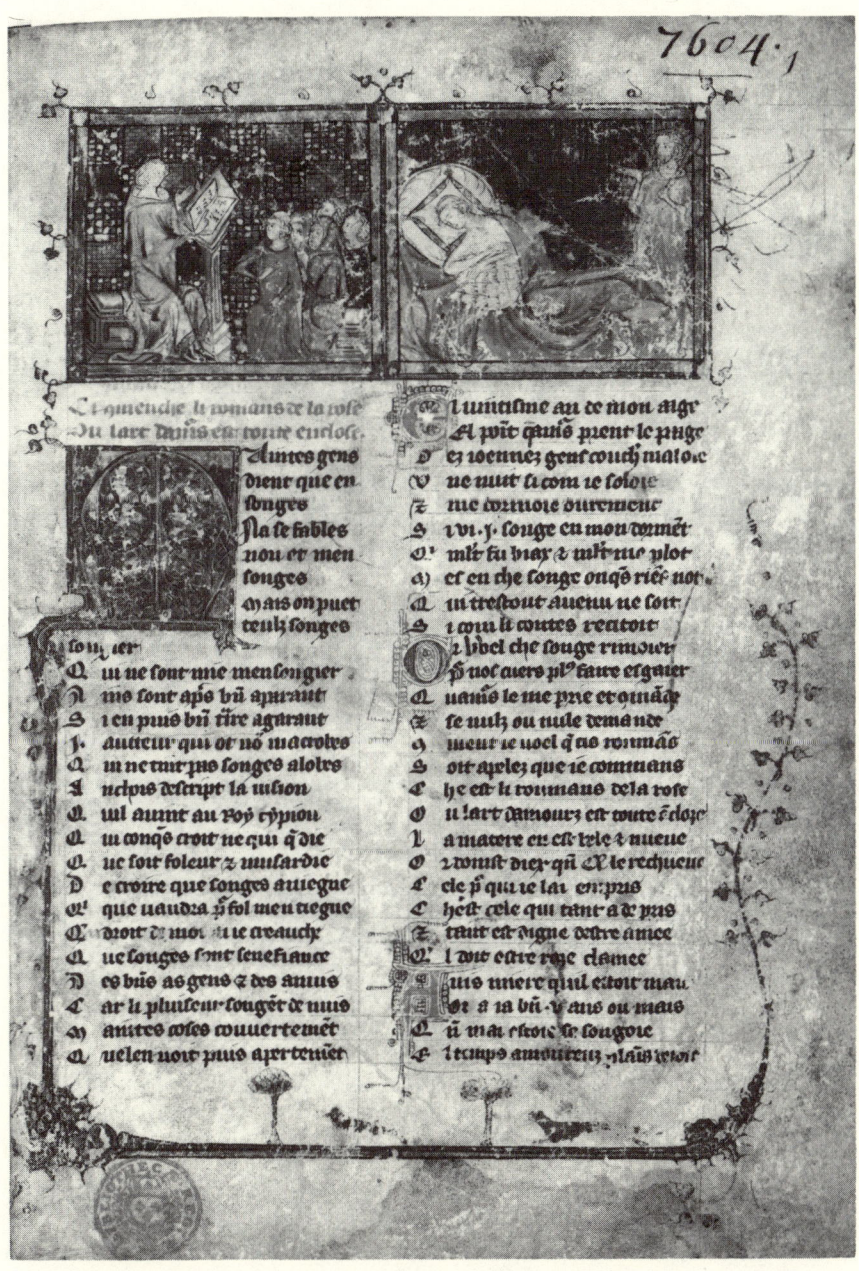

Figure 10. Left: Author reading text to a crowd. Right: Lover in bed, Dangier standing to one side. Bibliothèque Nationale Ms. Fr. 1569, Fol. 11r°. Phot. Bibl. nat. Paris.

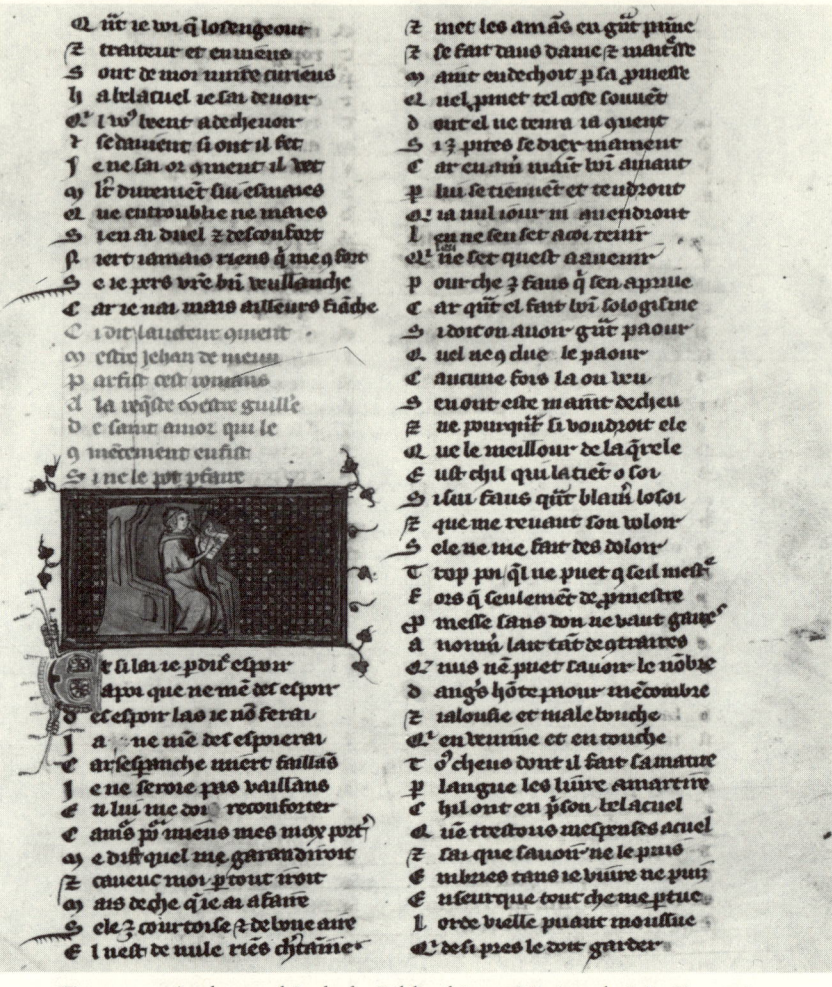

Figure 11. Author at his desk. Bibliothèque Nationale Ms. Fr. 1569, Fol 28r°. Phot. Bibl. nat. Paris.

the continuation are described at length) than a thematic one (suggestive rather of the abstract idea of continuation and its relation to writing), some scribes seem to have taken the midpoint in Amor's speech (also the midpoint of the entire poem) as the moment where one author took over from the other. In any event perfect consistency is not to be expected: At least one manuscript (B.N. Ms. fr. 1569) indicates Jean de Meun's continuation taking place in *both* spots (the rubric on fol. 28r° states, "Ci dit l'aucteur

[?] comment mestre Jehan de Meun parfist cest romans a la requeste mestre Guillaume de Saint Amor [!], qui le commencement en fist, si ne le pot parfaire" ["Here the author tells how Master Jean de Meun completed this romance at the request of Master Guillaume de Saint-Amour, who composed the beginning of it but could not bring it to completion"], while the rubric immediately preceding the authorial illumination on fol. 68v° [Fig. 9] reads, "Ci commence mestre Jehan de Meun"). The unusually complex succession of portraits in this manuscript (compare Figs. 9, 10, and 11) suggests a thematization of the authorial role and its use as a device for textual partitioning that surpasses even the textual indications.

It remains to be seen how the authorial appellations introduced by the God of Love can be related to the various types of textual units which the manuscript tradition of the *Roman de la Rose* has handed down to us. If the validity of "Guillaume de Lorris" as an authorial designation is placed into question, what consequences, if any, will follow in terms of our traditional partitioning of the text(s)? The *Rose* text as we know it is composed of a distinct number of separable textual "modules." Following are the various arrangements of these modules as they are found in the body of over 250 manuscripts:[138]

R1	(1 presumed example: B.N. f.fr. 1573, cf. above)
R1 + R2	(1 example)
R1 + R2 + R3	(6 examples)
R1 + R3	(over 250 examples)
	where R1 = lines 1–4028, ed. Lecoy
	R2 = "anonymous conclusion," 78 lines
	R3 = lines 4029–21750, ed. Lecoy).

Traditional views consider the fourth possibility as *Le Roman de la Rose*, made out of two parts treated as if they were two chapters of the same work. Does it not make sense, however, to see that there are *several* textualities, each of which merits a separate treatment? In fact, there are many *Roses*, depending on whether we

---

[138] Ibid., pp. 2–212. The shorthand used to designate the various textual modules is borrowed from Paul Zumthor, "De Guillaume de Lorris à Jean de Meun," in *Etudes . . . Félix Lecoy* (Paris, 1973), pp. 609–20.

accord to R1 an ending or not, and *which* of the endings we designate.

Traditionally, we attribute R1 to Guillaume de Lorris, R3 to Jean de Meun, and R2 is considered of anonymous authorship. The names, as we have seen, function primarily as tags designating distinct discursive modules. Each name thereby governs a separate conceptual framework. R1 is only named within R3; the appellation associates a proper name (Guillaume) and a place name (Lorris) with R1. The only substantial conclusions we can draw are of the vaguest geographical and social nature. In spite of the utter impossibility of getting anywhere close to an intentionality, the name endows the text with a personality as well as a kind of uniqueness. R2, no less textually defined from within than R1, *has* no designation, and therefore joins for modern readers the nebulous world of anonymous continuations and insignificant discourses. While on occasion R1 and R2 have been associated with the name "Guillaume" and thus considered of homogeneous authorship, certain effects of style and tone (as well as their own desire to find, or invent, a different ending for the *Rose*) have led most scholars to separate their attribution. Thus, Guillaume's name disguises a literary conventionality based upon tradition, convenience and a stylistic uniqueness which separates R1 from other textual groupings.

The history of R3 proves to be quite different. First of all, R3 designates its author from within the text. As has often been noted, it even provides a revised title or perhaps a subtitle: *Le Miroer aus Amoreus* (10621) which, significantly, occurs in the same section as Amor's authorial digression. In addition, "Jean de Meun," as a proper name and classifier of discourse, carries with it certain additional associations, both literary and historical. The fact that several Latin-French translations, a testament, a codicil, and R3 are usually grouped under this name (although the *Testament* and *Codicile* might in fact have been written by someone else) relates them all in a fashion that Foucault terms (after Saint Jerome) the "principe d'une certaine unité d'écrire."[139] Whereas R1 is an almost anonymous, completely isolated shred of discourse, R3 takes part in a network of textual associations, an

---

[139] Foucault, "Qu'est-ce qu'un auteur?" p. 87. (English translation, p. 128.)

intertextual framework which circumscribes and helps define the text. We should remember, moreover, that this sense of homogeneity functions as an inner property of the texts being treated: That is, certain stylistic similarities, thematic consistencies and preoccupations allow us to group together the texts attributed to Jean de Meun: If there were too much difference, the attributions would be declared apocryphal and we would again be dealing with falsely attributed, anonymous texts.

When sorting through the variety and multiplicity that are such an essential part of the presentation of the medieval literary text, the reader must necessarily make choices that place boundaries around his critical purview. Otherwise, in a conceivably infinite expansion of textual variants and combinations, one could never distinguish one work from another. By focusing our attention on the definition of a particular level of intentionality and relating it through certain logical criteria to the demarcation of a specific textual space, the modern reader can arrive at a solution to the misleading belief in the author and his intention as the primordial definition of a text's unity. As we have attempted to demonstrate, the priority and uniqueness of authorial intention are not only historically inconsistent with medieval usage, but also as easily swayed as a "sleeve in the wind," inevitably molding the "intention" around that of the critic.[140]

Part of the "logical" process of textual definition I am suggesting would involve an attention toward the ways in which the text is treated on the macroscopic level among the various manuscripts. The *Roman de la Rose* provides a convenient and particularly rich example. Even though, for the purposes of the above analysis, we were able to abstract three "discursive modules," our evaluation of the *Rose* text could not logically be based on a separate study of the three. The logical restraints of what constitutes a story, along with the medieval scribe's "authority" come into play. In no way can R2 or R3 be considered apart from R1, upon which both are predicated. By purporting to *continue* the

---

140 Cf. Gottfried von Strassburg, *Tristan* (ed. Werner Schröder [Berlin, 1969]), line 15740. Although the situation in Gottfried is quite different, the mechanism is the same: the use (or abuse) of a particular rhetorical structure which totally contradicts its methodological bases. Isolt, however, uses her rhetoric "en toute connaissance de cause."

previous work — even if the success or the direction of that continuation remains questionable — R2 and R3 incorporate R1 into their own redefined textuality. In this sense, their use of R1 functions as a type of quotation, a re-citation. Were we to deny that Jean de Meun's *Rose,* conceptually and logically speaking, contains the entire work (R1 + R3) because he *did not write* the first part, then we would perhaps be forced to delete other sections of his poem that are explicit borrowings from still other *aucteurs.* The argument based on originality or "first" writing, as we saw above, is not pertinent in a medieval context. The point is that the open-ended and profoundly intertextual nature of medieval literary creation forces us to eliminate boundaries that a modern legal view of literary appropriation has forced upon our modes of thought. In this sense, our naming of the author (Jean de Meun = R3) is at odds with our logical constitution of the work (R1 + R3).

The reverse, however, is not true. That is, R1 can stand alone, there being no immediate need for the reader to attach either R2 or R3 to it. This view has scarcely been given credit by any of the readers of the *Rose,* medieval or modern, and yet the manuscript evidence allows for such an interpretation: R1 *does* occur by itself in one manuscript and independent of R3 in another. The fact that in the overwhelming majority of cases R1 and R3 are presented as inseparable says more about the history of the texts' reception than anything else. And here we must make a careful distinction between text reception as a historical criterion and text reception as an inner function related to the aesthetic appreciation of literature.[141] Our enterprise in this first chapter, indeed, involves making sure that the latter conception not be mistaken for the former. We must, in other words, insure that our interpretation rest firmly rooted in the text and its givens, eschewing impositions from the outside, be they the result of medieval readers, modern editors, or latent interpretive preconceptions. Inasmuch as our discussion through authorship and the literary work has led us full circle to the point at which we started — the feasibility of "reading" Guillaume de Lorris's *Rose* as an independent text — it is perhaps here that we should reevaluate Amor's discussion in view of the numer-

---

141 Cf. Hans Robert Jauss, *Literaturgeschichte als Provokation* (Frankfurt-am-Main, 1974).

ous difficulties and dark passages that lie at the heart of the handwritten medieval text.

MEDIEVAL TEXT/MODERN READER

It should at present be clear that Amor's authorial excursus, above and beyond the information it provides, calls directly into question the possibilities and modalities of our reading of the medieval text. Especially the *Roman de la Rose,* which, for better or for worse, through centuries of textual, scribal, and critical accretions, rests upon a firmly established readerly tradition whose authoritative weight has become overwhelming and definitive. We must take care, therefore, that the dictates of this tradition not preempt any contrary judgments that might result from a close textual reading. As we discussed above, the principal causes of the modern reader's distance are twofold: the documentary insufficiency; and the remoteness of the linguistic and referential frameworks supporting the literary production of the period. Such impediments to our constitution of an adequate conceptual model risk becoming all the more acute through the modern reader's reluctance to negotiate or even to acknowledge the insuperable distance facing him. The reader must at this point exercise caution so as not to fall prey to the inevitable double bind awaiting all those who balk at the seemingly insoluble paradox of desiring to subscribe to a foreign system of cultural values while retaining one's own personal sensibilities. To carry the *caveat* to its limit, refusing the modern reader and his interpretation *any* possible validity inasmuch as he could not possibly perceive or appreciate the work precisely as if he were a medieval reader/listener, would of course constitute an abusive exercise in self-defeat. To insist, on the other hand, that such an enterprise – the modern reading of a medieval text – *is* possible without the introduction of some anachronistic perspective, necessarily involves an underlying attribution of identical craft, techniques, and intentions to the medieval writer which is at best misleading. Indeed, in the latter case, our very terminology – by its disguising of the vital differences – serves to betray us. An answer to the perennially divisive problem of the dichotomy between a strictly historical and an exclusively subjective view can, in all likelihood, best be approached through a compromise that would attempt to incorporate the conceptual adjustments necessitated by the above-mentioned socioliterary differences, while at the same time allowing for the modern reader's own ever-present point of view. To reject *any* subjective approach in the name of a scrupulous objectivity would merely substitute one conceptual framework — perhaps no less anachronistic — for another. We can avoid falling into an epistemological impasse as long as we admit the impossibility of a total adequation between reader and text.

･･････

From the most narrowly historical (or situational) point of view, the actual place of the author in the concrete business of writing, as well as his creative role, seem rather effaced next to the all-important radiating figure that the modern tradition has forged. Accordingly, such resultant concepts of literary interpretation as "originality" and "intentionality" — so basic as to partake of our automatic and unquestioned critical vocabulary — need to be re-evaluated as to their relevance for the medieval model. In a more insidious way, as the example of Gui de Mori suggests, the manuscript copy of an authorial hand might bear witness to an underlying tension in the deployment of a poetic "I" or, at the very least, to a conflation of roles, whose realization depends greatly on a substratum of cultural and literary stereotypes.

More importantly, perhaps, the radical displacement of the author-figure forces an adjustment of the common philological "chain" (writer-text-reader), which purports to explain the production and communication of meaning via the literary text. Whereas traditional philology considers the author and his intention as the origin of the literary work, and its description by the passive reader as the ultimate goal of literary studies, an acquaintance with the medieval tradition and its authorial attitudes imposes a decided shift toward the reader and his active participation. Indeed, authors are frequently seen as readers of other texts, manifesting an originality that consists in the imaginative refashioning and reinterpretation of inherited materials. Based squarely upon the model of the scribe, as well as on that of the oral performer, the medieval author-figure places himself in a communicative framework whose ultimate fruition is to be situated within the dialogue established between writer and reader.

Nowhere perhaps do we get a better sense of the medieval vernacular author's self-situation than in the richly nuanced prologue that Marie de France appended to her collection of *lais*. She first of all justifies her literary creation by indicating that its social significance, that is to say its placement in a framework of reception and exchange, is its primary *raison d'être*:[142]

> Quant uns granz biens est mult oïz,
> Dunc a primes est il fluriz,
> E quant loëz est de plusurs,
> Dunc ad espandues ses flurs.

(When a great good is widely heard of, then, and only then, does it bloom, and when that good is praised by many, it has spread its blossoms.)

The activation of meaning which results from the text's reception proves to be essential. Predicated on the image of the flowering plant, her metaphor, interestingly, qualifies poetic genius *not* as a result of some inner quality or effort but rather through the external stimulus: The final stage of the flowering beauty of the work is a direct tributary of the listeners' active appreciation and widespread reception of the work ("Quant uns granz biens est mult oïz . . . " ["When a great good is widely heard of"]).[143]

---

142 *Les Lais de Marie de France*, ed. Jean Rychner, CFMA 93 (Paris, 1968), Prologue, lines 5–8. English translation by Robert Hanning and Joan Ferrante (New York, 1978), p. 28. Cf. Tony Hunt, "Glossing Marie de France," *Romanische Forschungen*, 86 (1974), 396–418.

143 The importance of the work that follows the listening of the story, the listener's active participation, is recalled toward the end of the Prologue, where Marie explains her own work:

> Des lais pensai, k'*oïz* aveie.
> Ne dutai pas, bien le saveie,
> Ke pur remambrance les firent
> Des aventures k'il *oïrent*
> Cil ki primes les comencierent
> E ki avant les enveierent.   (33–8)

(Then I thought of the *lais* I'd heard. I did not doubt, indeed I knew well, that those who first began them and sent them forth composed them in order to preserve adventures they had *heard*. [trans., p. 29])

"Listen and then retell" seems to be the message of this activity, which is seemingly without end.

Marie pursues the same idea in a slightly different context when she turns to what has been interpreted by many as an orthodox rendering of the allegorical method.[144] Most recently, Tony Hunt has placed into question the identification of Marie's allegorical method with the commonly practiced exegesis of Holy Scripture.[145] Whether or not Marie is thinking of scriptural allegorizing, she is quite specific as concerns the precise manner of approaching the text. The *purpose* of obscurity in written texts ("Es livres") is to elicit the reaction and commentary of future readers. She makes use of the verb *gloser*, which could apply equally to a religious or secular context. Moreover, the commentary, rigorously personal, must stem from each reader's individual capacity ("de lur sen"). She goes on to indicate that the effect of such commentaries does not lead to a dead end, a terminal, definitive *sen* or meaning, but rather an escalation in the perceptive capacities of those to come:

> Plus serreient sutil de sens
> E plus se savreient garder
> De ceo k'i ert a trespasser.

(the more subtle their minds would become and the better they would know how to keep themselves from whatever was to be avoided.)

The repetition of *plus* emphasizes the cumulative and endless character of such acquisition of knowledge.[146] Furthermore, the *sen*

---

144 Custume fu as ancïens
Ceo testimoine Precïens,
Es livres ke jadis feseient,
Assez oscurement diseient
Pur ceus ki a venir esteient
E ki aprendre les deveient,
K'i peüssent gloser la lettre
E de lur sen le surplus mettre. (9–16).

(The custom among the ancients – as Priscian testifies – was to speak quite obscurely in the books they wrote, so that those who were to come after and study them might gloss the letter and supply its significance from their own wisdom. [trans., p. 28])

145 Hunt, "Glossing," 415–18.
146 *Lais*, ed. Rychner, lines 20–2 (trans. p. 28). Not only does the repetition of *plus* seem to bespeak a forward-moving escalation over and against a retrospective recovery (for a recent statement of this latter interpretation, cf. Alfred Foulet and K. D. Uitti, "The Prologue to the *Lais* of Marie de France: A Reconsideration," *Romance Philology*, vol. XXXV, no. 1 [August 1981], 242–9), but the echo of "surplus" (16) adds the dimension of an undefinable, unmentionable cache of treasures. In their redefinition of

offered by some readers will have a distinct outward effect on the *sens* of others. As Hunt rightly points out, Marie is totally ambiguous as concerns whether this increase in *sen* occurs over the lifetime of an individual reader, or in the collective lifetime of the series of successive readers. In any event, Marie refuses to designate such a concept as might be alluded to by the term *verité*, an ultimate truth; rather, she characterizes what is "in" the text by the expression "ceo k'i ert", surely an invitation to a broad spectrum of reader interpretation.[147]

If the vernacular writer saw himself in such a reader-oriented reception situation, then the allegorical text, as suggested by Marie, is surely the literary form *par excellence* that urges the reader toward an active participation. The self-proclaimed allegorical text treats its fiction as a mere pretext for the doctrinal message, which will come about through a collusion between writer and reader.[148] In conjunction with the pleasure that will be accorded the reader in the course of his own allegorical journey, there is an implicit communicative pact between writer and reader that underlies any allegorical text. It is no wonder, then, that the author appears so often as a character in the midst of the allegorical fiction, his communicative desire constituting the ultimate justification for the very literary fiction he is recounting. Now, inasmuch as *any* fictional text is allegorical in the broadest sense – that is, inviting interpretation above and beyond "what is there" – the underlying communicative act cannot be totally excluded from our consideration of the fictional whole.[149]

> "lur sen" (16) – applying it to the Ancients and *not* to the Moderns – Foulet/Uitti have totally neglected the sexual connotations (or at least associations) of "surplus," which in courtly vocabulary designates the favors, unambiguously carnal, of the Lady. Inasmuch as "surplus" suggests a rather unthinkable and extravagant excess, it is difficult to justify translating the line as "complete the meaning of what they [the ancients] had said," a simple reconstruction or restoration of what is already known.
>
> [147] One should note the subtle ambiguity inherent in "ceo ki ert a trespasser" (22), greatly dependent on the punctuation chosen by the reader: (a) ceo k'i ert a trespasser, (b) ceo k'i ert, a trespasser, (c) ceo ki ert a trespasser; (a) (that which was there [in the book] meant to be avoided), (b) (to avoid that which was there [in the book]), (c) (that which was to be avoided [in a general sense]).
>
> [148] As Hunt rightly points out ("Glossing," 415 ff.), and in spite of his desire to reject a "scriptural" reading of Marie's prologue, there are many similarities between the views expressed therein and St. Augustine's extremely influential, programmatic statement of allegorical composition in his *De Doctrina Christiana*.
>
> [149] For the most cogent and influential formulation of the written text as a communication act, cf. Roman Jakobson, "Closing Statement: Linguistics and Poetics," in T. A. Sebeok, ed., *Style in Language* (Cambridge, MA, 1960), pp. 350–77.

Correspondingly, the medieval conception of the literary work was neither so monolithic nor so definitive as we are wont to think. The problem of delineating medieval textual combinations is to be sure an active (not passive) one, amply reflected in the century-long methodological debate over the modern critical edition of the medieval text. An indispensable research tool, the critical edition results nonetheless from just such a compromise between medieval and modern aesthetics. The extremes in editorial methodologies, represented by the Lachmannian and the Bédierist schools — that is, a maximal intervention and reconstruction by the modern editor *versus* the unretouched transcription of a single manuscript exemplar — are in most cases eschewed in favor of a middle-of-the-road combination of the two.[150] Whatever the proper amount of modern intervention might be in the establishment of the critical text, it is important to realize that the very existence of the mechanically reproduced format and all that it implies (exact reproduction of the text, elimination of errors, faithful reporting of an authorial intention or hand, mass circulation to a reading public, ready accumulation and disposal of books printed on paper) ideologically and pragmatically falsifies what we know to have been the historical conditions of literary creation and appreciation in the Middle Ages.

If we, as modern readers of medieval texts, had only this historico-cultural problem to surmount, our task would be formidable enough, but superimposed upon that is our own problematical use of the terms "author" and "work." Ostensibly, the words refer, respectively, to a human originator, a creator of a particular discourse, and to the written result of this creation. This is an accurate description insofar as we attempt the description of the creative act in a historical fashion. Seen from the other end, however — that is, from the reader's point of view — the terms take on a different meaning. When we come upon a text, we *assume* the agency of an author who will in most cases be absent from the activity of reading. In practice, only in our imagination does the

---

[150] Bédier's most complete statement of his editorial method, which was crucial in the twentieth-century development of text editing, can be found in his *La Tradition manuscrite du Lai de l'ombre: Réflexions sur l'art d'éditer les anciens textes* (Paris, 1927). For a brief, convenient recent summary of the evolution of text editing since Lachmann, with several important bibliographical references, see Foulet and Speer, *On Editing*, pp. 1–39.

author speak the text; the essence of literary communication resides in the nonimmediate, nonvocal aspects of the message. This is not to deny the actual historical preexistence of the person who wrote the text, whose existence may be more (massive amounts of corroborative biographical information) or less (complete anonymity) verifiable. Rather, it suggests that our perception of an authorial figure results largely from our conceptual totalization of the work. The text constitutes, pragmatically speaking, a disembodied voice, and it is upon this undifferentiated discourse that we erect an author-idea, an imitation based upon our preconceived models of human motivation and psychology. In effect, then, whatever the "reality" surrounding the creative act, our *re*creative interpretive faculty perceives and reconstructs the initial act in a virtually backwards fashion. The work, paradoxically, precedes the author.[151] The author figure represents an anthropomorphization of the literary work, an abstraction, an allegory, which provides a biological referent for the otherwise distant collection of written signs constituting the work as a concrete entity. To speak of an author, in other words, already implies an interpretation.

To the extent that fiction represents an aesthetic judgment aimed at contradicting a text's historical referentiality, it denies the simple existence of a reality statement in the written word. The idea of an unbridled fictionality, an unbounded discourse with no absolute truth value, is inherently unsettling. As a result, fiction and reality must be carefully differentiated in order that both be safely maintained. The border around fiction has as its analogue the frame in painting and the proscenium arch in theater. While we might say that, physically speaking, the cover of the book marks the limits of fiction, in a more abstract sense it is the figure of the author that provides the guarantee of an exterior reality, along with the needed connection between fictional discourse and reality statement. The global fictional work, taken as an artistic expression, thus becomes a sort of reality statement at a secondary level. The entire critical activity, in fact, can be characterized as a

---

[151] C. S. Lewis develops some important insights on this topic in his "The Genesis of a Medieval Book," in *Studies in Medieval and Renaissance Literature* (Cambridge, 1966), 18–40: "In my opinion all criticism should be of books, not of authors" (p. 38).

struggle to transform fiction into history (that is, reality statement).

While the economics of modern literary production depend greatly upon the history/fiction dichotomy, and therefore on the clear and easy denomination of the author, it is not at all certain that such was the case for medieval vernacular literature. The freedom in dealing with the authorial persona in a stereotyped, fictional mode, accompanied by the multiplicity and intangibility of scribal layerings, would seem to indicate the contrary. In this sense, Jean de Meun's play with authorial and fictional characters, in spite of its deliberate excesses, coincides nicely with other characterizations of medieval authors, both real and fictional. The ultimately disruptive nature of Amor's speech resides in its unabashed flouting of one of our most precious critical commonplaces: Authors must remain outside the fictional realm. The simplest way to handle the situation thus described is either to accept the historical referentiality of Amor's discussion (thus leaving aside what we have discovered to be the scene's multiple complexities) or merely to ignore it — two reactions which explain virtually all critical response to the passage. We are perfectly ready to accept the fictionalization of any element of experience, provided that it excludes the very categories that establish the fictional space, marking its separation. What eludes us in this narrowed critical purview is, of course, any attempt to thematize or to allegorize the very process of fictionalization, along with the attendant motifs of creation and closure. For the critic, the risk of losing his own sober position of distanced and enlightened exteriority is too high.

The approach to Amor's speech through the perception of a floating fictional boundary should lead us to see, in fact, that it governs two epistemological levels that deserve to be maintained as distinct. Amor's speech functions simultaneously as a poetic element interior to Jean de Meun's work *and* as an *exterior* agent of textual designation and delimitation. A clear understanding of medieval authorship and textuality here becomes essential, for it shows us that "textual" historicity is not to be confused with "authorial" historicity. Or, rather, the two are not coextensive. Let me explain. When Amor tells his tale of Guillaume de Lorris's plight, we on the one hand interpret it as the biographical outline of a historical personage. Then, we apply that biographical scheme to the characterization of the literary work: Most notably, the fact that Guillaume de Lorris died prematurely translates as the incompletion of the literary work. As we are now prepared to articulate the question, it is not that the authorial discourse of Amor *cannot* be read historically, but rather that its historicity has always been misread. If we are correct in suggesting that the characterization of a text that proceeds uniquely from a preliminary sense of authorship is profoundly non-medieval – that the constitution of the text as an object of study must proceed in some more pragmatic way, taking account of the material filters determining its transmission in manuscript form – then we must eschew such information as that given by Amor. The slippage that we have just described, from authorship to textual definition, is comprised in the functional ambiguity of the authorial name. "Guillaume de Lorris" refers both to a person and a text. However, once we have been enabled to isolate a specific text from all other conceivable combinations (and we have seen the difficulties in doing that), then we must base ourselves on inner criteria for the judgment and characterization of that text. The vagaries and complexities of a manuscript tradition will justify nothing else. Through a paradox of vertiginous proportions, Amor's discussion, by singling out the text we refer to as "Guillaume de Lorris," precludes the validity of its own commentary on the text. The logic of the medieval manuscript tradition – wherein the fiction safely admits of no exterior determination, even that of authorship – dictates such a paradoxical stance. Moreover the insidious, because unstated, interpretive patterns imposed by a modern use of the word *author* call for an additional measure of caution. Amor, as the repository of a certain tradition of readership – which by its inherent circularity constantly reconfirms its own presuppositions – represents the paradigm for all external impositions and restructurings. If Jean de Meun "re-opened" or reactivated a text perhaps already closed, Amor effects a new, definitive closure that locates the work, once isolated, in a redefined interpretive dimension.

Left with the solitary text R_1, which may conveniently although arbitrarily be identified with the name "Guillaume de Lorris," we need to consider the implications for our reading of the text. In the broadest sense, thanks to the influence of Amor, we have been accustomed to reading R_1 as a text with a lack, with pieces missing that need to be supplied in order that the operation of reading and interpretation be fulfilled. This is true in the case of both the "author" (whose name, once supplied, negates its own validity) and the ending of the *Rose*. Let us consider briefly the status of these two absences, one after the other.

In the modern view, textual anonymity appears as a sort of aberration. It is virtually unthinkable that a text might remain unclaimed by someone. As a result, the sole meaning of anonymity in our contemporary critical vocabulary is that of a lack, marking the absence of information that *should* be there. It is all too easy in a medieval context to blame such lacunae on accidents of manuscript transmission or authorial negligence. The problem, however, only *appears* solved before we confront it. As we said above, the presence or absence of authorial naming in a medieval context was not a matter of automatic determination. Authorial naming potentially fulfilled an internal function of literary fictions, becoming one of a number of stereotypical elements differentiating the various literary genres. While the authors of the *fabliaux* and the *chansons de geste,* as part of their generic pose, often did not name themselves, the authors of romances typically introduced themselves into their fictions. Authorial naming thus operates as a poetic strategy, taking its place as one of the expressive registers used to characterize discrete literary works.

Similarly, to see in anonymity *not* an accident of chance but a sort of "unavowed authorship," a specific choice open to the author, must necessarily direct our attitude toward the text. Anonymity itself can become a poetic effect. Even knowing the name of the anonymous author from another source, whether doubtful or certain, would not change that effect. For example, our knowing that John Jones sent a letter of complaint anonymously to his boss does not make that letter any less anonymous in character. Other events might be contingent upon the eventual uncovering of the author in this case (Mr. Jones might lose his job) but that does not change the nature or the intention of the document itself. Were we to see anonymity as a distinctive feature of R1, related in some thematic or other way to the poem's meaningful structure, we might be further along in perceiving the "intention" of the supposed fragment. Moreover, R1 is certainly not the work of a careless author, given that the latter takes great pains to introduce and entitle his work in a fairly elaborate prologue.

The problem of textual unity and totality poses an even more formidable theoretical challenge. The assumption of the *Rose's* lack of completion is based primarily upon three varieties of information. First, the dream account does not end. That is, narratively speaking, not all of the plot elements are tied together ("noué") by the last line of R1. Second, the *verité* that has been alluded to throughout is never articulated in any explicit way. Third, and perhaps most important, Amor tells us, through his biographical fable, that it was left incomplete. The instinctive desire of any reader to fill the blank of an apparently unfinished narrative, officially sanctioned and ultimately validated by Amor, provides nonetheless only one of several possible readings (and perhaps not the most reliable). While we would never think of adding any words to the textual space of other literary works, we do so automatically for R1. The critical risks of such a move should be obvious.

And yet, do we have a choice? How does one interpret an incomplete, unclosed text? My suggestion, or working hypothesis, would be to verify first whether or not the work is indeed unambiguously an incomplete fragment. We might begin by asking what are the standards by which we measure textual completion, or closure. Is the outcome of plot the only way? In a culture so foreign as that of the Middle Ages, it is probably unwise to apply from the outset a preconceived notion of closure to what might originate in a quite distinct poetic perception or intentionality. One might add, somewhat facetiously, that R1 does not overtly declare its lack of completion. Of course, logically speaking, no text ever would (or, at least, such a statement would be highly questionable) but, on the other hand, texts rarely state explicitly the fact of their completion either. Characteristically, it is the scribe in the medieval tradition who demarcates textual closure through his EXPLICIT. Lacking this, might there not be some other sorts of textual signals by which the fact of completion would be marked?

It is these two points, or hypotheses, that I hope to explore in the following two chapters. In Chapter Two I will approach the problem of closure from a purely internal point of view, testing stylistic, thematic, and narrative elements for some kind of totalizing or unifying effect. In Chapter Three, R1 will be placed in its literary context, against which the intertwined notions of closure and anonymity will perhaps appear in greater relief and suggest certain ways of understanding a medieval poetics. The applicability of these hypotheses, radical in their departure from traditional views of the *Roman de la Rose*, can be judged through the success or failure of the enterprise that follows.

In a curious move of negation, then, we totally eliminate any consideration of that which served as our point of departure in the discussion of authorship. Does this demonstrate a lack of unity on our part, a miscalculation? Perhaps and yet, in another way, we have done nothing but repeat the steps taken by those readers who have preceded us. No statement, perhaps, could be more cogent than that which retraces traditional movements only to lift the veils covering them. Even though I am suggesting that we *must* read the text attributed to Guillaume de Lorris to the exclusion of Jean de Meun's interpretation, it is nonetheless a fact that, traditionally speaking, his imposition cannot be avoided. We must eliminate the name "Guillaume de Lorris" while at the same time we have no choice but to maintain it. Such is the difficulty – and the fascination – of our rich literary tradition, which is built upon layers of readers every bit as much as it is on texts and authors. This is perhaps the ultimate failure, and strength, of the first *Roman de la Rose*.

TWO

The narration of allegory

[...] jou ne sai proier
Se si haut non que jou ne doi finer.
             (Richard de Fournival, V, 15–16).

Nimirum hoc die uno plus vixi mihi quam vivendum fuit.
             (Macrobius, *Saturnalia*, II, vii, 3)

ALLEGORY AND INCOMPLETION

In a short essay concerning man, Fortune, and the final judgment imposed by other men, Montaigne writes, "les hommes, quelque beau visage que fortune leur face, ne se peuvent appeller heureux, jusques à ce qu'on leur aye veu passer le dernier jour de leur vie, pour l'incertitude et varieté des choses humaines, qui d'un bien leger mouvement se changent d'un estat en autre, tout divers."[1] He understood that men's lives, in this as in other ways comparable to fictions, are only truly interpretable through the final form granted them by the unexpected peripeties of the "dernier acte de sa comedie." Moreover, making use of the subtle grammatical oscillation inherent in the phrase "ne se peuvent appeller heureux" – simultaneously passive and reflexive – Montaigne alludes to the excruciating human desire to judge one's own life, to tell one's own ending, which is thwarted by the confrontation with an inescapable paradox: One can *never* "call oneself fortunate" if death is a necessary corollary to judgment; one must wait to be called fortunate by someone else.[2] Montaigne saw that the only valid

---

1 Michel de Montaigne, *Essais* (I, xix), ed. Pierre Villey (1924; Paris, 1978), I, pp. 78–9. The quotation is from Ovid's *Metamorphoses*, III, 135. Shortly thereafter, Montaigne reiterates this idea in other words: "ce mesme bon-heur de nostre vie ... ne se doive jamais attribuer à l'homme, qu'on ne luy aye veu joüer le dernier acte de sa comedie, et sans doute le plus difficile."
2 Montaigne applies this difficulty to his own contemplative effort later in the same essay: "Je remets à la mort l'essay du fruict de mes etudes. Nous verrons là si mes discours me partent de la bouche ou du coeur" (p. 80). Aside from the fact that the key word "essay," normally applied to Montaigne's own literary text, is here referred to his future readers' activities, one is led to ask whether Montaigne is not from the outset addressing his remarks to some literary, quasi-fictional concept of wholeness. His allusions to theater as well as to his own *Essais* would seem to argue for such an interpretation.

judgment results from an after-the-fact *vue d'ensemble,* a situation rendered even more complex in view of the masks that all men wear up until the last day of their life.[3]

The bulk of Montaigne's comments are indeed applicable to the evaluation of men's fictions, with one important difference: The "last sentence" of a man's life is easily verifiable. The finality of death can scarcely be placed into doubt. Textual endings, however, can never be so clear-cut or absolute, particularly in a manuscript culture such as we attempted to describe in Chapter One, characterized by a limited sense of authority and a radically open textuality. Someone can always take it upon himself to add another sentence and the later reader might never suspect (indeed, *should* never suspect). Once one can no longer be assured of a text's completion — where there is no legal or practical guarantee — the task of judging or interpreting becomes all the more complicated. *And* all the more central for, as Montaigne sees it, it is the *perception* of finality and its relation to previous moments of a man's life that is of ultimate importance in the scheme of things. This specific difficulty, characteristic of human fictions, arises when one can no longer call upon God or Fortune as the author of a work.

Whereas any work of art, even a modern "completed" one, risks incurring a judgment of fragmentariness or incompletion, Montaigne reminds us that an aesthetic appreciation of fiction is largely contingent upon the reader's capacity to erect boundaries around the literary object. Our work in Chapter One was that of isolating physically and conceptually, albeit through somewhat arbitrary means, the potentially lacunary text within an open-ended tradition of writing, in which it is perhaps impossible to treat *any* text as other than lacunary in some sense. One must inevitably base oneself upon a criterion *exterior* to the work (or life) in question — be it an act of God (death), of the printer or of the scribe — since inner determination of an ending is either impos-

---

[3] Montaigne in fact gives two reasons for this end-oriented necessity. Superficially, unexpected last-moment occurrences, the works of Fortune, can adversely change any situation. More perniciously, it is the problem of man's duplicity, even vis-à-vis himself, which prevents a true contemporary assessment. The end signifies unambiguously the moment of unmasking, the interruption of the "comedie."

sible or potentially a mask, a type of deception. Having performed this demarcation of the literary text, as we have done in the difficult case of the *Roman de la Rose* through the hypothetical designation of R1 as a complete(d) work, the reader must then address the question of how to appreciate, evaluate, or simply to understand it, especially when it openly defies the most common narrative logic or reasoning.

It is the problem of the literary text's very borderline that, initially at least, differentiates our own enquiry from that of Barbara Herrnstein Smith in her seminal study of poetic closure.[4] Smith develops some important insights relating to varieties of closure in a broad corpus of poetic texts, but perhaps her most important contribution is her characterization of closure as a function of readers' perceptions of artistic works.[5] Closure is an aspect of the experience of works of art and, I would add to that, a necessary corollary to their interpretation.[6] But the fact that Smith's corpus consists only of manifestly complete poetic works steers her investigation in the direction of "how poems end," while the status of those endings is itself taken very much for granted. Our initial remarks concerning the *Roman de la Rose* and its manuscript context have led us to a total uncertainty as to the "ending" of the poem attributed to Guillaume de Lorris and thus a question as to *whether* its closure can be evaluated. Can a poem remain unended and yet achieve closure? What, in fact, is the relative status to be accorded to "ending" and "closure" in a given work when neither of these is certain? The potentially dynamic interaction between ending and closure points up the two terms' relativity and, more than Smith had realized, the reader's role in predetermining the shape of the text. These questions are well worth asking and the necessary arbitrariness of our decision to declare that R1 is complete can perhaps be justified if we consider the unfortunate critical consequences of calling it a fragment. Whereas one ought to be able to evaluate a literary fragment on its own terms and with-

---

[4] Barbara Herrnstein Smith, *Poetic Closure: A Study of How Poems End* (Chicago, 1968).
[5] Ibid., p. 36: "Closure occurs when the concluding portion of a poem creates in the reader a sense of appropriate cessation."
[6] Ibid., pp. 212–13. See also my prefatory remarks to a special issue of *Yale French Studies*, no. 67 (1984), entitled "Concepts of Closure."

TWO: THE NARRATION OF ALLEGORY

out reference to its missing parts, readings of the first *Roman de la Rose* inevitably supply an ending (usually the plucking of the rose, or at least the Lover's fulfillment in some way) before proceeding to an exegesis of the poem. This is largely due to the "end-oriented" nature of the text, its allusions to a meaning that will be revealed at the end, and to the fictional plot that remains unresolved as of the final lines. But what if the overwhelming push to reach the end were itself being undermined by the work's structural and thematic principles? A question such as this one has scarcely ever been asked, for the initial supposition that the *Rose* is a fragment functions as an optical illusion, making the reader "not see" certain other potential contours of the text.[7] The reader tacitly adds the missing part and thereby alters the work's overall structure. What I am suggesting here is that the reader must temporarily suspend his conviction that R1 is a fragment by creating a fiction of its completion in order, quite literally, to see it for what it is. The stakes are high, involving the possible revision of an entire poetic tradition of which the *Roman de la Rose* has always been considered the capstone, and so my hope is that the "end" will justify the rather devious means.

Having established the necessarily exterior determination of the literary object, it should be stressed that the project of aesthetic appreciation or judgment must be pursued along an *interior* space, as a sort of mediation between that which is *pro*posed by the text and that which is *im*posed by the reader. While readers of fiction are always tempted to apply external models of various sorts, they must take care not to misapply or misjudge the text's own use of these models. The types of model will of course vary from fiction

---

[7] A visual example might here be appropriate. Suppose that a partially disklike object were found in the archaeological excavation of some long-lost culture: ☙ If we decide that this object is a fragment, there are two normal ways of approaching an aesthetic evaluation: (1) the beholder automatically "adds" the part that completes the circle, and pretends that this is the object: ○ Or, (2) not wishing to be so bold, he merely intuits the missing part: ☙ In either case, the jagged edge, which might potentially have an aesthetic or utilitarian value, is eliminated. Short of the object being placed on a pedestal, or surrounded by a frame, the jagged edge will in all likelihood not even be "seen." For a fascinating discussion of the intricacies of perception in the visual arts and its dependence upon previously known models, the reader is referred to E. H. Gombrich's seminal study, *Art and Illusion: A Study in the Psychology of Pictorial Representation,* 2nd ed. rev. (1961; Princeton, 1972).

to fiction. The dominant formal model for the *Roman de la Rose,* that which has given the strongest evidence for its incompletion, is that of the dream. It is indeed natural to assume that the account of a dream which does not end with the dreamer waking up is unfinished or fragmentary. The most common-based logic of dream experience dictates that for someone to tell about a dream he must be awake and that, even if it was interrupted, the dreamer had to wake up. Not surprisingly, the final line attributable to Jean de Meun, "atant fu jors et je m'esveille" (21750) ("Straightway it was day, and I awoke" [p. 354]), functions very nearly as a scribal rubric or EXPLICIT, thanks to its outright closing of the dream-as-narration. By its formal implications, Guillaume's choice of the dream nearly overdetermines its own end, since there is virtually no other "natural" mode of closure.[8] We are reminded, nonetheless, of Montaigne's word of caution, to the effect that no man can tell his own end and that if he does, it risks being a deceptive mask. Is the analogous possibility of ending a dream as unproblematical as it seems? Must the dreamer always state programmatically that he has awakened? In a more general sense, what does it mean to pass from dream to wakefulness? When a dream prophesies the dreamer's future experience, can one tell one's own dream *and* complete it?

The first few lines of the dream narration might give us a better idea of the possibilities and limitations of the Narrator's task. Certain of the problems involved in passing from dream to wakefulness via the narrative medium are adumbrated in the first section of the dream account, that part which should, when confronted with the end, prepare a liaison between wakefulness and dream, between Narrator and Lover – for what Guillaume re-

---

[8] A. C. Spearing (*Medieval Dream Poetry* [Cambridge, 1976]) suggests: "Compared with other poems, it [the dream vision] makes us more conscious that it has a beginning and an end (marked by the falling asleep and awakening of the narrator)" (p. 4). As Spearing rightly points out, it is the dream vision's need to justify itself, to emphasize its naturalness, which, paradoxically, accentuates its fictionality. This does not lead, however, to the conclusion that all dream poems had to stipulate their coordinates in such a narrow vision of *vraisemblance*. For significant variations on the model, see Pierre-Yves Badel, *Le Roman de la Rose au XIVe siècle: Etude de la réception de l'oeuvre* (Geneva, 1980), pp. 332–53.

TWO: THE NARRATION OF ALLEGORY

counts here at the outset is the ending of a dream, that is, the moment of waking up:[9]

> Avis m'iere qu'il estoit mais,
> il a ja bien .V. anz ou mais,
> qu'en may estoie, ce sonjoie
> [. . .]
> En icelui tens deliteus,
> que toute rien d'amer s'esfroie,
> songai une nuit que j'estoie.
> Lors m'iere avis en mon dormant
> qu'il iere matin durement;
> de mon lit tantost me levé [. . .]. (45–7; 84–9)

(I became aware that it was May, five years or more ago; I dreamed that I was in May, . . . And so I dreamed one night that I was in that delicious season when everything is stirred by love, and as I slept I *became* aware that it *was* full morning; I immediately rose from my bed. [p. 31–32])

To be precise, the Lover does not wake up, but rather gets out of bed. The difference might appear inconsequential (of course the Lover woke up, or else he could not have arisen), and yet precisely the same critical strategy (proof by omission) has been used on a larger scale to show that the poem as a whole is not ended: It is a fragment since it does not explicitly declare its closure. However, this strategy of arising without awakening, as we shall see, could

---

9 Two recent articles that deal with the complicated problem of the narrative personae in the *Roman de la Rose* are Paul Strohm, "Guillaume as Narrator and Lover in the *Roman de la Rose*," *Romanic Review*, vol. LIX, no. 1 (Feb. 1968), 3–9; and E[velyn] B[irge] Vitz, "The *I* of the *Roman de la Rose*," *Genre* 6 (1973), 49–75. I am particularly indebted to the latter for a number of suggestive interpretations. Throughout this study, I will be using the following terms to refer to the various personae taking part in the narrative: "Narrator" will refer to the storytelling voice (and to be distinguished from the author who, for the reasons discussed above in Chapter One, will be referred to as "Guillaume"); "Dreamer," to the past self of the Narrator who had the dream; and "Lover," to the persona *in* the dream who directly experienced the various events (he who, for example, danced in the *carole* and kissed the rose). The reasons and justification for this division will be discussed later in this chapter. For the moment, suffice it to say that the distinctions are based upon a layering of distinct and yet coalesced perceptual vantage points. Vitz, pp. 52–7, posits four such personae, three of which, respectively, more or less coincide with those listed above: "Narrator," "Dreamer," and "Hero of the Dream." Her fourth, "Real-Life Hero," is virtually nonexistent and in any event does not take part in the narrative configuration; as we shall see later, the "Real-Life Hero" belongs to an implicit level of experience without being a narrative persona.

provide a key to the understanding of the poem as a whole. Certain other complications related to the perception and depiction of events begin to occur: First, it should be noted that the Narrator, after the lengthy springtime description found between these two passages (lines 48–83), reiterates the Dreamer's location in bed. Exact repetitions ("Avis m'iere"/"m'iere avis"; "estoie"/"estoie"; "songoie"/"songai") highlight the parallelism. By his placement of the Lover *also* in bed, the Narrator doubles the past occurrence to the point of confusion, spatially intermingling the two otherwise separate moments. The syntactic freedom of Old French verse, accompanied by a conspicuous absence of subordinating conjunctions, allows a further attenuation of what might be a straightforward localization: Does "en icelui tens deliteus" (84) refer to the *songai* (Dreamer) or to the *estoie* (Lover) of line 86? Whereas Modern French syntax would require an ironing out of the ambiguity ("songai *que* j'estoie en icelui tens deliteus"), Old French allows for a juggling of perspectivism, fully exploited in the present instance.[10] Furthermore, since Lover and Dreamer are manifestly in the same position, the line, "Lors m'iere avis en mon dormant" takes on a perfectly equivocal referentiality, applicable to either one of the two sleeping scenes. This in turn causes a perceptual slippage in the following line: Was it Lover or Dreamer who got out of bed? The answer is obvious, but only to the reader who has previously convinced himself of the situation. This ambiguity, coupled with the failure to mention a moment of awakening – an overture to the dream and hence to the poem – suggests an oscillation of levels that subtly undermines the clearcut dream situation being described. The Dreamer, once asleep, projects himself ahead to the moment of completing his present activity (sleeping), bypassing the nighttime hours while simultaneously blurring the transition from a state of sleep to wakefulness. Indeed, perhaps

---

10 One might compare this narrative perspectivism with that employed in the numerous manuscript illuminations. Frequently, the first page contains a large illumination divided into four sections, usually portraying the Lover/Dreamer in bed, the Lover getting dressed, walking in the woods, and coming upon the garden of Deduit. Not only is the figure in bed usually not distinguished from the Lover, but in many versions he is watched over by Dangier, the "vilain" who will only intervene much later in the dream. Cf. Alfred Kuhn, *Die Illustration des Rosenromans*, Jahrbuch der Kunsthistorischen Sammlungen des Allerhöchsten Kaiserhauses, Band XXXI, Heft 1 (Vienna/Leipzig, 1913–14), pp. 1–66.

TWO: THE NARRATION OF ALLEGORY

the problem with this transition — in sum, the problem of conclusion — needs to be confronted here at the poem's beginning and not at its end, which is nonetheless the most obvious place.

An additional confusion of levels is evident at the very beginning of the passage quoted, but there it straddles all three personae: Narrator, Dreamer, and Lover. Although "avis m'iere" ("I became aware" or "it appeared to me") clearly refers to the Dreamer's perception of the original scene, while "il estoit mais" ("it was May") describes the dream story itself, the application of the following line to one or the other level is nearly impossible. Did the dream occur more than five years ago (at a time when the Dreamer was twenty years old), did the Dreamer at the age of twenty dream of a period of five years earlier, when he would have been at most fifteen, or is the Narrator alluding to the dream's fulfillment, which occurred five years before the present moment? In other words, does the five-year anteriority refer to the Dreamer, the Lover, or the Narrator? Our incapacity to unravel the text's initial temporal intricacies in the face of such otherwise specific information (twenty years old; five years ago; the month of May) suggests either a careless (inconsistent) narrator or one who is deliberately blurring the distinctions he has just prepared so carefully.

The question of temporality is certainly pertinent to the study of *any* narrative work. At the very least, the reading experience, over and against that of the purely visual arts, orients the observer in a direction, a perceptual development, which is dictated by a specific chronology. If formal structure in the visual arts is the result of a simultaneous, totalizing perception, that of a written text depends necessarily on a sequential progression that the work itself dictates. Our taking in of a painting might also, in practice, result from a sequence of perceptual moments, but they are rarely imposed by the work. Unlike a painting, a literary work has a stipulated (even quantified) beginning, middle, and end, which must be followed at least in the first reading experience. Consequently, the beginning takes on an added importance, providing as it does the orientation and direction for what is to follow, as well as a measure against which the end will be evaluated. Inasmuch as no narrative can have a predetermined or "natural" end, that point which does form the terminus will create a sense of totality and completion once it is confronted, in a circular motion, with the text's overture. A sense of wholeness will, then, result from a certain disposition of elements rather than force itself upon them. This manner of approaching wholeness can be termed arbitrary only insofar as it refuses to obey a preconceived order, preferring description to prescription at least in the initial stages of the analysis: A disruption or inconsistency in temporal relationships is potentially as meaningful or as "complete" as a strict succession that follows normal (stereotyped) expectancies.

The beginning of any narrative provides a promise (or premise) whose fulfillment, in a profoundly allegorical movement, will only be actualized once the ending has been reached. We are fortunate in having for the *Roman de la Rose* a well-developed, formal prologue that demarcates and situates quite deliberately the initial steps of Guillaume's narrative undertaking. The inclusion of a prologue at the beginning of a narrative work had become a commonplace by the time of Guillaume.[11] While the most important Latin rhetorical treatises of the period prescribe prologues containing material of general interest as a proper beginning for literary works, one need go no further than Guillaume's illustrious predecessor, Chrétien de Troyes, for several examples of elaborate, ingeniously articulated prologues that frame ostensibly unrelated tales of adventure.[12] It goes without saying that the Narrator's self-conscious stance, his direct address to the reader – constitutive parts of the literary prologue – will initiate an implicit or explicit metadiscursive dialogue with the reader/listener.

Guillaume's prologue, which comprises the first forty-four lines

---

[11] For their treatment in the medieval Latin rhetorical arts, cf. Edmond Faral, *Les Arts poétiques du XIIe et du XIIIe siècle* (Paris, 1924), pp. 55–60. An extensive repertory of the prologues from vernacular works of this period can be found in Ulrich Mölk, ed., *Französische Literarästhetik des 12. und 13. Jahrhunderts: Prologe, Exkurse, Epiloge* (Tubingen, 1969).

[12] For a general overview of Chrétien's prologues and their relation to traditional materials, the reader is referred to two recent articles by Tony Hunt: "The Rhetorical Background to the Arthurian Prologue: Tradition and the Old French Vernacular Prologues," *Forum for Modern Language Studies*, 6 (1970), 1–23; and "Tradition and Originality in the Prologues of Chrestien de Troyes," *Forum for Modern Language Studies*, 8 (1972), 320–44. For the present purposes, I will define a prologue as an introductory passage in some way marked by the narrator's presence (discursive tenses, universalizing present tense, *je/tu*, and such enunciatory formulae as "or," "sachiez") and before the beginning of the narrative tale (marked by a passage from present to past, first- to third-person). For a fascinating variation on this paradigm, cf. the important discussion of the "prologue" to *Yvain* by Marie-Louise Ollier, "Le Discours en 'abyme' ou la narration équivoque," *Medioevo Romanzo*, 1 (1974), 351–64.

of the poem, launches directly into an articulation of dream thematics, which we have already perceived to be of an overriding formal importance:

> Aucunes genz dient qu'en songes
> n'a se fables non et mençonges (1-2)
> (Some men say that there is nothing in dreams but fables and lies [p. 31])

The rhyming pair *songe/mensonge* places the reader squarely in the midst of a vastly popular field of enquiry in the Middle Ages, and one that ultimately bears considerable importance for our reading and interpretation of the *Rose,* itself a poem that purports to recount a dream experience. In order to explore more fully the ramifications of this theme, we should perhaps take a brief look at the medieval tradition of dreaming before proceeding to an evaluation of Guillaume's own dream.

THE PROLOGUE: DREAMS AND THEIR SIGNIFICANCE

Guillaume's *songe/mensonge* association seems all the more negligible because it is a rather banal reference to a widespread convention of dream lore: According to this etymological proof, based on a paronomastic coupling of the two words, anything contained in a dream is a lie, a statement bearing no relation to reality (and, consequently, intrinsically untrustworthy and of little significance).[13] In contrast, Guillaume's treatment of the clichéd ex-

---

13 Cf. the discussion by Herman Braet, *Le Songe dans la chanson de geste au XIIe siècle,* Romanica Gandensia, XV (Ghent, 1975), pp. 56–9. Numerous examples of the *songe/mensonge* association in other Old French texts can be found in the Tobler-Lommatzsch *Altfranzösisches Wörterbuch* (Berlin/Wiesbaden, 1925–) under the articles "songe" (Band IX, cols. 841–2) and "mençogne" (Band V, cols. 1392–6). Cf. also Renate Blumenfeld, "Remarques sur *songe/mensonge,*" *Romania* 101 (1980), 385–90. For proverbs in Latin concerning *somnium,* cf. Hans Walther, *Carmina Medii Aevi Posterioris Latina,* Part II: *Proverbia Sententiaeque Latinitatis Medii Aevi,* Vol. 5 (Göttingen, 1967), pp. 71–4 (nos. 30020a–34). The use or "invention" of etymologies to provide such a proof was considered largely a rhetorical technique and had very little of the historical connotation which we accord to it. On this subject, see Paul Zumthor, "Fr. *Etymologie* (essai d'histoire sémantique)," in *Etymologica,* Festschrift for Walther von Wartburg, on his 70th birthday (Tubingen, 1958), pp. 873–93; and Robert Guiette, "L'invention étymologique dans les lettres françaises au moyen âge," in his *Questions de Littérature,* Romanica Gandensia, VIII (Ghent, 1960), pp. 87–98.

pression is nuanced by the fact that he presents a second assertion of sufficient generality to refute the initial maxim:

> mes l'en puet tex songes songier
> qui ne sont mie mençongier,
> ainz sont aprés bien aparant   (3–5)

(but one may have dreams which are not deceitful, whose import becomes quite clear afterward [p. 31])

The criteria that serve to evaluate dreams – indeed, upon which their very acceptability is based – according to Guillaume and the voices of tradition, can be articulated quite neatly in terms of truth and falsehood. In order to understand this fixation on truth, which will be reiterated later in the poem, we must first look at the dream experience in its most general manifestation.

A couple of fundamental distinctions must be made before one can approach an adequate evaluation of medieval dream literature, as well as Guillaume's place therein. A first distinction would mark the difference between dreaming as a universal human activity and the dream account as a conventional literary creation. The post-Freudian world has perhaps come to overemphasize dreams as a psychic manifestation, thereby eliminating the conventionalized literary significance granted to them in certain societies. If we posit from the outset that the two (dream activity and dream account) are separate and distinct, the question becomes *why* the dream experience would present a formal and perceptual model for literary expression and *how* the model functions differently from the actual experience.[14]

Dreams, through their ultimately personal, unseen, and unshared nature, present an aspect of mystery, of unknowing. Since a dream is necessarily inaccessible to all but the experiencing individual, it calls for communication at some level; one must tell

---

14 As will be abundantly clear from the discussion that follows, the treatment of dreams presents manifold problems, largely a result of the many possible fields of application: "real" perception; supernatural; fictional; psychic; metaphorical. It does not lie within the scope of the present work to touch upon all of these, but rather to suggest certain aspects of dream experience and dream literature which might enter into an understanding of Guillaume's poem. My biases will, of course, lead me to emphasize the fictional/metaphorical aspects at the expense of the others – that is, what the dream can suggest in the context of literary communication and expression.

one's dream or it does not exist.[15] A preliminary distinction therefore arises within the realm of dreams between the experience itself, radically immaterial, individual, and unique, and the dream account, an after-the-fact re-creation and description of the experience. While normally the telling of tales is an act that attempts to describe or recreate linguistically a prior event, the filters separating a dream account from the dream experience are considerably more complex. A dream account, as any other narrative, purports to describe an experience; this experience, however, has never taken place outside of the dreamer's mind. If, for most Western cultures, language can only be conceived as an instrument contingent upon real occurrences, then the dream experience, first imagined and then described, must eventually take place. This is the only way of justifying the dream's existence as a discursive event. Nonreferential language, in other words, cannot at the same time be acknowledged and tolerated.

In a so-called theological culture – one that posits the existence of a transcendent, omniscient deity – the dream occurrence often suggests a communion with the divine, inasmuch as the dream is not manifestly a product of the dreamer's conscious thoughts. In this way, the product of dreaming is quite distinct from that of pure imagination, which is considered to be gratuitous. Moreover, when the events of a dream do take place afterwards, dreaming can be construed as the human activity *par excellence* which, through its prophetic structure, bears witness to the workings of divine providence. It is at this stage of development that the criteria of truth and falsehood take their place as central and unavoidable points of judgment in the theological consideration and sanctioning of dreams. What does it mean to say that a dream "comes true," that it is not a lie (*mensonge*)? Guillaume's simple articulation of the answer gets at the heart of the theological stance: "tex songes . . . sont aprés bien aparant" ("such dreams . . . are afterward quite clear"). Making use of the oscillation between what is visible and what is hidden – reiterated later in the prologue through the rhymed pair *apertement/covertement* – Guillaume

---

[15] It does not exist, that is, for anyone but the dreamer. And even he must in some way reformulate it, re-cover it in his mind, for it to have a lasting effect on him. In this sense, of course, one could argue that no thought or idea or perception *really* exists before it has been externalized or expressed in some fashion.

shows that the *true* dream account is one that will make itself visible (*aparant*) at a moment chronologically posterior to (*après*) the telling of the event. By extension, a "false" or lying dream (*mensonge*) will *not* repeat itself after the telling. We shall hereafter refer to this iterative quality as the "prophetic" structure to which all dream accounts are implicitly answerable.

If a primary metaphoric value of the dream experience is that of its prophetic efficacy, a second association immediately asserts itself: As we mentioned above, that which makes a dream a dream is its *telling*. In this sense, dreaming can be seen as a paradigm for the human imperative to tell stories, to recount one's own experience (which otherwise would remain inaccessible to others). In fact, the dream, as a phenomenon that forms the crossroads between divine knowledge, individual creation, and worldly communication, represents for medieval and ancient society the point of juncture between the poet and the prophet.[16]

Guillaume's awareness of this cluster of meanings comes out in his addition of a third term to the *songe/mensonge* association: *fable*. The association between fables and lies is, to be sure, another literary commonplace, but the context of the present discussion, which situates lies inside dreams literally ("en songes ... n'a se fables non et mençonges" ["there is nothing in dreams but fables and lies"]) and dreams inside lies etymologically (men*songe*) – an intricate copenetration of the two terms – forces the dream account to fold out into a more general treatment of the possibility or desirability of literary recreation.[17] We might here recall the definition of fictional, as opposed to historical, discourse that we proposed in Chapter One: a discourse that manifestly reverses the

---

16 For an extensive discussion of this association among medieval theoreticians, see the unpublished doctoral dissertation of Francis Xavier Newman, "Somnium: Medieval Theories of Dreaming and the Form of Vision Poetry" (Princeton, 1963).

17 While the association between *fable* and *mensonge* is not original with Guillaume de Lorris (cf., e.g., Chrétien's *Yvain*, ed. Mario Roques, CFMA 89 [Paris, 1960], line 27), the linking of *songe* and *fable* via *mensonge* is provocative. All the examples given by T-L under the neutral definition "Gerede" (Band III, col. 1543) are formulated in the negative: e.g., "ne ferai pas fable." The implication is, of course, not that *all* speech is potentially duplicitous or tedious but that "fable" designates a necessarily negative variety. One might add that the word *fable*, derived from the defective Latin verb *for*, *fātus* via *fābŭla*, seems always to have been linked with the false or unreal. Cf. Varro, *De Lingua Latina*, VI, 55; *Rhetorica ad Herenniam*, I, viii, 13: "Fabula est quae neque veras neque veri similes continet res." ("A fable is that which contains neither true nor verisimilar things.")

secondary place of language in the order of things. Clearly dreams, through their characteristic reverse structure, which we have termed "prophetic," become a figure for the fictional imperative itself (and a contrary of history in the Aristotelian sense). In a very real sense, the problem of dreams is the problem of fiction. Whereas dreams, like works of fiction, are susceptible to frivolity, to a disassociation with real events, the theological model of language will only sanction a subservience of language to reality. This explains the hostility of medieval theologians toward dream interpretation, and the resultant *songe/mensonge* association that discredits them. Short of rejecting completely the validity of dreams, the assurance of dreams "coming true" is another way of handling the problem, an attempt to reinscribe the dream (or fiction itself, which it always risked becoming) in this theologically sanctioned system, making it once more a discourse ultimately contingent upon real events.

A clear justification for the dual perspective of dream accounts in relation to real events, prophetic (theological) and fictional (recuperated as allegorical expression), can be found in the problematical mention of Macrobius which occurs a few lines later in the prologue:

> si en puis bien traire a garant
> un auctor qui ot non Macrobes.   (6–7)
> (We may take as witness an author named Macrobius. [p. 31])

A mention of Macrobius is, on the one hand, quite natural – nearly a prerequisite – in a medieval discussion of dreams: The most widely read authority on the subject for nearly a thousand years, Macrobius had proposed an extensive categorization of the principal varieties of dreams.[18] Writing at the end of the fourth century, Macrobius undertook a lengthy commentary on a short text by Cicero, the "Dream of Scipio," itself in actuality part of a larger work, the *De Re Publica*. Macrobius's commentary, mostly

---

18 The edition of Macrobius to be used will be that of Iacobus Willis, Vol. 2, *Commentarii in Somnium Scipionis* (Leipzig, 1963) (hereinafter *Comm.*). An excellent general introduction to the place of Macrobius in early Christian tradition can be found in the English translation by William Harris Stahl, Macrobius, *Commentary on the Dream of Scipio* (New York, 1952), pp. 3–65; a useful discussion of Macrobius's sources is that of Pierre Courcelle, *Les Lettres grecques en occident: de Macrobe à Cassiodore* (Paris, 1943), pp. 3–36.

THE PROLOGUE: DREAMS AND SIGNIFICANCE

an excuse for the promulgation of neo-Platonic lore ranging from music to geography to a discussion of virtue, starts out with a statement of its own justification, based on the defense of dream accounts as a method of acquiring knowledge of the divine. According to Macrobius, there are five main types of dreams, two of which need not be considered since they have no prophetic qualities (*insomnium* and *visum*) and three that indeed do foretell the future (*somnium, visio,* and *oraculum*).[19] Macrobius devotes the bulk of his chapter to a discussion of the latter three and a demonstration of how Scipio's dream does relate to them. Briefly, Scipio's dream provides examples of all three types of prophetic

19 "aut enim est ὄνειρος secundum Graecos quod Latini *somnium* vocant, aut est ὅραμα quod *visio* recte appellatur, aut est χρηματισμός quod *oraculum* nuncupatur, aut est ἐνύπνιον quod *insomnium* dicitur, aut est φάντασμα quod Cicero, quotiens opus hoc nomine fuit, *visum* vocavit. Ultima ex his duo cum videntur, cura interpretationis indigna sunt, quia nihil divinationis adportant, ἐνύπνιον dico et φάντασμα. Est enim ἐνύπνιον quotiens cura oppressi animi corporisve sive fortunae, qualis vigilantem fatigaverat, talem se ingerit dormienti [. . .] φάντασμα vero, hoc est *visum,* cum inter vigiliam et adultam quietem in quadam, ut aiunt, prima somni nebula adhuc se vigilare aestimans, qui dormire vix coepit, aspicere videtur irruentes in se vel passim vagantes formas a natura seu magnitudine seu specie discrepantes variasque tempestates rerum vel laetas vel turbulentas [. . .] et est *oraculum* quidem cum in somnis parens vel alia sancta gravisve persona seu sacerdos vel etiam deus aperte eventurum quid aut non eventurum, faciendum vitandumve denuntiat. *visio* est autem cum id quis videt quod eodem modo quo apparuerat eveniet [. . .] *somnium* proprie vocatur quod tegit figuris et velat ambagibus non nisi interpretatione intellegendam significationem rei quae demonstrato, quod quale sit non a nobis exponendum est, cum hoc unus quisque ex usu quid sit agnoscat." (*Comm.,* I, iii, 2–10; emphasis mine)

"There is the enigmatic dream, in Greek *oneiros,* in Latin *somnium;* second, there is the prophetic vision, in Greek *horama,* in Latin *visio;* third, there is the oracular dream, in Greek *chrematismos,* in Latin *oraculum;* fourth there is the nightmare, in Greek *enypnion,* in Latin *insomnium;* and last, the apparition, in Greek *phantasma,* which Cicero, when he has occasion to use the word, calls *visum.* The last two, the nightmare and the apparition, are not worth interpreting since they have no prophetic significance. Nightmares may be caused by mental or physical distress, or anxiety about the future: the patient experiences in dreams vexations similar to those that disturb him during the day [. . .]. The apparition (*phantasma* or *visum*) comes upon one in the moment between wakefulness and slumber, in the so-called 'first cloud of sleep.' In this drowsy condition he thinks he is still fully awake and imagines he sees specters rushing at him or wandering vaguely about, differing from natural creatures in size and shape, and hosts of diverse things, either delightful or disturbing. [. . .] We call a dream oracular in which a parent, or a pious or revered man, or a priest, or even a god clearly reveals what will or will not transpire, and what action to take or avoid. We call a dream a prophetic vision if it actually comes true [. . .]. By an enigmatic dream we mean one that conceals with strange shapes and veils with ambiguity the true meaning of the information being offered, and requires an interpretation for its understanding. We need not explain further the nature of this dream since everyone knows from experience what it is" (Stahl, *Commentary,* pp. 87–90). For a discussion of Macrobius's system with regard to previous dream theories, see Stahl's introduction to Macrobius, *Commentary,* and Braet, *Songe,* pp. 17–33.

dreams, containing simultaneously an outright portrayal of the future, a disguised, or figurative, portrayal, and the verbal announcement by an authority figure of future events.[20]

Guillaume's reference to Macrobius immediately begs the question of how *his* tale relates to the latter's commentary. Accordingly, most scholars have applied themselves to the categorization of the *Roman de la Rose* dream according to Macrobius's scheme. The answers have varied but mainly oscillate between *somnium* and *insomnium* as guiding principles.[21] It has been placed into doubt whether Guillaume's account, in spite of the reference to Macrobius, is even worth interpreting according to his scheme.[22] Aside from the difficulty of choosing the proper category, however, numerous other problems impede our attempt to categorize Guillaume's dream according to Macrobius. First of all, it is far from certain whether Guillaume's mention of Macrobius arises from a studied reading of the *Commentary* or simply an association between a well-known name and the general topic of dream lore. Even granting Guillaume's familiarity with the *Commentary*, none of the categories applies unambiguously and exclusively to Guillaume's account. Indeed, as with Scipio's dream, several or perhaps *all* of the categories apply: It is a *somnium* because of its allegorical, figurative expression of future events; a *visio*, insofar as it portrays specific actions of the narrator himself, who is not treated figuratively; an *oraculum*, because of Amor's lengthy instructions; an *insomnium*, by virtue of its being an erotic dream. In fact, only the *visum* does not initially seem to apply. A reading of Guillaume according to Macrobius calls for considerably more discretion than has heretofore been exercised.

Moreover, a careful reading of the *Commentary* reveals an emphasis that has scarcely been considered in discussions of the *Ro-*

---

20 "hoc ergo quod Scipio vidisse se rettulit et tria illa quae sola probabilia sunt genera principalitatis amplectitur, et omnes ipsius somnii species attingit." (*Comm.*, I, iii, 12) "The dream which Scipio reports that he saw embraces the three reliable types mentioned above, and also has to do with all five varieties of the enigmatic dream." (Stahl, *Commentary*, p. 90)

21 See Charles Dahlberg, "Macrobius and the Unity of the *Roman de la Rose*," *Studies in Philology*, 58 (1961), 573–82; D. W. Robertson, Jr., *A Preface to Chaucer* (Princeton, 1962), p. 103; and Rupert T. Pickens, "*Somnium* and Interpretation in Guillaume de Lorris," *Symposium*, 29 (1974), 175–86.

22 As Dahlberg suggests, if Guillaume's dream is an *insomnium* then, according to Macrobius's authority, it allows for no interpretation.

THE PROLOGUE: DREAMS AND SIGNIFICANCE

man de la Rose.[23] We must not forget that Macrobius's discussion of dreams is *not* the central focus of his commentary, but rather a preliminary methodological enquiry on the feasibility of his own exegetical undertaking. For Macrobius, the major question, of which dreams form only a part, becomes that of the appropriateness of fables as a means of demonstrating philosophical truths:[24]

> Fabulae, quarum nomen indicat falsi professionem, aut tantum conciliandae auribus voluptatis, aut adhortationis quoque in bonam frugem gratia repertae sunt.
> (Fables – the very word acknowledges their falsity – serve two purposes: either merely to gratify the ear or to encourage the reader to good works.)

To this end, and after a preliminary rejection of those fables which only "please the ear," Macrobius distinguishes between the *fabula* and the *narratio fabulosa,* the former being frivolous and improper to philosophical discussions while the latter is a construct fitting to the expression of philosophical doctrines (within certain limitations). It should be obvious that already in Macrobius dreams are construed as a literary device and *not* as a feature of human experience: He treats Cicero's use of a dream and Plato's use of the myth of Er as interchangeable and equally fictive:[25]

> Hanc fabulam Cicero licet ab indoctis quasi ipse veri conscius doleat irrisam, exemplum tamen stolidae reprehensionis vitans excitari narraturum quam revivescere maluit.
> (Cicero, as if assured of the truth of this tale, deplored the ridicule it received at the hands of ignorant critics and yet, fearful of the unwarranted censure that was heaped upon Plato, preferred to have his account given by a man aroused from sleep rather than by one returned from the dead.)

Whatever we think of dreams as a supernatural phenomenon is clearly irrelevant: their importance resides in their efficacy as an expository technique. Not only, then, does Macrobius make the

---

23 See, however, Pickens's remarks on the exegetical levels of Guillaume's account.
24 *Comm.*, I, ii, 7. Stahl, *Commentary*, p. 84.
25 *Comm.*, I, i, 9. Stahl, *Commentary*, p. 83.

concepts of dream and *fabula* coincide, but he emphasizes their utilitarian role in the formation of the literary/philosophical enterprise.[26]

Macrobius provides an important example of what we have termed the theological attitude toward dream accounts and their utility: Their function is that of an instrument, a tool, with a further applicability – either the communication of some "higher" truth or to "encourage one to good works." The fable itself, according to this theological perspective, can be of no worth and, moreover, those fables that do arrest the reader's interest or stimulate his pleasure (those, in other words, that do not remain transparent) are to be shunned. That we are coming close to a discussion of allegory as an exegetical mode should come as no surprise – Macrobius, one of the major sources of neo-Platonic thought for Western Christianity, will later discuss figurative thought (with of course an emphasis on dream figuration) and the interrelation between soul and body, closely approximating more strictly theological discussions of the relationship between meaning and text in the exegesis of Biblical accounts.

The programmatic statement – certainly the most influential – of the dual-level allegorical method of reading the Bible is that of St. Augustine in his *De Doctrina Christiana,* a central text of study

---

[26] "utraque enim sub adposito argumento electa persona est quae accomoda enuntiandis haberetur" (*Comm.,* I, ii, 5). "In either case [Plato and Cicero] the author justified his choice of character as suited to the expression of his doctrines" (Stahl, *Commentary,* p. 84). It should be added that Macrobius's addition of the term *narratio fabulosa* is certainly an attempt to straddle conflicting associations within the more basic word *fabula,* which while meaning most literally *any* tale, had certainly acquired an indelibly negative connotation (see note 17, above). The contradiction shows itself more clearly once one realizes that the *narratio fabulosa* is at once a subset of the general field of *fabula* and *not* a *fabula* ("non fabula," *Comm.* I, ii, 9). One might add to this terminological confusion the fact that Plato's story of Er, certainly considered legitimate by Macrobius, is designated by the term *fabula* up to the moment where the latter is distinguished from the *fabulosa.* A twelfth-century realignment of Macrobius's ambiguous distinction between *fabula*-as-fiction (in its broadest acceptance) and *fabula* as vain or philosophically unworthy narrative (as opposed to *narratio fabulosa*) by William of Conches is discussed by Peter Dronke in his *Fabula: Explorations into the Uses of Myth in Medieval Platonism* (Leiden, 1974), pp. 13–78. One might suggest that Macrobius's subsequent dream categorization results from a similar desire to categorize and legitimize, except that a commonly accepted generic term for dream (equivalent to *fabula*) seems to be lacking (what is translated by Stahl as "dream" at the beginning of Chapter Three is actually the quite elliptical "omnium quae videre sibi dormientes videntur" ["of all those things which those who are asleep think they see"]). While a form of the verb *somnio* is used in this general sense ("somniandi modos," *Comm.* I, iii, 1), the noun *somnium* is used to refer to the allegorical dream or to Scipio's philosophical one.

at least through the thirteenth century.[27] A number of fascinating metaphors going back to classical and Biblical texts were developed to express the fundamentally intangible relationship between letter and spirit, between obvious meaning and revealed truth (which could appear to contradict each other).[28] Not only is Macrobius's definition of *somnium* a rhetorical imitation of this fundamentally neo-Platonic vision of meaning as a veiled truth ("tegit figuris et velat ambagibus" ["it conceals with strange shapes and veils with ambiguity"]) but the rest of his discourse is laced with analogous expressions. For instance, nature prefers to maintain her secrets veiled before men, much as she disguises her naked body:[29] "sciunt inimicam esse naturae apertam nudamque expositionem sui, quae sicut vulgaribus hominum sensibus intellectum sui vario rerum tegmine operimentoque subtraxit (. . .)" ("[philosophers] realize that a frank, open exposition of herself is distasteful to Nature, who, just as she has withheld an understanding of herself from the uncouth senses of men by enveloping herself in variegated garments [. . .]"). There is even a certain sense in which *no* meaning is communicated directly, without such a cover: Numenius, after having revealed (vulgarized) the secrets of the Eleusinian goddesses, is visited in a dream *not* by the naked goddesses, but by the latter travestied ironically as prostitutes:[30] "somnia prodiderunt, viso sibi ipsas Eleusinias deas *habitu meretricio* ante apertum lupanar videre prostantes, admirantique et causas non convenientis numinibus turpitudinis consulenti re-

---

27 For a thorough and fascinating analysis of the fourfold method of Biblical exegesis, cf. Henri de Lubac, *Exégèse médiévale: les Quatre sens de l'écriture*, 2 vols. in 4 (Paris, 1959–64) who, while stressing particularly the importance of Origen in the elaboration of the fourfold method, states that, "De l'oeuvre augustinienne à l'oeuvre origénienne les correspondances abondent, dans les idées, dans les thèmes, parfois jusque dans l'accent et le mouvement spirituel [. . .]. Dans ses grandes lignes, les meilleures comme les plus contestables, leur herméneutique est la même" (I, i, p. 214).
28 For a series of such examples, see Jean Pépin, *Dante et la tradition de l'allégorie* (Paris/Montreal, 1970), pp. 89–92; D. W. Robertson, Jr., "Some Medieval Literary Terminology with Special Reference to Chrétien de Troyes," *Studies in Philology*, 48 (1951), pp. 669–92, as well as his *A Preface to Chaucer*, pp. 315–17; and de Lubac, *Exégèse*, who states most succinctly, I, i, pp. 307–8: "L'intelligence spirituelle vient ôter le voile de la lettre, ou le voile qu'est la lettre, afin d'en dégager l'esprit; ou bien, au contraire, elle vient couvrir la pauvreté de la lettre d'un manteau royal qui la transfigure. Sans elle, on voit l'Ecriture encore sans la voir. Elle découvre l'esprit comme le soleil sous la nuée, comme la moelle sous l'écorce, comme le grain sous la paille."
29 *Comm.*, I, ii, 17. Stahl, *Commentary*, p. 86.
30 *Comm.*, I, ii, 19. Stahl, *Commentary*, p. 87, emphasis mine.

spondisse iratas ab ipso se de adyto pudicitiae suae vi abstractas et passim adeuntibus prostitutas." ("The Eleusinian goddesses themselves, *dressed in the garments of courtesans,* appeared to him standing before an open brothel, and when in his astonishment he asked the reason for this shocking conduct, they angrily replied that he had driven them from their sanctuary of modesty and had prostituted them to every passer-by.") In what amounts to an allegory of allegorical expression, Macrobius seems to be suggesting, most paradoxically, that the truth is *never* perceived without its figurative covering — that a truth denuded is simply a truth that has donned another type of clothing.

One final example from Macrobius deserves mention here, insofar as it relates directly dreaming and allegorical covering, his interpretation of Virgil's twin gates:[31]

> "siquis forte quaerere velit cur porta ex ebore falsis et e cornu veris sit deputata, instruetur auctore Porphyrio, qui in commentariis suis haec in eundem locum dicit ab Homero sub eadem divisione descriptum: "Latet," inquit, "omne verum. hoc tamen anima cum ab officiis corporis somno eius paululum libera est interdum aspicit, non numquam tendit aciem nec tamen pervenit, et cum aspicit tamen non libero et directo lumine videt sed interiecto velamine, quod nexus naturae caligantis obducit." Et hoc in natura esse idem Vergilius asserit dicens,
>
>> Aspice, namque omnem quae nunc obducta tuenti
>> Mortales hebetat visus tibi et umida circum
>> Caligat nubem eripiam.
>
> Hoc velamen cum in quiete ad verum usque aciem animae introspicientis admittit, de cornu creditur, cuius ista natura est ut tenuatum visui pervium sit; cum autem a vero hebetat ac repellit optutum, ebur putatur, cuius corpus ita natura densetum est ut ad quamvis extremitatem tenuitatis erasum nullo visu ad ulteriora tendente penetretur."
>
> (Someone may take the occasion to enquire why false dreams are allotted to the gate of ivory and truthworthy ones to the gate of horn. He should avail himself of the help of Porphyry, who, in his *Commentaries,* makes the following remarks on a passage in Homer presenting the same distinction between

---

31 *Comm.,* I, iii, 17–20. Stahl, *Commentary,* p. 92.

gates: 'All truth is concealed. Nevertheless, the soul, when it is partially disengaged from bodily functions during sleep, at times gazes and at times peers intently at the truth, but does not apprehend it; and when it gazes it does not see with clear and direct vision, but rather with a dark obstructing veil interposed.' Virgil attests that this is natural in the following lines: 'Behold — for all the cloud, which now, drawn over thy sight, dulls thy mortal vision and with dank pall enshrouds thee, I will tear away.' If, during sleep, this veil permits the vision of the attentive soul to perceive the truth, it is thought to be made of horn, the nature of which is such that, when thinned, it becomes transparent. When the veil dulls the vision and prevents its reaching the truth, it is thought to be made of ivory, the composition of which is so dense that no matter how thin a layer of it may be, it remains opaque.)

Even the clearest perception of truth is mediated by the "transparent veil" of the gates of horn. Macrobius shows us that to speak of dreams and prophecy, particularly in their capacity as philosophical instruments, is to speak of allegory. Furthermore, through their fundamental structuring of figuration and fulfillment, more than a convenient "vehicle . . . for allegory," a type of narrative container or pretext, dreams are a constitutive and privileged mode of allegorical writing.[32]

If we are at all, then, to pursue an interpretation of Guillaume according to Macrobius, it must be in light of the latter's major theoretical contribution, the theological recuperation of dreams as an expositional technique, and *not* through a vague belief in prophecy or the phenomenology of dream lore. It is important to see that the dream, an allegorical structure, presents a radically *prophetic* narrative configuration, one based on the eventual iteration of a narrated account. This is indeed the principal quality of dreams articulated by Guillaume ("sont aprés bien aparant" ["they are afterward quite clear"]). The only way for a dream to maintain its validity, to avoid the accusation of falsehood, to justify its very existence, is to repeat itself at a later time; moreover, inasmuch as the dream account implies the prior existence of the dream experience (the original, preverbal apparition or vision), a three-tiered program of temporally developed sequences is set up,

---

[32] Cf. Constance B. Hieatt, *The Realism of Dream Visions* (The Hague, 1967), p. 13.

TWO: THE NARRATION OF ALLEGORY

a point x along any one of the lines finding a correspondence — if not identical, at least analogical — in the other lines:

$$\underset{A_1}{*}\underline{}\underset{x_1}{*}\underline{}\underset{B_1}{*}\quad\text{DREAM EXPERIENCE (prelinguistic)}$$

$$\underset{A_2}{*}\underline{}\underset{x_2}{*}\underline{}\underset{B_2}{*}\quad\text{DREAM ACCOUNT}$$

$$\underset{A_3}{*}\underline{}\underset{x_3}{*}\underline{}\underset{B_3}{*}\quad\text{REAL EVENT}$$

A larger chronological imperative imposed by the logic of the dream sequence dictates that each line follows the next without overlapping, that is, that any point on the line A_1–B_1 occurs before any point on the line A_2–B_2 (how could one tell one's dream before the dream itself was concluded?). Similarly, the sequence from A_2 to B_2 must be accomplished before its effectiveness as a prophetic tale is realized by the events following upon A_3.[33]

At the outset, then, we must conclude that it is totally uncertain to what extent Guillaume "knew" or applied the rules of Macrobius's treatise. Our understanding of the potential influence must come from indications in Guillaume's text, and certainly requires more than a mere citation of the renowned authority's name. Second, if we do concede a familiarity with Macrobius, then the only likely conclusion that is justifiable on methodological grounds is Macrobius's emphasis on dreams as a mode of allegorico-narrative *prophetic* expression, whose didactic function does not differ substantially from other such modes as visits to the other world, descents to hell, and so forth.[34]

---

33 This is of course only the most simple and least complicated of schemes, that which presupposes a separation among the levels, along with a parallelism. The simplicity of this ideal scheme will however allow us better to perceive potential aberrations in the system, interferences among levels. Such would be the case were the dream experience or dream account to take place *during* the development of the "Real Event" (the dream experience or account forming a point x_3 along the line A_3–B_3), not to mention the possibility of an interruption of dream experience or dream account. In general, once the dream (experience or account) is perceived as an *event* and no longer simply as a *discourse,* the sequence of parallel levels will necessarily be altered.

34 It is clear that the allegorical tradition upon which Guillaume predicated his account alternated between visits to the other world and dream occurrences. The Classical example of the former, which held sway for most of the Middle Ages, was Aeneas's descent to Hell in the sixth book of the *Aeneid.* As for Guillaume's contemporaries, one is immediately reminded of Huon de Méry's *Tornoiement d'Antecrist,* in which a first-person narrator tells of an allegorical adventure that occurred to him when out walking

THE PROLOGUE: THE AUTHORITY OF WRITING

The transfer from a phenomenal universe of divine prophecy to one of narrative prophecy suggests an oscillation within the dream construct between a God-centered theological universe and the writer-oriented universe of fiction, where the author replaces God as the omniscient controlling figure. By way of illustrating this basic difference between the dream as divine prophecy (theological context) and dream as narrative prophecy (allegorical context), we might take a look at the principal ways in which dreams may be manifested in a work of literature. There are two major types of dream portrayals in medieval literature: the dream as a narrated element in a larger narrative scheme; and the dream itself as a narrative frame (hereafter called the "dream vision"). While both refer to the same human activity that we have described above and demonstrate the same aspects of iteration that normally adhere to any dream construct, their poetic use is quite distinct. The interpretation of dreams is a radically contextual exercise, depending as it does on the actualization (fulfillment) of the dream's promise (prophecy). Within a narrated poem, such as the *chanson de geste,* which Herman Bract has carefully analyzed, the dream and its fulfillment, while signifying a sort of divine intervention, the all-knowing providence of God, attest as well to the poet's omniscience, his knowledge (and our belief in his knowledge) that the dream will indeed be realized in some way (either in an outright or an ironic fashion).[35] Such literary dreams are virtually

---

in the forest: Inasmuch as a dream framework is lacking, the otherwise similar vision of the two poems leads one to ask whether Guillaume's dream pretext was absolutely essential for the expression of *his* allegory. Cf. the important tradition of love debates that frequently involve the first-person narrator in a dreamlike experience (texts collected in Charles Oulmont, *Les Débats du clerc et. du chevalier dans la littérature poétique du moyen-âge* [Paris, 1911]). For a more detailed analysis of the relationship between Guillaume and his allegorical forebears, cf. Marc-René Jung, *Etudes sur le poème allégorique en France au moyen-âge,* Romanica Helvetica, 82 (Bern, 1971), esp. pp. 227–328; and the important article by Hans Robert Jauss, "La Transformation de la forme allégorique entre 1180 et 1240: D'Alain de Lille à Guillaume de Lorris," in Anthime Fourrier, ed., *L'Humanisme médiéval dans les littératures romanes du XIIe au XIVe siècle* (Paris, 1964), pp. 107–46.

35 Braet, *Songe,* p. 46: "Or, il s'avère que les textes que nous avons examinés contiennent sans exception des présages véridiques. [. . .] l'auteur épique manifeste une foi inébranlable dans les présages oniriques. [. . .] On croit parfois déceler chez l'un ou l'autre personnage une attitude de refus. Cela ne signifie nullement que le poète partage

never random or pointless. And yet we do know by experience that not all dreams are indeed prophetic; it is through the poet's selectiveness that our belief in prophecy is bolstered. As readers of the epic poem (especially outside of the rigid context of medieval Catholicism), we maintain our assurance of the dream's fulfillment *not* through a belief in God but, somewhat more subtly, through our belief in the narrator's belief in God. The theological model of divine prophecy is subsumed under the literary model of allegory once the story is told and not lived. The poet makes use of divine intervention in order to adumbrate in a gesture of incomparable finesse his own narrative omniscience.[36]

The dream vision goes one step further in its magnification of the narrator's authority. There, inasmuch as the fulfillment of the dream is not recounted (the poem normally ends where the dream ends), one must lend all the more credence to the narrator and his assurance (explicit or implicit) that the tale did or will come true. If the epic poet makes use of dreams as a coy statement of his own authority within the global narrative context, the dream vision brings the question of authority clearly to the fore. All the more so in the important innovation made by Guillaume de Lorris, whereby the Narrator's own personal experience and feelings occupy the center of the account. Once prophetic dreams are included within a secular context, the questioning of authority becomes crucial: Do such dreams really "come true"? How do we know for sure? If the dream as a narrative structure works intrinsically at disrupting the normal chain of linguistic authority (and therefore promoting its fictionality at the expense of its historicity), how does this affect the ultimate divine authority that sanctions (authorizes) all human works? Can the dream signify or have value outside of a structure

---

cet avis." Whether or not the epic poet has a real faith ("foi") in the irrational, divine origin of dream prophecy, as Braet asserts, is a moot point. Similarly, to tell stories filled with fantastic elements such as fairies, magic rings, and disappearing castles does not mean that one "believes" in them. When Braet here insists on the seriousness and naïve faith of the epic poet over and against the rational, skeptical vision of the romance writer, he is merely falling back into a cliché enshrined in literary histories; moreover, the tacit assumption that medieval poets were necessarily "serious" when treating divine topics needs to be questioned.

36 It is not therefore a coincidence that the central portion of Braet's thesis is devoted to the dream as a storytelling device: "Nature et fonction de l'annonce épique" (*Songe*, pp. 63–109).

of prophecy such as we have just described? I would suggest that Guillaume's enterprise – investigating the realm of human love – simultaneously presents certain precise obstacles to the prophetic endeavor (Guillaume perhaps having become a victim of his model) while giving him a way out of his very real predicament. The prologue taken as a whole is in this respect central, for it shows Guillaume grappling with the question of his own authority and, indeed, the very reason behind the narrative tale, the goal toward which it is projecting.

As we mentioned above, the typical role of an initial *sententia* was that of enunciating some sort of moral or doctrinal theme that would thereafter be illustrated in the narrative account.[37] Significantly, in the case of Guillaume, the initial maxim touches neither moral nor doctrinal codes but rather a metadiscursive theme: It serves to comment upon the signifying possibilities of the poetic strategy itself which is being utilized. In other words, from the first, the project of dream interpretation as a narrative strategy is explicitly thematized. Might this not suggest the elaboration of the theme of interpretation within the romance itself? In this context, Guillaume's mention of Macrobius takes on an added dimension, forcing us to alter a first perception that placed him in a strictly doctrinal framework. Literally, Guillaume does not cite Macrobius on account of his authority in matters of dream interpretation, but rather because he *wrote down* ("escrit") Scipio's dream. Guillaume states,

> ... Macrobes,
> qui ne tint pas songes a lobes,
>ançois escrit l'avision
> qui avint au roi Scypion. (7–10)

(Macrobius, who did not take dreams as trifles, but instead wrote of the vision which came to King Scipio. [p. 31])

---

[37] Hunt, however, insists that the proverb or *sententia* is merely a *captatio benevolentiae* and "need have no direct connexion with the ensuing *narratio*" ("Rhetorical," p. 9). His assumption that only a prologue that *explicitly* comments upon the way a work is to be read (to be distinguished from a *proemium*, which is merely decorative – literally, an *hors d'oeuvre*) had a connection with the romance itself is clearly reductive and at the very least a simplistic view of the complexities of Chrétien de Troyes and his literary followers.

In Old French, expressions of the type

$$\begin{array}{c}\text{Negative}\\\text{Statement}\end{array} + \begin{array}{c}\textit{ainz}\\\textit{ançois}\end{array} + \begin{array}{c}\text{Positive}\\\text{Statement}\end{array}$$

place the two statements on a parallel plane of meaning, as reverse equivalents of each other.[38] For instance, "li entr'ieuz *ne fu pas petis,*/ainz *ert assez grant* par mesure" (528–9) ("The space between her eyes was not small but very wide in measure" [p. 38]), or "El mantel *n'ot pas penne veire,*/ainz *fu vil et de povre afeire*" (215–16) ("The mantle had no fur linings, but very poor and shabby ones" [p. 33]). On occasion the equivalence is less literal, although nonetheless implicit, as in an example that we have already seen: "qui *ne sont mie mençongier,*/ainz *sont aprés bien aparant*" (4–5) ("[dreams] which are not at all deceitful, but which are, rather, afterward quite clear" [p. 31]), which, through the negative equivalence, gives us an adequate definition of what true dreams are. In the Macrobius example, "ne tint pas songes a lobes" is juxtaposed with "escrit l'avision" by means of an identical construction with *ainz*. Essentially, "escrit" ("wrote") is equated with the expression "ne tint pas . . . a lobes" ("did not take . . . as trifles"): While finding its basis in a subjective appraisal of veracity, the act of writing, once accomplished, founds its own discursive veracity and becomes in turn a *garant*. Macrobius, according to Guillaume's expression, is a *garant not* because of what he said (the contents of his commentary) but by the fact of his having placed it into writing. The philosophical relevance of Macrobius and his dream commentary is undermined in no uncertain fashion.

The enigmatic position of Macrobius with regard to his posterity calls for still another measure of caution. At least since the time

---

38 On this point, see the rich discussion by Paul Imbs, *Les Propositions temporelles en ancien français: La Détermination du moment*, Publications de la Faculté des Lettres de l'Université de Strasbourg, fasc. 120 (Paris, 1956), pp. 419–26. Imbs shows how the use of *ainz* (Latin *ante*) passed from a relation of chronological anteriority between two propositions to one of opposition, indicating that the choice between the two is contingent upon the meaning and tense of the two verbs thus opposed. In a recent article ("Sur l'emploi adversatif de *mais* et de *ainz* (*ainçois*) en ancien français," *Travaux de linguistique et de littérature*, XVI, No. 1 [1979], 271–92), Georges Kleiber describes even more fully the way in which *ainz*, as an "opérateur d'inversion," can associate two clauses which would not normally be opposed and thus produce a specific stylistic effect: "la rectification est un renchérissement" (p. 283).

THE PROLOGUE: THE AUTHORITY OF WRITING

of Langlois, scholars have been aware that Guillaume gives false information concerning his acknowledged *auctor:* Not only was Scipio not a king, but Macrobius did not write the dream of Scipio; Cicero did.[39] If we attribute this to a mere oversight, we are perhaps missing Guillaume's point. We remember that Cicero's complete *De Re Publica* was lost for a period of several centuries, a nearly complete text having only been found in a palimpsest in the early nineteenth century. In fact, the only fragment of Cicero's work available to the Middle Ages was the final section, the Dream of Scipio, preserved thanks to Macrobius's commentary and its considerable success. Somewhat paradoxically, in this specific case, the commentator allowed for the preservation and, ultimately, the very existence of his primary text. For Guillaume, in a distinctly nonhistorical sense, Macrobius *did write* the Dream of Scipio. Moreover, if we remember that Cicero is already imitating Plato's *Republic,* which itself tells of a man (Er) telling a story, and that Macrobius, as we have seen, discusses the storytelling efficacy of *both* his forebears (myth versus dream), it is easy to see that a lineage of authorial begetting is implicit in Guillaume's evocation of Macrobius, based on the writing, preserving, and rewriting of texts.

If, through his mention of Macrobius, Guillaume is attempting to establish a particular authority of the writing subject, he also calls on the voices of anonymous, traditional authority: "Aucunes genz" ("some people"); "l'en puet" ("one can"). However, pursuing a second movement as of line 11, Guillaume subtly shifts his tactic. While reiterating the premonitory efficacy of dreams, already proven through anonymous and written authority, Guillaume establishes his own subjective voice: "endroit moi ai ge fiance/que songes est senefiance" (15–16) ("for my part, I am convinced that a dream signifies" [p. 31]). In a passage strewn with verbs and expressions of opinion ("cuit" ["think"] [11]; "die" ["say"] [11]; "croire" ["believe"] [13]; "tiegne" ["consider"] [14]; "fiance" ["confidence"] [15]), the impersonal, indeterminate voice ("Qui c'onques" ["whoever"] [11]; "qui que" ["whoever"] [11]; "qui" ["who"] [14]; "as genz" ["to people"]

---

39 Cf. Ernest Langlois, *Origines et sources du Roman de la Rose,* Bibliothèque des Ecoles françaises d'Athènes et de Rome, fasc. 58 (Paris, 1891), p. 69.

131

[17]; "li plusor" ["most people"] [18]; "l'en" ["one"] [20]) is opposed to the Narrator's own defined *je,* which is doubled in line 15 for added emphasis ("endroit *moi* ai *ge*") ("for *my* part, *I*").[40] Whereas many points can be proven by general statements of opinion (for example, the irreconcilable pair of maxims that open the poem), the Narrator's subjectivity can be unified and consistent. The assertion of authorial attitude at the expense of authoritative discourse can also be perceived in a remarkable shift in expression: "*sont* aprés" ("*are* afterwards") (5) finds itself reformulated as "*l'en voit* puis" ("*one sees* afterwards") (20); the being or existence of events is reiterated as a seeing, a perceiving (a passage from object to subject). One can see this identical oscillation in the Narrator's assertion of his own folly – "por fol m'en tiengne" ("[he] may think me a fool") (14) – which might be considered a counterpart to the reasoned argumentation and rhetorical precision of the opening.[41]

Taking a third step after line 20, the Narrator passes from a general to a specific discourse. At this point, he attempts to prove his ideas concerning dreams by telling of his own personal experience on one specific occasion. After adding a precise temporal indication ("el vintieme an de mon aage" [21]) ("In the twentieth year of my life" [p. 31]), the Narrator tells us that he went to bed, fell asleep, and, finally, that he had a dream (literally, he *saw* a dream). The subject of the dream (or the dream experience itself) was beautiful and pleasant ("mout fu biaus et mout me plot" [27]) ("it was very beautiful and pleased me a lot"), *but* ("mes") there was nothing in the dream that did not later take place exactly as the dream told it. Instead of the conjunction one would expect at this point, *et,* Guillaume here places a *mes,* conjunction of exclu-

---

40 The effect is all the more pronounced since the inclusion of the subject pronoun is already emphatic.
41 The following remarks by Montaigne are in this regard enlightening: "les poëtes sont espris souvent d'admiration de leurs propres ouvrages et ne reconnoissoient plus la trace par où ils ont passé une si belle carriere. C'est ce qu'on appelle aussi en eux ardeur et manie. Et comme Platon dict que pour neant hurte à la porte de la poësie un homme rassis, aussi dit Aristote que aucune ame excellente n'est exempte de meslange de folie. Et a raison d'appeler folie tout eslancement, tant loüable soit-il, qui surpasse nostre propre jugement et discours. [. . .] Platon argumente ainsi, que la faculté de prophetizer est au dessus de nous; qu'il nous faut estre hors de nous quand nous la traittons: il faut que nostre prudence soit offusquée ou par le sommeil ou par quelque maladie, ou enlevé de sa place par un ravissement céleste." (*Essais,* II, ii, ed. Villey, vol. 1, pp. 347–8).

sion, which seems to suggest that the beauty inherent to the dream and its realization are incompatible. Moreover, by marking this exclusion, the question of beauty is immediately placed aside at the expense of still another statement of the dream's eventually coming true. If "beauty" refers to all that is intrinsically attractive within the dream tale, such appears not to be the interest of the Narrator, who once again returns to the statement of the dream's properties, its function of iteration – which, as we have seen, is equivalent to a fixation on truth interpreted as prophecy. Indeed, it seems to be the dream's intermediary space (between lies and truth, between fable and experience, between interiority and exteriority) that attracts the Narrator – that intermediary space of ultimate authority which, as we shall discover further on, is the *mise en écrit*.

By way of summarizing the first three movements of the prologue (equal in length, we might add), one could interpret them as a continuous sliding from one proof to another. The Narrator passes from a purely exterior form of authority (the use of the *sententia* and the appeal to an *auctor*'s name, Macrobius) to the authority of subjective experience and ends with the account of a specific, unique occurrence. In each case, it is a matter of seeking a *garant*, a base upon which the Narrator's own discourse may rest and in which it may find its justification. Justification is, after all, one of the principal reasons for any prologue's existence. But the instability of the Narrator's passage from one justification to another suggests a problem in the nature (or perhaps even the actuality) of the truth that is being sought, to the extent that the word "truth" ("verité"), whose shadowy form is constantly being alluded to, is not mentioned in the prologue. The resolution of the Narrator's quest for truth and authority will only come in the prologue's fourth and final movement.

In line 31, the Narrator makes an abrupt perceptual leap without offering any explanation. He says, "Or veil cel songe rimeer/por vos cuers plus feire agueer" (31–2). The placement of *or* at the beginning of the line, accompanied by a move from past to present verb tense, emphasizes the temporal shift from the Narrator-as-Dreamer (in the past) to the unavoidably present Narrator, whose situation is here indicated explicitly for the first time. The two *personae* will hereafter find themselves neatly and necessarily de-

TWO: THE NARRATION OF ALLEGORY

marcated. In addition, for the first time, an addressee is alluded to ("*vos* cuers"). In spite of the fact that the dream and its realization, the prophetic dimension, have a real interest for the Narrator to the point of obsession, this is not the moment where his attention comes to rest. Rather, it is the present instant of poetic creation ("rimeer") which occupies him and out of which the joy of his listeners will come. Directly accompanying the writing and creation of the poem is its reception by others.

The Narrator's overt shift in the fourth part of his prologue tells us that neither the dream experience itself, nor its eventual fulfillment are important, but rather the after-the-fact consideration of these interrelated events by way of poetic composition. And at least one of these products is the joy of those who will receive the work.[42] We should not wonder why the entire last movement of the prologue revolves around questions of the poem's creation, its reception and its denomination. Those who think that the poem is primarily a treatise on the art of love have only read a limited – indeed, isolated – portion of the prologue: The several expressions of the Narrator's desire in this final section refer specifically and consistently to the interrelated themes of writing and poetic reception: "Or *veil* cel songe rimeer" (31) ("Now I *wish* to tell this dream" [p. 31]); "*je veil* que li romanz/*soit apelez*" (35–6) ("*I wish* the romance *to be called*" [p. 31]); "*doint Dex* qu'en gré *le receve*/cele" (40–1) ("*God grant* that *she may receive it* with grace" [p. 31]). By contrast, the role of the poem's doctrinal content, to which most modern (and medieval) readers have called attention, inasmuch as they can only appreciate the doctrinal at the expense of the communicative (fictional), could be characterized as highly passive, if not an afterthought: "ou l'art d'Amors est tote *enclose*" (38) ("in which the whole art of love *is contained*" [p. 31]). The ambiguity of the word *enclose*, which could mean "contained," "hidden," or even "imprisoned," adds to the difficulty. Moreover, if we notice that here Guillaume is quoting

---

42 The use of the verb "aguëer" in line 32 of the Lecoy edition, soon followed by the word "gré" in line 40, suggests a profound interpenetration between the roots *gai, joi,* and *gré*, and hence between the work's reception by both Lady and listeners. Tobler-Lommatzsch lists only the verb *agreer*, while Langlois includes "esgaier" in his edition of the *Roman de la Rose*, SATF (Paris 1914–24). Clearly scribes copying the poem had no fixed idea, writing *aguëer, esjoier, esgaier, esgeer,* or *agreer* in free variation: Joy and the poem's reception are one and the same.

the well-known title of Ovid's most popular work in the Middle Ages (*L'Ars d'Amor*), we might entertain even more seriously the possibility that Guillaume is articulating an intertextual relationship of authority: Explicitly, Guillaume's own title, *Le Roman de La Rose*, has replaced (or subsumed) the *Art of Love;* implicitly, romance has replaced art (doctrine), and the Rose – the ultimate symbol – has replaced Love.

While "vos cuers" refers us to a group of people (at least two) addressed by the poet and not necessarily defined by their belonging to one sex or the other ("nule ne nus" [34]) ("any woman or man"), we have yet to look at another person to whom the poem is eventually destined – "cele por qui je l'ai empris" (41) ("she for whom I have undertaken it"). Whereas the above-mentioned group of persons is localized spatially and chronologically through the Narrator's direct address (*vos* + present tense) – as a public audience – the other *destinataire* is specifically single, a woman, and not present (she is referred to in the third person). At this point, a significant overlapping occurs, private concerns complementing what had been a public address. Even though love/Love (is the Narrator referring to personal feelings or to Cupid at this moment? Has the allegory yet begun?) has ordered him to write the poem, it is for *her*, ultimately, that he has done it. While the Lady ousts love as a motivating factor, she also replaces the audience, in a sense *dis*placing the doctrinal aspects of which they are the receivers as well as the safeguards. Now, the question might be asked why he has written a poem to this Lady and, moreover, why this particular variety of allegorical poem. First of all, it is easy to recognize in this Lady the stereotyped recipient of the courtly lyric, the far-off lady, usually anonymous, who is continually sought after and who eventually becomes the target of the poet/lover's lyric outpourings. The poem serves in theory as a kind of *gage* which, if the Lady approves, will lead to her fair welcome and, perhaps, eventually, her love. Expressed in the most succinct manner, the poem, it is hoped, will win the Lady.

That the Narrator should tell us all this is quite revealing. First of all, he is pursuing an amorous affair and wishes to instill a feeling of gratitude and acceptance (*gré*) within his Lady. Now, he goes on further to state that she is so worthy of being loved that she must (or ought to) be called "Rose." The poet does not hesitate to pass from implicit to explicit, voicing the connection between the Lady being addressed by the Narrator, and the object, obviously of high value, pursued by the Narrator's past dream self in the poem. In other words, the present (but absent) Lady is figured by the rose in the poem. We recall, however, that the dream took place some time in the past (five years earlier) and that everything in the dream has already taken place. Given this, it should be clear that the Narrator is between experiences, having already pursued the rose in the dream and lived out the action in real life. *Now* he is telling the dream and expects to live it out a second time with a (presumably) different Lady. Taking up the scheme of prophetic levels that we have sketched for the most simple dream account, here is the multiplicity of levels implicit in Guillaume's complex telling of the dream:[43]

$$\overset{*}{A_1}\underline{\qquad}\overset{*}{x_1}\underline{\qquad}\overset{*}{B_1} \quad \text{DREAM EXPERIENCE} \quad \text{(PAST)}$$
$$\text{(prelinguistic)}$$

$$\left[\overset{*}{A_2}\underline{\qquad}\overset{*}{x_2}\underline{\qquad}\overset{*}{B_2}\right] \quad \text{DREAM ACCOUNT (1)} \quad \text{(PAST)}$$

$$\overset{*}{A_3}\underline{\qquad}\overset{*}{x_3}\underline{\qquad}\overset{*}{B_3} \quad \text{REAL EVENT (1)} \quad \text{(PAST)}$$

$$\overset{*}{A_4}\underline{\qquad}\overset{*}{x_4}\underline{\qquad}\overset{*}{[B_4]} \quad \text{DREAM ACCOUNT (2)} \quad \text{(PRESENT)}$$

$$\overset{*}{[A_5]}\underline{\qquad}\overset{*}{[x_5]}\underline{\qquad}\overset{*}{[B_5]} \quad \text{REAL EVENT (2)} \quad \text{(FUTURE)}$$

By setting up the situation in this fashion, Guillaume is making a subtle, profane, and rather deliberate use of what we have seen to be the traditionally theological and philosophical value accorded to dream accounts. Not content to proffer an empty *gage,* he has undertaken a work whose relation to reality is even more overdetermined than we expected at the beginning. First of all, not

---

[43] This chart is to be read as the first one, with each level repeating analogically or mimetically the other levels. Those sections within brackets are either hypothetical (A_2–B_2, a previous retelling of the dream before its "first" fulfillment, might or might not have taken place) or future. Insofar as x_4 represents our present moment at the reading of the romance, B_4 (the end of the dream account) is yet to come, as well as A_5–B_5, which should follow upon the dream events in accordance with the prophetic imperative.

only are dreams iterative, necessarily and by definition, but they are also end-determined. As dreams must end, so must the events that they foretell reach a culmination. The Narrator has taken care of the problem of authority or justification in his prologue, we have seen, by coyly playing out the various voices of authority and ending up ultimately with only his own. Lest it go unnoticed, the Narrator's careful dispensing with Macrobius (who, as it turns out, fades into the background of the multiple voices of opinion) leads into his own aggrandizement via the title of his work, which replaces that of another, authorless, antique model. The Narrator's act of *rimeer* carefully bypasses Macrobius's *escriture*. By setting up the situation in this fashion, the Narrator is stacking the cards in his favor, describing as it were a series of events which on the one hand he hopes will take place but which also, according to the prophetic stance of his writing authority, cannot help but take place. If Guillaume has started with a specific theological model, it is clear by the end of the prologue that he has turned the model upside down, pointing it toward a fundamentally personal and profane use, one that indeed contradicts all the intentions voiced by Macrobius in his treatise.

AUTOBIOGRAPHICAL PROPHECY: GATES OF HORN OR GATES OF IVORY?

On the one hand, Guillaume's tale obeys the iterative structure characteristic of prophetic narrative by dint of the dream form and the pseudotheological support provided in the prologue: All the events recounted in the dream will take place at some future time. Guillaume's project of personal prophecy and poetic utility is as subtle as it is terribly convincing. By means of the intricate play of levels, he manages to multiply his *persona* in such a way that it occupies positions before, during, and after the desired event — essentially encompassing all of time. The ingenious scheme, however, runs across a precise obstacle for two distinct reasons. First, even if Guillaume has intuited a multiplicity of perceptual levels, the linguistic means at his disposal are inadequate to safeguard the distinctions. The dissection of his being into several *personæ* necessarily collapses when confronted with the fact that only one pronoun, *I* (or *je*), is available, and that moreover the verb tense system will not maintain the multiple levels of temporality. The linguistic apparatus open to the Narrator necessarily reduces, or at least alters, the storytelling possibilities. We saw this problem at work as of the first few lines of the dream account, where a distinct ambiguity arises as to the respective perceptions of Narrator, Dreamer, and Lover. Although each *persona* perceives the same events at a different moment and from a different perspective, their eventual grammatical collusion prevents a consistently clear demarcation.[44]

A second reason for Guillaume's narrative complications results from his own logic of seduction. Guillaume's apparently seamless subversion of the traditional dream structure follows a temporal logic that orients the account outward, toward a fulfillment independent of the text (and of which the text itself becomes a participant). We have seen the series of justifications meant to insure the narrative's efficacy: the Narrator's own personal opinion; the fact that it is the Narrator's own dream; the authority of Macrobius. At the risk of overstating his case, the Narrator adds to the list — somewhat ingenuously — the statement that every event that was portrayed in the dream occurred later in real life. This reminds us of the all-important iterative aspect of the dream account, the assurance of which is all the more crucial where the dream is clearly not sanctioned by God. Paradoxically, the overpowering need to justify the prophetic weight of his account forces the Narrator to emphasize the retrospective nature of his tale — he is now recognizing not a single but a *double* past occurrence (dream and fulfillment). It is primarily for this reason that Guillaume must tell his prophetic account in the past and not in the future tense. As such, whatever the prophetic resonances might be, the romance is formally an autobiography — the Narrator's retrospective account of an event which he not only personally experienced but in which

---

44 "I dreamed that I was there" finds itself inevitably reduced to "I was there" in the telling of the tale. What we have already seen to be a typical looseness in the use of subordinating conjunctions ("en may estoie, ce sonjoie" ["I was in May, this I dreamed"]) accentuates the collapsing of the narrative *personae*. A failure to perceive this fundamental difference between narrative voices and implicit past selves explains the inconsistencies in Vitz's schematization alluded to above (note 9): Whatever the number of past selves we might be able to intuit, the narrative configuration can never handle more than two voices at once, the present narrator and a past self.

he was the central actor (or hero).⁴⁵ It remains to be seen in what sense the formal autobiographical structure, fundamentally retrospective, might influence the forward-looking prophetic account.

It has become common in narrative analysis to distinguish between two basic levels of discourse: the direct speech of the narrator, along with all indications of his storytelling presence (*discours*); and the message or story being conveyed, normally conceived as other than the instance of narration (*histoire*).⁴⁶ Any narrative will incorporate aspects of both levels, being characterized by the relative emphasis placed on one or the other. The distinctive quality of autobiography results from these two levels of literary perception being assumed by a single character, the narrator. Or, rather, the narrator must split his own perceptual capabilities in order to play two parts at two distinct temporal moments: the *I* of the past account; and the *I* of the present communication (or moment of enunciation). By its very nature, autobiographical narration slips into a strict dichotomy of perceptual levels, past and present, which immediately sets it apart from the prophetic dream model and its characteristic multiplicity of levels.

Whereas in the nonautobiographical fictional mode, the narrator can be obscured or eliminated to the point of being impli-

---

45 Jean Starobinski provides the following working definition: "[. . .] les conditions générales (ou génériques) de l'écriture autobiographique [. . .] exigent d'abord l'identité du narrateur et du héros de la narration; elles exigent ensuite qu'il y ait précisément narration et non pas description" ("Le Style de l'autobiographie," *Poétique*, 3 [1970], 257). Since the concerns of the present study are primarily formal (and not historical), the distinction often made between autobiography and the autobiographical novel is irrelevant. Phillipe Lejeune, for example, in his *Le Pacte autobiographique* (Paris, 1975), considers reference to a verifiable "external reality" to be the distinguishing characteristic of autobiography. This corollary, however important for modern texts, is insufficient for the Middle Ages. Abelard's *Historia Calamitatum* is indisputably an autobiographical text even though its attribution is not certain. See, on this point, Evelyn Birge Vitz, "Type et individu dans l'autobiographie médiévale," *Poétique*, 24 (1975), 426–45. My use of the term "autobiography" will thus coincide roughly with what Genette calls "autodiegesis" (cf. *Figures III* [Paris, 1972], p. 253) and will not deal with any consequences that might be drawn from the medieval, essentially Augustinian, tradition of contemplation of the self.

46 The terms are those of Emile Benveniste, *Problèmes de linguistique générale*, I (Paris, 1966), pp. 238–50. The articulation of these two narrative "moments" goes back at least as far as Plato's discussion of *mimèsis* and *diegèsis* in the *Republic*, Book III (392d and following), and corresponds to the showing/telling distinction made common in Anglo-American critical discourse by Henry James. For an enlightening reappraisal of Plato's classification, cf. Gérard Genette, "Frontières du récit," *Communications*, 8 (1966), 152–63.

cated solely by the material existence of his story (for example, Hemingway), the autobiographical account constantly makes reference to the narrator's present situation insofar as, grammatically, the *I* designates both *personae* at once. The autobiographical narrator finds himself in the difficult position of treating himself as the "other," looking back on his past as if it were that of someone else. In this sense, the task of the autobiographical narrator, while requiring a greater effort of distancing, is analogous to that of any fictional narrator. Jean Pouillon, pursuing a similar point, insists that artistic (novelistic) creation of any kind is not so much a matter of *remembering* past events as of *reinventing* them: "Le souvenir n'est pas une réalité, mais une opération; il n'y a pas de souvenir, on se souvient."[47] As does any narrator, the autobiographer gives meaning to the past that he reconstitutes. Pouillon concludes "il n'y a pas de différence radicale entre la compréhension de soi et celle d'autrui."[48]

Although it is essential to keep in mind the profoundly fictive nature of any autobiographical account, the creative distance that separates narrator from past self, its ramifications as a narrative form are quite distinct from those of a third-person narrative. As we have seen, the autobiographical form requires that there be simultaneously an identity and a distance between narrator and past hero. Were the narrator not able to distance himself in this temporal manner from the story he is telling, there would be no narrative. However, the implication is that, because of the irrefutable identity of the two *personae*, eventually the two levels will come together: At some point, by the logic of the account, the past self must "become" the present narrator. Hence the "work" (or challenge) of the autobiographical narrative is in part that of bringing the two narrative levels, *discours* and *histoire*, together, showing thereby how the narrator reached point B (his present state) from point A (the moment of the past self). As in most narrative fictions, the autobiographical account is usually a tale of upward development (education, maturation, social ascension, and so on) or downward decline (through growing deprivation, error, and so on), but with the following crucial difference: It must

---

[47] Jean Pouillon, *Temps et roman* (Paris, 1946), pp. 52–3.
[48] Ibid., p. 67.

find its endpoint in the narrator's present state. Even when such a narrative limits itself to an event far off in the narrator's past, the reader's curiosity is elicited as to the tale's relevance to the present narrator: Were there no such relevance, why would the narrator use the first-person? Why, that is, would he tell a story from his past and characterize it as such? The narrative motor, as it were, is predicated upon the suspense elicited in the reader as to how the two levels will come to be associated — all the more so when, as in the *Rose*, the allegorical narrative's fulfillment is based upon just such a coalescence of narrative voices.

The narrator, having perforce lived through the experience he is recounting, is in a position of omniscience. The account is inherently circular: The narrator departs from the present, recuperates the past, and returns to the present. However, the narrator can remain neither aloof nor static. He has of course some reason for telling his own story, and the very fact of his telling it has an effect on him. If he is indeed reinventing his past experience, as Pouillon suggests, placing it in a fictional mode, then it is certainly accompanied by a personal reevaluation. Rarely does the autobiographical narrator remain the same at the end of his tale as at the beginning. His traversing of the fictional moment, his reliving of the past, *the very telling of the tale,* becomes a part of the movement of reflection and discovery, itself an element of the autobiographical quest.

In the most elementary sense, the manner by which Guillaume has chosen to tell his dream clashes with the very dream structure he has so carefully established. The prophetic dream structure, while calling for a later repetition of the dream events, demands a discontinuity between narrator and dreamer. The dream account must necessarily conclude, there must be an awakening, and the events must be repeated in the narrator's future. By this device, the narrator remains distanced from his account, exculpated from criticisms of indiscretion or indelicacy that any text of seduction takes the risk of eliciting. Thus, strangely enough, the fact that the narrator is using the dream structure denies that he is telling his own story. The realization, the fulfillment, the "end" — ultimately independent of the dream vision — will occur elsewhere. The contrast with autobiography, where the fulfillment takes place as a part of the story, could not be more pronounced.

TWO: THE NARRATION OF ALLEGORY

Guillaume has in effect concluded two separate fictional pacts with his reader from the poem's opening, each of which projects to a distinct resolution. Not only are two conclusions possible, but they are mutually exclusive: The ultimate closing-off of the dream account certainly obviates an eventual cotermination of the two *personae*. Ultimately, the project of telling one's own story as a prophecy (or allegory) creates a double-bind situation that stretches narrative possibilities to their limits. It places the storyteller in the unique situation of living both after the completion of an event and before it. The *Rose* narrator has forged himself a position out of time by means of his careful, even overstated, emphasis on temporality and iteration. In a secular, narrative context, Guillaume has reformulated the philosophical paradox of divine omniscience and free will as a problem of temporality and conclusion.

Whether or not Guillaume works himself out of the paradox philosophically is one question, but at the very least we can attempt to chart the eventual resolution or nonresolution of the two narrative structures. Although there is an implicit tension or contradiction between the two fictional structures from the outset, the conflict is stabilized, the commingling of the two structures carefully maintained, by means of the grammatical separation between the levels of *discours* and *histoire*. As long as past self and narrator occupy two distinct perceptual planes, we need not confront the temporal paradox and the incumbent problem of conclusion. Moreover, we as readers do not want to do that. Our awareness of the dream and prophecy is so strong, has been so carefully programmed by Guillaume, that we have no choice but to seek its outcome – in other words, to deny the autobiographical dimension.

Benveniste has provided a clear idea of how grammatical elements can play a crucial role in the formation of discursive patterns.[49] Certain categories are more important than others: Among the personal pronouns, *je* and *tu* designate the level of *discours*, pointing as they do to the function of direct address and communication, while *il*, a fundamentally nonpersonal grammatical marker, is constitutive of *histoire*. Of verb tenses, the present, passé

---

[49] See especially Section V of Benveniste's *Problèmes*, entitled "L'Homme dans la langue," pp. 225–85.

composé, and future are associated with *discours,* while preterite (passé simple) and imperfect indicate *histoire.*[50] Clearly, the autobiographical narrative mode, which makes use of *je* throughout, will shift an even greater functional burden on the variation in verb tense as a way of differentiating past and present *personae:* As we saw, because of the autobiographical narrator's need to divide himself perceptually, the pronoun *je* will not apply unambiguously to the level of *discours,* as it would in other types of narrative. Rather, *je* plus the present tense will in theory mark the level of enunciation and *je* plus the past will qualify the level of past perception. Table 1 indicates frequencies of selected verb tenses and their general distribution throughout the *Rose.* In the discussion that follows, we propose to study the precise functioning of a limited number of narrative verb tenses in the romance and their placement in the broader patterning that can be derived from the table.

It should be mentioned initially that the relative amounts of text devoted to straight narration (that assumed in the Narrator's own voice) and to dialogue (direct quotations of others' discourse) will influence the proportions of the various verb tenses, since the latter will effect an increase in the markers of *discours.* One observation gleaned from the table is immediate and striking: Between the first section of 500 lines and the final one there is a distinct shift, indeed a reversal, in the proportion of past (preterite and imperfect) to present (present and future) verb tenses in all persons (185 versus 145 in the first section; 70 versus 305 in the last section). This reversal is mirrored in the first-person sequences: 35 versus 17 in the first section; 14 versus 65 in the final section. Before interpreting these global results, we need to take a look at specific instances of tense usage in context.

Whereas the morphology of verbs in Old French has been amply studied, their transphrastic syntactical usage remains a relatively unexplored field.[51] In any event, the medieval writer did not control

---

50 Ibid., pp. 225–57.
51 See, most recently, André Lanly, *Morphologie historique des verbes français* (Paris, 1977), for a formal description of Old French verb forms. On syntactic verb usage we have, for Middle French, Robert Martin, *Temps et aspect: Essai sur l'emploi des temps narratifs en moyen français* (Paris, 1971). While there is no comprehensive work dealing with the tense system in Old French, there are several isolated studies: D. R. Sutherland, "On the Use of Tenses in Old and Middle French," in *Studies in French*

TWO: THE NARRATION OF ALLEGORY

his usage with a grammar book and, consequently, there are bound to be a number of apparent irregularities. The safest approach is undoubtedly that which attempts to describe distinctions which can be seen to function within the text. At the start of the dream, it is usually quite easy to distinguish the two basic levels of narration in spite of an occasional random tense usage. Present, passé simple, passé composé, and imperfect can all be used to designate the Lover's actions or perceptions, but with precise nuances. The imperfect tends to be used in descriptive settings, iterative and "imperfective" passages, much as it is in Modern French; this explains the relatively high number of occurrences in the first section. The passé simple is the base tense of past actions, but can also be used in extended descriptive passages (for example, lines 525 ff.). The use of the present in the context of past actions has been termed the "historical present," insofar as it clearly can be detected to follow the level of narrated action; in these cases, it is normally not confused with the ordinary present, which would indeed refer to the moment of enunciation. The use of the "historical present" adds a nuance of immediacy to the otherwise distanced account. Following is a passage taken from the beginning that illustrates the interweaving of the three tenses:

> Lors m'*iere* avis en mon dormant
> qu'il *iere* matin durement;

Language and Medieval Literature, presented to Mildred K. Pope, by Pupils, Colleagues and Friends, Publications of the University of Manchester, No: 268 (Manchester, 1939), pp. 329–37; Anna Granville Hatcher, "Tense Usage in the *Roland*," *Studies in Philology,* 39 (1942), 597–624; Tatiana Fotitch, *The Narrative Tenses in Chrétien de Troyes,* the Catholic University of America Studies in Romance Languages and Literatures, vol. 38 (Washington, DC, 1950); Manfred Sandmann, "Die Tempora der Erzählung," *Vox Romanica,* 16 (1957), 287–96; H. Yvon, "Emploi dans la *Vie de Saint Alexis* (XIe siècle) de l'imparfait, du passé simple, et du passé composé de l'indicatif," *Romania,* 81 (1960), 244–50; Mitja Skubic, "Le Passé simple et le passé composé dans la langue des troubadours," *Linguistica,* 5 (1964), 61–70; M. H. A. Blanc, "Time and Tense in Old French Narrative," *Archivium Linguisticum,* 16 (1964), 96–124; Friederike Stefenelli-Fürst, *Die Tempora der Vergangenheit in der Chanson de Geste,* Wiener Romanistischen Arbeiten, 5 (Vienna, 1966); and H. Saunders, "The Evolution of the French Narrative Tenses," *Forum for Modern Language Studies,* 6 (1970), 141–61. Finally, a work that I have found particularly suggestive in its discussion of discursive verb tense modeling is that of Harald Weinrich, *Le Temps: Le Récit et le commentaire,* trans. Michèle Lacoste (original title: *Tempus,* 2nd ed. [1964; Stuttgart, 1971]) (Paris, 1973). An important discussion of the differences between the French "translation" and the German original can be found in Maureen O'Meara, "From Linguistics to Literature: The Un-Time-Liness of Tense," *Diacritics,* vol. 6, no. 2 (Summer, 1976), 62–8.

Table 1. Frequency of selected verb tenses in the Roman de la Rose by 500-line groupings

LINE NOS.	A 0–500	B 501–1000	C 1001–1500	D 1501–2000	E 2001–2500	F 2501–3000	G 3001–3500	H 3501–end
FIRST-PERSON (je)								
Present	15	15	10	40	45	40	40	55
Future	2	10	1	10	10	2	10	10
Passé Composé	2	2	1	10	5	10	15	10
Passé Simple	25	35	10	50	5	20	30	10
Imperfect	10	3	0	10	5	5	5	4
Total (All Tenses)	60	75	30	140	85	85	125	100
ALL PERSONS								
Present	140	65	60	170	240	225	245	280
Future	5	10	4	20	100	35	25	25
Subtotal (discours)	145	75	65	190	340	260	270	305
Passé Simple	70	130	135	100	25	60	75	55
Imperfect	115	105	100	50	5	25	25	15
Subtotal (histoire)	185	235	235	150	30	85	100	70
Passé Composé	5	4	3	40	15	30	40	40
All Subjunctives	60	35	40	40	70	60	65	50
Imperative	10	10	3	10	50	25	25	20
Dialogue (No. of lines)	0	51	0	107	475	331	295	195
Narration (No. of lines)	500	449	500	393	25	169	205	333

Note: All figures numbering verb tenses that total more than five are rounded off to the nearest five.

> de mon lit tantost me *levé,*
> *chauçai* moi et mes mains *lavé;*
> lors *trés* une aguille d'argent
> d'un aguillier mignot et gent,
> si *prins* l'aguille a enfiler.
> Hors de vile *oi* talant d'aler
> por oïr des oisiaus les sons,
> qui *chantent* desus les buissons
> en icele saison novele.
> Cousant mes manches a videle,
> m'an *vois* lors tot sol esbatant,
> et les oiseleiz escoutant,
> qui de chanter mout s'*engoissoient*
> por les jardins qui *florissoient*. (87–102)

(I *became* aware that it *was* full morning. I *got up* from bed straightway, *put on* my stockings and *washed* my hands. Then I *drew* a silver needle from a dainty little needlecase and *threaded* it. I *had* a desire to go out of the town to hear the sound of birds who, in that new season, *sing* among the trees. Stitching up my sleeves in zigzag lacing I *set out*, quite alone, to enjoy myself listening to the birds who *were straining* themselves to sing because the gardens *were bursting* into bloom. [p. 32])

It is easy to see not only how the sequence of verb tenses forms the infrastructure of the narrative movement, but also the ease and subtlety with which Guillaume manipulates them. Their frequency alone should alert the reader to their organizing function.[52] In the passage cited, the imperfects refer to the Dreamer/Lover's perceptions ("iere" "iere") and to the descriptions of the surroundings ("engoissoient," "florissoient"); the passé simple, to the narrated actions ("levé," "lavé," "chauçai," "trés," "prins," "oi"); the present as "historical present" ("vois"); and the present as general or universal statement ("chantent"). The only usage that might lead to misunderstanding here is the detection of the historical present. As a general rule, we might say that a present tense bear-

---

[52] One should note in addition the placement of the verbs in the passage above: either at the end of the verse or in first- or second-syllable position (preceded by a weak, unaccented particle such as *si, lors,* or *qui*) – the two principal positions of emphasis in the Old French octosyllable. The only verb not falling into one of these two positions, "oi" (94) has an infinitive that receives the emphasis at the end of the line, "aler."

ing no semantic marks of the level of enunciation and which finds itself in the midst of a past sequence will be interpreted as the "historical present." An example several lines later does not fulfill these conditions and can thus be interpreted as a true present, marker of *discours:*

> Les ymages et les pointures
> dou mur volentiers *remirai;*
> si vos *conterai* et *dirai*
> de ces ymages la semblance,
> si com moi *vient* a remenbrance.   (134–8)

(I willingly *admired* the images and paintings, and I *shall recount* to you and *tell* you the appearance of these images as they *occur* to my memory. [p. 32])

Having interrupted his past narration with two verbs in the future, which semantically refer in an obvious manner to the enunciation of the story ("conterai," "dirai"), the Narrator has created a new localized context to which "moi vient a remenbrance" ("[it] occurs to my memory") also applies. Two further examples show how, even without the creation of a new context, a true present *discours* can be detected:

> car tel joie ne tel deduit
> ne *vit* mes hom, si com je *cuit,*
> come il *avoit* en cel vergier.   (473–5)

(for, as *I believe,* no man ever *saw* such joy or diversion as *there was* in that garden. [p. 37])

> Trop par *fessoient* bel servise
> cil oisel que je vos *devise*   (659–60)

(These birds that I *describe* to you *performed* a lovely service [p. 39])

Both present verbs ("cuit," "devise") mark, through their belonging to the enunciative context (thinking and describing), the level of narration.

Now, any use of the historical present in the first person will obviously provide a critical challenge to the separation between Narrator and Lover, inasmuch as we would normally expect *je*-plus-present to be a sure marker of the level of *discours.* The same transgression of levels does not occur with the historical present in the third person, which on the contrary provides a sense of relief in the narration, highlighting as it does past actions with a sense of immediacy. The following passage portraying the Lover's first approach to the rose will demonstrate this highlighting effect:[53]

> Entre les autres en *eslui*
> un si tres bel, envers celui
> nul des autres rien ne *prisé*
> puis que celui bien *avisé;*
> car une color l'*enlumine*
> qui *est* si vermeille et si fine
> con Nature le *pot* plus faire.
> Des fueilles i *a* quatre paire,
> que Nature par grant maistire
> i *ot asisses* tire a tire;
> la tige *ere* droite con jons,
> et par desus *siet* li boutons
> si qu'i ne *cline* ne ne *pent.*
> L'odor de lui entor *espent;*
> la soautume qui en *ist*
> tote la place *replenist;*
> et quant jou *senti* si fleirier,
> je *n'oi* talant de repairier,
> ainz m'en *apressai* por le prendre,
> se g'i *osasse* les mains tendre.   (1653–72)

(Among these buds I *singled out* one that was so very beautiful that, after I *had examined* it carefully, I *thought* that none of the others was worth anything beside it; it *glowed* with a color as red and as pure as the best that Nature *can* produce, and she *had placed* around it four pairs of leaves, with great skill, one after the other. The stem *was* straight as a sapling, and the bud *sat* on the top, neither bent nor inclined. Its odor *spread* all around; the sweet perfume that *rose* from it *filled* the entire area. And when I *smelled* its exhalation, I *had* no power to withdraw, but *would have approached* to take it if I *had dared* stretch out my hand to it. [p. 53])

---

53 In this passage, as elsewhere, Dahlberg regularizes the present tenses to conform to the surrounding past framework. The temporality of the narrative is maintained but the Narrator's poetic effects are lost. Whereas in the case at hand this is an understandable translation device, it falsifies later sections of the narrative; accordingly, I have on occasion retranslated certain of the verbs to reflect the appropriate Old French tense.

The short episode is sustained by a series of actions in the preterite ("eslui," "prisé," "avisé," "senti," "oi," "apressai") that frame and situate the event. A suspension in the dynamism of the scene is effected by a description that lingers on the form of the rose, principally translated by the present; the latter serves additionally to provide the nuance of the vivid memory which the Narrator has retained. Even there, however, the Narrator is selective, concentrating his present descriptions around the color ("enlumine," "est"), the leaves ("a"), the placement of the bud ("siet," "cline," "pent"), and the smell ("espent," "ist," "replenist"). The erectness of the flower's stalk, perhaps of less interest, is rendered by the imperfect ("ere"). In this passage, the description of the rose is no less "past" (as indicated in Dahlberg's translation), but made more brilliant through Guillaume's tense modeling.

Following is an example of the present used historically to translate actions and not simply description:

> tot adés la ou il *tendoit*
> m'*estovoit* aler tot a force.
> Mes li archiers, qui mout s'*esforce*
> de moi grever et mout se *poine*,
> ne m'i *let* pas aler sanz poine,
> ainz m'*a fet*, por mieuz afoler,
> la tierce floiche ou cors voler,
> que Cortoisie *ert* apelee.
> La plaie *fu* parfonde et lee ...   (1758–66)

(I *had to* go perforce, always where it *aspired* to be. But the bowman, who *strove* mightily and with great diligence to wound me, *did not let* me move without hurt in that direction. To madden me further, he *caused* the third arrow, called Courtesy, to fly to my heart. The wound *was* deep and wide ... [p. 55])

Chronologically speaking, all of these actions take place at the same level and in a strict sequence. The virtuosity of the tense variation allows us to "presentify" the hunt of Amor, placing it into a perceptual relief against the background of the Lover's state of mind. Moreover, the fact that the major action, "a fet," is in the passé composé, further broadens or universalizes what can be described as the attitude of the God of Love toward *all* lovers (although here the Narrator is obviously only speaking of himself).

Significantly, the "historical present" in the first person scarcely occurs in the first 2,000 lines. Of all instances of the first person present tense in the first 2,000 lines (72 in all), after eliminating those that are included in direct discourse and those that are overt discursive markers (for example, "ce cuit" ["this I believe"], "vos voil dire" ["I wish to say to you"], "que je vos devise" ["that I am describing to"], "si com je recors" ["as I remember"], "n'en sai pas dire" ["I can't say"]), only nine could be considered the "historical present." Two occur in the very first lines of the poem (lines 99, 104, quoted above), and the remaining seven are clustered in the following passage just before Amor's speech:

> La grant dolor me renoveile
> de mes plaies de maintenant,
> .III. foiz me *pasme* en un tenant.
> Au revenir *plains* et *soupire,*
> car ma dolors croist et empire
> si que je n'*ai* mes esperance
> de garison ne d'alijance;
> mielz voudroie estre morz que vis,
> car en la fin, ce m'est avis,
> fera Amors de moi martir,
> je ne m'en *puis* par el partir.
> Il a endementiere prise
> une autre floiche, que mout *prise*
> et que je *tien* a mout pesant,
> c'est Biau Samblant. . . .   (1826–40)

(Immediately the great anguish of my wounds begins again. I *swoon* three times in a row. Upon reviving, I *wail* and *sigh,* for my anguish is growing so much worse that I *have* no hope, either of cure or of relief. I would rather be dead than alive, for, in my opinion, Love will make a martyr of me in the end. I cannot *part* from him by any other means. Meanwhile he has taken another arrow, one that I *value* highly and *consider* very powerful. This arrow is Fair Seeming [p. 56])

This is obviously an emotionally charged moment, the Lover having been gravely wounded by Amor's first four arrows, and at the point of being hit by the fifth, which, while bringing him an "oignement precieus" to soothe his wounds, will also confirm him as

Love's man. The effect is all the more striking when we notice that the Narrator has consistently refused to use the first-person historical present up to this point, even in passages that, as above, make use of the present in other persons.

What keeps the reader from being dislocated by this first person historical present, which should somehow disrupt the careful balance we have described between Narrator and Lover, is his innate desire to maintain the levels as separate and thereby continue reading the dream account – which is, after all, the overriding structure – through to its end. In other words, as long as he can perceptibly reinscribe the historical presents within the past moments, and not mix them up with the Narrator's present voice, the separation will continue to function. In the above passage, "prise" ("I value") and "tien" ("I consider") possibly refer to the Narrator, involving as they do a sense of opinion or judgment, but the others are unambiguously to be situated at the level of past action. What effects the final recuperation of the separation of levels, however, is the return to a sequence of past tenses, first passé composé, (1837, 1855, 1856), the imperfect (1851) and pluperfect (1845, 1852), and finally passé simple (1857, 1858). The encroachment upon the primary grammatical marker of enunciation is temporary and takes its place as a special and isolated stylistic effort.

One relevant tense that we have not yet mentioned and that involves special problems in medieval tense usage, is the passé composé. If we take the present and passé simple as polar oppositions in a dual temporal and perceptual system, it is easy to see that the passé composé, formed as it is from a present verb form (auxiliary) and a past participle, forces a liaison between the two. The fluidity of the verb/participle relationship in Old French is here particularly important, a fact that undoubtedly explains the tense's fluctuating use before the Renaissance. As opposed to a single, unified form (which, in a sense, it has become in modern usage), the passé composé overtly involves both past and present: "En effet, le passé indéfini renferme toujours l'indicatif présent d'*estre* ou d'*avoir,* et le participe étant, comme nous le savons, très indépendant en vieux français, l'auxiliaire, envisagé à part, est ainsi un véritable présent, qui précédera ou suivra tout naturellement un présent de l'indicatif ordinaire."⁵⁴ Foulet indicates clearly that in Old French the passé indéfini expresses the present perfect. Ménard concurs, "le passé composé est un *perfectum praesens*. Il marque le résultat présent d'une action passée. Il souligne qu'un événement passé a des conséquences durables et encore perceptibles dans le présent. C'est un temps actuel et vivant qui par excellence jette un pont entre le passé et le présent."⁵⁵ Theoretically, then, the passé composé will be used for a past action, but one whose effect is still felt in the present, much as the English present perfect. In a certain sense, the passé composé is the most appropriate tense to translate the tentative position of our Narrator, allowing both temporal dimensions and denying neither one. As was true of Guillaume's manipulation of the present, the passé composé, which also has strong links with the level of enunciation, is often used to designate a narrated past act. Inasmuch as it is slightly less transgressive than the first-person historical present, the historical usage of the first-person passé composé, while rare, does occur in more varied contexts. Again, either the lexical denotation of the verb used (verbs such as "ai devisé" or "ai . . . dite" obviously apply to an enunciatory situation) or the context will give the major clue: a series of consecutive past actions will normally be interpreted as the remote past regardless of the variation in verb tense. For example:

> a la querole me *sui pris*,
> si ne *fui* pas trop entrepris,
> mes sachiez que mout m'*agrea*
> dont Cortoisie me *prea*
> et me *dit* que je querolasse,
> car de queroler, se j'ousasse,
> *estoie* envieus et sorpris.   (787–93)

(I *joined* the carol, where I *was* by no means at a loss. You may know of course that I *was* very pleased when Courtesy

---

54 Lucien Foulet, *Petite Syntaxe de l'ancien français*, 3rd ed., CFMA 21 (Paris, 1930), p. 229.

55 Yves Lefevre, ed., *Manuel du français du moyen âge:* Vol. 1: *Syntaxe de l'ancien français,* par Phillipe Ménard, Nouvelle édition entièrement refondue (Bordeaux, 1973), pp. 140–41. While most of the linguists mentioned in note 51 are in agreement, Robert Martin (pp. 377 ff.) adds the observation that the fate of the passé composé is intimately related to that of the "présent historique" in its opposition with the passé simple, and that, moreover, the passé composé always had the potential to be used as a preterite.

> *asked* me and *told* me to join the carol, for I *was* eager and longing to carol if I had dared. [p. 41])

Aside from a nuance of the Narrator's continued involvement in the *querole,* the passé composé of line 787 fits snugly into the temporal context.

The Narrator's use of the passé composé adds something to the tense structure of this first half of the poem in a couple of ambiguous cases, where the lexical meaning of the verb is in the domain of telling and perception, thereby causing an ambiguity. On line 856, in the context of describing Leesce, one of the participants in Deduit's *carole,* the Narrator says:

> s'ot un chapel d'orfrois tot nuef.
> Je, qu'en ai veü .XX. et nuef,
> a nul jor mes veü n'avoie
> chaspel si bien ovré de soie.   (855–8)

(she had a brand new chaplet of gold embroidery. I have seen twenty-nine of them, and never had I seen a chaplet so beautifully worked in silk. [p. 42])

In addition to the metrical highlighting of the pronoun *je,* the passé composé prompts us to ask which *persona* (past or present) is responsible for this opinion. On the one hand, line 856 in isolation would lead us to think that the Narrator is talking from his own personal experience (in the interval between the dream and his present moment), in which case we would expect a continuation of the dream's effect in the present. When he continues with a pluperfect ("veü n'avoie" ["I had not seen"]), the reader's expectation is shifted and he realizes that it is really the Lover's opinion localized in the past. Is the passé composé, then, a mistake, a measure of expediency, or is there some more convincing explanation?

Another grammatical tool at the Narrator's disposal serving to specify the application of the passé composé is the adverb *puis,* roughly translated "since that time," which emphasizes the present perfect use of the passé composé. For example:

> Mes de fort eure m'i miré.
> Las! tant en ai puis soupiré!   (1605–6)

(but it was a painful hour when I admired myself there. Alas! How I have sighed since then! [p. 52])

TWO: THE NARRATION OF ALLEGORY

The perfective use of the passé composé is indicated by the placement of *puis* between auxiliary and participle, which isolates and thereby accentuates the presentness of the verb form.[56] One would say that, here, in a moment of high emotionalism, at the moment of seeing the rose for the first time in the fountain, the Narrator is not only involving himself, but personally excited and perhaps even participating. However, by the same process of recuperation that we saw in the case of the first-person historical present, and through a desire to maintain the Narrator at a remove outside of the dream, we attribute it to a kind of dramatic participation. In no case do we seriously suspect that the Narrator might be describing his own recent past, bringing forth his own feelings. Inasmuch as such expressive openings are quite rare in the first part of the poem, they are easily forgotten; the carefully wrought system of tenses and the incumbent narrative separation sustain themselves with great ease.

Amor's speech, lines 1882–2748, provides a lengthy hiatus (nearly a quarter of the entire poem) that interrupts the narrative progression, constituted by the Lover's movement in the garden. This massive shift to basic dialogue, direct address, explains the sudden drop in historical tenses and the concurrent increase in discursive verb tenses (present, future, passé composé, imperative) found in the table under sections D, F, and, most particularly, E. We might mention that from this point until the end of the romance the proportion of dialogue to narration is progressively less.

After Amor's interlude, we find a distinct alteration in what had been a stable and mostly reliable system of narrative tenses (more reliable, in fact, than the Middle Ages is usually given credit for). As we noted at the outset, there is a tendency to use increasing

---

56 Imbs, *Propositions*, pp. 392–3: "A mesure que l'on avance dans le XIIe et surtout dans le XIIIe siècle, *puis* préposition s'emploie de moins en moins au sens de 'après' pour se cantonner de plus en plus dans celui de 'depuis' [. . .] *Puis* adverbe suit le mouvement et signifie très anciennement 'depuis' [. . .] *Puis* 'après' n'a plus dès lors qu'une valeur très affaiblie [. . .] *Puis* 'après' n'est plus finalement qu'une conjonction de coordination, marquant la simple succession, et à peine plus fort que *alors* ou même *et*." While *puis* in combination with a passé simple could easily mean "afterwards" (were the present instance, for example, "tant en soupirai puis" ["so much did I sigh afterwards"]), its separation of the two components of the passé composé here unambiguously dictates a translation of "since" and thus a presentifying of the sentiment expressed by the verb.

numbers of discursive tenses in all grammatical persons, even as we are moving away from a concentration on dialogue. Narration, still principally in the passé simple is more and more frequently punctuated with present and passé composé, even in the first person:

> Atant Reson s'*est departie,*
> qu'el *voit* bien que por sarmoner
> ne me *porroit* de ce torner.
> Je *remés* d'ire et de duel plains,
> sovent *plorai,* sovent me *plains,*
> car de moi ne *soi* chevisance,
> tant qu'il me *vint* en remenbrance
> qu'Amors me *dit* que je *queïse*
> un compaignon qui je *deïse*
> mon conseil tot outreement.   (3080–9)

(Thereupon Reason *left,* since she *sees* that by speech she *could* not turn me from my purpose.
   I *remained,* full of anger and sorrow, often weeping, often complaining, for I *knew* of no way of getting out of my plight by myself, until it *came* to my memory that Love had *told* me that I *should seek out* a companion to whom I *might say* quite openly what I thought. [p. 75])

As this continues, the reader's recuperation process, his attempt to maintain the strict systematization of the narrative levels, becomes increasingly difficult. There are even entire passages where the Narrator slips into a complete and rigorous system of discursive tenses. A short example should suffice:[57]

> Or *ai* par tot d'aler congié,
> or *sui cheoiz,* ce m'*est* avis,
> de grant enfer en paradis,
> car Bel Acueil par tot me *moine,*
> qui de mon gré fere se *poine.*   (3334–8)

(Now I *have* leave to go everywhere; now I *have fallen,* as I think, from deepest hell to paradise, for Fair Welcoming, *troubling* himself to do what pleases me, *is leading* me everywhere. [p. 78])

---

57 Cf. lines 2930–54; 3204–30; and 3468–92.

TWO: THE NARRATION OF ALLEGORY

And yet, however fragmentary or irregular it has become, the Narrator still maintains a foothold in his structure of historical tenses. One can hardly call these passages interventions of the Narrator, since one is bound to interpret even the most blatantly discursive passages which take part in the action as historical. One must assume that the confusion in tense structure is somehow meant to duplicate the Lover's confusion, who is at this point in the account (lines 3000–700) encountering the numerous obstacles to his attainment of the rose. It should be noted that throughout this lengthy passage, the few first-person passé composés that occur in the narration refer unambiguously to the Lover's story; there is, in other words, no further usage of the passé composé as a discursive marker for the Narrator.[58]

A decisive cleavage in the total narrative structure, in the face of which no rationalization of the previous system can possibly continue, occurs after Dangier's speech, on line 3737. We have, as before, an interlude of discursive tenses but it never gives way to a narration in the past. As corroborated by the numbers in the last section of our table, the present has become the framing narrative tense, definitively taking over the role of the passé simple. The passé simple has not disappeared in the final section, but its functional load has been greatly reduced and its point of reference has

---

58 Our observation of a shift in the functional role of the passé composé is confirmed by Guillaume's manipulation of another grammatical marker of *discours*: the conjunction *or*. *Or*, literally "now," is normally accompanied by the present, imperative, or future tense, drawing attention to the speaker or storyteller – that is, to the act of narration. Of the fifty-six occurrences of *or* in the *Roman de la Rose*, forty occur inside speeches (direct discourse), as would be expected, and sixteen are spread throughout the narrative (lines 31, 40, 354, 985, 1313, 1747, 2847, 2850, 3334, 3335, 3414, 3743, 3771, 3779, 3927, and 4022). Of the first seven occurrences of the latter (lines 31 through 1747), five explicitly refer to the moment of enunciation, and two are found in the midst of descriptive passages accompanied by past tenses: There they pass as phrase attacks, divested of their enunciatory association in the way that the passé composé can take on a strict preterite sense in the context of a past narration. Of the final nine (lines 2847 through 4022) the balance is reversed: Only two manifestly indicate a shift of reference to the speaking voice. And these are, not surprisingly, found in passages marked by a return to a consistent sequence of preterite tenses: "[. . .] el n'*iert* pas de religion./Ne *ferai or* pas mancion" (3413–14) ("she *was* not a religious. I *shall* not *now* mention her dress" [p. 79]); "Des *or* est droiz que je vos conte/coment je *fui* melez a Honte" (3481–2) ("From *now* on it is right for me to tell you how I *struggled* with Shame" [p. 80]).

In both cases, one could suggest that the enunciatory function of *or*, greatly lacking in this second part of the poem, is being called upon as a way of reinforcing the former tense structure and, hence, the separation of narrative levels. In this way, Guillaume's stylistic use of *or* parallels exactly his use of the passé composé.

been overtly readjusted. Immediately following Dangier's speech, the latter's actions are described totally in the present tense. Then the Narrator intervenes with an expression which might be a way of indicating this crucial point of rupture: "Des or est changiez mout li vers" (3743) ("From now on the situation is very much changed" [p. 84]). Although this line has been typically translated to read that the Lover's "situation" has changed, I would suggest another reading: In the most literal sense, the *vers,* or poem, has changed its visage and at this point will not revert;[59] a new ordering has taken place. What follows is a lengthy passage, we assume in the Narrator's voice, in which he recounts his sorrows and in which he emphasizes his memories of actions which he has already recounted in the dream:

> quant il *me menbre*
> de la rose que je soloie
> veoir de pres quant je voloie.
> Et quant du bessier *me recors,*
> qui me mist une odor ou cors
>
> quant il *me sovient*
> que a consirrer m'en covient (3752–6; 3761–2)

(when I *remember* the rose that I used to see nearby when I wished; and when I *recall* this kiss that placed in my heart an odor ... when I *remember* that I must be separated from it [p. 84])

Indeed, we might ask, is this the present voice of the Narrator, the present voice of the Lover (therefore to be placed in quotation marks), or merely another sequence of discursive tenses interpretable as historical tenses? A few lines later, we find the echo of a previous line, but with a distinctly altered import in the new context: "car *je sui* en enfer *cheoiz*" (3775) ("for I *have fallen* into hell" [p. 84]). We are reminded of lines 3335–6: "or *sui cheoiz,* ce

---

59 Certainly the most common and widespread meaning of *vers/versus* from classical times was a line of verse and, by extension, a poem. Cf. Walther von Wartburg, *Französisches Etymologisches Wörterbuch* (Bonn/Leipzig/Basel, 1928–) (*FEW*), Band XIV, pp. 315–17. It is significant that the only examples of *vers* meaning "état, situation" provided by Godefroy (*Dictionnaire de l'ancienne langue française,* 10 vols. [Paris, 1880–1902]) come from the *Roman de la Rose* – the present instance and two quotations from Jean de Meun's continuation. It is thus quite possible that the metaphorical extension of the word was invented by Guillaume de Lorris.

m'est avis,/de grant enfer en paradis" ("Now I *have fallen,* it appears to me, from deeper hell to paradise"). As if in direct response to a faulty interpretation imposed by the previous line, accompanied by a judicious splitting apart of auxiliary and participle, Guillaume provides us with a palinode indicating the correct destination of the fall (Fall?) and the correct grammatical understanding of his passé composé.

Up to this point, it is still in the Narrator's powers not to change the *vers,* but then he recounts the further narrated action *in the present tense:*

> Des or *est* tens que je vos die
> la contenance Jalousie,
> qui *est* en male soupeson.
> Ou païs ne *remaint* maçon
> ne pïonier qu'ele ne *mant,*
> si *fet* fere au comencemant
> entor les rosiers uns fossez
> qui *costerent* argent assez,
> qu'i *sont* mout lé et mout parfont.   (3779–87)

(From now on it *is* time for me to tell you of the activities of Jealousy, with her foul suspicion. There *remains* no mason or ditcher in the country that she *does not send for,* and, for a beginning, she *has* them construct ditches around the rose-bushes. They *cost* a great deal of silver, for they *are* very wide and deep. [p. 85])

Indeed we do find here one verb in the passé simple, but its relative isolation shows us that it and the present have changed positions – we must now rationalize or explain the existence of the passé simple in the midst of a regularized system of present, discursive tenses, and not the contrary. From this moment until the end of the romance, the twenty-odd examples of the passé simple will refer to the moment of the castle building, now inexorably present, or, interestingly enough, to previous moments that have already been recounted in the poem. At this point, as we saw with the series of reminiscences above, the Narrator reaches back once more in a movement which in some sense reduplicates the events he has already repeated by telling the story. By means of a highly intricate narrative transformation, the dream, barrier to autobiographical continuity, has been removed and the two once-separate levels of perception now merge in a relationship of equivalence and univocal destiny. The autobiographical contract — as we have described it, a circular movement — has now been completed.

If at the outset the reader was somewhat certain of a specific verbal and conceptual patterning, according to the following scheme:

je plus present tense   level of narration
je plus passé simple   level of narrated action (Lover)
je plus passé composé   level of narrated action (Lover) *or* recent past of Narrator

he must now readjust his interpretation of the tense system:

je plus present   present of Lover *and* Narrator
EX: "je, qui *sui* dehors le mur" (3920)
("I who *am* outside the wall")

je plus passé simple   Dream events already recounted — Remote past for Lover *and* Narrator.
EX: "Mar *touchai* la rose a mon vis" (3764)
("It *was* an evil hour when I touched the rose to my face")

je plus passé composé   Recent past for Lover *and* Narrator.
EX: "la joie que j'*ai perdue*" (3929)
("the joy that I *have lost*")

What is past for the Lover is now doubly past for the Narrator, for included in his reliving of the events is his writing of them. Curiously, the final passé simple in the text, a sort of endpoint to the reiterated assessments of the Lover/Narrator's involvement, deals with the storytelling, perhaps the romance whose conclusion is only a few lines away:

c'onques par moi ne fu retrete
chose qui a taire feïst   (4004–5)

(for I never mentioned anything that should have been kept hidden [p. 88])

TWO: THE NARRATION OF ALLEGORY

Storytelling has acquired a past significance much as the story itself. The Narrator's experience as a writer, which previously only paralleled the Lover's quest, now becomes a figuration within the story as the Narrator takes up his rightful position – indeed, the one he has occupied from the start – outside the castle walls. The object of storytelling has now become identical with the object "inside" the story.[60]

THE ALLEGORY OF INCOMPLETION

Why this narrative convergence is significant and whether it is indeed necessary are two questions that immediately proceed from our recognition of the *Rose*'s stylistic closure. We discover by the end that the Narrator has all along been telling his own story, a series of past events leading up to his present moment, but under the cover of a dream. The emphasis placed on the dream's prophetic and doctrinal value in the prologue stresses the "otherness" of the account, its existential distance from the Narrator. The five-year remove of the dream, as well as its allegorical veneer, further accentuates the Narrator's position of objectivity, which is a necessary corollary to his writing authority. A clean opposition between the narrative levels of *discours* and *histoire* substantiates and maintains the Narrator's fictional pretext. The Narrator makes use of still another technique to mark his authoritative distancing: The romance is interrupted periodically by pauses wherein the Narrator extends his own commentary, developing the discursive voice at the expense of the historical one. These interludes effectively continue the narratorial voice that was initiated in the prologue, thereby recalling along with the enunciatory situation those prophetic and authoritative aspects that attach themselves to the dream structure. The interventions are frequent and important enough to justify the perception of a continuous,

---

[60] The confusion between Narrator and Lover is mirrored in a number of rubricated manuscripts that attempt to distinguish between the two by means of the titles *Aucteur/Acteur* and *Amant*. While the differentiation is made easily at the beginning, toward the end there is usually some confusion or simply an elimination of one of the titles. The definitive collapsing of the tense structure is further confirmed by Jean de Meun's need to bracket Guillaume's poem as a quotation. For a discussion of these two points, see my "Closed Quotations: The Speaking Voice in the *Roman de la Rose*," Yale French Studies 67 (1984), 248–69.

ever present discursive thread that, woven around the story being told, throws it into relief.

Leaving aside those short interventions (fewer than two lines) that are either stylistic remnants of the *jongleur*'s oral art of storytelling, or incidental markers of *discours* as mentioned above (compare "si vos dirai"), as well as those statements of a general nature that only allude to the presence of a narrator (for instance, "il n'est nus graindres paradis/d'avoir amie a son devis" [1297–8]), there are six such prolonged narratorial excursuses, five of them in the first half of the poem (up to Amor's speech). The first of these occurs at the moment of the Lover's introduction into the garden:

> Des or mes, si con je savrai,
> tot l'afeire vos conterai.
> Primes de quoi Deduiz servoit
> et quel compaignie il avoit
> sanz longue fable vos voil dire,
> et dou vergier trestot a tire
> la façon vo redirai puis.
> Tot ensemble dire ne puis,
> mes tot vos conteré par ordre,
> que l'en n'i sache que remordre.   (689–98)

(From now on, I shall recount to you, as well as I know, how I went to work. First I want to tell you, without any long story, about what Diversion served and about his companions, and then I will tell in a full and orderly way about the appearance of the garden. I cannot speak of everything together, but I will recount it all in such order that no one will have any criticism to make. [p. 40])

The placement of this passage is certainly suggested by the context – following upon a long passage describing the birds' singing in the garden:

> Il chantoient un chant autel
> con fussent angre esperitel;
> . . .
> que mes si douce meloudie
> ne fu d'ome mortel oïe.
> Tant estoit cil chanz doz et biaus
> qu'il ne sembloit pas chant d'oisiaus,

> ainz le peüst l'en aesmer
> au chanz des seraines de mer,
> qui par lor voiz qu'eles ont saines
> et series ont non seraines.
> A chanter furent ententif
> li oiselet (. . .)   (661–2; 665–74)

(they sang a song as though they were heavenly angels

. . .

for mortal man never heard so sweet a melody. It was so sweet and beautiful that it did not seem the song of a bird; one could compare it rather with the song of the sirens of the sea, who have the name *siren* on account of their clear, pure voices. The little birds were intent on their singing [p. 39–40])

As if this repetitive series were not sufficient, Guillaume follows the excursus with a further development on the type of songs being sung:

> Grant servise et doz et plesant
> aloient li oisel fesant;
> lais d'amors et sonoiz cortois,
> chantoient en lor serventois,
> li un en haut, li autre en bas.
> De lor chant, n'estoit mie gas,
> la douçor et la melodie
> me mist el cuer grant reverdie.   (699–706)

(The birds went along performing their wondrously sweet and pleasing service, in which they sang love lays and elegant songs, one high, the other low. Without joking, the sweetness and melody of their singing brought great joy to my heart. [p. 40])

Guillaume is here referring to the well-known metaphoric association between birds and courtly poets, first implicitly in a naturalistic description that through the etymological play on sirens links up singing and seduction, and then explicitly when the birds actually sing poems from the courtly repertoire ("lais d'amors," "sonoiz cortois," "serventois," "reverdie"). In the midst of this carefully orchestrated "poet's" context, the Narrator steps out in his own voice to discuss the present song of seduction. In a not infrequent move by Guillaume, metaphor calls forth (evokes, realizes) its referent.

THE ALLEGORY OF INCOMPLETION

The Narrator's intervention provides two types of information: First, he comments upon the manner of telling his tale, stressing the completeness of his undertaking ("tot l'afeire") as well as the natural requirements of chronology that prohibit a simultaneous view of the situation in its totality ("Tot ensemble dire ne puis,/mes tot vos conteré par ordre" [696–7]) ("I cannot speak of everything together, but I will recount it all in order" [p. 40]). A sense of totality can only be grasped through a movement, an accumulation of distinct moments. We are reminded of the related problems of chronology and narrative point of view which appeared as early as the prologue. A second type of information gives a specific résumé of what is to follow within the story ("de quoi Deduiz servoit" ["about what Diversion served"], "quel compaignie il avoit" ["about his companions"], "dou vergier . . . la façon" ["about the appearance of the garden"]), a plan that the Narrator does indeed observe subsequently.

The second excursus, of similar length, punctuates the Narrator's discussion and explanation of Amor's arrows:

> mes ne dirai ore pas toute
> lor force ne lor poësté.
> Bien vos en ert la verité
> contee et la senefiance,
> nou metrai pas en obliance,
> ainz vos dirai que tot ce monte
> ainçois que define mon conte.
> Or revendrai a ma parole.   (978–85)

(but I shall not now tell all about their force and power. I shall indeed recount to you the truth about them and their significance, and I shall not forget to do so; before I finish my story I will tell you what all this signifies. I shall come back now to my account. [p. 44])

Here the view is slightly altered, bringing us back somewhat to the discussion in the prologue. Unlike the first excursus, here it is a matter of the poem's *meaning*, its "senefiance," and the apprehension of that aspect that was so cautiously alluded to in the prologue, "verité." While the truth went unnamed, or tacitly understood, in the prologue, we also detect a slight shift in the use of the word "senefiance." We recall that in the latter the Narrator claims "songes est senefiance"; a subtle ambiguity in the word places it at the juncture between a creation of meaning (a process [prologue]), and an answer, a fulfillment that will come afterwards and is exterior to the account (result). Along with this dual strengthening of the poem's doctrinal importance, some terminal meaning being valorized at the expense of poetic process, the Narrator brings up still another key concept that was only implicit in the prologue's dream structuring: the end ("ainçois que *define* mon conte") ["before I finish my story"]. What we saw as a constitutive aspect of the dream structure, and perhaps inherent in the notion of totality, is here spelled out and linked irremediably to the doctrinal message. Moreover, the choice of telling the answer — indeed the very ability to do so — is clearly placed in the hands of the Narrator: "ne dirai ore pas. . . . nou metrai pas en obliance . . . ainz vos dirai" ("I shall not now tell. . . . I shall not forget. . . . I will tell you"). The Narrator has chosen to hold back some information which will only be disclosed at the end.

The third intervention is a moral appended to the lengthy retelling of the Narcissus legend, which will be discussed along with that episode in Chapter Four.

The fourth intervention gives a brief explanation of the fountain's designation, just after the discussion of the crystals' optical properties and leading into the vision of the rose:

> Por la graine qui fu semee
> fu ceste fontaine apelee
> la Fontaine d'Amors par droit,
> dont plusor ont en maint endroit
> parlé en romanz et en livre.
> Mes ja mes n'oroiz mielz descrivre
> la verité de la matere,
> quant j'avré apost le mistere.   (1593–1600)

(Because of the seed that was sown this fountain has been rightly called the Fountain of Love, about which several have spoken in many places in books and in romances; but, when I have revealed the mystery, you will never hear the truth of the matter better described. [p. 52])

Not only does the Narrator seem to take his function as a donor of secrets more and more seriously (we are reminded of his deft appropriation of authority in the prologue), endowing the *verité* with a kind of quasi-mystical status ("mistere"), but he begins to resituate himself with respect to a tradition of writing where he finds himself without equal, either in the vernacular ("romanz") or in Latin ("livre").

The fifth intervention, of considerably greater length, directly precedes Amor's commandments:

> Li diex d'Amors lors m'encharja,
> tot issi com vos oroiz ja,
> mot a mot ses comandemenz.
> Bien les devise cist romanz;
> qui amer veut, or i entende,
> que li romanz des or amende.
> Des or le fet bon escouter,
> s'il est qui le sache conter,
> car la fin dou songe est mout bele
> et la matire en est novele.
> Qui dou songe la fin ora,
> je vos di bien que il porra
> des jeus d'Amors assez aprendre,
> puis que il veille tant atendre
> que je die et que j'encomance
> dou songe la senefiance.
> La verité, qui est coverte,
> vos sera lores toute overte
> quant espondre m'oroiz le songe,
> car il n'i a mot de mençonge. (2055–74)

(The God of Love then charged me, word by word, with his commandments; this romance portrays them well. Let him who wishes to love give his attention to it, for the romance improves from this point on. From now on one will do well to listen to it, if he is one who knows how to recount it, for the end of the dream is very beautiful, and its matter is new. I tell you that he who will hear the end of the dream can learn a great deal about the games of Love, provided that he wishes to wait until I tell the tale and begin [to explain] the dream's significance. The truth, which is hidden, will be quite open to you when you hear me explain the dream, for it doesn't contain a lying word. [p. 59])

Not only does this intervention continue the line of thought that we have seen in the previous interventions, but it also strengthens the ties with the prologue. First, we recall that in the prologue, one of the two motivating forces for the creation ("rimeer") of the poem was love ("amor"); as if in direct reply, Amor, without question the personification of love, "charged" the lover "with his commandments." In a certain sense, what we have here is *not* the God of Love (personification of a specific erotic doctrine) but rather the poetic motivation made flesh. With the introduction of Amor, the Narrator states most openly, we are getting closer to the kernel of the dream (the "art d'amors" of the prologue?), the reason for writing and reading the text ("qui amer veut, or i entende,/que li romanz des or amende" [2059–60]) ["Let him who wishes to love give his attention to it, for the romance improves from this point on"]. By emphasizing the "fin dou songe" ("end of the dream") not once but twice, the Narrator seems to be demarcating this vital locus of truth and meaning, while associating narrative spacing with signification.

And yet this is not the end. Not only would an ending at the moment of Amor's speech be unsatisfactory from a narrative point of view, but the *verité*, the "fin du songe," is to be told by the Narrator: "que *je* die et que *j*'encomance dou songe la senefïance" ("until *I* recount and start [telling] the significance of the dream"). While Amor's commandments will be of interest, they must be contextualized so that we as readers can understand the "jeu d'Amors." Might this imply that Amor, the motor of narrative creation, the seeming *détenteur* of truth, is trying to trick his faithful suppliants? Moreover, whereas previously the meaning had merely been located at the end ("ainçois que define mon conte" ["before I finish my story"]), here, by the Narrator's parallel expressions, the meaning seems to be *equivalent to* the end: "dou songe la fin" ("the end of the dream"); "dou songe la senefiance" ("the significance of the dream"). Only now, the meaning/end has a beginning: "que j'encomance" ("until I begin").[61] The more materialized this truth gets, a progression we have seen from the prologue (where truth is not mentioned), to the second intervention (where the truth is vaguely at the end), to this fifth

[61] An important variant for Lecoy's line 2069, "que je die et que j'encomance," is to be found in Langlois's edition (line 2071): "que j'espoigne et que j'enromance" ("until I explain and tell in French"). But in both cases the preceding "atendre que" ("wait until," and not "wait while," as Dahlberg would have it) implies that this part of the Narrator's task has yet to be begun.

intervention (where truth has a beginning and is coextensive with an ending), the more we seem to get caught up in a confusion of beginnings and ends. How will we know when the Narrator "begins" telling the truth? Has he already begun? Is it clear that the truth is different from (coming after) or coextensive with the poem's end? Is Amor, is love, the beginning or the end (in both senses) of the *Roman de la Rose?* Where may we locate the game, the "jeu d'Amors"?

A second important development in this final intervention before Amor's speech is the reiteration of the romance's utility and its eventual audience. Not only will the romance profit those who pay close attention, becoming thereby a pedagogical tool, but the profit must come in a particular way: Readers must wait ("atendre"); in other words, they must allow themselves to be put off, to flounder (or luxuriate?) in a state of ignorance. The Narrator here articulates what was only expressed indirectly through his apparently capricious desire *not* to tell everything at a given moment. Even here, at the overture to Amor's speech, where we think we will be getting the fruit of this authority's wisdom, we are mistaken: The meaning will come later. One of the "laws" of this narrative is the eliciting of suspense in the reader, as a way of keeping him reading – a particular exercise of power or, in the case of Guillaume, authority.[62] This in fact explains the allegorical movement, a profoundly narrative motivating force that puts off the secret, the message, the doctrine, the "end," as long as it can. Guillaume's *Rose* is an allegory in two senses: as a metaphorical enigma, where substances stand for other things (the symbolic dimension of personified qualities); and as a narrative enigma, where the attainment of an end, of a "goal" will explain the machinations of an inscrutable narrator. In order to maintain his power, the Narrator must hold off the end for as long as possible – the ultimate accomplishment being that ending which does not give the appearance of being one. It is in this sense that the *Rose,* as any allegory, paradoxically "means" by not meaning, by not revealing its "truth" – and, accordingly, by not ending. What,

---

62 Cf. Roland Barthes's superb analysis of this aspect of fictional writing in *S/Z* (Paris, 1970). Following upon Barthes, one might suggest that detective fiction, an outright distillation of this narrative constant, represents a kind of paradigm for any novelistic reading experience.

after all, could be more faithful to Guillaume's forebear, Macrobius?

There is a fundamental lack of logic to Guillaume's enterprise that is inexplicable unless we take account of this narrative allegorization. We remember from the prologue that the Narrator first experienced the dream and that every event foreshadowed in the dream later came true. Now, given this evidence of past fulfillment, why would the Narrator choose to recount the dream, pale image or reflection of an event that actually took place, instead of the event itself? Obviously, obscurity has a value of its own, and will serve the poet and his audience. Perhaps the move we must make in untwisting the courtly rhetoric is that of realizing that the value of the allegorical narrative, the fundamentally endingless, meaningless text, is distinct from the expression of traditional doctrinal values. If the apprehension of doctrine is at stake, the pedagogical imperative of the narrative text, its attainment, is something else and certainly not a part of the text's movement. Allegory is, then, synonymous with mystification, with not-knowing – but, paradoxically, necessitates the assurance that the meaning or doctrine is there.

The Narrator makes one other curious statement when he calls into question the capacity of someone (or anyone) to recount the present romance: "s'il est qui le sache conter" (2062) ("If he is one who knows how to recount it"). Now *conter* is ambiguous, meaning both "to tell" (in the sense of creating or composing) and "to deliver orally" (someone else's text). Since Guillaume is not here referring directly to Amor's doctrine (in which case he might be placing into doubt his own capacity to formulate it) but rather to the romance, as an object already in existence, he seems to be giving to *conter* the second definition. According to this interpretation, he is alluding to the *jongleur*, or other literate person, who would promulgate the text, reading it aloud for the audience to enjoy. We have seen in Chapter One to what extent this oral reproducer of the literary text was emblematic of a typical readership in the Middle Ages: Reading implied reception, reproduction, and, eventually, interpretation. Guillaume is simultaneously throwing out a challenge to his future readership, implying that even his ultimate explanation is none too explicit, *and* revealing that the true understanding will result from an active rereading, the activity that this text will produce in its readers.

Let us summarize: The *discours/histoire* distinction that we perceived at the outset as two grammatico-discursive constructs plays itself out within the narrative as two complementary threads: the past level of action (the hero of which is the Lover) whose path we have charted above; and the present voice of the Narrator, which punctuates the first structure regularly in the first half of the poem, and functions *grosso modo* as a commentary to the text as well as a constant reminder of the poem's discursive situation. Parallel to the narrative separation that maintains itself up to the point of Amor's speech, the interventions stress clearly and consistently the Narrator's exterior and fundamentally doctrinal orientation. From the prologue through to the last of these interventions, we find an outward strengthening of the Narrator's position of authority, with a concurrent realization or concretization of the concept of *verité*, which was only indirectly perceived at the outset. The Narrator's omniscient backward glance safeguards, *guarantees,* the existence of a *senefiance* for the poem, which is in turn irremediably linked to the poem's end. The necessity for poetic meaning or justification becomes indistinguishable from the problem of poetic closure; closure, or lack of it, becomes a figure for meaningful discourse. We are assured of the dream's ending as we are of the *senefiance*. One difficulty arises, however, from within the discourse of authority: as the idea of truth or doctrine becomes more and more materialized, so does it become more and more distanced. With the Narrator's appropriation of authority, and his incumbent concentration on the manipulation of his readership, an undeniably personal, or arbitrary, dimension invades the account. One notices specific delaying tactics that, while fundamental to allegorical exposition, seem illogical and inconsistent in a linear narrative account, especially in one purporting to tell everything ("tot") in a concise manner from start to finish.

As we are soon to discover, the Narrator's attempt to distance himself is only illusory. Through the layers of dream, prophecy, and temporal distancing, he is really telling his own story, which is clearly not yet finished. The closer his story approximates his present moment, the more difficult the maintenance of the two

TWO: THE NARRATION OF ALLEGORY

levels becomes. Hence, the growing confusion, the incapacity to maintain a distance, and the increasing participation of the Narrator *in* the story (via present and passé-composé tense usage). What we are witnessing is *not* a dream account, and not even a discrete tale from the Narrator's past, but the Narrator's present drama of consciousness being worked out on the field of his memories, both distant and recent. Theoretically, and insofar as he is capable of vouchsafing his stance of prophetic authority, the Narrator attempts to bring his own story to a conclusion, projecting ahead to an end that has not yet taken place. The Narrator has constructed as many barriers as possible in order to insure this conclusion, the attainment of the goal, but has not considered the ultimate risk: the loss of himself. To conclude the tale would be to render the text invalid in its context.

Indeed what *is* the poem's context? We too easily forget – the Narrator in fact induces us to do so – that the written narrative has a place in the Narrator's story: Its function will be that of gaining the *merci* of his Lady, as he told us in the prologue. Through the first three-quarters of the poem, we completely lose sight of the present Lady, ultimate *destinataire* of the poem, forgetting that the rose figures Rose ("el doit estre Rose clamee"). The Narrator recalls her in his final intervention (significantly, the only one in the last half of the poem) which is also perhaps the most perplexing of them all:

> Des or est droiz que je vos conte
> coment je fui melez a Honte,
> par qui je fui puis mout grevez,
> et coment li murs fu levez
> et li chastiaus riches et forz,
> qu'Amors prist puis par ses esforz.
> Tote l'estoire veil parsuivre,
> ja ne m'est parece d'escrivre,
> por quoi je cuit qu'il abelise
> a la bele, que Dex guerisse,
> qui le guerredon m'en rendra
> mieuz que nule, quant el voudra.   (3481–92)

(From now on it is right for me to tell you how I struggled with Shame, who gave me a lot of trouble afterward, and how the walls were raised and how there rose the rich and powerful castle that Love seized later through his efforts. I want to pursue the whole history, and I shall never be idle in writing it down as long as I believe that it may please the beautiful lady – may God be her cure – who better than any other shall, when she wishes, give me the reward. [p. 80])

Strategically placed at a moment immediately following the kiss of the rose, an emotional highlight, this passage marks a pause in order to take stock and look forward to the rest of the story. Curiously, neither truth ("verité") nor meaning ("senefiance") nor even the end ("fin") is specifically named. A summary of the rest of the narrative is given, nearly all of which is ultimately carried out: "coment je fui melez a Honte" (recounted in lines 3543–82) ("how I struggled with Shame"); "par qui je fui puis mout grevez" (3620–3712) ("who gave me a lot of trouble afterward"); "coment li murs fu levez" (3779–99) ("how the walls were raised"); and "li chastiaus riches et forz" (3800–48) ("the rich and powerful castle"). The only part of the program not fulfilled is the final part, "qu'Amors prist puis par ses esforz" ("that Love seized later through his efforts"), a line that has not unexpectedly contributed to a number of interpretations of the poem's projected ending.[63]

By way of seeing how this problematical line fits into the narrative as Guillaume has constructed it, we must first note that, while this final intervention follows upon a passage predicated mainly on the present tense, one of the many discursive outpourings in this central section of the account, the Narrator gives his plot summary in a perfectly regular sequence of preterites ("fui," "fui," "fu," "prist"). Having been made aware of the Narrator's tense manipulations, we can easily interpret this as a reassertion of the authoritative, prophetic voice in the midst of an encroaching

---

[63] See especially Douglas Kelly, "'Li chastiaus . . . Qu'Amors prist puis par ses esforz': The Conclusion of Guillaume de Lorris' *Rose*," in Norris J. Lacy, ed., *A Medieval French Miscellany*, University of Kansas Publications: Humanistic Studies, no. 42 (Lawrence, KS, 1972), pp. 61–78. Most *Rose* scholars have assumed, first, that this line proves the eventual ending of the poem and, second, that it confirms Jean de Meun's fidelity to Guillaume's "plan." Kelly, while not really confronting the problem of the poem's closure, uses the fact that Amor, and not Venus, is mentioned, in order to place into doubt the latter contention.

subjectivity. Moreover, with its concentration on events, the Narrator's voice is turning away from his previous doctrinal orientation. Then he simultaneously alludes to the totality of the story ("tote l'estoire") and its seeming openness or undeniability ("ja ne m'est parece d'escrivre"). Finally, he proceeds to the important recall of the poem's eventual purpose, adventuring somewhat further than in his prologue. There, his hope was that she would receive it with a positive attitude ("qu'en gré le receve"); here, he repeats the desire to please his Lady ("por quoi je cuit qu'il abelise/ a la bele"), adding that if she desires, she will give him a recompense ("guerredon"). In other words, the writing ("escrivre") of the story ("l'estoire") can be exchanged ("*en* rendra") for a favor ("guerredon"). Nothing could be simpler and more explicit by way of explaining the poem's material existence, and yet few readers of the *Rose* have attended to this line. If we in turn ask ourselves exactly what the "taking of the castle" means (that is, translate the allegory), we understand that it does *not* designate the poet's physical consummation with the Lady (which would presumably find its figurative portrayal in some direct interaction between the Lover and the rose), but instead the winning over of the Lady's good graces (eliminating such adverse factors as Jealousy, Shame, Refusal, and liberating Fair Welcome). In fact, as we have just seen, this is precisely the object of the written poem as Guillaume has articulated it. The point of writing the poem (for the Narrator) coincides with that of the Lover outside the castle desirous of a friendly glance. Not only is their narrative coalescence not arbitrary in its placement, but absolutely necessary as a consequence of the relationship between erotic quest and poetic document.

The Narrator's prophetic stance, we have seen, is deceptive. The dream events, instead of foretelling future actions, actually recapitulate them *after the fact*. Even if the distance between the two is reduced to infinitesimal proportions, the dream portrayal will always trail behind the actuality.[64] This alteration in the narrative/dream structure can be perceived visually in reference to the

---

[64] For a stunning analysis of this problematic in a very different literary work, see John Freccero, "Zeno's Last Cigarette," *Modern Language Notes*, 77 (1962), 3–23.

schemes which we introduced above. Reproducing the second one (without the hypothetical "first" telling of the dream A_2–B_2) we have:

$$
\begin{array}{ccc}
\underset{A_1}{*} \quad \underset{x_1}{*} \quad \underset{B_1}{*} & \text{DREAM EXPERIENCE} \text{ (prelinguistic)} & \text{(PAST)} \\
\\
\underset{A_2}{*} \quad \underset{x_2}{*} \quad \underset{B_2}{*} & \text{REAL EVENT (1)} & \text{(PAST)} \\
\\
\underset{A_3}{*} \quad \underset{x_3}{*} \quad \underset{[B_3]}{*} & \text{DREAM ACCOUNT} & \text{(PRESENT)} \\
\\
\underset{[A_4]}{*} \quad \underset{[x_4]}{*} \quad \underset{[B_4]}{*} & \text{REAL EVENT (2)} & \text{(FUTURE)}
\end{array}
$$

Now, according to this scheme, x_1 (a given dreamed event) will be imitated verbally – expressed – by x_3 (a linguistically recounted event, part of the dream account). X_1 has already prefigured the real event x_2, which has taken place, and will similarly prefigure x_4, which has manifestly *not* taken place. The entire structure is altered by what we find out as of the end of Guillaume's poem: First, A_1–B_1 is eliminated. In other words, we discover that there never was a dream. Second, chronologically speaking, the three other axes collapse into each other: Not only is there no *completed* past affair, as would be indicated by A_2–B_2, but the story supposedly in the future is already under way (A_4, the beginning of the love affair, has already taken place – thus explaining the very possibility of addressing a love poem). In sum A_2–B_2 and A_4–B_4 are one and the same love story (we find out at the end) which the Narrator doubled and reoriented chronologically at the outset in order to justify his initial prophetic claims. Not only has the "future" story already begun but the "past" story has never ended. A_3–B_3, the dream tale whose writing we are in the process of following, has itself become an event, a part of the love story exercising a particular function, and therefore ultimately finds itself reinscribed in a considerably simplified schematic representation. A_3–B_3, no longer solely analogical, assumes its place as an event, and hence as a point along the unique evenemential line A'–B'. A new schematization representing the collapsing of these once-separate levels could look something like this:

TWO: THE NARRATION OF ALLEGORY

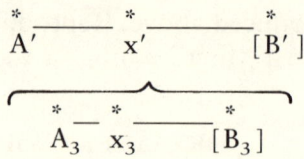

Such a graphic and hopelessly reductionist scheme might nonetheless provide a clearer idea of the Narrator's impasse. While A' and A_3, B' and B_3, still correspond to each other in a mimetic or analogical fashion, the progress through the writing of the narrative poem from A_3 to B_3 takes its place *as an event* x' along the other axis. Moreover, insofar as A_3 manifestly imitates and does not prophesy the real event A' (the love affair was under way before the beginning of the poem), in order for B_3 to be written, *necessarily* before the event B', the Narrator would have to switch at some moment from the mode of imitation to that of prophecy, as it were stepping outside of himself (from an inner, involved, narrative stance to one of omniscience). Where, one might ask, would this passage take place? As is clear from the above discussion, the Narrator chooses not to abandon his persona and consequently ends at that point where his narrative catches up with his actual point of experience – schematically, where x_3 coincides with x', the moment of writing the love poem.

Hence, we witness the paradox of projecting to an end that is contingent upon the very act being accomplished (that of writing a poem). Since the Narrator is using the written document to attain his goal, the story *must* remain in a state of suspension, for the reaching of the goal can only be portrayed after it has happened. But, once the Narrator has achieved his goal, there would be no more reason, no further pretext, to continue writing. The Narrator's allusion to an ending, the taking of the castle, slyly hints at the poem's potential effect, its favorable reception by the Lady – but this can never be expressed as other than a faint pseudoprophecy ("quant el voudra"). The allusion can never become a narrated element within the confines of the poem, for the latter must be received by her before the "castle is taken." The poet hovers at a moment of stasis, literally out of time, beyond which only an after-the-fact, exterior continuation can proceed. The impossibility of an overt ending generated from within seals the closure of the *Rose*.

AN ALLEGORY OF LOVE

To assert categorically that the *Roman de la Rose* is an unfinished poem is at best a naive judgment that takes little account of the intricacies latent in a tale whose self-conscious manipulation of a sequence of narrative voices risks threatening, if not eradicating, a single authoritative voice. In this sense, and according to the terms which we set up in Chapter One, the *Roman de la Rose* is a profoundly medieval poem, one which functions within a tradition of writing for which authorship is not a simple, external guiding factor behind fictional works. The poem, as we have seen, is closed, but not in the conventional narrative fashion which we would expect. Closed, perhaps, but not ended, inasmuch as the narrative threads are left manifestly unresolved. In a narrative whose point, however, happens to be the impossibility of resolution, of the attainment of a goal, no approach could be more effective (or more seductive). One related point pertaining to our perception of narrative completion deserves to be mentioned here: To insist that the *Rose* as we have it is a complete text is not equivalent to saying that it could not have been any other way, that it could not be ended in a conventional manner. A convenient proof to the contrary can be found in the form of the "anonymous conclusion" found in a half dozen *Rose* manuscripts.[65] A specific difficulty in recent studies of poetic closure is related to the methods of evaluation: Should we attempt to describe closure effects in a more or less passive way or should we establish a set of normative rules and guidelines that will serve as points of judgment for the closure of narratives?[66] Clearly, authors make various choices in the construction of their narratives and, however spectacular or fitting or perfect, their ending always partakes of the arbitrary as does any facet of literary composition. Here we come to another point of judgment related to the authorial problem of Chapter One – the mistaking of the author for God, so that we assume his creation to be preordained, flawless and eternal.

---

65 *Roman de la Rose*, ed. Langlois, vol. II, note to line 4058, pp. 330–3.
66 Two recent books on narrative closure approach the problem in quite different ways: Whereas Marianna Torgovnick, in her *Closure in the Novel* (Princeton, 1981), chooses to develop a formalistic critical vocabulary tending toward the dogmatic, D. A. Miller (*Narrative and Its Discontents* [Princeton, 1981]) offers a considerably more subtle demonstration of how closure becomes an ultimately antagonistic and yet essential variable in the entire novelistic endeavor.

TWO: THE NARRATION OF ALLEGORY

This is, in other terms, the Platonic problem raised in considering the relationship between Ideal forms and individual objects, abstract and concrete perceptions. To read the *Roman de la Rose* according to an Ideal model of narrative unity is very simply to ignore a carefully prepared choice that openly defies any judgment grounded in preordained closural rules and notions of linguistic meaning or finality.

Whereas the theological mode of dreams as prophetic structures argues for the objective distancing of the account, the eventual meaning that the text will produce — its outcome — autobiography, through a radical dissolution of objectivity, stresses the personal, the anti-doctrinal phenomenon of literary acts and their hypothetical referents. What we perceived initially only as two structures, complementary in their articulation of a narrative relationship, but ultimately antagonistic, subtends a chain of dualities — the universal versus the individual; public versus private; doctrine versus antidoctrine; fiction versus experience — that are being played out in the *Rose*. A grammatical analysis demonstrates perhaps the most apparent of the solutions (or resolutions) reached by the text, through the eventual choice of one of the narrative options, but the ramifications of such an observable transformation extend much further. If the Narrator's ultimate solution is that of eliminating the doctrinal aspects of this poem, the so-called Art of Love, there is nonetheless a lengthy segment that not only constitutes the primary statement of instruction on love, but also breaks through the narrative configuration in the form of a lengthy, nearly unwieldly, quotation. We have already noted that there is an implicit authoritative rivalry instituted between Amor and the Narrator in the latter's intervention immediately preceding Amor's instructions. By virtue of this rivalry, and insofar as it is the only textual element susceptible of placing into question the Narrator's otherwise all-inclusive stance, Amor's speech takes on an added importance. If, as suggested above, Amor functions as a kind of narrative motor, he is also the ultimate authority figure, replacement for the single "God" who does not have a part in the adventure.[67] Moreover, actualized as a prophecy, Amor's speech

---

[67] Amor is alternately called the "dieu d'Amor"; it is clear, moreover, that in many instances where the word "Dieu" is used in isolation, it refers to him and not to the Christian God.

provides an inner mirror, a *mise-en-abyme*, of the entire dream framework, a model provided by an acknowledged authority on such matters. Not surprisingly, the information that it sets forth will also become a reflecting mirror for the totality of the poem.

Amor's speech can be neatly divided into three major sections: Amor's commandments of love (2075–252); Amor's prophetic, or anticipatory, tale of the Lover's trials (2253–566); and Amor's account of the consolations available to his faithful lovers (2567–748).

The first section, cast mainly in the subjunctive and imperative modes, presents a series of commands and prescriptions meant to prepare the Lover for an amorous existence. The commandments recapitulate precisely the progress that the Lover has made right up to this point, that of submitting himself to Amor. The goal of this first part: to give one's heart "en don" (2241) ("as a gift"). This is precisely what the Lover did once Amor had shot him with his five arrows: "'li cuers est vostres'" (1983) ("'My heart is yours'").

The speech of Amor turns to the prophetic mode in the second section, by way of informing the Lover – in the future tense of course – how his love affair will progress from that point. The passage from the first to the second section is marked by a careful and consistent shift from imperative to future, as well as by the recapitulative marker, "Quant tu avras . . .":

> Donc le done tot quitement
> si le fai debonairement
> . . .
> Quant tu avras ton cuer doné,
> si con je t'ai ci sarmoné,
> lors te vendront les *aventures*.   (2247–8; 2253–5)
>
> (Then give it fully and freely, and do so with an easy manner,
> . . .
> When you have given your heart away, as I have been exhorting you to do, things will happen to you. [p. 80])

The *aventures* are, to be sure, the events that will follow and that will present obstacles for the Lover, as in any quest. In a gesture befitting the romance, instruction turns to anecdote, philosophical truth to narrative. By couching his prophecies in the future tense and with a direct address ("tu"), Amor portrays directly, and not figuratively, our specific Lover's trials: illness; pilgrimage to the beloved; hot and cold spells; sight of the beloved; memory; regrets; renewed visits to the beloved; direct address; erotic dreams; vigil outside the beloved's house (under cover of night). Amor's future account ends on the following note:

> Une eure *iras* a l'uis derieres
> savoir s'il *est* remainz desfers
> et *jucheras* ilec defoirs
> touz seus a la pluie et au vent;
> aprés *vendras* a l'uis devant,
> et se tu *treves* fendeüre,
> par fenestre, par serreüre,
> *oreille* et *escoute* par mi (. . .)   (2504–11)

(One hour you *will go* to the back door to see if it *has been* left unclosed, and there you *will perch* like a crane all alone, outside in the wind and rain. Afterward you *will come* to the front door, and if you *find* a chink, a window or lock, *put* your ear to it to hear [pp. 65–6])

The passage from "iras . . . jucheras . . . vendras" to "treves . . . oreille et escoute" marks the movement from prophetic narrative back to commandments in the style of the first section. If we are right in assuming that Amor's account provides a model for the entire narration, it is certainly significant that it culminates at the moment where the Lover is pining away outside the door of the beloved's house waiting to catch a glimpse of her.[68] This is, needless to say, precisely the position of the Narrator/Lover, portrayed from the inside, at the close of Guillaume's poem. So, in fact, Amor's prophecy *does not end* in the same way that Guillaume's poem does not end, for both come to a point of stasis that can be interpreted as a type of closure while at the same time they allude to possible developments that might occur subsequently.

The final section of Amor's speech consists in the presentation

---

[68] Several manuscripts in which the portrait of the author has not been chosen as the illumination to be placed between the two parts of the poem include instead an illumination of the Lover pining away below the tower with a head looking at him from the window, evidently Bel Acueil.

of the varieties of consolation available to the unfortunate lover, he who is left outside and apart from the object of his affections. The gifts that he grants are, first, Esperance, and a group of three further gifts: Douz Penser, Douz Parler, and Douz Regart. Curiously, Amor is in a way reaching back to his prophetic tale of the Lover's trials, for each one of these gifts was already available: No advance seems to have been made. The one thing over and above these, which Amor only alludes to, seems scarcely realizable, and certainly dependent upon his whims:

> Chascuns de ceus veil qu'i te gart
> jusque tu puisses mieuz atendre,
> qu'autre biens, qui ne sont pas mendres,
> mes greignor, avras ça avant.   (2744–7)
>
> (I want each of these to watch over you until you can expect something better, for in the future you will have other good things, not less but greater. [p. 69])

These other gifts, better ("mieuz") and greater ("pas mendres," "greignor"), obviously exist and yet have no identity, allegorical or otherwise. They are never named. Amor's discourse vis-à-vis the disconsolate Lover reminds us of the Narrator's own discourse, withholding information from his readers until the proper moment, and leaving them in a position of waiting ("atendre"). Once we perceive the vital link between Amor and the Narrator – both figures of authority, controllers of information, tellers of tales, ostensibly arbitrary – we can begin to guess the "jeus," not only of Amor, but also of his imitator. Not the least of which is the latter's managing to place on stage in a central confrontation his authoritative double (Amor) and his subservient double (Lover). This is the vital moment of decision, for once the Narrator has subsumed the roles of master and servant, beloved and lover, author and reader, there is no place to go. In a certain sense, the Narrator must recognize a higher authority, or else his work will have no meaning.

It is in this context that one of Amor's comments takes on an added cogency, above and beyond his description of the Lover's trials. In detailing the lover's various acts of remorse, Amor indicates that the lover will have a wish-fulfilling dream that will turn out to be only a lying illusion:

> tel foiz sera qu'il t'ert avis
> que tu tendras cele au cler vis
> entre tes braz trestote nue
> ausi con s'el fust devenue
> dou tot t'amie et ta compaigne.
> Lors feras chastiaus en Espaigne
> et avras joie de noiant
> tant con tu iras foloiant
> en la pensee delitable
> ou il n'a que mençonge et fable.   (2425–34)

(there will be a time when you will think that you are holding her, with shining face, quite naked in your arms, just as if she had become wholly your sweetheart and your companion. Then you will build castles in Spain and will take joy in nothing as much as in going around deluding yourself with this delectable thought that contains only lies and fables. [p. 64])

First, this statement is in direct contradiction to a doctrine we have been induced to believe since the first words of the prologue: the prophetic efficacy of dreams. Amor makes this clear through his repetition of the phrase "mençonge et fable," reversed and divested of the third term, "songe." We recall that the *songe/mensonge* model, initial truism of the dream account, and repeated in the fifth narratorial intervention (2073–74), served as a foundation for the dream account, the Narrator's authority, and everything that the prophecy implies. In one clear moment of reinscription, Amor pinpoints the Narrator's folly and the invalidity of his narrative undertaking. Not only can our Lover not enjoy his beloved in the same way (embrace a naked rose?), but it shall soon become apparent that he is not the one who will build the castles. Moreover, there is an implicit return to the truth of Macrobius. The dream here described by Amor does indeed fit squarely into Macrobius's scheme, the category termed *insomnium*.[69] But there is more: The *avis/vis* rhyme in the above-quoted passage recalls the one Macrobian dream category that we definitively excluded at the outset: *visum*. The *visum*, for Macrobius,

---

69 "est enim ἐνύπνιον, quotiens cura oppressi animi corporisve sive fortunae, qualis vigilantem fatigaverat, talem se ingerit dormienti: animi, si *amator deliciis suis aut fruentem se videat aut carentem*" (*Comm.* I, iii, 4; emphasis mine).

comes upon one in the moment between wakefulness and slumber, in the so-called "first cloud of sleep." In this drowsy condition he thinks he is still fully awake and imagines he sees specters rushing at him or wandering vaguely about, differing from natural creatures in size and shape, and hosts of diverse things, either delightful or disturbing.[70]

One can, on the one hand, recognize in the "specters rushing at him or wandering vaguely about" the allegorical inhabitants of Deduit's garden; more importantly, however, this "moment between wakefulness and slumber" is exactly the space in which, as we have attempted to show, the *Rose* drama unfolds. The dissolution of the dream barrier is a way of acknowledging this incapacity to distinguish perceptually between dream and wakefulness, imagination and reality. In spite of the Narrator's attempts to appropriate authority and undo such *magistri* as Macrobius, here is found the return and eventual triumph of the Macrobian system by way of still another authority, Amor.

If we learn anything about the "Art of Love" from Amor, it is that there is no such thing. Although predicated by analogy on other philosophical, religious, or ethical schemes, whose "answer" is known in advance and can be formulated in all its generality, love does not lend itself to a doctrinal summary as would be implied by its designation as an "art." As we gather from Amor's exposition, love is predicated upon individual comportments and experiences, finding itself ultimately subject to his own arbitrary caprices. His teachings ("comandements") can only go a certain distance before they are forced to discontinue by the sheer multiplicity of possible outcomes. The workings of lovers are ultimately based upon individual experience and not universal doctrine. Love, in other words, cannot be prophetic. The Narrator's stance of authority, his claims to the truth and the art of love, turn out finally to be themselves the "jeus d'Amors," a game of bluff. For what he forgets is, finally, that he cannot step outside of himself. If, on the one hand, love is being characterized as an irrational,

---

"Nightmares may be caused by mental or physical distress, or anxiety about the future: the patient experiences in dreams vexations similar to those that disturb him during the day. As examples of the mental variety, we might mention the *lover who dreams of possessing his sweetheart or of losing her*" (Stahl, Commentary, p. 88).
70 *Comm.*, I, iii, 7; Stahl, Commentary, p. 89.

undefinable experience, it is likewise a figure for the incapacity to codify or to express knowledge. Insofar as the Lover wishes to address his Lady, he cannot maintain a pedagogical discourse, which puts him in the position of both lover and beloved (authority figure). If he is to be "true" to his own Rose, then he must submit himself.

At one point, as a means of consolation, Amor provides a stunningly direct formulation of all the difficulties we have found in the Narrator's discourse:

> nes qu'em puet espuisier la mer,
> ne poroit nus les maus d'amer
> conter en romanz ne en livre.
> Et totes voies covient vivre
> les amanz, qu'il lor est mestiers.   (2591–5)
>
> (No more than one can empty the sea could any man recount in a romance or a book the woes of love. And in any case, lovers must live, for life is their occupation. [p. 67])

In an oblique reflection upon the Narrator's impossible task ("ne poroit *nus* les maus d'amer/conter"), Amor makes use of the Narrator's own previous formula, which had been directed toward the latter's forebears in the poetic endeavor: "plusor ont . . . /parlé *en romanz et en livre*" (1596–7). Moreover, Amor revitalizes a rhyming couplet ("mer"/"amer"), made famous presumably by Thomas's poetic development in his version of the *Tristan,* through his emphasis on the complementary actions "espuisier"/"conter."[71]

---

71 Although not preserved among the fragments of the *Roman de Tristan* that have come down to us, the passage was well-known enough to be parodied in Chrétien de Troyes's *Cligés* (ed. Alexandre Micha, CFMA, 84 [Paris, 1957]):

> Ne ne set por coi il le font
> fors que por la mer ou il sont.
> Espoir bien s'an aparceüst,
> Se la mers ne la deceüst;
> Mes la mers l'angingne et deçoit
> Si qu'an la mer l'amor ne voit;
> An la mer sont, et d'amer vient,
> Et d'amors vient li max ques tient.
> Et de ces trois ne set blasmer
> La reïne fors que la mer . . . .   (537–46)

(Nor does she [Guenevere] know why they are doing it except for the sea [*mer*] where they happen to be. Indeed, she might possibly have realized it, had the sea not deceived her. However, the sea has fooled and tricked her in

What image could be more vital to the present discussion than that of the storytelling activity compared to the extraction of water from a well ("es*puisi*er"), which is magically transformed into the sea with its endless possibilities (just as "l'amer" has limitless stories to be told about it)? Furthermore, the abstract extension of *espuisier* (closer to the modern French meaning, "to exhaust") coincides nicely with a strict utilitarian view of language, according to which its purpose, paradoxically, would be to do away with itself, to create a situation in which it would no longer be necessary or useful. Amor's point, to the contrary, is that the possibilities of language are limitless, or rather end-less; in this he agrees totally with the *Rose*'s closural strategy. One is likewise led to consider, through Amor's metaphor, those qualities of the sea that pertain to the *éternel retour* of the writer: What, at least visually, seems to prevent the sea from being emptied, indeed which perhaps emblematizes the infinite expanses, is the wave pattern, the continual and unceasing retreat and return. If this observation serves to explain why one cannot exhaust the water in the sea, it also offers a satisfying analogue to the Narrator's curious predicament: the inherent circularity of the erotic quest, the perhaps inevitable return to the same point, which translates itself narratively as an inability to end (the dream, the love story) and a concurrent return to the past, to the source, which is inevitably the Narrator's own voice.[72]

such a way that she does not see love [*l'amor*] on the sea [*la mer*]. They are on the sea [*la mer*] and it is the result of bitterness [*amer*] [or "of loving": *amer*], and the illness which has taken hold of them comes from love [*amors*]. And the queen doesn't know which of these three to blame except the sea . . .)

as well as in Gottfried von Strassburg's Middle High German adaptation of Thomas's poem, ed. Werner Schröder (Berlin, 1969), lines 11990–12032.

72 As if in direct response to Amor's metaphoric extension of the sea image, the Narrator inserts the following lines in a strategic position, immediately after the kiss of the rose and just before his apocryphal prophecy of the taking of the castle by the god of Love:

> La mer [l'amer?] n'ert ja si apesie
> qu'el ne soit troble a poi de vent:
> Amors se rechange sovent,
> il oint une eure, autre eure point,
> Amors n'est gueres en un point.   (3476–80)

(The sea will never be so calm that it may not be a little troubled by the wind. Love changes often: one hour he soothes, another pierces; he is rarely in the same situation. [p. 80])

Could any critique of the poem's hypothetical closure be more devastating than this recall of Amor's fickleness, by way of the sea's perpetual motion – in short, the god of

In the midst of this discussion, Amor quietly switches gears and via a new rhyme ("livre"/"vivre") passes from the telling of erotic tales to the living of them, which was after all his point of departure. The space between *livre* and *vivre,* writing and experience, is specifically what our Narrator attempts to straddle through his very poem. It is not irrelevant that Amor forecast his failure, inevitable in any such endeavor, while at the same time insisting upon the unceasing nature of his activity. We have here in a marvelously compact expression the discernment of, and justification for, the *Rose*'s closure mechanism. As if in reinforcement of the *livre/vivre* association, there is a double enjambment in the passage, a relatively infrequent stylistic device of Guillaume:

> ne poroit nus les maus d'amer
> *conter* (. . .)   (2592–3)
>   (. . .) covient vivre
> *les amanz* (. . .)   (2594–5)

Metrically separated from the balance of their clauses, *conter* and *les amanz* crystallize the complementarity of the two concepts of writing and living (loving).

In a considerably more direct expression than we have seen up to now, Guillaume is here telling us that to love is to remember, to recall past moments while maintaining the dream or illusion that a term can be sought and attained. By internalizing the inevitability of the *échec,* while maintaining the hope (we recall Amor's final concession: Esperance) thanks to an open-ended narrative/dream configuration, Guillaume has brilliantly imitated in his allegorical rendering the futility *and* utter necessity of a goal-oriented approach to desire and to linguistic meaning. Not to end is not to exhaust one's meaning (or write oneself out of existence); that which dislocates an otherwise untenable impasse is the intercession of the written document, the ended and unendable narrative. If we say that the Narrator at the end has abandoned the allegorical veneer, the dream framework, in order to speak forth in his own voice, we are only partly correct, for he has simply passed to another mode of allegorical expression, where he himself *as nar-*

Love's refusal to terminate anything – which occurs only six lines before the sole allusion to the poem's conclusion (again, supposedly brought about by the very same Amor)?

rator becomes the figure for any such endeavor. His confusion becomes our confusion, his quest our quest. This stepping back from his own voice is in fact one of the primary features of literary memory: the quotation. While the Narrator has quoted a number of characters, he is in the final lines quoting himself, taking himself as an exemplary figure, one whose well-established rhetoric inheres in the *I* speaking voice. After all, the voice at the end, the solitary lover's plaint, is the traditional poet's voice in the surprisingly cohesive corpus of courtly lyric poems (*chansons*). Far from being a text in isolation, an eccentricity, Guillaume's *Roman de la Rose* provides through its allegorization of a significant poetic legacy a poignant and essential reading/reinterpretation of the single most important erotic conception in the western world. If the Narrator returns to himself, in so doing he returns to the expression of tradition, which will never again be the same. It is in this sense, as a reinterpretation of, and commentary on, the intertextual ramifications of this allegory of love (allegory of allegory?) that we will investigate in Chapter Three the courtly *chanson* and its poetic expression.

THREE

Lyric and romance

> ... tout mon aé
> D'amour ne joï
> Fors qu'en pensé
> (Richard de Fournival, XIII, 6–8)

THE GENRES OF COURTLY LITERATURE

The analysis of the last chapter has demonstrated, using grammatical and structural coordinates inherent in the formal makeup of the *Roman de la Rose,* that the poem does achieve a type of closure. As a work that brings into play two different modes of narrative participation, and ultimately opts for one of them, the *Rose* subtly manipulates the way in which a poetic message is to be construed and thereby reflects upon its very reception. Such a noncontextual analysis – one that largely eschews outside cultural determinants – is, I believe, important for our detection of the work's contours apart from the prejudices imposed upon our vision by an inherited tradition of literary studies. Nonetheless, a strictly narrative analysis merely scratches the surface of a work that is so heavily steeped in codes and *topoi* derived from a rich poetic tradition developed over the preceding sixty or seventy years. Furthermore, the question remains as to whether this vision of the first *Rose* and its paradoxical closure-in-suspension is a modern imposition or whether it can be substantiated by reference to the poem's most likely literary contexts. If the perception of narrative structures and their manipulation is, as I have suggested, predicated to a great extent upon the reader's capacity to recognize them, then we should expect to find such patterns of expectation encoded in other literary works of that period. The following pages will be devoted to an investigation of the generic background of the *Rose,* especially in light of the above narrative analysis, and the relevance of the "matter" of courtly love to the author's strategy.

As far as the study of literary genres is concerned, a few preliminary remarks are in order. Our initial reaction to the problem of genres tends to be dictated by a sense of preestablished codification, characterized by lists of topical elements or structural guidelines the replication of which across a body of works constitutes that genre; and yet this conception greatly misconstrues the dynamic play of imitation and variation which has shaped our literary heritage. With the exception of certain fixed poetic forms that are by definition predetermined (for instance, sonnet, rondeau, *chant royal*), most generic categories are heuristic constructs formulated by the reader or critic as based upon the work's reception within a given context. To be sure, what the reader understands to be the constituent parts of a given genre helps inform his interpretation of new works added to that genre, but that does not of course imply that these very same rules were followed in order to create each of the works "belonging" to that genre. More importantly, it will often be the case that in the historical development of a genre innovative works will challenge the norms that have been handed down and thus alter the rules previously attributed to that genre. Boundaries between genres will also change over the course of history, so that distinctions or definitions valid at one time period will no longer pertain in a later one.[1] To view genres as immutable constructs amounts to an ideal (in the Platonic sense) vision of literary creation that remains theoretically resistant to chronological movements and individual aberrations. In order to preserve the dialectical movement that is proper to a historical and historicizing vision of generic construction and mutability, the essentially fluid constructs known as genres must not be allowed to coagulate, to turn into a system, and should, in the felicitous expression of Fredric Jameson, "be understood . . . as mere ad hoc, experimental constructs, devised for a specific textual occasion and abandoned like so much scaffolding when the analysis has done its work."[2]

---

[1] Cf. Hans Robert Jauss, "Theory of Genres and Medieval Literature," in *Toward an Aesthetic of Reception*, trans. Timothy Bahti (Minneapolis, 1982), pp. 76–109; and my "The Limits of Mime(sis): Notes Toward a Generic Revision of Medieval Theater," *L'Esprit Créateur*, XXIII, No. 1 (Spring 1983), 49–63.

[2] Fredric Jameson, *The Political Unconscious* (Ithaca, NY, 1981), p. 145.

THREE: LYRIC AND ROMANCE

Hans Robert Jauss has been instrumental in the formulation and application of this approach to the study of literary genres.[3] His expression "horizon of expectations" most appropriately displaces the normative connotations of the word "genre" by situating the productivity of literary codes precisely at the point of intersection between public expectation or foreknowledge (based upon a reception of previous works) and the singular difference of a new work. Expressed most succinctly, a work's meaning, or significance, resides in the space separating the known from the unknown. By mapping interpretation onto history, which amounts to a relativizing of the production of meaning, Jauss's formulation allows us to evaluate with considerably more sophistication than in traditional views of genre the relative import of conformity and innovation, general and individual expression. This is especially important for an understanding of medieval works of fiction, which are largely conceived in the spirit of imitation and repetition of previous works outside the confines of a classical canon.[4] An important space is nonetheless reserved for innovations in structure (*conjointure*) and meaning (*sens, entencion*), which promote distinctions among works and authors.[5] The recently developed notion of the intertext will be of some help inasmuch as it allows for the evaluation of poetic similarities or borrowings outside of the narrow confines of a source-oriented tradition of philology. As defined by Michael Riffaterre, the term designates "l'ensemble des textes que l'on peut rapprocher de celui que l'on a sous les yeux, l'ensemble des textes que l'on retrouve dans sa mémoire à la lecture d'un passage donné."[6] As an approach to reading, intertextuality studies the rhetorical productivity of language across texts without seeking the genetic or historical reasons for the expressivity of a given work, the implication being that style and rhetoric are immanent possibilities

---

3 In addition to Jauss's "Theory of Genres," particularly important theoretical formulations are to be found in his "Literary History as a Challenge to Literary Theory," in *Toward an Aesthetic*, pp. 3–45; and "The Alterity and Modernity of Medieval Literature," *New Literary History*, X, no. 2 (Winter 1979), 181–229.
4 Peter Haidu, "Repetition: Modern Reflections on Medieval Aesthetics," *MLN*, 92 (1977), 875–87.
5 The terms are of course borrowed from Chrétien de Troyes, for whom there seems to be no contradiction between the existence of a source and novelty in composition. For a sensible discussion of the terms' application, see F. Douglas Kelly, *Sens and Conjointure in the Chevalier de la Charrette* (The Hague, 1966).
6 Michael Riffaterre, "L'Intertexte inconnu," *Littérature* 41 (1981), 4–7 [4].

of language prior to any concrete realization. The circulation of texts and fluidity of imitation (in modern terms, plagiarism) that we have seen to characterize the medieval literary work suggest that there is much to be gained in the application of such a notion to that corpus for, while it does not invalidate the importance of source study, intertextuality does allow us to navigate in territories where unverifiable textual dating, anonymity, or large-scale rhetorical borrowing makes it unfeasible to formulate textual similarities as a function of one author's influence upon another. To give only one example pertaining to our enquiry, never has the influence of our *Roman de la Rose* upon the romance of the same name composed by Jean Renart (also known under the title *Guillaume de Dole*) been ascertained, nor has the converse been proven; there are, nonetheless, significant thematic, symbolic, and writerly features that unite the two texts and can enrich our understanding of the contemporary literary scene.[7] Studied as part of a broad intertext, these features can be developed and allowed to reverberate; within a strict chronology, only hypotheses, mostly unrelated to the poetics of the texts, are possible.[8]

Accordingly, an attempt to construct a generic horizon for the *Rose* might include certain works the direct influence of which cannot be ascertained, or even ones that, strictly speaking, could not have influenced it. To put it a slightly different way, whether or not we know that the author of the first *Rose* had read one or another given works, this uncertainty should not prevent us from perceiving shared themes and expressions that make up part of their inherited language and rhetoric. While it has always been acknowledged that the *Roman de la Rose* is about love, two other factors, principally rhetorical in nature, have recently oriented the search for its generic horizon: the special position of the first-person narrator; and the allegorical framework characterized by an extensive use of personification allegory. The influential studies by Hans Robert Jauss and Marc-René Jung have amply documented and analyzed the important tradition of vernacular allegories by way of proving their relevance to the composition of the

---

[7] Michel Zink, *Roman rose et rose rouge: Le Roman de la Rose ou de Guillaume de Dole de Jean Renart* (Paris, 1979), pp. 69–93.
[8] Ibid., pp. 7–16.

Rose.[9] The similarities are striking, but even more so is the conceptual and literary gap separating the *Rose* from the other works included in this corpus. The association nonetheless carries with it significant interpretive consequences. By situating the *Roman de la Rose* in this primarily religious, didactic lineage, Jauss is for instance led to formulate its alteration of the generic horizon as "the ostentatious appropriation and conscious literarization of a method proper to the spiritual tradition," laying claim "to the same allegorical truth for the poetry of courtly love that the spiritual tradition of textual exegesis had reserved for itself."[10] But is this totally justified? Our analysis in the previous chapter would lead us to believe that, contrariwise, and in spite of a conscious incorporation of the tactics of biblical exegesis, the rhetorical structure of the *Rose* formally undermines the initial typological construct in favor of an unmediated, personal poetic address. While well aware of the confluence of literary types in the *Rose,* Jauss has failed to take account of the possibility that "courtly love" might not simply be a didactic content-form waiting to be legitimized in a framework conceived for the expression of spiritual truths — that it might in fact carry with it certain ideological biases countermanding the spiritual order that would attempt to subsume it. Before settling for the ultimately superficial features uniting the first *Roman de la Rose* with the allegorical didactic tradition represented by such authors as Raoul de Houdenc, the Reclus de Molliens, and Huon de Méry, it is perhaps advisable to investigate the field of courtly literature for elements which might have suggested, if not generated, the allegories of the *Rose.*

The first-person participatory narrator is a very likely and possibly essential contribution of these allegorical traditions, but we can already see models for this type of narrative in early courtly, or even precourtly, poems. The "romances" and *pastourelles* such as

---

9 Hans Robert Jauss, "La Transformation de la forme allégorique entre 1180 et 1240: D'Alain de Lille à Guillaume de Lorris," in *L'Humanisme médiéval dans les littératures romanes du XIIe au XIVe siècle,* ed. Anthime Fourrier (Paris, 1964), pp. 107–46 (an expanded and somewhat revised version was written for the GRLMA, entitled "Entstehung und Strukturwandel der allegorischen Dichtung," and is now available in Jauss's *Alterität und Modernität der mittelalterlichen Literatur* [Munich, 1977], 154–218); Marc-René Jung, *Etudes sur le poème allégorique en France au moyen âge,* Romanica Helvetica 82 (Bern, 1971).

10 Jauss, "Theory of Genres," p. 104.

are found in the collection of Karl Bartsch,[11] and which Zumthor has classified as the "Encounter-type,"[12] display a highly codified narrative framework involving a first-person, generally anonymous, narrator's awakening in the Springtime, his venturing out into nature and subsequent encounter with a woman. The outcomes are varied, but the opening sequences follow a uniform pattern of which the following is quite typical:[13]

> Ce fu en tres douz tens de mai,
> que de cuer gai
> vont cil oiseillon chantant,
> en un vergier pour lour chant
> oir m'en entrai,
> tant que la regardai
> en ce jardin,
> desoz un pin
> bien rame,
> pucele de grant biaute. . . .

(It was in the very mild Maytime season, when the little birds go on singing, gay of heart. In order to hear their song I made my way into an arbor, when I fixed my eyes on her in this garden beneath a pine tree thick with branches – a young girl of great beauty . . .)

The influence of the "Encounter-type," one of the oldest and most widely spread in the courtly tradition, is observable in other poems such as the love debate: Whereas in the earlier poems (*Concile de Remiremont, Altercatio Phyllidis et Florae, Florance et Blancheflor, Hueline et Aiglantine*) the tale of the dispute over the relative merits of *clercs* or *chevaliers* is told with little or no authorial intervention, later versions (the Anglo-Norman *Blancheflour et Florence, Melior et Ydoine*) frame a virtually identical story with the first-person narrator's account of how he happened on the scene and witnessed the event.[14] The large corpus of love encoun-

---

11 Karl Bartsch, *Altfranzösische Romanzen und Pastourellen* (Leipzig, 1870).
12 *Essai de poétique médiévale* (Paris, 1972), p. 298 and passim.
13 Bartsch, *Altfranzösische Romanzen*, pp. 24–25.
14 The texts are conveniently collected in Charles Oulmont, *Les Débats du clerc et du chevalier dans la littérature poétique du moyen-âge* (Paris, 1911). Cf. Edmond Faral, *Recherches sur les sources latines des contes et romans courtois du moyen âge* (Paris, 1913), pp. 191–303; and Jung, *Etudes*, pp. 192–226.

ters thus provides a significant intertext for the *Rose*, as well as for the thirteenth-century vernacular allegories.[15]

A further important model for the first-person narrator is to be found in the stereotyped persona that had developed in the body of courtly romances dating back to the third quarter of the twelfth century.[16] The *Roman de la Rose* does, after all, situate itself in the romance tradition by virtue of its verse form (rhymed octosyllabic couplets), its length, and of course its very title. Perhaps as early as Chrétien de Troyes's composition of the *Chevalier de la Charrete* (about 1181) we witness the narrator of chivalric romance establishing parallels between his own allegiance and service to his Lady and the love affair within the romance.[17] The singer's presentation of a poem as *gage* to his mistress extends to the less personal, but ideologically more complex, creation of romance fiction. This thematic is elaborated in a variety of ways in other romances: Renaut de Beaujeu, in a well-known epilogue appended to his *Bel Inconnu* (about 1190), tells his lady that the romance ending he has conceived and written down can be altered if his lady so desires:[18]

> Quant vos plaira, dira avant,
> U il se taira ore a tant.
> Mais por un biau sanblant mostrer
> Vos feroit Guinglain retrover
> S'amie, que il a perdue,
> Qu'entre ses bras le tenroit nue.

(If it pleases you, he [Renaut de Beaujeu] will speak further; otherwise he will remain silent for now. But in return for your display of a favorable countenance he would, for your sake, have Guinglain recover his ladyfriend, whom he has lost, in such a way that he would hold her naked in his arms.)

---

15 Paul Zumthor, *Essai*, p. 371; and *Langue, texte, énigme* (Paris, 1975), p. 170.
16 Pierre Gallais, "Recherches sur la mentalité des romanciers français du moyen âge," *Cahiers de Civilisation Médiévale*, 7 (1964), 479–93, and 13 (1970), 333–47; Marie-Louise Ollier, "The Author in the Text: The Prologues of Chrétien de Troyes," *Yale French Studies* 51 (1974), 26–41; and Michel Zink, "Une Mutation de la conscience littéraire: Le langage romanesque à travers des exemples français du XIIe siècle," *Cahiers de Civilisation Médiévale*, 24 (1981), 3–27.
17 Jean Rychner, "Le Prologue du 'Chevalier de la charrette,'" *Vox Romanica*, 26 (1967), 1–23.
18 Ed. G. Perrie Williams, CFMA 38 (Paris, 1929), lines 6253–8. Cf. Alice M. Colby-Hall, "Frustration and Fulfillment: The Double Ending of the *Bel Inconnu*," *Yale French Studies* 67 (1984), 120–34.

The anonymous author of *Partonopeu de Blois* (before 1188), in a similar vein, expresses his incapacity to finish as a consequence of his sorrow:[19]

> E od cest aise le vos lais,
> Nïent por ce que n'en sache mais,
> Ains le fait cele que j'ain si
> Qu'en si grant paine sui por li
> Ne puis riens faire fors plorer . . .
> Tot ai perdu, mais neporquant
> Tant la redot et tant la crien
> Et tant a son lige me tien
> A son servise sens orguel,
> Que s'ele me gignot de l'uel
> Que je die l'ystoire avant,
> Faire m'estovra son commant.

(I leave him to you in such a pleasurable state, not at all because I do not know any more of the story but on account of the woman whom I love so much that I can do nothing but weep, so great is my suffering over her . . . I have lost everything, but nonetheless so much do I feel consternation and fear over her, so much do I count myself her vassal, humbly at her service, that if she were but to signal me with a wink of her eye to go on further with the story, I would be obliged to do her bidding.)

The author/narrator brings the tale to a satisfying conclusion, contrasts his own melancholy situation with the fictional lovers' happy ending while alluding to a possible extension, and then proceeds to outline later events which might be recounted. Five manuscripts of *Partonopeu* include a sizeable continuation, by the same author or another, presented as a response to his lady's wish for him to continue.[20] In a similar elaborate scheme, the anonymous narrator of *Joufroi de Poitiers* (ca. 1250) repeatedly breaks through his narrative with plaints directed towards his beloved.[21] The groundwork in romance fiction for the parallel between

---

19 Ed. Joseph Gildea, O.S.A. (Villanova, PA, 1967), lines 10607–24.
20 Cf. Anthime Fourrier, *Le Courant réaliste dans le roman courtois en France au moyen-âge*, I (Paris, 1960), 315–446.
21 John L. Grigsby, "The Narrator in *Partonopeu de Blois, Le Bel Inconnu*, and *Joufroi de Poitiers*," *Romance Philology*, 21 (1968), 536–43; and Roger Dragonetti, "Joufroi, Count of Poitiers and Lord of Cocaigne," *Yale French Studies* 67 (1984), 95–119.

knightly feats and clerkly service, between actions and words, loving and singing, had thus been carefully laid by the first quarter of the thirteenth century.

Whereas the narrative tradition of courtly literature, largely but only partially represented by the romance, provides the most convincing analogue for the commenting I-narrator, the literary type coming closest to the plaintive I that assumes the stance of direct address at the end of the *Roman de la Rose* is the singer of the lyric *chanson*. Rita Lejeune has recently compared these final lines to an *envoi* and Michel Zink, in a more global statement, has qualified the *Rose* as "le développement narratif, organisé autour d'une allégorie cohérente, du décor, des images, des lieux communs de la poésie lyrique."[22] Especially in view of the narrative distinction elaborated in our last chapter, it seems tempting to see in that division a basic generic crisscrossing between narrative and lyric, the romance and the *chanson*. It is this topic that will occupy our discussion for the balance of this chapter.

From the earliest discussions of lyric poetry in the North and South of France, the *chanson* has always been accorded a privileged position in the large corpus of courtly works.[23] The highly stylized codification of its rhetoric approaches the "courtly" love relationship from one specific point of view and at one precise temporal moment.[24] Expressed most simply, the vision of the *chanson* en-

---

22 Rita Lejeune, "A Propos de la structure du *Roman de la Rose* de Guillaume de Lorris," in *Etudes de langue et de littérature du moyen âge offertes à Félix Lecoy* (Paris, 1973), 315–48; and Zink, *Roman rose*, p. 80. Following the lead of Lejeune, L. T. Topsfield demonstrates the affinities between the *Rose* and a variety of troubadour motifs found in the *canso*, as well as the pertinence of the genre known as the *domnejaire* or *salut d'amour* (an address to the lady culminating in a plea for mercy), in his "The *Roman de la Rose* of Guillaume de Lorris and the Love Lyric of the Early Troubadours," *Reading Medieval Studies*, 1 (1977), 30–54.
23 Cf. Dante, *De Vulgari Eloquentia*, II, chapters 3 and 8. For modern studies, the reader is referred to the seminal essay by Robert Guiette, "D'une Poésie formelle en France au moyen âge," *Revue des Sciences Humaines* (April–June 1949), 61–8 (rpt. with additional notes in his *Questions de littérature*, Romanica Gandensia, 8 [Ghent, 1960], pp. 9–32), which influenced Roger Dragonetti's important study, *La Technique poétique des trouvères dans la chanson courtoise: Contribution à l'étude de la rhétorique courtoise*, Rijksuniversiteit te Gent, Werken uitgegeven door de Faculteit van de Letteren en Wijsbegeerte, 127 (Bruges, 1960); and Paul Zumthor's "De la circularité du chant (à propos des trouvères des XIIe et XIIIe siècles)," *Poétique*, 2 (1970), 129–40 (incorporated into his *Essai de poétique médiévale*).
24 I knowingly place the word "courtly" in quotation marks to reflect the probable intention of Gaston Paris when he unwittingly coined the phrase some one hundred years ago – namely, to refer to the variety of love relationships and fictional accounts conditioned by the sociocultural milieu of the medieval court.

compasses that timeless (both infinitely expansive and fundamentally atemporal) moment of suspense, of waiting, before the suppliant lover has achieved the favors of the lady — these latter constituting a goal that, it might be added, is sufficiently vague to allow for constant redefinition. Whatever the psychological, physiological, or cultural reasons might be for this obsessive centering around what becomes a privileged moment of expression and experience, the courtly *chanson* expands and elaborates this moment to the extent that an entire rhetoricized mythology is developed to sustain it. In terms of narrative description, the *chanson* displays two basic and virtually unchanging coordinates. First, the expression takes place in an "eternal" present tense, admitting of an occasional memory of the past, and hope (optative) for the future, but remaining essentially static. If there is a measurable progression (from one stanza to the next), it is purely asymptotic and involves no completely developed action. As Zumthor puts it, "La chanson cesse; mais elle n'a pas de fin."[25]

Second, this form of expression constitutes the direct address of a lyric I, the voice of the poet himself. More than simply the narrator of a story, the poet himself becomes the actor within the highly simplified plot structure. His voice is both vehicle for expression and the very act of that expression, *énoncé* and *énonciation*.[26] The terms of the argument oscillate continually between reflections of a general nature and expressions of personal feeling. It is not surprising that, divested of almost any possibility of a peripety or of a cast of individualized characters, the *chanson* should become the most highly codified (and, in less positive modern terms, repetitive) of all medieval literary forms. Furthermore, the requirement of anonymity, which passes from its initial *raison d'être* as a factor of social decorum to a poetic element in its own right,[27] accentuates the free-floating quality of these quintessential texts of desire.

---

[25] Zumthor, *Essai*, p. 217.
[26] Cf. Jean Dubois, "Enoncé et énonciation," *Langages*, 17 (1970), 100–10: "L'énonciation est présentée soit comme le surgissement du sujet dans l'énoncé, soit comme la relation que le locuteur entretient par le texte avec l'interlocuteur, ou comme l'attitude du sujet parlant à l'égard de son énoncé" (p. 100).
[27] This would seem to be confirmed by a much less frequent use of the *senhal*, a pseudonym for the poem's female addressee, in the trouvère *chansons* than in those of the troubadours. For instance, of the thirty-three *chansons* included in Alain Lerond's critical edition of the Châtelain de Coucy (Publications de la Faculté des Lettres et

THREE: LYRIC AND ROMANCE

Possibly one of the earliest of the troubadour poetic forms imitated in the North of France, the *chanson* was cultivated side by side with courtly romance in the late twelfth century. The manuscript tradition of the *chansonniers* tells us that the lyric corpus, in many cases transcribed with melodies, was grouped separately from works of narrative fiction composed in rhymed octosyllabic couplets. But the fact that both types of works, romance and *chanson*, could be attributed to the hand of one and the same author (for example, Chrétien de Troyes, Renaut de Beaujeu) suggests that a sense of personal expression was of considerably less importance than the adherence to precise formal rules. The narrator's voice in Chrétien's romances has nothing whatsoever in common with the lyric voice of the two *chansons* attributed to him, a fact that, along with many others, argues for the conventionality of the speaking voice even in early examples of medieval composition.[28] The importance of conventionality as a determinant of poetic content provides a simple and yet unimpeachable answer to the much overblown debate over courtly love. Most approaches to the question, assuming automatically that courtly love represents an ideological or moral stance towards eroticism, never consider that whatever doctrine might be implicit in the text does not dictate circumstantial plot developments (for instance, adultery) but rather attitudes and types of behavior. Courtly love applies to a wide range of literary fictions written within a specific cultural context and which tell of love and the social rules guiding it.[29] While the extremely varied corpus displays a uniform lack of moral judgment, no matter how antisocial, religiously unor-

---

Sciences Humaines de Rennes, 7 [Paris, 1964]), only one *envoi* contains a woman's name (XVII, line 46: Hersent) and even that is included in only two of the poem's ten manuscripts. Furthermore, the addressee is usually not to be identified with the poet's patroness (Dragonetti, *Technique*, pp. 321–4), a fact that bespeaks a conventional, gamelike atmosphere of poetic performance.

28 Leo Spitzer, "Note on the Poetic and Empirical 'I' in Medieval Authors," in *Romanische Literaturstudien: 1936–1956* (Tubingen, 1959), pp. 100–12.

29 Cf. Robert Guiette, "Observations sur l'âge courtois," in *Questions de littérature* (seconde série), Romanica Gandensia, 13 (Ghent, 1972), pp. 17–32; and Jean Frappier, "Vues sur les conceptions courtoises dans les littératures d'oc et d'oïl au XIIe siècle," *Cahiers de Civilisation médiévale*, IIe année, no. 2 (April–June, 1959), 135–56 (later reprinted in his *Amour courtois et table ronde* [Paris, 1973], pp. 1–31). For an especially lucid account of the various critical debates which have plagued the topic of courtly love, see Roger Boase, *The Origin and Meaning of Courtly Love: A Critical Study of Recent Scholarship* (Manchester, 1977).

thodox, or even destructive a given situation might prove to be, the reader soon detects certain behavioral norms, subsumed under the larger rubric of "courtliness," which place lovers alternately in a favorable or unsympathetic light. Such possible fictional outcomes as marriage, adultery, death, or unfulfilled longing are incidental to the more important question of how one is to act in given situations; it is not so much what the characters do, but how they do it, which merits our attention. When different works tell, somewhat inevitably, different stories, the authors are not arguing for one "type" of love, adulterous over marital, for instance, or mystical over carnal. Instead, such diversity represents an attempt to approach certain commonly felt social and personal conflicts through the language of fiction. Even the most rigorously doctrinal approach to the "discipline" of loving, exemplified by Andreas Capellanus's *De Arte Honeste Amandi,* can be shown to reenact, through its own recourse to fictional portrayals, a failed attempt to codify love.[30] It is not my point here to provide another assurance of the existence of courtly love, nor to account for the intentions behind all erotic literature written in the twelfth and thirteenth centuries, but rather to stress the importance of various horizons of expectation that had become fixed by the last quarter of the twelfth century and to insist upon the generic determination of specific fictional content independent of a didactic purpose. The *chanson* and romance depictions of love do not differ because the one bespeaks an ideal of marriage while the other promotes the virtues of unrequited love longing or adultery; they simply approach the question from different angles and with a quite distinct set of rhetorical and narrative rules. Thus, the sort of unrealized love longing endlessly depicted in the *chanson* is in its essence neither purer nor more mystical than passions that are eventually fulfilled in romance depictions: The chronological restriction and practical role of the *chanson,* as supplication, by definition limit its sphere of action but not the implied expectation of later events.

Jean Frappier's well-informed discussion of the contrast between the courtly ideal in the North of France and in the South takes an all but acknowledged turn toward a distinction between

---

30 Paule Demats, "D'*Amoenitas* à *Deduit:* André le Chapelain et Guillaume de Lorris," in *Mélanges de langue et de littérature du moyen âge et de la Renaissance offerts à Jean Frappier,* Publications Romanes et Françaises, 112 (Geneva, 1970), I, 217–33.

literary genres: lyric in *langue d'oc* and romance in *langue d'oïl*.[31] While his scheme possibly explains the absence of romance in the South, it is undermined by the concurrent popularity of lyric and romance in the North. Frappier extends the argument to a consideration of the social classes involved in the creation of such literary works: aristocrats in the South and clerks in the North. Later, while according the genre distinction a minor role, he will qualify the Northern *romanciers* as "less lyrical" and "more psychological" than their Southern counterparts.[32] Had he been a bit more circumspect about his own terminology, Frappier would have noted that his casual use of the term "lyrical" is itself an offshoot of genre characteristics and that the linguistic tools of analysis do not necessarily differ in the two cases: The adjective "lyrical" merely refers to a "psychological" portrayal pursued from an interior point of view. The terms of Frappier's argument fall into a neat set of dichotomies: *oc* versus *oïl*; *chanson* versus romance; noble versus clerk; lyrical versus psychological. While the tautological nature of his description of poetic effect suggests that he is saying much more about the aesthetics of courtly genres than about divergent ideologies, his inclusion of the artist's social affiliation merits further comment. Had he pursued the analogy, he would have come across the potential paradox of Northern clerkly poets cultivating the *chanson,* a genre developed within an aristocratic, knightly class. Indeed, how does this genre fit into the new context of the clerkly writer?

One part of the answer is certainly to be found in the popular debate tradition mentioned above, dealing with the relative merits of knights and clerks as lovers. While the lines of the debate can certainly be traced to actual social differences between the two classes,[33] the argument quickly takes on a more abstract significance. As far as specifics are concerned, knightly valor is overshadowed by their flightiness, their frequently penurious way of life, their indiscretion, and occasional physical shortcomings resulting from the hardships of constant battle; clerks, by contrast, are well-to-do, faithful, discrete, and spiritual. On a more abstract

---

31 Frappier, "Vues," p. 137 and passim.
32 Ibid., p. 144.
33 Giuseppe Tavani, "Il dibattito sul chierico e il cavaliere nella tradizione mediolatina e volgare," *Romanistisches Jahrbuch,* 15 (1964), 51–84.

level, the knight represents the principle of physical action or direct participation, while the clerk embodies verbal prowess, mediation, and spiritual development:[34]

>Factus est per clericum miles Cythereus.

(The amorous knight was created by the clerk.)

>... chevalier ne sevent rien
>Ne de deduit ne de franchise,
>Se il ne l'ont de clerc aprise.

(Knights know nothing of pleasure nor of forthrightness, unless they have learned it from a clerk.)

Thus, the clerk assumes the role in these debates of worldly instructor. Furthermore, his privileged domain of writing and documentary preservation entitles him to a place of pride as creator and perpetuator of social truths, the ironic limit being of course that in his capacity as writer of courtly fiction he is himself responsible for the creation and perpetuation of knightly virtues. According to one extreme formulation, the clerk is seen as indistinguishable from the very meaning of courtliness and love:[35]

>"Trestout le sen de nostre vie,
>Queintise e curtoisie,
>Valour e amur e druerie,
>C'est escrit de clergie."

("The entire meaning of our lives, elegance and courtliness, valor and love and gallantry, is contained in clerkly writings.")

Let us return to the social contradiction hinted at, but ultimately avoided, by Frappier.[36] It is tempting to ask whether the courtly *chanson* might not represent for the clerkly writer a prestigious yet unattainable genre to the practice of which he could only vainly aspire. The situation is complex, for, on the one hand, it appears that even when transposed to the context of the courts of *langue*

---

34 *Altercatio Phyllidis et Florae*, line 163, and *Florance et Blancheflor*, lines 290–2 (both quoted from Oulmont, *Débats*, pp. 114 and 136).
35 *Melior et Ydoine*, lines 331–4 (Oulmont, *Débats*, p. 194).
36 Basing himself rather loosely on John of Salisbury's belief that literary culture was important for temporal rulers, Frappier concludes that the clerk and knight end up being combined in a new ideal figure, "le gentilhomme cultivé et galant, héros du roman courtois" ("Vues," p. 149).

d'oïl the *chanson* was associated with aristocrats and/or knights.³⁷ On the other hand, the genre's careful rhetorical stylization and nonreferential qualities allow it to be sung, or assumed, by any poet. The characteristic anonymity of the lyric voice insures the imperative of secrecy while providing a kind of moral shield protecting the identity (and social affiliation) of the artist. A hint at potentially critical attitudes toward amorous clerks occurs for instance in the later love debates; while the clerk is still deemed the better lover, shame would result were the affair to become public knowledge:³⁸

> E si clerc eime apertement
> Dame ou pucele gent,
> Meintenaunt serra esclaundré
> E par le païs toute escrié,
> E ele hunny a touz jours.
>
> (And if a clerk loves a noble lady or maiden openly, he will immediately be greeted with public outrage and be thoroughly defamed throughout the country; *she* will forever be disgraced.)

In short, whereas a general perception of courtly generic horizons in the late twelfth and thirteenth centuries would have it that the *chanson* was an aristocratic, knightly literary creation, the terms of the clerk/knight debate poems (which all but deny any verbal or poetic capacity to the latter) would seem to bespeak a determined effort on the part of clerks to lay claim to all poetic activity.

There are several possible reasons for the appeal of the *chanson*. First the genre's predetermined stylistic parameters place a heavy burden on the poet's powers of expressivity and virtuosity, even more so than in narrated genres. The expression of one's own originality and poetic skill becomes itself a stereotyped amplification of the lover's plaint, in such a way that verbal resourcefulness, understood as a sign of sincerity, comes to be equated with the

---

37 Dragonetti, *Technique*, pp. 573–80. Not only do many *chansonniers* accord precedence to known, aristocratic *trouvères* (such as Thibaut de Champagne or Gace Brulé), but the illuminated portraits tend to depict them as knights while clerk/poets (such as Richard de Fournival or Adam de la Halle) are shown at their desk, with book or scroll. I am indebted to Sylvia Huot for sharing this information with me.

38 *Melior et Ydoine*, lines 221–5 (Oulmont, *Débats*, p. 190). This view is, needless to say, expressed by Ydoine, lover of the knight.

poet's worthiness in the domain of love.[39] Furthermore, the passage of the I to a position of centrality, as actor in his own love plot, marks the possibility of transcending the stance of mere description and becoming an active participant in affairs of the heart. The *chanson* thus would allow the clerkly poet to put into practice the superior position he had marked out for himself in the context of the love debate. A second characteristic of the *chanson* actually draws the written poem into the plot, insofar as it exercises a persuasive function in the love pursuit. The *chanson*, as a document – on occasion, nearly an epistle – aimed at the lady and the reception of which will help further the love service by its rhetorical powers, takes on a logical priority vis-à-vis the outcome of the lover's suit. If the poet's rhetorical virtuosity was necessary, as mentioned above, for the distinction of his poetic creation, it was doubly so in order to set him apart from his rival poetic suitors. The need to disparage rivals, along with that of insisting on one's own merits, becomes a central feature of the *chanson*.[40] This is an acute problem, for it provokes what might be called a "crisis of

---

39 Dragonetti, *Technique*, pp. 29–30 and 539 ff. Since the beautiful and potentially persuasive poetry of *other trouvères* must by definition be considered less sincere and worthy than one's own, a logical counter-topic is developed early on, according to which clever poetry is a sure sign of insincerity. The following stanza of the Châtelain de Coucy (ed. Lerond, VI, lines 17–24) provides a brilliant example:

> As fins amans proi qu'il dient le voir:
> Li queuz doit mieuz par droit d'amours joïr,
> Cil qui aime de cuer sanz decevoir,
> Si ne s'en set mie tres bien couvrir,
> Ou qui prie sanz cuer pour decevoir
> Et bien s'en set guarder par son savoir?
> Dites, amant, qui vaut mieuz par raison:
> Loiauz folie u sage trahison?

(I implore all true lovers [*fins amans*] to tell the truth: Which one has more right to delight in love, he who loves from the heart without deceit and who does not know very well at all how to cover it up, or he who entreats insincerely [*sanz cuer*: lit. "without heart"] with the intention of deceiving and who is smart enough to make sure he's not caught? Tell me, lovers, by all reason what is worth more, loyal extravagance or clever betrayal?)

40 The *losangier*, or slanderer, takes his place next to the lover and his lady as part of the eternal love triangle. Cf. Dragonetti, *Technique*, pp. 23–4 and 272–8; and Erich Köhler, "Observations historiques et sociologiques sur la poésie des troubadours," *Cahiers de Civilisation Médiévale* 7 (1964), 27–51 (esp. pp. 43–4). Köhler will speak of the *lauzengier* figure (in the troubadour tradition) as a personification of adverse forces facing the lover in the world, an undifferentiated actor more than an individual personage, and as an "indispensable third person" in the *chanson*. Even more interesting is the reciprocity inherent in the *lauzengier*'s status as rival: "chacun est toujours le *lauzengier* de quelqu'un" (Köhler, "Observations," p. 43).

sincerity;" when one is making use of a highly stylized, essentially stereotyped mode of expression, how does one prove one's own authenticity, separate oneself from the common mass, and, with that, establish one's rights to the lady's favors? If everyone insists that he is sincere and that the others are not, how does one manage to tell the difference? There is of course no simple answer, all the more so since, once an answer were found, it would be copied by all the others and cease to be an answer. The theoretical limits can indeed never be reached and a careful balance must therefore be maintained between new types of expression proving the poet's singularity (and authenticity), and the basic intelligibility that comes from a shared rhetoric. Along with the escalation in the value of poetic finesse, there follows a continual drawing back from any remnants of a descriptive stance and the search for progressively more adequate means of personal expression. The extreme limit of the lyric pursuit, then, is *not* to talk about oneself in relation to one's external actions, but rather as a function of one's own private, unique emotions.

This very special, highly literary sense of the lyric poet's persona probably has a lot to do with its rapid, and occasionally contrived, assimilation to the rhetorical self-representation of the romance narrator, as exemplified by the examples drawn from *Le Bel Inconnu* and *Partonopeu de Blois* quoted on pages 192–3. And while this mutation in poetic functions is thus observable as of the last decades of the twelfth century, the first quarter of the thirteenth century will witness an even more intense production of works playing on the relationship between lyric and romance. Most famous and influential of these was Jean Renart's *Roman de la Rose,* into which are inserted forty-six lyric pieces of varying genres – *chansons de toile,* dancing songs, as well as sixteen *chansons*. The lyrics function alternately as entertainment interludes punctuating the oral declamation of the romance, as lyric expressions of personal emotions, and very possibly as generators of the fiction itself, as is suggested in the prologue:[41]

> Cil qui mist cest conte en romans,
> ou il a fet noter biaus chans

[41] Jean Renart, *Le Roman de la Rose ou de Guillaume de Dole,* ed. Félix Lecoy, CFMA 91 (Paris, 1962), lines 1–5, 8–15, and 24–9.

> por ramenbrance des chançons,
> veut que ses pris et ses renons
> voist en Raincïen en Champaigne . . .
> car aussi com l'en met la graine
> es dras por avoir los et pris,
> einsi a il chans et sons mis
> en cestui *Romans de la Rose,*
> qui est une novele chose
> et s'est des autres si divers
> et brodez, par lieus, de biaus vers
> que vilains nel porroit savoir. . . .
> Il conte d'armes et d'amors
> et chante d'ambedeus ensamble,
> s'est avis a chascun et samble
> que cil qui a fet le romans
> qu'il trovast toz les moz des chans,
> si afierent a ceuls del conte.

(He who turned this tale into a romance [or possibly: translated this tale into French], wherein he has had beautiful melodies transcribed in remembrance of the songs, wishes his value and renown to spread to Reims, in Champagne . . . for just as they put cochineal dye in fabrics by way of garnering praise and prestige, so has he placed songs and melodies in this *Romance of the Rose,* which is a new item and is indeed so different from the others, embroidered as it is with beautiful poems, that a churl would never comprehend it. . . . It tells of arms and of love, and sings of both together; moreover, everyone has the impression that he who made the romance composed all the words to the songs, so much do they conform to those of the tale.)

The songs not only appeal to the audience's collective memory, but they also provide costly ornamentation, as the brilliant red dye ("graine") does to cloth. Perhaps more importantly, the songs function as an instrument of social exclusion; a *vilain* might conceivably understand the events of a romance, but he will not decipher the courtly code of the lyrics. Such literary and cultural elitism, implicit in our discussion of poetic virtuosity, recalls the important troubadour style known as the *trobar clus,* predicated upon hermeticism and exclusion as a way of increasing poetic value.⁴² While not widely cultivated among the *trouvères,* such tactics are not totally absent, as we can judge from the following lines by Gautier de Dargies, in which he tells us that facile poetry is not adequate to the gravity of love:⁴³

> La gens dient pour coi je ne faiz chanz
> Pluz legiers et meilleurs a retenir;
> Maiz ne sevent qu'Amours me fait sentir:
> Quar de celui dont l'amours est plus granz
> Convient mouvoir les chans fors et pesans;
> Qui mainz aime, de lui convient issir
> Les febles chanz que chascuns puet furnir . . .

(People ask me why I don't make songs that are lighter and easier to retain; but they don't know what it is that Love makes me feel, for the person whose love is the most intense must put out the most forceful and weighty songs. He who loves less is destined to issue those weak songs that anyone can compose . . .)

Similarly, Jean Renart extends the sense of poetic subtlety to the dynamic play between lyric and romance which he has created.

Finally, Jean Renart tells us, the romance story and lyrics cohere so well that the latter, while clearly not of the poet's invention, could appear to be so. The implication is that, more than simply a juxtaposition of discourses, the two poetic types mutually explicate each other. And given the fact that the songs were written before the romance, many belonging to the popular *trouvère* repertory, it is even possible to infer that the romance is in some way beholden to the songs for its very plot.⁴⁴ Gerbert de Montreuil's *Roman de la Violette* (ca. 1227–30) is only one of several works that copied this technique of song and narrative intermingling.⁴⁵ We are probably not mistaken in detecting within Jean Renart's prologue some sense of nostalgia toward earlier or different poetic traditions: Zumthor, in demonstrating the fundamentally lyric

---

42 Cf. Erich Köhler, "Zum 'Trobar Clus' der Trobadors," in *Trobadorlyrik und Höfischer Roman* (Berlin, 1962), pp. 133–52; and Ulrich Mölk, *Trobar Clus – Trobar Leu: Studien zur Dichtungstheorie der Trobadors* (Munich, 1968).
43 *Chansons et descorts de Gautier de Dargies,* ed. G. Huet, SATF (Paris, 1912), pp. 14–15.
44 Zink, *Roman rose,* pp. 17–44.
45 Ed. Douglas Labaree Buffum, SATF (Paris, 1928). Buffum provides an extensive list of Renart's other imitators, p. lxxxiii.

nature of one of the most popular thirteenth-century novellas, *La Chastelaine de Vergi* (which itself quotes a *chanson,* one written by the Châtelain de Coucy), has persuasively argued that such penetration of narrative by lyric represents a reaction against the contemporary historicizing trend in chivalric romance, most noticeable in the expansion and popularity of the prose cycles.[46] The reference to song, to the *chanson,* is for Zumthor a return to the dynamic source of courtly inspiration.

A parallel phenomenon relating lyric works with narrative fiction is to be found in the *vidas* and *razos,* pseudobiographical prose compositions created for the purpose of presenting the troubadour authors and explaining the context and meaning of their poems.[47] In most cases, they merely elaborate or restate information from within the poem and relate it to a purported real exis-

---

[46] "De la chanson au récit: La Châtelaine de Vergi," in Zumthor, *Langue,* pp. 219–36.

[47] J. Boutière and A.-H. Schutz, ed., *Biographies des troubadours* (Paris, 1964). While no precise equivalent to the *vidas* and *razos* is to be found in the *trouvère chansonniers,* a persistent biographical interest in the thirteenth century is evident from our discussion of authors in Chapter One. A work such as the *Jeu du Pèlerin,* appended to Adam de la Halle's *Jeu de Robin et Marion* as a prologue, was meant to inform spectators in a theatrical setting of Adam's fame. We might also mention a curious anonymous prologue included in one manuscript of Richard de Fournival's *Bestiaire d'Amours* (Pierpont Morgan Library 459), which attempts to identify the unnamed narrator of the allegorical bestiary and explain how he came to write it (ed. Cesare Segre [Milan, 1957], pp. lviii–lix):

> il aunt chose en la contree defrance que uns philosophes del ordre des iacobins qui ert apelez danz Helyes et ert uns des plus sages gentils hom dou monde. si sen amora dune dame qui ert apelee yselt. et ert une des plus beles gentils renomee de tote cele contree. et. amee lauoit longement de merueilleus amor. demorant en la religion souffrant por li poines innumerables. Mes por la tres grant amors que il uers li auoit si ne pot demorer por rienz. ainz issi hors de son ordre por achaison de li solement . . . et fist por li maintes chanconetes et lays et pastoreles et autres paroles . . . Et uoiant il que les soes amors ausi aloient et que il aroit sa paine perdue si pensa et mist tote sentente afaire cest liure que il fist en leu de son arriere ban ce est adire enleu de son derain secors aconquerre la soe amor . . .

> (It happened in the country of France that a philosopher of the Jacobin order who was named Lord Helyes and was one of the wisest gentlemen of the world fell in love with a lady named Yselt, who was one of the most beautiful noblewomen, renowned throughout the country. And he had loved her with astonishing devotion for a long time, remaining in his religious order and suffering innumerable torments for her sake. But because of the great love he felt for her nothing could make him remain, and so he left his order for her alone. . . . and he composed many little songs and lays and pastoreles and other works for her . . . And seeing that his love was going poorly and that he might find all his effort wasted he reflected and put all his skill into composing this book which he conceived as his *arrière-ban* ["call-to-arms"], which is to say as his last succor in conquering his love.)

THREE: LYRIC AND ROMANCE

tence. If narrative works incorporating lyric poetry such as *Guillaume de Dole* or *Le Roman de la Violette* can be seen to represent an antihistorical trend in the domain of courtly literature, the *vidas* and *razos* are perhaps best understood as examples of an opposite movement — a recuperation of anonymous, atemporal, free-floating texts within a biographical, historical continuity. While demonstrating an unquestionable reverence for the lyric texts, the authors of the *vidas* and *razos* clearly want to know the "whole" story and that story, so conceived, belongs to the real existence of poets. But however different their intentions might have been, all of these lyric/narrative pieces occupy a common ground insofar as they juxtapose, and thereby contrast, the unlocalizable speaking voice with a commentative historical discourse. At its most intense, we are aware of the contradiction between a fascination with the speaking voice and the push toward a historical comprehension of events.

This tension playing itself along the lines of genre stereotypes that were well-established by the first quarter of the thirteenth century was thus probably quite in vogue at the time the *Roman de la Rose* attributed to Guillaume de Lorris was being composed. The persona of the lyric poet and the kinds of manipulation to which the first-person speaking voice lent itself provide a convincing explanation, through a specific horizon of literary expectations, for the subtle intermingling, and ultimate conflation, of speaking voices in the *Rose*. An attentive courtly reader, not a *vilain* (to borrow Jean Renart's characterization of one facet of his own probable readership), would with little difficulty have recognized the profusion of rhetorical ornaments borrowed from the *chanson* register, which crop up in the poem's final lines: Avowal of fear (lines 3921–3, 4006–8, 4010, 4013–14); Sorrowful plaint (lines 3929–30, 3943–4, 4026–8); Memories (lines 3945–9, 3964, 4011–12); Prayer for assistance (lines 3489–92, 3975–86); Request for pardon (lines 3997–4009); *Addubitatio* (lines 4022–4); Repetition (lines 3764–5, 3771–4, 3878–9, 3977–86/93, 4016–17); Interrogation (lines 3931, 4015–18); Sententious style (lines 3932–42, 3953–7, 3987–8); Antithesis (lines 3960–2); Apostrophe (line 3975, and the string of imperatives which follows, lines 3977, 3978, 3983, 3986, 3991, 3993, and 4019); and

Exclamation (lines 3871, 3893, 3902).[48] But, somewhat paradoxically, this same literary fashion (or the inner impulses that it represents) explains why our *Roman de la Rose* would have been perceived as unfinished, or at least treated as such. The widespread desire to subsume anonymous lyric pieces under the aegis of some kind of historicizing fiction explains why the *Rose* could not be left alone, why it also had to be historicized and the story finished. The same move in the thirteenth century to preserve and comprehend the lyric voice is the one that had the effect of altering that voice in the history of the perception of that poem. Typical of an ambivalence as to the author's intention is the following statement by the scribe of an early *Rose* manuscript (B.N. fr. 378), who explains Guillaume's failure to write any more (and not his failure to finish or end the poem) as the result of either a lack of will or of capacity: "Ou pour ce quil ne vost ou pour ce quil ne pot" (Either because he did not wish to [write any more] or because he could not do so).[49] The space between not wishing and not being able is precisely the space that separates inscrutable lyric desires from historical rationalization. The hesitation between the two explanations for Guillaume's poem lasted but a fleeting moment for, as the *Rose* was acquiring popularity and being transmitted by scribes, the conventions of courtly literature were probably becoming less and less understood.[50] And once Jean de Meun wrote his authoritative conclusion, complete with its own biographical explanation for Guillaume de Lorris, the perspective by which the poem's lyric inspiration might have been detected was definitively altered.

Whereas the voice of the lyric poet and its persistence in thirteenth-century courtly literature provides the most convincing analogue for the complex narrative structure of the *Rose*, the elaborate use of personifications, its second most striking characteristic, remains to be evaluated. Specifically, while it is clear that the *Rose*

---

48 For a discussion of these various types of ornamentation, see Dragonetti, *Technique*, pp. 32–59 and 146–57.
49 Quoted *in extenso* in Chapter One, above, p. 78. The scribe actually says that Guillaume finished the romance ("fina . . . cest roumanz").
50 Cf. Nancy Freeman Regalado, *Poetic Patterns in Rutebeuf: A Study in Non-Courtly Poetic Modes of the Thirteenth Century* (New Haven, CT, 1970), pp. 1–14.

shares many features with the vernacular allegorical tradition, the question remains as to whether this mode is quite as incongruous with the lyric *chanson* genre as is normally supposed. It would be unwise to insist that this personification mode has its origin in the *chanson,* and that is not our intent here. Rather, the question to be asked is to what extent the preoccupations of the lyric poet might be susceptible to expression couched in terms of extended personification. It is to this question that we turn in the following section.

THE LYRIC *ROSE*

The use of personification in the *Roman de la Rose* is in some ways inseparable from its fictional context, the springtime opening. The initial nature description, or *Natureingang,* was a regular ornamental feature of the lyric *chanson* and acquired such popularity that its influence can be felt in nearly every courtly genre of the late twelfth and early thirteenth centuries.[51] It could with little difficulty be demonstrated that a large portion of the descriptive elements in the first 1,500 lines of the poem are drawn from the lyric repertoire of nature *topoi* – flowers, birds, fountains, trees, and so forth. But perhaps of more importance is the manner in which their poetic role shifts from a lyric to a romance context. Dragonetti has shown that the *trouvère* attitudes toward the role of nature description in the *chanson* are scarcely uniform; several of the more illustrious *trouvères* (Gace Brulé and Raoul de Soissons, for instance) express scorn for poets using nature description as facile ornamentation for its own sake.[52] The true and worthy poet subordinates such motifs to the central discussion of love and personal sentiment. This show of poetic elitism offers an adequate explanation not only for the gradual turning away from such nature motifs in the thirteenth-century *trouvère chansons,* but also for the simultaneous popularity of lyric genres incorporating them into a narrative framework, such as the *pastourelle* and the *reverdie.*[53] The best way to preserve the *chanson*'s "purity," which

---

51 Found in works as diverse as the *Prise d'Orange* and Chrétien de Troyes's *Conte du Graal,* the *Natureingang* has been analyzed by Dragonetti, *Technique,* pp. 169–93.
52 Ibid., pp. 186–93.
53 Judging from *Guillaume de Dole* and *Le Roman de la Violette,* "popularizing" lyrics such as the *chansons de toile,* the *pastourelle,* the *reverdie,* and various dancing refrains were enjoyed in the same milieux as the more stately *chanson d'amour.*

resides in a highly metaphorical, nonreferential mode, is to exclude those elements that could lead to the construction of a concrete world beyond the confines of the poet's creative faculties. As Dragonetti so eloquently puts it, "le trouvère loyal porte la saison dans son coeur."[54]

In principle, the limited space of the *chanson* should allow room for the introduction of only a few nature motifs and the latter, occupying stanzas rhythmically isolated from each other, should only be linked by an associative bond. It is the juxtaposition of stanzas, rarely with any provision for precise ordering (stanzas of a given *chanson* appearing in multiple manuscripts are frequently ordered in different ways), which allows the metaphorical suggestiveness of the image to float in the absence of temporal or causal succession. Very early in the tradition, the link between the poet's feelings and the objective surrounding had become so indelible, that the next step in poetic one-upmanship became the reversal of automatic rhetorical responses, such as the change of season from spring to winter or the denial of the flowers' and birds' capacity to inspire love. One out of many possible examples of this trend is the following opening to a poem by the Châtelain de Coucy:[55]

> L'an que rose ne fueille
> Ne flour ne puet paroir,
> Que n'oi chanter par brueille
> Oisel n'au main n'au soir,
> Adonc flourist mes cuers en un voloir
> De fine amour ki m'a en son pooir . . .

(In the season when neither rose nor leaf nor flower can appear, when I can hear no bird singing in the forest, at morning or at night, it is then that my heart burgeons with the desire for precious love [*fine amour*], which has me in its power . . .)

The literal, absent flower has been verbally transformed into the present, "flowering" ("flourist") action of the poet's heart; the

---

54 Dragonetti, *Technique*, p. 192.
55 Ed. Lerond (see note 27 above), Chanson IV, lines 1–6.

internal field of emotion has in some way usurped the primacy of natural functions. With that, any perception of natural elements fades away.

The change which these elements undergo when transposed into the romance format is dramatic and irreversible. The chronological requirements of the romance-I, the spatial localization imposed by the experiencing observer, the Lover, combine with the formally progressive, continuous octosyllabic rhymed couplet to recover the mimetic, descriptive function of objects which in the lyric tradition had become purely emblematic. The lyric *Natureingang* did not signify primarily a naturalistic description nor did it locate a precise setting; rather, it intimated the joy and fervent effusion of love, directly or *a contrario*, within the poet/lover. Once the images pass from the domain of metaphor to that of metonymy, from intuitive, haphazard association to a strictly physical, spatially determined one, they abruptly lose their attachment to emotional states. Moreover, whereas in the lyric it is clear that in most cases the images simply *exist* in the broadest metaphysical sense, in the *Roman de la Rose* they are being looked at, contextualized in all of their mortal contingency. The force of the lyric, moreover, is not in numbers but in technically persuasive recombinations. The contrary is true of romance, where, since no residue is left after the objects are described, more must be added. Paradigmatic, as opposed to metaphorical, association becomes the rule, and the more the better. The risk is, of course, that the reader will pass over the images as quickly as the Lover walks right by them. It is perhaps for this reason that Guillaume found it expedient to include no fewer than four successive Springtime "openings"; as an introduction to the dream account (lines 45–52); as the Lover's own experience with nature (lines 87–97); at the entry to the garden (lines 469–84); and at the Lover's departure from the *carole* (lines 1321–7).

What our Narrator *does* do in order to obviate the potential trivializing of his descriptive enumerations is to isolate and emblematize individual elements from within each series: There are several disparate floral images at the opening of the poem, a number of which happen to be roses; at a certain point one particular rose is singled out as the poem's titular and spatial center, leaving the previous occurrences of flowers but a faint memory.[56] Not only do several examples of innocuous bodies of water occur before the fountain of Narcissus is highlighted, but the variegated forest within the garden is reduced in the same episode to a single pine tree. Birds of various sorts appear incessantly in the first thousand lines, and it is perhaps in *this* series that the Poet/Narrator's own final self-insertion finds its emblematic justification.[57] Finally, the God of Love, who might have appeared simply another member of the courtly company in spite of his fantastic garb, is singled out as the Lover's master, even when the rest of the dancers in the *carole* have been totally forgotten. The progression through to the second half of the poem strikes the reader as a voluminous experimentation, a gradual sifting, out of which the few principal elements of the main narrative to follow were extracted.

As we suggested above, the move to eliminate nature descriptions from "serious" love poetry possibly explains the popularity of quasi-narrative lyrics devoted largely to encounters in nature as related by a first-person narrator. This casual walk in a natural setting (either in a dream or not) appears increasingly to have been associated with a fantastic or allegorical encounter, as can be judged not only from its assimilation to the vernacular allegory tradition, but also to the love debates and poems telling of the

---

56 Oiseuse wears a "chapel de roses tot frois" (553); Deduit also has a "chapel/de roses" (827–8) made for him by Leesce, who herself resembles a "rose novele" (838); Amor's cloak is tressed with flowers interspersed with "fueilles de roses" (894) and he is wearing, again, a "chapelet/de roses" (895–6). Given Guillaume's subtlety, and the association between roses and garb, one might suspect a foreshadowing effect in the first lines of the poem, where the earth ("terre") is personified with a multicolored "robe" and covered by dew, "rosee."

57 The play of birds in the first thousand lines of the poem is extremely complex and merits a study of its own. Aside from the Lover/Poet's association with birds, as we noted in Chapter Two, it might be mentioned that it is the song of the birds that first attracts the Lover to the garden (476–98). Guillaume goes on to describe the beauty of the birds' singing, comparing it coyly to that of the "seraines de mer" (670), which as archetypal figures of erotic temptresses, are iconographically related in the Middle Ages to Venus and, through the mirror motif, to Oiseuse. For a discussion of this question, with ample bibliography, see John B. Friedman, "L'Iconographie de Vénus et de son miroir à la fin du Moyen âge," in *L'Erotisme au Moyen âge*, ed. Bruno Roy (Montreal, 1977), pp. 51–82. By way of attenuating an interpretation *in malo*, Guillaume provides a fantastic etymology of the name "seraine," which is explained by the "saine" (pure) and "serie" (sweet) quality of their voice (671–2).

court of Cupid (probably based on Ovidian models). The intermingling of types was quite advanced by the second quarter of the thirteenth century, and so the question of probable influences on the *Rose* becomes a sticky, if not insoluble one. What we can affirm is that fantastic allegorical encounters of the sort so elaborately detailed in the *Tornoiement d'Antecrist* are not absent from the purely courtly tradition. Witness a popular *reverdie,* in the second stanza of which the wandering narrator meets the God of Love and becomes his squire:[58]

> Je m'en alai soz la flor
> por oir joie d'amor:
> tout belement par un prael
> le deu d'amors vi chevauchier.
> je m'en alai a son apel,
> de moi a fet son escuier.
> ses chevaus fu de deporz,
> sa sele de ses dangiers,
> ses escuz fu de cartiers,
> de besier et de sozrire,
> ses hauberz estoit
> d'acoler estroit,
> ses hiaumes de flors
> de pluseurs colors.
> sa lance est de cortoisie,
> espee de flor de glai,
> ses chauces de mignotie,
> esperons de bec de jai.

(I went off beneath the flowering branches, in order to hear sing of the joy of love. I saw the God of Love ride his horse most nobly through a meadow. I came running to his call and he made me his squire. His horse was of enjoyment, his saddle of domination, his shield was divided in quarters, made of kisses and smiles, his halberd was of tight hugs, his helmet of multicolored flowers. His lance is of courtliness, the sword of gladiolus flowers, his hose of coquetry, the spurs of crows' beaks.)

In what is clearly a fanciful list of disparate elements rather mechanically attached to the pieces of knightly attire, we can see the

---

58 Bartsch, *Altfranzösische Romanzen,* p. 27.

kinds of playful imagination which would lead to allegorical elaborations within an exclusively courtly, nondidactic mode.

And within the *chanson* tradition itself, the thirteenth century will witness a widespread introduction of personification allegory.[59] Thibaut de Champagne, one of the most famous of all the *trouvères* and very likely a contemporary of Guillaume de Lorris, made extensive use of allegorical personifications in his lyric poetry. The following *chanson,* which has frequently been compared to the *Roman de la Rose,* offers some important insights into the courtly use of personification:[60]

> Ausi conme unicorne sui
> Qui s'esbahist en regardant,
> Quant la pucele va mirant.
> Tant est liee de son ennui,
> Pasmee chiet en son giron;
> Lors l'ocit on en traïson.
> Et moi ont mort d'autel senblant
> Amors et ma dame, por voir:
> Mon cuer ont, n'en puis ravoir.
>
> Dame, quant je devant vous fui
> Et je vous vi premierement,
> Mes cuers aloit si tressaillant
> Qu'il vous remest, quant je m'en mui.
> Lors fu menez sanz raençon
> En la douce chartre en prison
> Dont li piler sont de talent
> Et li huis sont de biau veoir
> Et li anel de bon espoir.
>
> De la chartre a la clef Amors
> Et si i a mis trois portiers:
> Biau Senblant a non li premiers,
> Et Biautez cele en fet seignors;
> Dangier a mis a l'uis devant,
> Un ort, felon, vilain, puant,

---

59 Dragonetti, *Technique,* pp. 226–48.
60 *Les Chansons de Thibaut de Champagne, Roi de Navarre,* ed. A. Wallensköld, SATF (Paris, 1925), No. 34 (pp. 111–16). While Lecoy places the date of composition of Guillaume's *Rose* between 1225 and 1230, Poirion situates it later, from 1230 to 1245. According to Wallensköld, Thibaut de Champagne, a verifiable historical figure, lived from 1202 to 1253 and would have started his poetic career prior to 1234, the year of his succession to the throne of Navarre (Introduction, pp. xii–xxvii).

Qui mult est maus et pautoniers.
Cil troi sont et viste et hardi:
Mult ont tost un honme saisi.

Qui porroit sousfrir les tristors
Et les assauz de ces huissiers?
Onques Rollanz ne Oliviers
Ne vainquirent si granz estors;
Il vainquirent en conbatant,
Mès ceux vaint on humiliant.
Sousfrirs en est gonfanoniers;
En cest estor dont je vous di
N'a nul secors fors de merci.

Dame, je ne dout mes riens plus
que tant que faille a vous amer.
Tant ai apris a endurer
Que je sui vostres tout par us;
Et se il vous en pesoit bien,
Ne m'en puis je partir pour rien
Que je n'aie le remenbrer
Et que mes cuers ne soit adès
En la prison et de moi près.

Dame, quant je ne sai guiler,
Merciz seroit de seson mès
De soustenir si greveuz fès.

(I am just like the unicorn who is stunned in the midst of his glance, when he proceeds to gaze at the maiden. So joyous is he over his pain that, in a dead faint, he collapses into her lap. Then he is killed by betrayal. So have they wounded *me* in a similar fashion — Amor and my lady, to be sure. They have my heart and I cannot get it back.

My lady, when I was before you and saw you for the first time, my heart went on performing such flipflops that it ended up remaining with you when I went off. Then it was led off as a prisoner without possibility of bail, into the sweet prison which has pillars made of desire, doors of pleasurable vision and shackles of fair hope.

Amor has the key to the prison and has placed three gatekeepers there: The first is named Favorable Glance, and [s]he [Amor] has made Beauty lord of the castle; Resistance was placed at the front door — a foul, villainous, churlish and putrid fellow who is quite evil and mean. These three are as agile as they are bold. Very quickly have they taken hold of a man.

Who could stand the sorrows and assaults inflicted by these guards? Never did Roland or Olivier win such a great battle; *they* won through fighting but these characters are conquered through the exercise of humility. Steadfastness is our standard-bearer. In this battle I am telling you about, there is no aid except grace [*merci*].

My lady, I no longer fear anything so much as the possibility that I might cease loving you. So much have I learned to endure that I am in every way yours. And even if it really grieved you, I could not for anything separate myself from you without retaining my memory and without my heart being at once in prison and close to me.

My lady, since I know nothing of trickery, your grace [*merciz*] would at present be appropriate, for my having borne such a heavy burden.)

A comparison of this poem with the allegory of Guillaume de Lorris's *Rose* yields a number of interesting observations as to the personification of erotic emotions. The first stanza takes as its point of departure the well-known bestiary example of the unicorn, who is caught and killed as a result of gazing at the *pucele*, object of fascination. The steps of the unicorn's increasing involvement are the glance ("regardant"), the fascinated gaze ("mirant"), the joy-in-suffering ("liee de son ennui"), fainting or lack of consciousness ("pasmee chiet"), and death ("l'ocit on"). The plight of the unicorn, as recounted in bestiary lore, provided a direct parallel to the lover's situation.[61] Actually, the unicorn is at once a metaphor and a substitute for the human lover, inasmuch as both fall for the same object, the human female (Lady).

Thibaut makes the comparison explicit when he says that he also has been wounded ("mort") by Amor and his Lady. It should be noted that while *morir* does in this context, and tense, refer to a

---

61 Wallensköld, *Chansons*, pp. 115–16. See also *Li Bestiaires d'Amours di Maistre Richart de Fornival et Li Response du Bestiaire*, ed. Cesare Segre (Milan, 1957), pp. 42–6. Cf. Florence McCulloch, *Mediaeval Latin and French Bestiaries*, University of North Carolina Studies in the Romance Languages and Literatures, 33 (Chapel Hill, 1960), pp. 179–83; McCulloch states that the unicorn was "doubtless the best known of fabulous animals" (p. 179).

deep wound,[62] the full force of death is indicated through the close proximity of "ocit" (line 6). The unicorn's story, presumably an exemplum of common currency, is expressed in even metrical units, each line comprising a complete, self-enclosed clause. With the introduction of the poet, the rhythm changes; the next sentence extends over two lines (7–8), isolating through inversion the harmful agents ("Amors et ma dame" [8]) from the *moi* (7), here placed in a position of emphasis. The two sets of agents are juxtaposed in the final line, by means of the paratactic inclusion of two separate clauses: "Mon cuer ont, n'en puis ravoir" (9). The *cuer*, object of attention for both sides, will constitute the poetic battlefield in the following stanzas.

The second stanza, addressed to the Lady ("Dame . . ." [10]), institutes a swift succession of preterites with one imperfect ("fui," "vi," "aloit," "remest," "mui," "fu"), describing the poet's past *innamoramento* and the allegorical fate of the heart. The abrupt switch from present (first stanza) to past (second and following) is analogous to Guillaume's use of the preterite at the end of his poem in order to describe events that have already been recounted (compare Chapter Two); the past events are clearly not remote but rather moments leading up to the present irresolution ("n'en *puis* point ravoir" [9]). The development of the well-known "separable heart" *topos* is here pursued.[63] After Ovidian models, the heart, as seat of the lover's emotions, is conceived of as the locus of all metaphorical descriptions of falling in love. Either the heart is wounded (by Amor or the lady) and must be cured, or the heart is separated from the body in order to attend the object of its affections. Guillaume prefers the image of the heart being wounded and locked up (lines 1688–2008). The motif of the separable heart, particularly fruitful in view of the proximity in Old French of the key words *cuer* (heart) and *cor* (body), was presumably made famous by its use in the *Tristan* of Thomas. Contrary to most lyric figurations of the separable heart (where, according to Dragonetti, the heart is more or less a *gage* granted by the lover to his lady in hope for some recompense), in Thibaut's poem the poet is removed from consideration ("je m'en mui" [13]) in order to con-

---

[62] Wallensköld, *Chansons*, p. 116.
[63] Cf. Jung, *Etudes*, pp. 183–5; and Dragonetti, *Technique*, pp. 85–113.

centrate on the allegorical development and personification of the imprisoned heart itself ("il vous remest. . . . Lors fu menez" [13–14]). Such a move will allow for greater allegorical coherence than, for instance, the poet's direct interaction with personifications in the *Rose*.

The static allegory of the prison is elaborated by means of an enumeration of the attributes which correspond to each part of the prison (16–18). These attributes are all functions of the poet's own experience: *talent, biau veoir,* and *bon espoir*. The prison is founded on the poet's desire ("li piler sont de talent"), which is aroused by the sight of the Lady ("li huis sont de biau veoir"); the Lover's hope for attainment only keeps him more firmly entrapped ("li anel [sont] de bon espoir"). Thibaut attenuates the sense of an unjust victimization (which is so essential to Guillaume's account) by acknowledging that his own qualities form the material of the heart's prison.

From this static allegory, Thibaut turns to an allegory of personages in the third stanza – the enumeration of the prison guardians. It is at this point that the strongest resemblance with the *Roman de la Rose* occurs. Not only has Amor locked the prison with his key (compare the complicity between Amor and the lady in the first stanza), but the three guardians (Biau Senblant, Biauté, and Dangier) are constantly on the lookout to trap men ("Mult ont tost un honme saisi" [27]). These three are, of course, attributes of the Lady, and occupy their stations *outside* of the prison, which is itself a construct of the lover/poet. In contradistinction to Guillaume's allegory, here the prison is assumed under the aegis of Amor; such a prison is thus considered the typical fate of the lover, and not the circumstantial result of an antithetical force (for example, Jalousie). Moreover, of the Lady's attributes, two are passive virtues (Biau Senblant and Biauté) related to physical appearance, and the third is the ultimate obstacle, Dangier. As such, it is understood that the Lady's refusal is "built into" the system, and that Bel Acueil, as a positive force working to unite the two, has no place in Amor's scheme.

A further contrast results from the fact of the rose's imprisonment in Guillaume's allegory, with the Lover remaining on the outside; for Thibaut, the lover's plight results from an assault on the part of Amor, the Lady, and her allegorical attributes. The lover is clearly on the defensive, and the essential integrity of his heart is contrasted with the fragmented portrayal of the female qualities. The lover's battle, as compared with the battle fought by Roland and Olivier, is won, paradoxically, by waiting ("Sousfrirs" [34]) and not by fighting ("conbatant" [32]). The answer to this paradox can be found in a closer look at the misleading question posed by Thibaut.

Thibaut does not really ask how to win this battle, but how to withstand the assault ("sousfrir . . . les assauz" [28–9]). Logically, the result of winning or losing the battle would be, respectively, either freeing oneself of the Lady's influence or forever remaining in her thrall. The first choice is obviously out of the question, inasmuch as the basis of the *trouvère*'s longing is founded in his desire for the lady. And yet the specious comparison with the battle of Roland is suggested, a battle which, in the poet's case, cannot be won without a rejection of the very premises of the poem. What results is a feint revealing the inherent contradiction of the poet's condition in terms of the battle metaphor: He desires, and yet by prior definition, cannot attain his desire. If he "wins," he "loses" and, in a way, if he "loses," he also "loses." In fact, the poet tells us that the only help ("secors" [36]) possible is *merci* (36), which, as he indicates in the *envoi*, is to be the reward for his ability to "soustenir si greveus fès" (48). In fact, the outcome of the battle "plot," conceived of in terms of a winner and a loser, is clearly incompatible with the poem's courtly underpinnings.

The final full stanza momentarily departs from the prison allegory in order to return to the poet's plaint in his own voice. His major fear is to be out of love (allegorically, for his heart to escape from the prison, no longer to be held). His present position of security is such that his whole being belongs to the Lady ("je sui vostres" [40]), as a result of what he has undergone ("Tant ai apris a endurer" [39]). The poet has apparently gone through a period of transition only to settle down in his state of mental serfdom. A return to the previously developed allegory assures this when we see that paralleled to the poet and his memory are his heart and the prison:

> Ne m'en puis je partir pour rien
> Que *je* n'aie le *remenbrer*

> Et que *mes cuers* ne soit adès
> *En la prison* et de moi près. (42–5)

A literal translation for these lines is as follows: "I cannot take my leave from there (*en:* undoubtedly referring to the Lady's sphere of influence) for anything, without retaining my memory and without my heart being at once in the prison and by my side." These lines are thus based on a double movement: that of the lover *spiritually* away from his beloved, and that of the heart *physically* between the prison and the lover's body. An additional difficulty is introduced by an important variant reading: Some manuscripts have, instead of "de moi près," "de vos près." Insofar as the separable heart's prison is roughly equivalent to a proximity with the lady ("il [le cuer] vous remest" [13]), the second choice makes the most immediate sense, "en la prison" and "de vos près" occupying the same spatial locus. However, the *lectio difficilior*, "de moi près" (logically, how can the heart be both away from the body in its prison *and* with the poet?), gives a more nuanced and satisfying reading in that it forces together the two contradictory realms of which a choice cannot in fact be made (just as the battle cannot be won). If the heart leaves the woman in order to reunite with the poet, his memory ("remembrer") will without delay return the heart to its prison, and then, simultaneously or subsequently, back to its original place. The perennially circular, and not unidirectional, movement transforms the initial martial image into a visual paradox representing the aporia of the desiring subject. This development of the heart image is fulfilled by the poet's narrative stance in his own poem, returning in this fifth (and last) stanza to the initial personal poetic voice that has been largely suspended for the sake of the allegorical, more impersonal, and manifestly deceptive tale.

On a greatly reduced scale, Thibaut's poem presents a precise parallel to the movement of the *Roman de la Rose:* an extended allegorical/narrative development translating the poet's amorous struggle and, ultimately, ending up with the poet's own personal voice. Unlike Guillaume, however, Thibaut reminds us at every point that the logic implied by the narrative materials (escape from prison) is undermined by the inherent resistance to such a conclusion: implicitly, the fact that the prison is a construct whose foundation is the poet's own desire, and whose principal guardian under the aegis of the God of Love is Dangier, refusal or resistance; explicitly, by his comments on what type of war is being waged. The irreality of the situation is accentuated by two important factors: First, the separation and personification of the poet's heart, thus acting as an agent apart, represents narratively the undesired and yet absolutely essential abjection of the lover. Second, the attainment of a goal, the reaching of the lady, is conceptually impossible, insofar as there is no place in the allegorical "geography" for the woman's body, which dissolves before the fragmentation of the allegorical figures.

Now, Dragonetti tells us that personification allegories such as this one have an ornamental use, contain no enigma (as would be required in an exegetical framework), and are purely ends in themselves.[64] I would suggest on the contrary that the growing exploitation of personification allegory in the *chanson* reflects an increasingly sophisticated fascination with poetic forms of expression and their adequacy to the expression of internal emotional states. Indeed, the personal expression of emotions through an abstract vocabulary turns perhaps inevitably to personification when it is syntactically combined with verbs of action.[65] To name an abstract quality, to nominalize it, is already to grant it an

---

64 Dragonetti, *Technique*, pp. 247–48.
65 Cf. Richard Glasser, "Abstractum agens und Allegorie im älteren Französisch," *Zeitschrift für Romanische Philologie*, 69 (1953), 43–122; and Siegfried Heinimann, *Das Abstraktum in der Französischen Literatursprache des Mittelalters*, Romanica Helvetica, 73 (Bern, 1963), esp. pp. 101–17. Both concur that personified qualities, the *abstractum agens*, are not the same as personification allegory but that the line between the two is difficult, if not impossible, to draw. Out of a multitude of studies on allegory and personification, I have found most useful for the following discussion, Morton W. Bloomfield, "A Grammatical Approach to Personification Allegory," *Modern Philology*, 60 (1963), 161–71; and Jauss, "Transformation." It is important to keep in mind that personification is first and foremost a rhetorical mode of expression, related simultaneously to *prosopopeia*, metaphor, synechdoche, and metonymy – and as such is quite distinct from the rhetorical figure called *allegoria* or to the hermeneutic exercise known as figural interpretation. In the following pages the word "allegory" will be used in its widest and most general acceptation, that is, as a discourse that says something and means something else (*alieniloquium*) – a vision of linguistic expression that encompasses simultaneously the speaker and the listener, the creator of speech and its interpreter. On this last point, see the lucid discussion of Jean Pépin, *Dante et la tradition de l'allégorie* (Montreal/Paris, 1970), esp. pp. 11–31. For a study of the romance tradition of personified psychological expression, see Charles Muscatine, "The Emergence of Psychological Allegory in Old French Romance," *PMLA*, 68 (1953), 1160–82.

existence as some-thing separate, apart. From there to what one calls personification is merely a development of that quality's thingness into a mode of action metaphorically borrowed from some other experience or circumstance. Perhaps an example of one possible transformation might here prove helpful. At the most basic level, before nominalization, one might say,

> An idle man will fall in love.

Having nominalized the quality — once "idle" becomes "idleness" — the point of view as well as the action in the sentence necessarily change:

> Idleness makes a man fall in love.

Even though most readers would not consider this a personification at all, the agency inherent in the verb "make," accompanied by a shift in responsibility (from interior to exterior causality) suggests a radical difference. From there, to embroider metaphorically is a simple task:

> Idleness leads to love.
> Idleness opens the door to love.

At this point, allegory is officially created and we are confronted with the basic sentence whose expansion forms the first real episode in the *Rose,* the Lover's encounter with Oiseuse. If the creation of allegorical expression involves the conjunction of two elements, an abstract quality and a narrative situation to which it is metaphorically adjusted, then there are clearly two paths of development: An elaboration of the narrative action(s) being accomplished; and an extended description of the personification (physical features, clothing, attributes, and so forth). Inasmuch as a concentration on the former will tend to obscure the allegorical "meaning," while a concentration on the latter will accentuate it (through a description which evokes in more or less direct physical terms the quality), some sort of equilibrium between the two fields needs to be found for the allegory to maintain its dual purpose of telling a story and conveying a general meaning.

The possibility of describing the quality, of finding physical human (or nonhuman) traits which will in some way suggest the quality, varies of course according to the nature of that quality, the degree of its abstraction. "Idleness" provides an interesting example, for it is simultaneously a state resulting from a matter of circumstances (nothing to do) *and* it implies as well a disposition to do nothing when such situations arise, similar in this respect to the concept of "laziness." Guillaume's solution in presenting Oiseuse is to describe a stereotypical courtly lady who *is* idle, who spends all her time grooming herself and looking into her portable mirror. Guillaume's lengthy description of her, therefore, centers upon a physical portrait that, except for the fact that extreme beauty implies the free time in which to attain that state, is typical of romance treatments; the portrait is then combined with a list of the character's day-to-day actions, all an empirical result of idle behavior.[66]

This initial episode of Guillaume's *Rose* is a pleasant *tour d'esprit* whose intent is fairly clear, but it does bring into focus certain of the inherent allegorical shortcomings that only appear, perhaps, in a lengthy treatment. Now, with respect to the initial declarative sentence, "An idle man will fall in love," it is clear that the man himself is idle. In the above "personified" episode, the lady Oiseuse is, strictly speaking, idle, and even though she serves as the Lover's gatekeeper, it is hard to see how he would thereby be infected with the quality of idleness; moreover, except for the fact that he has the time to wander about (which indeed he had even before reaching the garden) he never seems to be, or at least become, idle. One could possibly imagine the personifications initially as miniature demons

[66] Several recent critics have attempted to apply techniques of scriptural exegesis to the character of Oiseuse, finding in her a figure of the contemplative life or more specifically *in malo* (via the iconographic tradition of the handheld mirror) as a representation of the vice Luxuria. For these various interpretations, see especially Erich Köhler, "Lea, Matelda and Oiseuse," *Zeitschrift für Romanische Philologie*, 78 (1962), 464–9; Herbert Kolb, "Oiseuse, die Dame mit dem Spiegel," *Germanisch-romanische Monatsschrift*, NF 15 (1965), 139–49; John V. Fleming, *The Roman de la Rose: A Study in Allegory and Iconography* (Princeton, 1969), pp. 73–81; and John B. Friedman, "Iconographie." For a fuller bibliography, cf. Shigemi Sasaki, "Sur le personnage d'Oiseuse," *Etudes de Langue et de Littérature Françaises*, 32 (March 1978), 1–24 (esp. n. 7, pp. 6–7). Need we mention that these various figural interpretations seek to apply a moral or religious context that is scarcely justified in Guillaume's text taken as a whole? As is clear from the "seraine" example (note 57, above), Guillaume is deliberately rejecting such a reading. Moreover, these moral interpretations foresake the basic value of the personification, which is at bottom the expansion of a figure of speech. In the sensible words of Sasaki, p. 23, "Le loisir est une valeur et une vertu que Guillaume intègre à bon escient dans l'éthique courtoise traditionnelle."

or spirits inside the head of an individual that "determine" his actions.[67] To portray them as human figures *outside* of someone's head, and in fact standing next to the person they are supposed to affect, is a basic move of doubling that does not in fact go further than an "inner" description in explaining allegorical causality. On the contrary, by juxtaposing a man supposedly idle, or becoming idle, with a woman who *is* idle (and, in addition, idleness itself) is merely to suggest affinities by way of material contingency, thus attenuating the causality otherwise inherent in the notion of psychological transformations. If it is unclear how idleness will affect the man, since the man will be(come) idle independently of this outside correlative, the action so allegorized becomes merely emblematic within its own context, a reduplication of a transformation that has already taken place (or will take place) on another psychic "battlefield." The problem here (which is avoided by many personification allegories) is, of course, that a personification and a total human being exist on two different planes of conceptualization, the one being in some sense a subspecies of the other, and to place them side-by-side, to cause them to interact, is to undermine the conceptual criteria underlying both of them. The resulting tension – between "human" (that is, inner, inscrutable, intangible, and ultimately, inexpressible) and allegorical motivation – will assume a central position in the later developments of the *Rose* allegory.

Guillaume's description of the portraits outside the garden wall, the reader's first encounter with the mode of personification, provides an extreme limit of the breadth of possibilities outlined above: If the two major directions in which one can expand an initial allegorical "sentence" are, on the one hand, the narrative elaboration of the metaphorized action and, on the other, exterior physical description, it results that the expressive results are also double. Inasmuch as the narrative development dwells on the initial situation borrowed from another domain for the purpose of the metaphor (in the above example, "opening the door"), it tends to detract from a concentration on the abstract quality itself. Or, rather, an effort must be made in order to retranslate the actions as metaphor. In the static description, however, the reader will find

---

[67] On various aspects of allegorical agency, cf. Angus Fletcher, *Allegory: The Theory of A Symbolic Mode* (Ithaca, NY, 1964), esp. pp. 25–69.

direct insights concerning the specific quality, elaborated through its physical, exterior effects or the comportment of someone who has that quality. It is undoubtedly for this reason that personification allegories whose thrust is primarily doctrinal lean heavily on static elements (physical description, enumeration, allegorized naturalistic settings, debates [where direct speech conveying doctrine comes directly out of the characters' mouths]). As can be seen through Guillaume's portraits of the courtly vices, the description will depend largely upon the nature of that quality being treated. Vieillesse (Old Age) and Pauvreté (Poverty) seem to pose the fewest descriptive problems, since, already being exterior, physical states, their very description coincides precisely with the requirements of personification. Vieillesse *is* an old woman, and Pauvreté *is* a poor, abject woman. On another level of understanding are the bulk of the remaining personifications, those which are decidedly inner, immaterial qualities, such as Haine (Hatred) or Envie (Envy); Guillaume's solution is to portray them as people who possess these qualities and who act upon them (although occasional eccentric physical attributes are added to fortify the correspondence between interior and exterior).[68] Another type of vice, unique in the series of wall paintings, is Papelardie, who seems to

---

68 Consider, for instance, the following physical description of Envie:

> ele ne regardast neant
> for en travers, em borneant;
> et s'avoit trop mauvés usage,
> car el ne peüst el visage
> regarder rien de plain em plaing,
> ainz clooit un oil en desdaing,
> qu'ele fondoit d'ire et ardoit
> quant aucun qu'ele regardoit
> estoit ou preuz ou biaus ou genz
> ou amez ou loez de genz.   (281–90)

(She looked at everything obliquely, and she had this bad habit because she could not look anything straight in the face, but closed one eye in disdain; for she burned and melted with rage when anyone at whom she looked was either wise, fair, or noble, or was loved or praised by men. [p. 34])

The portrait serves two distinct purposes: First, it presents a general ugliness that would be appropriate to any of the vices (as beauty will be generally applicable to the *carole* dancers); second, her one-eyed physiognomy is a physical result of some imaged statement such as the following: "She could not stand to *see* anyone be happy." The idea of "seeing" in this statement is already a metaphor that is further extended or concretized by portraying Envie as someone whose deformity makes it that she is incapable of looking directly at such people.

represent simultaneously an inner quality (which could be termed "Religious Hypocrisy"), possibly a manner of behavior (in the words of C. S. Lewis, the hypocritical attitude of "ladies who supported their unkindness with moral or religious pretensions"), and a specific social group (nuns).[69] While the relative weight to lend to these three possibilities is uncertain, Guillaume's descriptive task is made simple as a result of the accoutrements belonging to the latter, easily identifiable, religious social group.

An interesting fact to keep in mind is that these vices are not personifications in the fullest sense of the word; they are manifestly painted, immobile images resulting from artifice, a fact which is repeated on several occasions:

> si vi un vergier grant et lé,
> tot clos de haut mur bataillié,
> portret dehors et entaillié
> a maintes riches escritures.
> Les ymages et les pointures
> dou mur volentiers remirai;
> si vos conterai et dirai
> de ces ymages la semblance. . . . (130-7)

(I saw a large and roomy garden, entirely enclosed by a high crenelated wall, sculptured outside and laid out with many fine inscriptions. I willingly admired the images and paintings, and I shall recount to you and tell you the appearance of these images. [p. 32])

> Mout bien sot poindre et portroire
> cil qui sot tele image feire. . . . (163-4)

(He who could produce [such] an image . . . knew how to paint and portray. [p. 33])

> Ces ymages . . .
> furent en or et en azur
> de totes pars pointes ou mur. (461-4)

(the images . . . were done in gold and azure, painted all along the wall. [p. 37])

Works of art, man-made abstractions, the images are not even exclusively pictorial: The "escritures" mentioned in line 133 are clarified in one of the subsequent descriptions as the name of each

---

69 C. S. Lewis, *The Allegory of Love* (Oxford, 1936), p. 127.

quality, which is appended to the portrait: "son non desus sa teste lui,/apelee estoit Felonie" (154–5) ("I read her name, Felony, beneath her head" [p. 33]). It is not clear, in fact, whether the characters are identifiable visually or simply because their name is there: Indeed, this same "Felonie," whose name had to be read in order for the quality to be identified, is not described. Aside from the inner reflection of our own poet's verbal artistic endeavor, the self-conscious use of rhetorical ecphrasis, there is a further complication brought in by the juxtaposition of word and image, name and quality. The uncertain interaction between the two, the hazy question of identification (via word or image?) — not without recalling the symbiotic relationship between word and illumination in medieval manuscripts, thanks to which the visual aspect of Guillaume's verbal portraits will later be restored — points to the larger problem of naming and its adequacy to convey feelings that are neither animate nor visible. At this moment, however, the problem is scarcely alluded to, since the Lover's reading of the portraits will never actively interfere with his thoughts or actions.

If the movement from outside to inside the garden marks a psychological and experiential rite of passage, it also signals a transformation in the allegorical figurative mode.[70] The characters in the *carole* are indeed virtues corresponding to the wall portraits, but, as with the first of the series, Oiseuse, they *are* real people who must physically confront the psychologically "complete" Lover. As such, when they are taken out of context, described physically (apart or in relation to other personifications) and according to their behavior, they cohere psychologically, adequately representing their respective qualities (Richece, Largesce, Franchise, and so forth). Through the elaborate figurative description of these characters' garments (where the word "portrete" discretely recalls the wall paintings), the painted bows of Amor, and the statement that Deduit, who had commissioned the portraits to be painted (595–6), himself "resembloit une pointure" (810) ("he looked like a painting" [p. 41]), the reader feels a sense of nostalgia for the figurative and intuitive simplicity of the initial static

---

[70] For the notion of multiplied barriers as a structural and conceptual pattern, developed in a slightly different sense, see the highly suggestive article by Paul Verhuyck, "Guillaume de Lorris *ou* la multiplication des cadres," *Neophilologus*, vol. LVIII, no. 3 (July 1974), 283–93.

personifications. The glance backwards is indeed justified, for, when placed into the mode of action, realized as the *carole* into which the Lover is invited (by Cortoisie, no less), their respective allegorical qualities (which inhere solely in their names) begin to fade away. One could easily take this scene for any of a number of joyous court scenes that wandering knights happen upon in medieval chivalric romances. If there remains an allegorical signification to the scene (that is, one that bypasses the physical setting in order to express something about mental states), it occurs at the global level of the entire event, and no longer within individual characters. To borrow the name of the garden's owner, it is an atmosphere of Deduit (Pleasurable Delight) propitious to the pursuit of amorous adventures. Here, whether or not the crowds of beautiful men and ladies are themselves personifications is of little relevance, a fact that is underscored by the introduction of numerous anonymous characters.[71] It becomes evident subsequently, once the *carole* is ended, that the personifications carry on sexually in a manner befitting any mortal; by this point, they have totally relinquished their initial signification:

> Les queroles ja remenoient,
> car tuit li plusor s'en aloient
> o lor amies ombroier
> soz ces arbres por donoier.
> Dex! com menoient bone vie!
> Fox est qui n'a de tel envie!
> Qui autel vie avoir porroit,

---

[71] Richece (1108), Largesce (1174), Franchise (1222), Cortoisie (1243), and Joinece (1266) all have anonymous boyfriends, two of whom are knights. Jung curiously insists (*Etudes*, p. 297) that the *carole* dancers do not correspond to the wall portraits, since there are more than ten of the former; if one counts only the courtly virtues which are named, however, one comes up with a list of precisely ten, as follows:

Haine	Oiseuse
Felonie	Deduit
Vilanie	Leesce
Covoitise	Cortoisie
Avarice	Amor (with Douz Regart)
Envie	Biauté
Tristece	Richece
Vielleice	Largesce
Papelardie	Franchise
Povreté	Joinece

>   de meillor bien se soufreroit,
>   qu'il n'est nus graindres paradis
>   d'avoir amie a son devis.   (1289–98)
>
> (Already they were stopping the carols, for most of them were going off with their sweethearts to shelter under the shade of the trees in order to make love. God! What a good life they lead! He who does not long for such a life is a fool. He who could have such a life might dispense with a greater good, since there is no greater paradise than to have one's beloved at one's desire. [p. 48])

In this scene, the personified characters are performing an activity the Lover would gladly himself be involved in. The basis of their relationship has shifted from the in-spirational (conveying a sense of psychological causality) to the imitative. The metaphorized décor of the courtly social gathering has taken over, and the characters pass from personification to *exemplum*.

Is it a touch of irony, or merely of contrariness, that the Lover at this juncture, having found precisely what he wants ("Fox est qui n'a de tel envie!"), decides to turn around and explore the rest of the garden? It might be suggested that the Lover's move translates a fatigue not only with the superficial courtly society therein depicted, but also with a particular figurative mode that was beginning to show signs of wear. If the spatial marking of the garden wall indicated a transcendence from the initial, static, "pure" mode of personification – totally emblematic and descriptive – the physical turning away from the dance ("D'ileques me parti atant" [1299] ["At this point I left there" (p. 48)]) to the rest of the allegorical countryside is perhaps a further topographic analogue to a revised poetic artifice, whose ultimate function is that of persuasion. The abandoning of one figurative framework for another is substantiated by the significant fact that the personifications just described virtually disappear from the scene, never to return – stuck to their initial canvas just as the portraits are forced to maintain their static surveillance outside the walls.[72]

An alteration is marked by two additional factors: the final

---

72 In addition to Amor, only Franchise will reappear, albeit briefly, accompanied by the previously unmentioned Pitié. Along with this unique reappearance, it might be mentioned that Franchise is also the name of one of Amor's arrows, subsequently renamed Cortoisie (see below, note 76).

"springtime opening," here consisting of the most ambitious enumeration of trees and flowers in the entire poem; and the singling out of the God of Love, Amor, who had merely been one of the dancers in the previous scene. One can see in the God of Love, along with the paraphernalia endowed upon him by an extensive literary tradition, an attempt to deal further with the problem of allegorical figuration and its relation to psychological motivation.[73] One might ask initially why the garden does not in fact belong to Amor, given that he certainly represents the governing principle of that which is to follow. An answer to this complicated question will only be apparent after more of his role in the poem is seen. In any event, at this point Amor becomes the central figure and transforms the allegorical context from the dance to the hunt:

> Et li dex d'Amors m'a seü
> endementieres aguetant
> con li vanieres qui atant
> que la beste en bon leu se meite
> por lessier aler la saeste.   (1418–22)

(And the God of Love followed me, watching me all the time, as does the hunter who waits until the animal is in good position before he lets fly his arrow. [p. 50])

As if in response to the initial difficulty of how Oiseuse could possibly make the Lover idle, how in any sense she could get inside of him when in fact she was a quality "removed" from him in order to facilitate her portrayal, Amor has the solution: Calling upon Ovidian sources, Guillaume shows in a grand departure from his accustomed naturalism how Amor's arrows strike his victims through the eyes and eventually reach the heart. It is significant that with the shift in allegorical causality, the Lover for the first time demonstrates something of a personal desire. The bulk of the narration up to the meeting with Amor and the fountain of Narcissus consisted almost exclusively of description and enumeration borrowed, as we saw, from the lyric stock of motifs – ultimately nonparticipatory in spite of the Lover's having joined in the dance.

The discovery of an adequate form of allegorical causality in the

---

[73] On the traditional portrayals of the God of Love, cf. Doris Ruhe, *Le Dieu d'Amors avec son paradis* (Munich, 1974).

present circumstance does not however eliminate all of the conceptual problems that were latent in the narrative from the start. First, even though the Lover is pierced by a series of arrows, which allegorically suggest a *punctual,* immediate falling in love, it is never stated clearly at what moment he actually does fall in love. It might here be helpful to retrace the sequence of events at this crucial turning point in the development of the Lover's desires:

1. Lover sets out to inspect the garden with no apparent motive in mind [1283–1417]
2. Lover encounters fountain/Tale of Narcissus [1418–1508]
3. Lover approaches the "Fontaine d'Amors" and looks in [1509–1612]
4. Lover perceives the rose bushes [1613–20]
5. Lover leaves the fountain and approaches the rose bushes [1621–34]
6. Description of rose bushes and "boutons" (general) [1635–52]
7. Lover singles out one particular bud [1653–78]
8. Amor pierces Lover with succession of arrows [1679–1878]
9. Amor exacts the Lover's pledge of homage and service [1879–1952]
10. Amor's demand for a hostage (Lover's heart) [1953–2008]

While it might be objected that to seek here a moment of falling in love is futile, inasmuch as a gradual process is being described, the problem of redundancy still remains. The same might be said of the objection that Amor does not signify a mere falling in love, but rather a refinement added on to a more primitive, brute emotion. Whichever way we read Amor's arrows, the fact remains that their allegorical expression of the *gradus amoris topos* (expressing the steps leading up to an eventual *innamoramento*) duplicates events that occur elsewhere in the narration.[74] A couple of Amor's arrows manifestly repeat events which have already taken place: Biautez recapitulates the Lover's first sight of the rosebud ("si tres bel"

---

74 Cf. Lionel J. Friedman, "Gradus Amoris," *Romance Philology,* 19 (1965), 167–77.

[1654]);[75] Simpleice, while not so outright in its duplication, is implicit in the Narrator's description of the rose ("tige . . . droite"; "des fueilles . . . quatre paire"; "li boutons . . . ne cline ne ne pent"). Moreover, this second arrow evokes the rose's odor, which the Lover had already discovered for himself (1666–9). The third arrow bears witness to a possible corruption in the transmission of the text: While it is first given the name Franchise (942) it is later referred to as Cortoisie (1765). Whatever might be the source of this confusion, both names duplicate participants in the *carole*, and both in some way return later in the tale.[76] Franchise herself comes back to help the Lover by persuading Dangier of his good will, and Cortoisie "reappears" in the person of her flesh-and-blood son, Bel Acueil, who becomes the object of the Lover's attentions. As for the Compaignie of the Lady/rose (fourth arrow), either of two correlated moments could be adduced: Possibly the previous first encounter with the rose, where the Lover approaches it and very nearly plucks it (1671–2); or, more likely, the later friendship with Bel Acueil, which does in fact explicitly yield this quality:

> . . . em Bel Acueil grant amore é
> et grant *compaignie* trovee. . . .   (3362–3)

(in Fair Welcoming I found much love and *companionship* [p. 79])

> Je [Dangier is speaking] veil qu'il ait la *compaignie*
> Bel Acueil, puis que il vos plest. . . .   (3306–7)

(Since it pleases you, I want him to have the *company* of Fair Welcoming [p. 78])

---

75 Biauté was also one of the *carole* dancers, a fact that is self-consciously pointed out in the text: "cele dame avoit non Biautez,/ausi come une des .V. floiches" (992–3) (that lady's name was Beauty, just like one of the five arrows) — as if in recognition of the arbitrariness of allegorical naming.

76 Is this second section, because of this allegorical "inconsistency," merely an interpolation (cf. Nicola Zingarelli, "L'Allegoria del *Roman de la Rose*," in *Studii dedicati a Francesco Torraca nel XXXVI anniversario della sua laurea* [Naples, 1912], esp. pp. 507–9)? I believe not, particularly in view of the otherwise careful coherence of the description, not to mention the later appearance of these two characters. Moreover, the concepts of "franchise" and "cortoisie" are associated in Guillaume's text from the beginning: "Franchise: cele iert empanee/de valor et de cortoisie" (942–3) ("Openness: this arrow was feathered with valor and courtesy" [p. 43]). In the description of the *carole* dancers, the portrait of Cortoisie follows immediately upon that of Franchise (lines 1189–1248).

Finally, the fifth arrow, Biau Samblant, likewise projects to a later event in the growing relationship between the Lover and Bel Acueil:

> Bel Acueil au comencement
> me salua mout doucement
> et me mostra plus *bel samblant*
> que onques n'avoit fet devant.   (3327–30)

(To begin with, Fair Welcoming saluted me sweetly. . . . he showed me an *appearance fairer* than he had ever shown before. [p. 78])

If Amor's five figurative arrows merely duplicate events that are recounted in another way elsewhere in the narrative, then the most we can say is that they increased the Lover's incipient desire ("lors fu graindre la volentez" [1750] ["my wish was greater now" (p. 55)]) but *they did not create it*. In an important aside, it is stated furthermore that the God of Love deliberately waited to attack until the Lover had chosen a specific bud:

> et quant il [Amor] ot aperceü
> que j'avoie ensint esleü
> ce bouton, qui plus me seoit
> que nul des autres ne fessoit,
> il a tantost pris une floiche. . . .   (1683–7)

(and when he saw that I had singled out the bud that pleased me more than did any others, he immediately took out an arrow [p. 54])

Thus the narrative, in an attempt to preserve the idea of a free, individual choice in love ("Entre les autres en eslui/un si tres bel" [1653–4] ["Among these buds I singled out one that was so very beautiful" (p. 53)]), ultimately undoes its own allegorical expression of erotic motivation (Love's arrows) – in much the same way that the love potion in *Tristan* displaces a more mystical, fundamentally inexplicable object choice.

It might be suggested additionally that Amor's shooting of arrows, in the measure that they merely duplicate episodic mental transformations that affect the Lover elsewhere and in different ways, functions much as his lengthy speech, offering simultaneously a narrative parallel and a doctrinal lesson that prove to be ineffective or irrelevant in terms of the Lover's actual experience. The dislocation between abstraction (in the case of Amor's discourse, a prophetic narrative *exemplum*) and event is perhaps most clear with the fifth arrow, the culmination of progress in love, Biau Samblant. Now, in the courtly stock of ideas, Biau Samblant would be the lady's favorable glance, adumbrating a positive acceptance, however limited, of the lover's pursuit. At the point of being struck by this arrow, the Lover has not received any such acceptance, nor is the arrow's attack likely to give it to him; in other words, the fact of being struck by the arrow has literally nothing to do with any eventual favorable glance he will receive in the dream tale. As we saw above, it is Bel Acueil who, in an independent move, will show the Lover a "plus bel samblant," a fact that is later disapprovingly underscored by Jalousie: "mar lor fist onques bel semblant" (3619) ("it was an unhappy day when he ever turned a pleasant face toward them" [p. 82]). The shooting of the arrows, their implicit analysis of the plot according to the *gradus amoris*, is simply that – an abstract analysis that is really only a prelude to Amor's lengthy teachings, but no less removed from the allegorical events experienced by the Lover. Thus, even when a mode of "injection" has been found to deal with the influence of personified qualities on real people, as is here the case, it can only be intellectualized, maintaining a strong foothold in the realm of abstract causality. Amor and his arrows do, however, play another role in the poem, which inaugurates a process governing the balance of the poem's elaboration; this new role, that of a physical displacement, ultimately mediates and redirects the Lover's desire, thus obscuring the initial object of fascination. Amor officially inserts himself in the path of the Lover's desire by means of the feudal oath and the locking up of the Lover's heart. Moreover, the repeated martial aspects of Amor's endeavor (the hunt motif, arrows, feudal submission) initiate a new story type, that of combat and allegiance, which ultimately vitiates the Lover's personal stance of nonconflictual longing.

After Amor's speech, which characteristically turns from strict doctrine to a hypothetical narration doubling the Lover's own experience (and lacking any allegorical veneer), the Lover discovers a new physical barrier ("Li roser d'une haie furent/clos environ" [2763–4] ["The rosebushes were enclosed about with a hedge" (p. 69)]), which had not been previously mentioned and which, not surprisingly, leads to a new cast of characters and a new figurative context: the guardians of the rose. In accordance with the gradations that have occurred up to this moment in the figurative expression of emotional states, the reader encounters here the most problematical one, and, indeed, the one that causes the entire structure to explode. Having passed from a series of vices, static and largely removed, through an assembly of corresponding courtly virtues which eventually fade into a larger tableau of elite society, to the central figure of Amor, who literally punctures his victim with his teachings, the reader here encounters personifications who correspond specifically to the emotions and sentiments of the actual erotic encounter. The first personification we meet is Bel Acueil, the son of Cortoisie, who grants the Lover immediate entry past the hedge to the rose bushes. The strategic mention of Cortoisie at this point unites the *carole* experience (Cortoisie, we remember, had invited the Lover to dance) with Amor's arrows and, genealogically, with the final quest—suggesting, if such were necessary, the persistent courtly mood of the Lover's endeavors. The latter's euphoria is abruptly curtailed as a result of the inimical guardians of the roses: Dangier, Male Bouche, Honte, and Peor. Corresponding to the brief genealogy of Bel Acueil, Guillaume here provides the family history of Honte (daughter of Reson and Maufez) along with a mythical prehistory of the keepers of the garden: Chasteez, "qui dame doit estre/et des roses et des boutons" (2830–1) ("who should be the lady of roses and buds" [p. 70]), once suffered attack (really plunder) at the hands of Venus and consequently asked Reson for the help of her daughter, Honte. Dangier and Jalousie appear simply to "be" there, receiving no mention in this brief mythology. It should be clear initially that what corresponds to an archetypal struggle between Chastity and Venus has evolved into a present-day tension between inimical and friendly personifications (Chasteez, although occasionally mentioned, never appears in the narrative). In spite of the individual qualities attributed to each of the personifications, they are globally categorized according to whether or not they are willing to help the Lover attain the rose. In this sense, Bel Acueil alone is to be included among the *pro* camp and the rest (Dangier, Male Bouche, Honte, Peor, and Jalousie) are unambiguously *contra*. There is, moreover, an initial distinction between Bel Acueil and Dangier, on the one hand, and the other, rather secondary, qualities. If, in the archetypal rose quest, Venus (very nearly "Luxure" [Lust], who is later mentioned as Chastity's mortal enemy) and Chastity represent two inimical and opposite dispositions, Bel Acueil and Dangier represent those dispositions translated into the mode of action. In other words, insofar as the latter are two types of behavior personified, they replace any external manifestations of the Lady's disposition, whether positive or negative, and thereby assume a pragmatic significance that the more cosmic forces "Lust" and "Chastity" could not convey.

The basic duality (Venus/Chastity; Bel Acueil/Dangier) governing the rose guardians constitutes a system in equilibrium, one in which it is not possible for one side to eliminate the other. It is crucial to keep in mind that the vices, those qualities that are incompatible with the courtly pursuit of desire, have already been excluded from the garden paradise. Logically, any quality inside the garden walls should, however negative in appearance, play a role in the love story. The question of how a "vilain" such as Dangier could maintain a place in the garden, which has seemed inconsistent to many readers, is explained by the simple observation that the woman's refusal is a necessary part of the lover's quest. The same can be said of Jalousie, a concept that has a long history in the courtly lyric tradition.[77] As such, these concepts cannot be excluded any more than that of Bel Acueil can. This sense of an unresolvable equilibrium between apparently good and bad qualities finds ample support in Amor's speech, which, in

---

[77] Andreas Capellanus is outspoken in this regard: "Qui non zelat, amare non potest" ("He who is not jealous cannot love"); "De coamante suspicione percepta zelus et affectus crescit amandi" ("Jealousy, and therefore love, are increased when one suspects his beloved") (*De Amore Libri Tres*, ed. E. Trojel [Hauniae (Copenhagen), 1892], pp. 310–11; English translation by John Jay Parry, *The Art of Courtly Love* [1941; New York, 1969], pp. 184–5). While certainly ironically intended, the chaplain's statements were probably aimed at what was a constant preoccupation in the literature. Cf. Moshé Lazar, *Amour courtois et fin'amors dans la littérature du XIIe siècle* (Paris, 1964), pp. 62–3; and Topsfield, "*Roman de la Rose*," pp. 32–4, who suggests that "jealousy" here might refer to the lady's worry for her own reputation. The interesting article by Erich Köhler, "Les Troubadours et la jalousie" (*Mélanges . . Frappier* [Geneva, 1970], I, pp. 543–59), shows how the contradictory perspectives of this concept (both vilified and in some ways indispensable) parallel the equally contradictory political situation of an upward-striving social class. However, this occasionally reductive analysis, for the purpose of showing the symptoms of a profound class struggle, tends to neglect or minimize the deep-rooted sense of individuality and rivalry that is so characteristic of troubadour poetry.

addition to its lack of conclusion, frequently mentions the mixed blessings of love, as for example in the following passage:

> nus n'a bien s'il ne le compere;
> s'en aime l'en mieuz le chaté
> quant l'en l'a plus chier acheté;
> et plus en gré sont receü
> li bien ou l'en a mal eü.   (2584–8)
>
> (no one has anything good unless he pays for it. Men love a possession more when they have bought it at a higher price, and the good things for which one has suffered are received with greater thanks. [p. 67])

This philosophy of Amor, realized in the two warring factions of rose guardians, explains why Amor never appears in order to help the Lover in his combat: It is simply not the place of Amor as overseer of this never ending conflict, to adjudicate, to choose one side over the other, much as the Lover/Narrator would like it to happen. Embodying that very principle of ambiguity and indecision that maintains the miserable Lover in a state of suspense, Amor cannot play a part in the Lover's narrative. The role that is frequently attributed to him, that of the Lover's eventual champion, actually falls to Venus, Amor's mother, and, as we have already seen, the embodiment of amorous conquest.[78] Accordingly, Amor's true contrary, insofar as it is expressed in the narrative, is Reson, that quality which apparently does not live in the garden and which opposes all of the Lover's efforts – opposition *not* in the sense of refusal but rather of a supernal kind that calls into

---

[78] Particularly interesting on the relationship between Amor and Venus in Guillaume's *Rose* is Douglas Kelly, "'Li chastiaus . . . Qu'Amors prist puis par ses esforz': The Conclusion of Guillaume de Lorris's *Rose*," in *A Medieval French Miscellany*, ed. Norris J. Lacy, University of Kansas Humanistic Studies, 42 (Lawrence, KS, 1972), pp. 61–78. I cannot agree with Hans Robert Jauss, who insists that Venus is substantially different from all the other personifications in the *Rose* because of her mythological background: cf. his "Allegorese, Remythisierung und neuer Mythus," collected in the author's *Alterität*, pp. 285–307. Jauss (pp. 290–1) calls attention to Venus's ambiguous description (as a "Göttin oder Fee") and her inability to act as or like the Lady for a justification of this view; in fact, her portrayal differs little from that of an outright personification such as Jalousie. Were one to change Venus's name to "Luxure," her actions and description would accord perfectly. Moreover, that Guillaume did not indiscriminately reduce his mythological characters to personification (in the words of Jauss, "Die antike Mythologie erlitt beim Absinken in den allegorischen Status der Personifikation eine Schrumpfung: der *Erzählzusammenhang* der Mythen wurde überflussig" [emphasis mine], should be manifest from his striking and highly ambiguous *narrative* retelling of the Narcissus myth (see Chapter Four, below).

question the very presence of the Lover in the garden. Reson in fact voices a direct opposition to love (Love?), which Lecoy decides not to personify in his edition:

> Or te veil dire et conseillier
> que l'amor metes en oubli
> dont je te voi si afoibli
> et si conquis et tormenté.   (3002–5)

(Now I want to tell you and advise you to forget the love by which I see that you are thus weakened, thus conquered and tormented. [p. 73])

> c'est li maus qui amors a non,
> ou il n'a se folie non.   (3025–6)

(that sickness [is] called love, in which there is nothing but madness. [p. 74])

> Or met l'amor en nonchaloir,
> qui te fait vivre, et non valoir. . . .   (3047–8)

(Now don't set store by the love that makes you live without worth [p. 74])

She then proceeds to vilify the part of the Lover which Amor had captured, his heart:

> Tu doiz metre force et desfense
> encontre ce que tes cuers pense.
> Qui totes eures son cuer croit
> ne puet estre qu'il ne foloit.   (3053–6)

(You must pit your strength and resistance against the thoughts of your heart. He who always believes his heart cannot keep from committing acts of folly. [p. 74])

Further parallels between Amor and Reson are striking. Both show themselves to be above the struggle for the rose by not taking part and by commenting on the very desirability of such a struggle. Moreover, the corporeal presence of both characters suggests an otherworldly aspect: Although the Lover first meets Amor dancing in the *carole,* the latter, at the end of his speech, disappears ("je ne soi mot/que il se fu esvanouiz" [2750–1] ["he vanished before I knew a word to say" (p. 69)]); Reson's abode is a tower above the garden ("Lors est de sa tor devalee" [2960] ["She then came down from her tower" (p. 73)]) and she departs just as abruptly ("Atant

Reson s'est departie" [3080] ["Thereupon Reason left" (p. 75)]) as she arrived. Whereas Amor is repeatedly called a "Dieu," Reson is herself a divinity:

> A son semblant et a son vis
> part qu'el fu fete ou paravis,
> car Nature ne seüst pas
> ovre fere de tel compas.
> Sachiez, se la letre ne ment,
> que Dex la fist ou firmament
> a sa semblance et a s'image.... (2969–75)

(By her appearance and her face it seemed that she was made in paradise, for Nature would not have known how to make a work of such regularity. Know, if the letter does not lie, that God made her in the firmament in his likeness and in his image [p. 73])

Finally, the repeated opposition between folly and reason is doubled by a more subtle one that will later take on added importance: that between the obsessively repeated memory characteristic of all lovers ("lors te vendra en remenbrance" [2421] ["Then you will remember" (p. 64)]) and the abrupt forgetfulness advocated by Reson: "que l'amor metes en oubli" (3003) ("that you forget love").

In this closed and insoluble system of opposing dispositions, the only narrative possibility is a series of inconclusive skirmishes; the assumption that the battle can be won is purely hypothetical. Dangier and Bel Acueil should enjoy alternating victories, but neither one can definitively destroy the other. Moreover, in order to be true to their personified qualities, Bel Acueil should always be welcoming, and Dangier should always reject the Lover. This is the way in which the narrative begins: Bel Acueil not hesitating to let the Lover in, and Dangier immediately chasing him away. Allegorically speaking this alternation in actions should translate the Lady's vacillating positions. And yet, the clarity of such a program shows signs of weakening even in the initial stages. Subsequent to the Lover's entry into the rose enclosure, but before any action on the part of Dangier, Bel Acueil voices a circumspect warning that is really counter to his allegorical quality:

> ... "Frere, vos beez
> a ce qui ne puet avenir.
> Coment! me volez vos honir?
> Vos m'avriez bien asoté,
> se le bouton aviez osté
> de son rosier; n'est pas droiture
> que l'en l'oste de sa nature.
> Vilains estes du demender!
> Lessiez le croistre et amender,
> nou voudroie avoir deserté
> dou rosier qui l'a aporté
> por nul home vivant, tant l'ains." (2892–2903)

("Brother, you aspire to what cannot take place. What! Do you want to disgrace me? You would indeed have made a fool out of me if you had plucked the rosebud from its bush. It is not just to strip it of its nature, and you are base to ask it. Let it grow and improve; I love it so much that for no living man would I want it exiled from the bush that bore it." [p. 71])

Venus later goes so far as to accuse Bel Acueil of having certain qualities of his supposed opposite, Dangier ("Por quoi vos fetes vos ... vers cest amant si *dangereus* ... ?" [3424–5] ["Why, fair sir, do you make such *resistance* to this lover ... ?" (p. 79)]). Is it consistent for Fair Welcome *in person* to call the Lover a "vilain" and to tell him to leave the rose alone? Indeed, this is the "job" of Dangier, who does immediately rear his ugly head and chase the Lover outside of the enclosure (2904–26). Clearly, as with Amor's arrows in relation to the Lover's amorous experiences, we have here another example of figurative doubling, but in this case the inconsistency takes place within a uniform level of personification.

What causes this duplication is the fact that Bel Acueil very quickly assumes generalized human characteristics and takes on a complete set of inner psychological motivations comparable to those of the Lover. As such, he rapidly takes the place of the rose as a figure for the immaterial Lady. This substitution is initially more satisfactory, for the fragmentation of the Lady's qualities creates at the very least an impossibility of communication for lack of any "center." As a result, one of the Lady's fragmented qualities, such as Bel Acueil, becomes that center and thereby assumes the complex psychological ramifications of its human form. In a more curious way, an identical transformation affects Dangier, who, in the absence of Bel Acueil, "becomes" the obdurate Lady. The latter transformation is apparent not only in the courtly plaint that the Lover addresses to Dangier ("Sire, or sui ici/venuz por vos crier merci . . ." [3143–4] ["Sir, I have come here to beg for your mercy" (p. 75)]) but also in Dangier's sudden change of heart a few lines later, which likens him to a welcoming figure. In one of the text's arresting self-reflective moments, Honte will later call attention to Dangier's having overstepped the bounds of his allegorical character: "'Il n'afiert pas a vostre non/que vos faciez se anui non'" (3677–8) ("It doesn't agree with your name for you to do anything but make trouble" [p. 83]).

It is perhaps natural that such characters representing the negative and positive reactions of the Lady should come to "be" the welcoming or rejecting lady, but what accompanies this transition in terms of the other personifications is even more astonishing. As Bel Acueil and Dangier become humanized, the secondary personified qualities, those standing for emotions and not primarily actions (for example, Honte and Peor), come to represent fragmented qualities *not* specifically of the Lady, but of the recently humanized primary abstractions Bel Acueil and Dangier. We will later find, for instance, Honte and Peor waking up Dangier to the Lover's encroachment (3651–712), while two personifications "brought by God," Pitié and Franchise, will provide an analogous contrary effect, briefly converting him to a welcoming disposition (3231–308). Moreover, a set of additional characters is introduced who assume functions once possessed by the two surrogate ladies: While Bel Acueil was first presented as a young valet, a companion who would do his best to aid the Lover in his quest, a similar role of male companionship is subsequently taken over by Ami (Friend or Friendship?), who, incidentally, seems like Bel Acueil to be intimately acquainted with Dangier. On the other hand, Jalousie, who received only a marginal introduction at first, assumes the primary role of the excluding force, vitiating Dangier's previous authority by becoming his "superior officer." In accordance with the revised physical barriers that succeed each other in the *Rose*, we encounter one final one: Jalousie's castle. If we are correct in assuming a correlation between physical barriers and figurative contexts, we might expect here still another shift, which does indeed prove to be the case. Although up till this point Bel Acueil and Dangier both adumbrated the disembodied Lady, the former comes more and more to be the sole substitute. Logically, if the Lover is about to address himself to a figure, should it not be the one who is likely to emit a favorable response? The natural preference for Bel Acueil is accentuated by the divergent physical descriptions of the two personifications: Dangier – ugly, hairy, and "vilain"; Bel Acueil – young, gracious, and handsome. In addition, the fragmenting and resultant copresence of two attitudes that would normally exclude each other in terms of the Lady's comportment allows for a double allegiance on the Lover's part and, eventually, the expression of a preference for one of the conflicting attitudes.

While in the preliminary stages Guillaume makes an attempt to eliminate this problem of copresence by having Bel Acueil flee when Dangier comes to repulse the Lover's first advance ("Lors s'en est Bel Acueil fuïz/et je remainz tot esbaïz" [2935–6] ["Then Fair Welcoming fled and I remained stupefied" (p. 72)]), a change begins to overtake the portrayal of Bel Acueil according to which he alone is reinterpreted as the object of worth, the person sought after. It might be noted, significantly, that in the second incursion of evil forces – following the Lover's kiss of the rose – Bel Acueil remains and the Lover flees (3541). Accordingly, Bel Acueil is addressed more and more as if he himself were the Lady, in ambiguous terms the delicacy of which ultimately avoids a direct contradiction or a compromising sexual situation; one example of Guillaume's subtle technique in this matter can be found in Venus's inflammatory address directed toward Bel Acueil:

> Por quoi vos fetes vos, biau sire,
> vers cest amant si dangereus
> d'avoir un bessier doucereus?
> Ne li devroit estre veez,
> car vos savez bien et veez
> qu'il sert et ainme en leauté,
> si a assez en lui biauté,
> por qu'il est dignes d'estre amez.
> Veez come il est acesmez,
> come il est biaus, come il est genz,

> et douz et frans vers totes genz;
> et avec ce il n'est pas vieuz,
> ainz est enfes, dont il vaut mieuz.
> Il n'est dame ne chastelaine
> que je ne tenise a vilaine,
> s'ele fessoit de lui dangier.   (3424–39)

(Why, fair sir, do you make such resistance to this lover's having a sweet kiss? It should not be forbidden him, for you know well and see that he serves and loves loyally and that he is beautiful enough to be worthy of being loved in return. See how graceful he is, how handsome, how pleasant, sweet, and open toward all men. Moreover, he is not old but rather a child, and therefore worth more. There is no lady, no châtelaine whom I should not consider base if she were to make any resistance to him. [p. 80])

In the context of Bel Acueil's uncharacteristic behavior, Venus mentions twice his inappropriate "dangier" (3425, 3439), the second time with regard to the comportment of a hypothetically resistant "dame" or "chastelaine." Venus describes at length the Lover's beautiful features, as if the latter's physical attraction could sway the Lady's male surrogate — a potential embarrassment if there ever was one. Venus's failure to mention the rose even once compounds the situation, rendering the frequent ambiguous references to the granting of a kiss tantalizing to say the least (is it Bel Acueil's own kiss or that of the rose?). Later references to the relationship between the Lover and Bel Acueil maintain an ambiguous hint of scandal and impropriety that, in the absence of a clear reference to the rose, takes on a broader significance than has heretofore been suspected:

> ... entre moi et Bel Acueil
> a un mauvés acointement.   (3506–7)

(there is an evil relationship between me and Fair Welcoming. [p. 81])

> [Jalousie addressing Bel Acueil]
> "Garz neanz, por quoi t'a failli
> sens, que bien fusses d'un garçon
> dont j'ai mauvese soupeson?"   (3518–20)

(Worthless wretch, why have you taken leave of your senses to become the friend of a boy of whom I suspect evil? [p. 81])

> [Bel Acueil] se fust alez repondre
> s'el ne l'eüst ilec trové
> et pris ovec moi tot prové.   (3536–8)
> (He would rather have gone to hide if she had not found him there and caught him with me and with full proof. [p. 81])

In this series of exchanges, the motivations of Bel Acueil are discussed with relatively little attention paid to the consequences as concerns the rose. One begins to wonder, in fact, wherein resides the apparent transgression, and why Jalousie's first reaction would be to imprison Bel Acueil and *not* the roses. Is there a need to protect Bel Acueil in some way? If Bel Acueil's fault lies exclusively in his having laid open access to the rose, why not simply expel him (as had previously been the case) and fortify the roses' protection?

These questions, which surround the motivation behind the building of the castle, the poem's final physical barrier, encounter difficulties, since they cannot be answered according to the initial logic of this scene. Bel Acueil and Dangier are no longer symmetrically balanced protectors of the desired rose: Bel Acueil has become the humanized substitute for the rose/Lady, and Jalousie has acceded to the position of command formerly held by Dangier. We note, moreover, that Male Bouche and Jalousie, who at this point become the primary excluding forces, both differ from the other personifications insofar as they certainly do not designate qualities originating inside the Lady. Construed more easily as exterior figures, not even personifications, they indicate a changed order, where, much as in the final stages of the *carole* scene, the personifications take on totally human dispositions and play their part in an everyday type of scene. This last part of the *Rose* has rightly been compared to a *fabliau* situation, where the young unmarried girl is locked up by members of her family in order that she not be swept away by a male intruder.[79]

And yet the rose does not totally disappear, a fact that brings even more radically to the fore the problems involved in conceptualizing its place next to the now surrogate lady, Bel Acueil. Obviously, from the outset, any type of sexual union between the Lover and the rose, or any implied union such as marriage, is

---

[79] Lewis, *Allegory*, pp. 130–36.

prohibited, even though the plot line of the *Rose* does not exclude such ideas. There are only two narrative conclusions to the Lover's quest: (a) that the Lover reach and pluck the rose; and (b) that the Lover never reach the rose. While the first possibility would seem to figure a physical union, it actually implies the death of the rose (or rather, both at the same time). Such would not be the case had a nonliving object, say a precious jewel, been chosen as the poem's central metaphor. If the Lover ever reaches the object of his desire, the poetic image created for the situation, he can only destroy it. This simple observation of a natural fact explains in some sense not only the conversion of Bel Acueil into a love object in his own right, but also his undeniable and yet unspeakable masculinity.[80] The poet's initial depersonalizing (or symbolization) of the beloved (into the rose) is accompanied by an emotional fragmentation which, as we have seen, has the ultimate effect of attenuating any true sense of causality or expressivity. The substitution of Bel Acueil is a manner of repersonification serving to restore a human-like center as the object of the Lover's quest. Additionally, Bel Acueil's masculinity, which might appear to be an impediment or a humorous mistake, in actuality serves the important purpose of rendering him totally untouchable, since such a homoerotic relationship is unthinkable in the expressive register of courtly poetry.[81] In this, Bel Acueil is the only possible choice of a human goal

---

80 In spite of the demands of grammatical gender in determining the personifications' sex, it appears that Bel Acueil's gender could be "altered" were such the poet's desire or need. Male Bouche is first introduced as a female ("la jangleor" [2819] [The scandalmonger]; "Avant que la chose soit fete,/l'a ele en .III. cenz leus retrete" [3019–20] ["Before anything can be done, *she* will have reported it in a hundred places" (p. 74)]) but is later manifestly portrayed as a male ("il fu fiuz d'une vielle irese" [3499] ["he was the son of an angry old woman" (pp. 80–1)]; "Male Bouche le losengier,/c'est uns hom qui ment de legier" [3551–2] ["Foul Mouth the scandal-bearer; he is a man who lies easily" (p. 81)]). This transformation, I would suggest, marks the passage of Male Bouche from a general principle of gossip (associated with women in medieval antifeminist lore) to a specific evil-tongued spoiler, in the words of Guillaume a *losengier* (who is always a man). This transformation, from abstract principle to individual, is moreover totally in keeping with the more general alteration we have noted in the allegorical configuration.

81 The theme of homosexuality is conspicuously absent from vernacular works before the mid-thirteenth century, and particularly so from courtly literature. This is especially evident in view of a relatively lively Latin tradition dating from the beginning of the twelfth century. On the latter point see the well-informed study by John Boswell, *Christianity, Social Tolerance, and Homosexuality* (Chicago, 1980), esp. Chapter Nine. Two twelfth-century texts that do bring up the topic in a most curious way are the anonymous *Eneas*, lines 8565–621 and 9130–88, as well as a short episode in Marie de

who, like the rose, is logically and programmatically unattainable. The sense of distancing and mediation initiated by Amor's intercession and advocated in his teachings, is carried out narratively by the set of antagonistic personifications, and hence integrated into the very development of the love affair. The progressive humanization of the personifications, moreover, goes hand in hand with the irretrievably impersonal, untouchable rose image. The Poet/Lover's incapacity to deal with (that is, physically overtake) such an image necessitates intermediary forms of experience for the narrative logic of the courtly situation to be sustained. The result is twofold: First, the rose as ultimate object is nearly obscured out of existence; second, the story degenerates into a *fabliau*-like (mock-heroic) situation wherein the Lover's task becomes that of rescuing his beloved male from the hands of his/her oppressors. The final indication of this, the last in a series of topographical barriers, is the aforementioned castle built by Jalousie to house Bel Acueil and the rose bushes. If the most typical plot-type used to portray the pursuit of amorous desire is that of the quest, here it has turned into one of armed combat, the imperative overwhelming and defeating of an entrenched enemy. That such martial allusions have always been applied to love affairs is beside the point; the resultant logic of action calls for defeat and destruction, clearly inappropriate in a courtly context based upon refined supplication, delicacy, and free choice.

The central problem in the *Rose,* that which causes in fact the various structural and figurative non sequiturs, is, not surprisingly, the presence of the Lover himself. The disjunction of perceptual levels noted at the outset, the impossibility of a "whole" human being interacting with a personified quality, presents a dislocation that cannot be resolved. For the narrative reasons analyzed in Chapter Two, the Lover, who happens also to be the Narrator, necessarily experiences his own feelings and emotions independently of their abstract outward expression. What the reader witnesses in the *Roman de la Rose,* through the continued revision of figurative modes, is a confrontation with the problems inherent in the attempt to accord personal expression with experience, rhet-

---

France's *Lanval* (lines 277–86), which was probably inspired by the *Eneas* passages. In both cases, men are accused of homosexuality for not being as ardent toward women as expected.

oric with feeling. For the courtly poet, words and their formation are always in some sense inadequate to the feelings they represent, and so, in an achievement of tremendous proportions, Guillaume gives this linguistic quandary a physical, spatial form. Moreover, with the presence and participation of the courtly observer, there is no systemic isolation of the sort that would allow the personifications to carry out their acts (that is, their meanings) unimpeded, as in previous allegories. Guillaume's investigation of courtly rhetoric, his attempt to manifest abstract notions visually, his unorthodox approach to interiority, have the effect of exploding that expression and thus demonstrating the limitations latent in the traditional discourse of affectivity. While the romance form argues for a recounted ending, the materials, all borrowed from the lyric tradition, resolutely demand that an ending not be recorded; such is the *raison d'être* of the lyric mode as it had come to be codified. Guillaume's absolute faithfulness to the demands of this same courtly rhetoric ensures simultaneously his work's failure as romance, but its ultimate success as poetic document and object of continued fascination.[82]

The grammatical merger of Lover and Narrator at the end is accompanied by a decisive reduction in the company of personifications, only four of which are mentioned in the final section (3921–4028): Amor, Fortune, Jalousie, and Bel Acueil. Amor is named but once, subsequently to be replaced by Fortune as the all-inclusive principle of unpredictability ("Ce est ausi con de Fortune" [3953] ["It is just as with Fortune" (p. 87)]). The relation of Fortune to her wheel, upon which all men are to be found tracing a circle from high to low, is equivalent to what we have seen as Amor's manipulative role, manifestly above the garden events, removed from the system. With that, the allegorical profusion is

---

82 Cf. the suggestive discussion by Roger Dragonetti (*La Vie de la lettre au moyen âge* [Paris, 1980], pp. 9–10), which evokes the multiple connotations of the typical romance ending formula "Ci falt" – situating a crossroads between a work's end, its failure (*faillir*) and a lack (*falloir*) of some kind. It can be supposed that inasmuch as "Ci falt" is an external scribal marker of closure it indicates some aspect which a work would not or could not evoke in and of itself. The truly exceptional work will be that one which manages to incorporate its own failure (or impossibility) to continue within its very rhetorical or imagistic structure – as a lack that *need not* name itself – a necessity and not an accident. And that is perhaps the most satisfying victory over the disappointment of closure. I have discussed a similar problem in my article " 'Ci falt la geste': Scribal Closure in the Oxford *Roland*," *MLN*, 97 (May 1982), 890–905.

reduced to its simplest coordinates, Jalousie, mentioned only once (3979), assuming the full weight of the collective antagonistic forces, and Bel Acueil becoming the central focus of desire and the sole addressee. The conflict having been reduced to lyric proportions (goal, obstacle, and overall principle of uncertainty), Bel Acueil is further decomposed in accordance with the requirements of a fleshed-out characterization, as would be the lady to whom a lyric is addressed. Not only is Bel Acueil's heart here separated from his body (3977–88) – a development recalling Jalousie's manifest imprisonment of Bel Acueil's body ("Je cuit si bien garder son cors" [3611] ["I plan to guard his body so well" (p. 82)]) – but the final desire of the Lover, neither the rose nor Bel Acueil himself, becomes a second level of "Bel Acueil," the "bienveillance" (4027) of the personification who should himself be a kind of benevolence. As in an infinite series of mirrors, or, more appropriately, an encasement of Chinese boxes, each successive quality, once objectified (or personified), becomes itself a container in which is to be found a further quality.

Moreover, a comparison of the poem's last lines with a similar, previously expressed desire demonstrates the considerable revision in the Lover's goals:

>*Ja mes n'iert* rien qui me confort
>se je pert vostre bienveillance,
>   car je n'ai mes aillors fiance.   (4026–8)

(*If I lose* your good will, *there will never be* any comfort for me, since I have no ties of faith elsewhere. [p. 88])

>Sire, fi ge, *ja mes n'avré*
>joie, *se n'est* par une chose. . . .
>*ja* les dolors *n'en seront* tretes,
>*se* le bouton *ne* me bailliez. . . .   (2870–1; 2886–7)

("Sir," I said, "*I shall never have* any joy *if it is not* through one thing . . . their pain *will never* cease *if you do not give* me the rosebud" [p. 71])

The formulaic repetition "*ja mes* + negation + future clause, *se* + present clause" assures the parallel of these two moments: From a direct desire to possess the rosebud itself, to a longing after the "bienveillance" of the "Bel Acueil" of the Lady/rose. While we might have gathered from his physical movements that the Lover was penetrating progressively into the center of a privileged world, we here understand that he is nowhere but outside, longing to get in. If the creation of allegorical expression entailed a turning inside out of what had been an interior analysis, the final lyric return marks a renewed interiority with the outside ultimately turned back inward upon one of the former abstracted elements. The Lover finds himself, much as at the poem's beginning, outside a hermetically sealed place (his privileged inclusion within the garden walls having been long forgotten) and unquestionably alone. All the personifications are locked up, safe behind the walls, a certain material sign that the *poet*'s attempt at personification has failed as well. It is therefore fitting that at this point the Lover-become-Narrator should return to the previous abstract vocabulary that served as his point of departure.

Let us summarize: From the outset, Guillaume's poem constitutes an attempt to treat manifestly lyric themes derived from the highly codified *chanson* genre (dedication to the lady, use of the participatory lyric I, proliferation of *Natureingang* elements, vocabulary related to emotions and development of love) according to a romance format (the reorganization of said elements into a particular temporal and spatial order). The notions of inclusivity and progression presupposed by this ordering are themselves voiced by the Narrator in one of his numerous interventions:

> *Tot ensemble* dire ne puis,
>   mes *tot* vos conteré *par ordre*. . . .   (696–7)
> (I cannot speak of *everything together,* but I will recount it *all in . . . order* [p. 40])

"Tot ensemble" clearly suggests the texture of the lyric treatment, where all the themes are present virtually, in a limited and yet expansive associative space; to tell "tot par ordre" is the romance imperative. One might ask *why* this undertaking should have been: Was it a deliberate desire to deconstruct or destroy a well-established poetic mode? Is it merely the development or extension of latent tendencies in the genre? Or is it, more practically, an attempt on the part of Guillaume to display his virtuosity in the original ("noviaus") manipulation of a venerable tradition? In the absence of one clearly stated motivation, perhaps all three apply in some measure.

While intention remains indeterminate, the results of this poetic experiment are more readily available for comment. To develop lyric sentiment into an "art d'amors" via the mode of personification profoundly alters, indeed contradicts, the uniqueness of individual affairs through its implicit generalization and codification. A move toward allegory, toward generalizing narration, ultimately endangers the lyric I and its pretension to individuality. The inherent impasse of erotic codification, no less obtrusive, likewise characterizes the treatise of Andreas Capellanus, forcing it to fragment into a series of individual judgments, opinions, and experiences; even within a specific dialogue, the contrast of the lady's free will with her stipulated "duty" toward her suitor is underscored.[83] It is precisely the same constraint that underlies Amor's didactic teachings, ultimately giving way to a nonallegorical narration concerning a specific troubled lover.

This potential impasse of generalization, hopelessly at odds with a type of courtly sensibility predicated at least fictionally upon the poet's personal uniqueness and a specificity of the love object, is nevertheless at the root of the lyric poet's very language. Guillaume's poetic experiment brings to the fore the disturbing truth that the lyric persona simply cannot interact physically with personified abstractions – meaning that the poet's unique "being" and the expression of emotions in a commonly shared vocabulary are two fields that cannot in the long run coincide. Indeed, two results are possible in this confrontation: Either the abstractions cease to be such, becoming complete autonomous human beings with their own foreseeable will; or they revert to their abstract, nonhuman state where confrontation is no longer a narrative necessity. And here, it should be insisted that the fact of physical confrontation is crucial, for what it provokes is a juxtaposition of those interior feelings and motivations that prove to be inscruta-

---

83 In the second dialogue, the Lady, in response to the Lover's implication that any suitor deserves to be loved in return, states: "cuiuslibet generaliter personae amor commisit arbitrio, ut, si velit, amet eum, qui petet amari, vel non amet, si nolit amare. Sed et, si hanc, quam dicis, regulam amor sine omni exceptione servaret illaesam, scilicet ut omnis semper, qui amat, ametur, alterius regulae cursui occurreret naturali" ("Love regularly leaves it to the choice of each woman whether to love or not, as she may wish, the person who asks for her love. And if this rule you mention, that everyone who loves is always loved, were kept unbroken without any exceptions, it would in the natural course of events run foul of another rule"). *De Amore*, ed. Trojel, p. 43 (trans. Parry, p. 47).

ble, with words purportedly equivalent to them. The utter failure to communicate, the irreducibility of the inside/outside dialectic, translates the fact that the only adequate expression of the lyric I is the literal repetition of that same iconic I along with an allusion to subjectivity via abstract terms, whose exterior correspondence is none other than the ever-turning, self-referential reservoir of rhetorical expressions.

The profound need *not* to explode what had been elevated to the status of an affective myth, to pull back, to preserve the tradition, is at the base of the image of the rose, inanimate correlative to the exterior courtly lady. The impact of the image arises from the simple fact that, in spite of individual wishes, it must remain intact or be destroyed. The *lyric* rose, as an allusive and fundamentally immaterial figure of speech, bespeaks such an inconclusive treatment; the *romance* rose begs to be plucked. The allegorical, *fabliau* expansion at the end results, paradoxically, from Guillaume's attempt to maintain the courtly end of the allegory, to resist plucking the rose by means of an interposition of mediating and contrary forces whose goal is to perpetuate the narrative action. The stakes of the conflict are high, and Guillaume's final reversal, a return to the lyric persona, signals the eventual withdrawal from a daring experiment whose logical conclusion risked bursting the bubble of the courtly dream.

CORPUS DOMINÆ

While the narration of the *Roman de la Rose* turns largely around the problems involved in expressing the Lover's emotions, and their subsequent fragmentation in language, a parallel difficulty arises in the portrayal of the Lady, to the extent that the perception of a corporeal locus is more or less definitively obstructed. The rose image has always raised questions, not only with regard to its "meaning," but also to its representational mode.[84] Is the rose the woman herself objectively perceived, a particular part

---

84 Cf., for example, Zumthor's distinction between *emblème* and *symbole* (*Langue*, pp. 249–53, a development from his remarks in the previous *Essai*), the former of which, applicable to a more or less decipherable figurative relationship, he applies to the rose. In this view, a *symbole* merely suggests an idea that would otherwise remain ineffable; the only example of the latter to be found in the *Rose* is, according to Zumthor, the fountain.

(emotional or physical) of the woman, or some abstract idea associated with the woman (such as her "love" or "femininity")? Certainly, as of the first lines of the poem, the Narrator makes the direct connection between his Lady in real life and the rose image:

> cele por qui je l'ai empris:
> c'est cele qui tant a de pris
> et tant est digne d'estre amee
> qu'el doit estre Rose clamee.   (41–4)

(she for whom I have undertaken it . . . It is she who is so precious and so worthy to be loved that she should be called Rose. [p. 31])

But, as so often happens in the course of allegorical (that is, analytical) decomposition, what was at one time an easy metaphorical association becomes problematized through a proliferation of details that are reinterpreted according to a rigorously material (spatiotemporal) logic. What *is* the relationship between the entire allegorical *paysage* and the woman's bodily representation? If characters such as Honte and Peor stand unambiguously for specific aspects of the Lady's psyche, can the rose possibly represent her in her entirety? If they are "parts" of her, then does the ground they walk on not also bear some kind of physical correlation to her body? Could the entire enclosure of roses "be" the Lady's body? One would suppose not, inasmuch as the Lover has been allowed to tread a path inside. The impossibility either of confining the Lady's body to the rose alone, especially in view of her abstract decomposition, or of determining some kind of physical border encompassing her, echoes the fluidity of the inside/outside rapport governing the major conceptual conflict that we have pointed out with regard to the *Rose*'s narrative transposition of lyric expression. What differs, however, is that the Narrator's view of his own qualities is an interior one, ultimately betrayed by the inadequacy of language to duplicate or substitute for emotional states, rigorously immaterial and mysterious in origin. But the woman, as object, is seen from the outside, and the attempt to portray her physical or mental locus becomes a nagging preoccupation not only here, but in the lyric enterprise as well. Certainly, much has been said about the idealized, dematerialized woman of the courtly tradition, elevated to the level of a divine figure (Mariology) or a metaphysical idea (for example, the *dolce stil nuovo*), and yet were the modern reader to assume that the woman and her body never existed in courtly love literature, he would be committing a grave error. On the contrary, courtly writers seem to have been fascinated with the complexities of physical representation and the eventual correspondences between parts of the body, elements of the material world, and ideas.[85] The ultimately unlocalizable, ineffable body of Guillaume's lyric love is directly related to her character, which, as per the God of Love, is defined as capriciously inscrutable; since the spatiality of the *Rose* portrayal results largely from a translation of mental characteristics into a physical imaginary world, what arises therefrom is a mental *utopia,* literally a no-place in which vague notions circulate but in which no representation of a governing, responsible center is to be found.

To locate the woman would be, in a sense, to vulgarize her, eliminating the inherent fascination of an unrevealed mystery. To situate her would be, in fact, tantamount to possessing her. It is this ineffable essence of the lyric lady that incites the poet to entreat her, to address her, but almost never to describe and attain her. And yet the desire to *see* the woman (compare Amor's last gift to the Lover, "Douz Regart"), to envisage a body, is overwhelming, and accounts for some of the more daring inventions in the corpus of courtly works.

The many affinities between the *Roman de la Rose* and Chrétien de Troyes's *Chevalier de la Charrete* — the romancier's only effort to portray, and perhaps to glorify, adulterous love — have never been clearly articulated. Most striking is the observation that Chrétien did not himself finish writing the romance, leaving that task to a clerk, Godefroi de Leigni, and that he stopped at the point when Lancelot was walled up in the tower by Meleagant:[86]

---

[85] For the versatility in treatments of the woman's body, two examples should suffice: the fantastic, lengthy portrait of Soredamor in Chrétien's *Cligés* in the course of which a description of Amor's fatal arrow is transformed into the woman's body, part by part; and Bertran de Born's poem of the "domna soisseubuda" ("Domna, puois de me no·us chal") in which, spurned by his beloved, the poet decides to compose a "borrowed" woman out of the features, both mental and physical, of several other women known to him.

[86] The text of the *Charrete* is quoted from the edition of Mario Roques, CFMA 86 (Paris, 1958).

> Godefroiz de Leigni, li clers,
> a parfinee LA CHARRETE...
> ...ç'a il fet par le boen gré
> Crestïen, qui le comança:
> tant en a fet des lors an ça
> ou Lanceloz fu anmurez,
> tant con li contes est durez.

(The clerk Godefroi de Leigni has brought *La Charrete* to a close... He did it with the good wishes of Chrétien, who began it; he did as much as was remaining in the tale from the point at which Lancelot was immured.)

No one has ascertained the exact line at which Chrétien broke off his romance, but this precision would add little to the basic significance of the tower captivity; the spatial closure suggested by Chrétien's fragmentary romance could very easily have served as an inspiration to Guillaume de Lorris. Were it just a matter of two prisons, the comparison would be rather tenuous, but in both cases the narrator tells of elaborate plans to construct the tower and a few of these descriptions reveal textual parallels:

> Ou *païs* ne remaint *maçon*
> ne pïonier qu'ele ne *mant*   (Rose, 3782–3)

(There remained neither a mason nor a worker in the country that she did not send for)

> si prist *maçons* et charpantiers...
> les meillors del *païs manda*   (Charrete, 6113, 6116)

(he acquired masons and carpenters... and sent for the best in the country)

> nule plus bele ne pot estre,
> qu'ele est *et* grant *et lee et* haute.   (Rose, 3818–19)

(there could be no more beautiful [tower], for is it large and wide and tall.)

> fu tote parfeite la torz,
> forz *et* espesse, *et* longue *et lee*.   (Charrete, 6128–9)

(the tower was completely finished, strong and thick, and long and wide.)

The word *enmurer* is used to designate Bel Acueil's imprisonment (line 3911), as well as that of Lancelot, quoted above. It is quite possible that Guillaume de Lorris saw in the elaborate narrative description of the prison motif an appropriate way to close his own narrative.

Chrétien's Arthurian context is of course quite different, and it is equally instructive to see the way in which he portrays a real woman, Guenevere. Critics have taken delight in discussing the comportment of Arthur's queen in Gorre, where she acts out the role of the domineering Lady, but little is said about Guenevere's actions in Logres, Arthur's kingdom. There is good reason for this, since in those scenes Chrétien seems intent upon stressing the queen's shadowy – even marginal – status in the court. The romance is, after all, about the queen's abduction, her nonpresence, and this theme seems to be elaborated on many other levels. Chrétien, absolute master of the literary portrait technique, somewhat curiously never describes Guenevere's physical appearance. In the first scene of the romance, during which she is at the center of the conflict (Meleagant's request to fight for the queen as the only condition under which he will release the prisoners in Gorre), she is only called into action as an odd surrogate for Arthur, who presumes that she will be more effective in persuading Keu to remain at court. She mechanically acts out Arthur's orders, uncharacteristically prostrating herself before the seneschal, and thus ends up, somewhat ironically, being the instrument leading to her own abduction.

Even more telling is the queen's triumphant return from Gorre in the company of Gauvain, a scene that is marked by a total failure on the Narrator's part to mention her physical presence. News ("la novele" [5303]) comes to court that they have penetrated into the realm. The people rush out to greet them and a discussion ensues with Gauvain, during which the queen's presence is never stated. The people come back to Arthur and his sentiments are reported, once again, in the total absence of Guenevere. He is happy to have the "thing" he wants the most: "la rien a que il plus vialt" (5357). "Where is she?" will become the insistent question in the last part of the romance.[87] No sooner has she

---

87 Godefroi de Leigni will teasingly articulate this problem in a sequence of questions asked in the last scene of the romance, the decisive combat between Lancelot and Meleagant: "Et la reïne n'i est ele . . . ?" (6820); "Dex, ou fust ele donques?" (6823); "Et li cors, por coi se celot?" (6832). ("And is the queen not there?" . . . "By God, where might she be then?" . . . "And why was her body hiding itself?") All this is meant to "show" Guenevere's absence.

returned, giving the king his great joy, than we come upon a reenactment of Arthur's mistake at the opening of the romance: He grants the ladies of Pomelegoi and Noauz a rash boon (lines 5389–91) which will turn out to be, not surprisingly, a turning over of Guenevere and her second departure from court.

Guenevere's final scene in the part of the romance attributed to Chrétien is not without its "conclusive" possibilities. Enshrined in her "loge" at the tournament of Noauz, Guenevere acts the part of the imperious lady once again. We in turn are treated to the repetition of a spatial configuration – the tower watch – the modalities of which have been repeatedly played upon in the romance.[88] Furthermore, Chrétien will not tell of her return to court, a fact that suggests that he wished to maintain her in this position, just as he had placed Lancelot in the tower. Godefroi de Leigni has been criticized for the turn he gives the plot in his continuation, but he seems to have understood perfectly Chrétien's politics of concealment and silence with regard to the queen. Immediately after the immurement of Lancelot, Meleagant comes back to court, bragging ostentatiously, in order to fulfill his part of the bargain to engage in single combat with Lancelot. Guenevere, making her last appearance, is verbally rebuffed by the king, and the narrator states quite simply "La reïne plus ne parole" ("The queen speaks no more").[89] What better way to resolve a politically insoluble and potentially disastrous conflict than by cutting off the flow of words?[90] Chrétien was well aware of the stakes of the conflict, one allowing of other outcomes in lyric poetry, and it is perhaps his idiosyncratic preoccupation with forms of physicality and their converse as expressed through Guenevere and Lancelot – prisons and defenses, presence and absence, speech and silence, body and heart, naming and anonymity – that Guillaume de Lorris will further develop in the allegories of the *Rose*.

---

88 Cf. Lancelot's first vision, from high above the damsel's tower, of Meleagant leading Guenevere away; Bademagu and Meleagant sighting from their tower Lancelot crossing the Sword Bridge; Guenevere watching the combat between Lancelot and Meleagant from the tower window.

89 Roques's text reads: "La reïne plus n'an parole" (6185) ("the queen speaks no more about it"). The variant reading "plus ne," accentuating the absolute nature of Guenevere's silence, is found in two manuscripts. Cf. Wendelin Foerster's edition, *Der Karrenritter* (Halle, 1899), p. 219.

90 The model of Wace's *Brut*, narrowly associating the queen's adultery with the end of Arthur's peaceful reign, would have been well known to Chrétien and his readers.

THREE: LYRIC AND ROMANCE

Both Chrétien and Thibaut de Champagne, in "Ausi com unicorne sui," provide an account of the lover trapped in prison. In Guillaume de Lorris's allegory, the rose, as a tangible goal, becomes a protected figure around which monumental barriers are constructed. In all cases, the directional force of the poet's quest is in some way obliged to adhere to a rhetoric of battle or penetration, where presumably brute strength will conquer. The logic of such a positivistic, objective, outward-turning aggression denies the inward lyric interrogation that can never, for the sake of propriety, amount to more than a humble request. Where Thibaut's account differs, and this is certainly due to the standardized lyric nature of his enterprise, is in demonstrating that being in love *means* unequivocally being a prisoner and never wishing to escape. This simple message explains Guillaume's allegorical discomfort, the narrative logic of conquest and personal liberty running counter to lyric subjugation; his only way out is to refashion the allegory by an assertion of the lyric voice while letting the central goal, the rose, drop out of the picture. It also suggests an answer for why Chrétien would have imprisoned Lancelot, silenced Guenevere, and stopped writing.

But this is not all, for in place of the rose, as we saw, Bel Acueil appears behind bars. Once a human object is reestablished, Guillaume can invent a new allegorical interiority through Bel Acueil's *bienveillance* and, not coincidentally, an insistence on the separable heart motif, suggesting an immaterial collusion between the two characters. Moreover, keeping in mind the imprisonment of Thibaut's heart, along with that of Lancelot, one can reach a better understanding of the *Rose*'s final lines. One naturally construes the castle walls painstakingly built by Jalousie as a protective measure; in the context of these textual analogues, however, one is led to ask whether it is here a question of defense or of prison, protection or subjugation, the outside looking in or the inside peering out. Such a conceptual about-face would explain Bel Acueil's anomalous masculinity, his growing assimilation to the Lover/Narrator, suggesting that along with the final narrative merger the physical barrier has also been reversed or at least relativized. In the contradictory expression of Thibaut, Guillaume would have realized the coinciding of "en la prison" and "de moi près." In short, what results is a recognition that the castle is a self-inflicted prison, that the lover is always the one who is entrapped, and, finally, that the vision of woman can only be a temporary and yet indispensable illusion.

The three works of Chrétien, Thibaut, and Guillaume – respectively, a romance with lyric overtones, a lyric subordinating romance (narrative) materials, and a virtually seamless combination of both – attest to the extreme vitality and irreducibility of literary imagination in the Middle Ages. Were one to investigate other works, one would find still other possibilities and combinations. What is particularly striking is the ease of passage between abstract and material relationships, the inevitable challenge of expressing the former in terms of the latter. As suggested at the beginning of this chapter, a sense of genre can at best constitute an interpretative signpost, ultimately transcended, or even dwarfed, by the individual work itself. The irreducible, nearly unspeakable, paradox of erotic passion that has always plagued and excited human imaginations, finds a worthy and adequate form of expression in the fluidity and versatility of the metaphoric imagination, which never allows itself to be trivialized before it switches gears, thereby instituting a new set of logical constraints that will themselves be bypassed. Indeed, a world of experience separates the quest of Lancelot from that of the rose, and yet a deeply felt conjunction of similarities – embarrassments of expression and situation coupled with conceptual trickery – allows us to perceive in the elaboration of stereotypes a profound dynamic of metaphorical evasion. Ultimately, what keeps the tradition alive, literally and figuratively, is the fact that the prison of love, the prison of language, is never a hermetically sealed space, but rather akin to a revolving door, whose turning and returning suggest a wealth of expression at least as broad as that which is to be found on the capricious wheel of Fortune.

༶

The narrative tension that we viewed in Chapter Two can thus be seen to parallel a crossover between two specifically medieval modes of poetic expression, the latter serving as an expression of the historically grounded *clerc/chevalier* rivalry, which, much more than a conflict between two social classes, represents ultimately two distinct principles of erotic participation – active and passive, lover *de facto* and lover in words. Be it a function of the social restrictions placed on clerks or a more strictly literary play with convention, the problem of loving via words, a central feature of the courtly *chanson*, exercises a great influence upon the clerkly writer. Insofar as the poem itself is incorporated into the love quest – its immediate *raison d'être* being the persuasion of the lady by means of a compelling rhetorical construct – factors of expressive virtuosity and personal sincerity assume a great importance. The adequacy of language to express personal *unique* feelings is severely placed into question when that language is a common, shared instrument. Any artifice can be copied, any voice mimed. The need for secrecy on all sides accentuates the crisis of individuality and sincerity in the face of an all-embracing expressive universe made up of generalizations and commonplaces.

Whatever Guillaume's intention might have been, his poem provides a unique and flawless superimposition of these two modes of vision. It is the tension produced by two antithetical points of view that constitutes the poem's dynamic, and their resolution that closes the poem. From the narrative point of view, the attempt to espouse two different voices is resolved by the disappearance, or suppression, of one of them; thematically, the poet's confrontation with elements of the rhetoric of love by means of a logic of material relations ends when those elements give up their qualities of concrete personification. Through the parallelism, and eventual collusion, between Lover and Narrator, one understands that while on one level (one hesitates in this case to say "literally") the poem is about an individual's erotic quest, it also relates the poet's struggle with his means of expression, his own rhetorical universe. The Narrator eventually pulls back for, in both cases, the logical outcome would be a type of self-destruction. It would be a mistake, however, to insist that this is the only possible ending. The attainment of the rose is narratively feasible, but Guillaume's uncommon adherence to his lyric persona indicates, ultimately, a rejection of this artistic choice. From this lyric solidarity there results a deep poignancy of expression with none of the ironic distance that a Chrétien de Troyes could establish with *his* fictional worlds. Guillaume's final move marks a return to a certain rhetorical security, which, while distancing the beloved, preserves the momentary integrity of the Poet/Lover.

With a little bit of reflection, it is easy to see that the sense of elitism cultivated within the courtly literary tradition, and which perhaps reached its utmost limit in the *chanson,* offers an explanation for the earliest reception of the *Rose*. The paradox of the most highly prized of literary preoccupations resides in the somewhat disquieting conclusion that the newest, most sincere poem will be the one that is the least understood by uninvolved, possibly pernicious, spectators. The paradox thus becomes a factor of poetic reception and transmission. Like the *chanson,* upon which its final narrative voice and a large number of its poetic and thematic elements are based, the *Rose* stops without ending. Readers familiar with the *trouvère* lyric easily recognize the terminating lyric voice and will also accept other givens of the genre, which include a suspension of chronology and a reduction of spatial coordinates. From the modern point of view, however, an attempt must be made to account for the very different reception met by the *Rose* in the century following its composition.[91] Whatever other affinities it might have, the *Rose* is in its metrical design and its likely performative characteristics (recited but not sung) not a *chanson,* and we know that formal characteristics such as verse and meter were extremely influential factors in the creation and reception of medieval poetry. Furthermore, largely owing to the intermingling of various sorts of topics among a broad spectrum of literary types as of the early thirteenth century, precise generic delineation is unfeasible. The *Rose*'s own brand of eclecticism situates it at a confluence of generic horizons, all much in vogue around 1235: vernacular allegory, courtly romance, lyrico-narrative fiction, "Encounter"-type verse, and didactic poems of the debate tradition. Now, Guillaume de Lorris's *Rose* is typically seen as the last work in the "classic" tradition of courtly literature, an ideological and cultural watershed. Throughout the mid-thirteenth century we bear witness to a disjunction between older works that were being copied and preserved, and current tastes, which were some-

---

[91] See the excellent recent study by Pierre-Yves Badel, *Le Roman de la Rose au XIVe siècle: Etude de la réception de l'oeuvre,* Publications Romanes et Françaises, 153 (Geneva, 1980).

times quite different. The period during which the *Rose* would first have been transcribed, from around 1235 to 1260, is characterized by a significant development in learning and a growing interest in the translation and transmission of erudite, hitherto exclusively Latin works: religious doctrine, philosophy, law, and what might in general be termed scientific disciplines. Historical accounts and chronicles written in the vernacular are becoming commonplace, and there is a renewed interest in the composition and compilation of *chansons de geste*. By all accounts, however, fresh inspiration in the "courtly" genres is scarcely to be found, and a new poetic style developed in the bourgeois entourage of the *puys* and the urban setting of Paris is emerging — one that either faintly imitates or boldly ironizes earlier courtly tradition. Originally amoral erotic concerns become subsumed under ethical or frankly religious ones. Given this enormous change in literary culture, which certainly was gaining momentum during the two decades following the composition of the first *Rose*, it is not at all surprising that the poem's brilliant strategy based on the subtleties of courtly expression was not perceived by most readers and, further, that it was reread against the backdrop of a quite distinct generic horizon. What *is* surprising, perhaps, is that the work would have been read at all after the thirteenth century, and this abrupt change in fortune can be interpreted as both the blessing and the curse bestowed upon the *Rose* by Jean de Meun.

The problem of the poem's ending, or closure, has occupied our attention repeatedly in the previous pages — in part because we are attempting to revise traditionally entrenched thoughts about the *Rose*'s completion, and in part because it seems likely that closure in its broadest sense is an explicit theme of the poem. Between absolute and partial closure there arises the significant difference between obliteration and perpetuation, finality and continuity. Insofar as literary perception is concerned, how does one know one is at the end of a poem . . . until one reaches it? When a distinct break from literary tradition occurs, such as we find in the *Roman de la Rose,* no amount of codification will provide an absolute answer. Someone must tell us that a work is ended in order for it to be perceived as such. But does that voice arise from the inside or the outside of a work? Is the closure thus effected a matter of *pre*ordained determination, or *post*poned indecision? The CI

FALT ending formula found in the manuscript tradition is here most instructive, for, in addition to its constituting an exterior voice recognizing the end and officially marking it – the scribal gesture *par excellence* – its etymology suggests that the end comes at a juncture where there is simply nothing more to say. *Le texte,* like Chrétien's Guenevere, *se tait.* And that is perhaps the only valid way of ending.

When we finally perceive the collusion between Narrator and Lover in the *Rose,* their radical interdependence, then it becomes obvious that at the end, at the moment where "Guillaume" purportedly stopped writing, there is literally nothing more to say. However, rather than a dead-end silence, the poem manifestly seeks an answer, a response – be it the *merci* or *guerredon* of one addressee, the Lady, or the fascinated adherence of its other audience (the *vos* of the prologue). The poem serves thus as a tool and the allegory, if anything, has been transformed into a figure for its own communication – an address that implies, but which cannot incorporate, its own response. The paradoxical non-ending of the romance elements, the incomplete quest, plays its part as a provocation to, or seduction of, would-be lovers and readers – soliciting, as it were, a reward (in one case) or a continuation (in the other).

The problem of incompletion, indeed ubiquitous, attaches itself to a larger question of the poetic expression of human desire. The *fact* of allegory, far from an accident or an arcane pastime, is actually the grammatical translation of a paradoxical, because intellectualized, erotic pursuit. The breakdown of the initial narrative scheme, while perhaps the most compelling sign of this expressive impasse, is only one symptom of a broader reinvestment in literary conventionality. To be sure, the reciprocity between Narrator and Lover echoes the distinction between lyric and romance expression, between subjective and objective vision, around which poles the articulation of love tends to gravitate. But it is important to notice that the very poetic materials of the *Rose* resist, by means of a logic of action and figuration, the romance treatment that they are forced to undergo. The consequences of the romance quest might be conceived in terms of failure or destruction, visualized as the fossilization or the plucking of the rose. In either case, these results are equally antithetical to the lyric enterprise, for which an indeterminacy is essential. In the psychological language of the courtly poet, *hope* must be maintained or the erotic dream cannot continue. This is the primary reason why nonattainment cannot be officially recognized, why the dream itself cannot close and why the effective closure must remain covert.

FOUR

Narcissus and the allegorical fountain

> Tant m'estoie amés toudis
> C'onqes mais ne me dounai
> (Richard de Fournival, VII, 28–9)
>
> "Iste ego sum"
> (Ovid, *Metamorphoses*, III, 463)

NARCISSUS, ECHO, AND THE ROSE

One important episode of Guillaume de Lorris's *Rose*, the tale of Narcissus, has been reserved for our final chapter, perhaps because it is the only way in which to conclude a book about the closure of an ostensibly unfinished, and unendable, poem. Indeed, it will be our task in the following pages to show how the example of Narcissus provides an answer to, and a justification for, the problematics of closure that have characterized our vision of the *Roman de la Rose* throughout this study.

It should first be mentioned that the modern fascination with the mythical Narcissus and the quality to which he lends his name, "narcissism," while of some relevance, is neither the primary motivation nor the inspiration for this chapter. On the contrary, one might say that the post-Freudian world has demythologized the myth, turned "narcissism" into a common noun, and thus emptied it of a great deal of its inherent polysemy. It might be added that the fascination with Narcissus has continued unceasingly since classical times and that it is itself an example of modern cultural narcissism to think that only the twentieth century has adequately uncovered the import of the myth.[1] We will, in the course of our discussion, have to deal with the fact that the most common reading of Narcissus in the courtly context treated him as an analogue to the courtly lover who cannot attain what he most desires (the

---

[1] The reader is referred to the convenient study by Louise Vinge, which contains texts and synopses of most major versions of the Narcissus legend from antiquity to the nineteenth century: *The Narcissus Theme in Western European Literature up to the Early Nineteenth Century*, trans. Robert Dewsnap and Nigel Reeves (Lund, 1967).

Lady).² Such a reading completely ignores what the modern world finds essential in the myth, the turning inward toward the self.

More importantly for our purposes, the Narcissus episode occupies an enigmatic and privileged position in the *Roman de la Rose*. One of the poem's earliest recorded readers, Jean de Meun, recognized this, having included a reply to the Narcissus example in the conclusion to his lengthy continuation of Guillaume's poem.³ As far as Guillaume is concerned, there are three principal factors that point up the singularity of Narcissus. First, in the midst of the various allegorical developments discussed in Chapter

---

2 For a comprehensive summary of these references, see the introduction to *Narcisus (poème du XIIe siècle)*, eds. M. M. Pelan and N. C. W. Spence, Publications de la Faculté des Lettres de l'Université de Strasbourg, Fasc. 147 (Paris, 1964), pp. 19–21.

3 In the final 500 lines of his 17,000-line continuation, Jean de Meun provides two direct palinodes to Guillaume's poem, which are connected in another way through their recall of Narcissus: First, Jean invents a paradisiacal space to replace Deduit's garden, the "biau parc" in which is to be found a precious fountain not at all like the one where Narcissus attempted to quench his thirst:

> c'est la fonteine perilleuse,
> tant amere et tant venimeuse
> qu'el tua le biau Narcisus
> quant il se miroit iqui sus.   (20379–82)

(It is the perilous fountain, so bitter and poisonous that it killed the fair Narcissus when he looked at himself in it. [p. 334])

Second, Jean tells a counter-myth, that of Pygmalion, in the midst of which the famous sculptor recalls Narcissus, having realized that his own fatal love bears certain similarities with that of the self-involved youth:

> "N'ama jadis ou bois ramé,
> a la fonteine clere et pure,
> Narcisus sa propre figure,
> quant cuida sa saif estanchier?"   (20846–9)

("Didn't Narcissus, long ago in the branched forest, when he thought to quench his thirst, fall in love with his own face in the clear, pure fountain?" [p. 341])

Particularly helpful on the nature of Jean's mythological reply to Guillaume are Daniel Poirion, "Narcisse et Pygmalion dans *Le Roman de la Rose*," in *Essays in Honor of Louis Francis Solano*, eds. Raymond J. Cormier and Urban T. Holmes, University of North Carolina Studies in the Romance Languages and Literatures, No. 92 (Chapel Hill, 1970), pp. 153–65; Thomas D. Hill, "Narcissus, Pygmalion, and the Castration of Saturn: Two Mythographical Themes in the *Roman de la Rose*," *Studies in Philology*, 71 (1974), 404–26; and Roger Dragonetti, "Pygmalion ou les pièges de la fiction dans le *Roman de la Rose*," in *Orbis Mediaevalis: Mélanges de langue et de littérature médiévales offerts à Reto Raduolf Bezzola à l'occasion de son quatre-vingtième anniversaire*, eds. George Güntert, Marc-René Jung, Kurt Ringger (Bern, 1978), pp. 89–111.

Three, the story of Narcissus is the only classical myth related in its entirety. Venus, whose roots are of course in the Graeco-Roman mythological tradition, is thoroughly assimilated to the personifications through her active participation in the Lover's quest; an additional sign of this is the absolute silence with regard to her mythic past. This observation leads to the second distinguishing feature of Narcissus's portrayal, namely that his story is totally isolated from the rest of the dream vision, both in terms of the events that occur *and* their narrative treatment. Narcissus and Echo do not interact with the Lover or with any of the personified qualities. They are clearly not present and, in fact, their story belongs to the shadowy past of the garden. In accordance with this discontinuous insertion, Narcissus will assume the function of a simple metaphor, with no hint of psychological causality. The narrative transition is equally abrupt, there being no introductory phrase of the sort that Guillaume uses quite frequently. Following upon the Lover's discovery of a sign identifying the fountain as the one at the edge of which "estoit morz li biau Narcisus" (1436) ("the fair Narcissus died" [p. 50]), the tale begins almost as if some other voice were telling it: "Narcisus fu uns demoisiaus . . . " (1437) ("Narcissus was a young man" [p. 50]). Finally, the story of Narcissus coincides with the crucial moment of the Lover's *innamoramento*. More precisely, as we shall see further on, it is through the fountain associated with Narcissus that the Lover views his beloved, a moment that is also distinguished by the Lover's first display of an active, willful desire.

After his delightful experience at the *carole,* the Lover makes a curious departure from what has turned into a refined orgy scene (lines 1285–92) and takes the opportunity to explore every square inch of garden property:

> . . . j'alai tant destre et senestre
> que j'oi tot l'afere et tot l'estre
> dou vergier cerchié et veü.   (1415–17)

(I went so far, to left and to right, that I searched out and saw the entire condition and nature of the garden. [pp. 49–50])

The Narrator, simultaneously with this perusal, informs us that the Lover has been followed all along by Amor wielding his bow and arrows, stating quite clearly, however, that the Lover (his past self) was unaware of this at the time: "Je, cui de ce ne fu noient" (1315) ("Knowing nothing of all this" [p. 48]). This is the first in a series of statements which emphasize the distance between Narrator and Lover, thus reinforcing our appraisal of them as two separate characters with two distinct points of view.[4]

Then the Lover comes upon a fountain in a large marble stone situated under a pine tree. The fountain, created by Nature, is clearly labeled as the one where Narcissus wasted away and died:[5]

> si ot desus la pierre escrites
> el bort amont letres petites,
> qui disoient, ilec desus
> estoit morz li biau Narcisus. (1433–6)
>
> (in the stone, on the border of the upper side, [Nature] had cut small letters saying that there the fair Narcissus died. [p. 50])

The setting of this scene has elicited a number of interpretations relating it to the Earthly Paradise, the garden of Eden. In an especially noteworthy article, Erich Köhler speaks of the archetypal fountain of life or regeneration, and of knowledge.[6] According to Köhler, Guillaume transforms the despairing image of Narcissus into one of hope and rebirth through the vision provided by the fountain, thereby acceding to the expression of a renewed Golden Age. A quite different interpretation, following upon the insights to be derived from Scriptural exegesis, views the story of Narcissus as a retelling of the Fall, and the Lover's experience as a repetition

---

4 For pertinent discussions of this perceptual distinction, see Stephen G. Nichols, Jr., "The Rhetoric of Sincerity in the *Roman de la Rose*," in *Romance Studies in Memory of Edward Billings Ham*, California State College at Hayward Publications, No. 2 (Hayward, CA, 1967), pp. 115–29; E. B. Vitz, "The *I* of the *Roman de la Rose*," *Genre*, 6 (1973), 49–75; Rupert T. Pickens, "*Somnium* and Interpretation in Guillaume de Lorris," *Symposium*, 28 (1974), 175–86; and our Chapter Two, above.

5 In addition to the articles cited in note 3 above, the following studies of the Narcissus episode in Guillaume de Lorris have been of most help in the present discussion: Jean Frappier, "Variations sur le thème du miroir, de Bernard de Ventadour à Maurice Scève," *CAIEF*, 11 (1959), 134–58; Erich Köhler, "Narcisse, la fontaine d'Amour et Guillaume de Lorris," in *L'Humanisme médiéval dans les littératures romanes du XIIe au XIVe siècle*, ed. Anthime Fourrier (Paris, 1964), pp. 147–66; Louise Vinge, *Narcissus Theme*, pp. 78–85; Frederick Goldin, *The Mirror of Narcissus in the Courtly Love Lyric* (Ithaca, NY, 1967), pp. 52–9; and, most recently, Jean Rychner, "Le Mythe de la fontaine de Narcisse dans le *Roman de la Rose* de Guillaume de Lorris," in *Le Lieu et la formule: Hommage à Marc Eigeldinger* (Neuchâtel, 1978), pp. 33–46.

6 Köhler, "Narcisse," p. 153.

of the original fault.⁷ Unfortunately, these ingenious interpretations place Guillaume's *Rose* in a theological context for which there is little textual evidence, occasionally confusing his poem with the continuation written by Jean de Meun.⁸ Finding the source of the garden imagery in exegetical commentaries is far less likely than the almost certain inspiration provided by the commonplaces of the courtly lyric and the highly rhetorical *Natureingang*.⁹ Interpretation of the poem in a Christian context, as if it were an orthodox religious expression, has been greatly encouraged by the repetition of the words *paradis* (found seven times in the text) and *Dieu* (thirty-nine times by itself and fourteen times in the expression "Dieu d'amor"). However, in most of its manifestations, "paradis" seems to designate a common rather than a proper noun, much as in modern English. Of the seven examples, only two appear to refer to a specific locality inhabited by God: Papelardie has been refused entry into the "porte . . . de paradis" (432–3) ("the door to Paradise" [p. 36]); and Reson was not created by Nature but rather "ou paravis" (2970) ("in Paradise"). In both cases, interestingly enough, the word refers to personages proscribed from the courtly garden in different ways and is totally inapplicable to any aspect of the Lover's quest. In the other five instances, the word *paradis* would simply translate as "delightful place": "je cuidai estre/por voir em paradis terrestre" (633–4) ("I

---

7 See D. W. Robertson, Jr., *A Preface to Chaucer: Studies in Medieval Perspectives* (Princeton, 1962), pp. 91–8; and John V. Fleming, *The Roman de la Rose: A Study in Allegory and Iconography* (Princeton, 1969), pp. 92–103.
8 The two studies mentioned in note 7, following upon the influential lead of Alan M. F. Gunn (*The Mirror of Love: A Reinterpretation of "The Romance of the Rose"* [Lubbock, TX, 1952]), treat the two "parts" of the *Rose* as a harmonious and consistent poetic unity, and consequently cannot help but read Guillaume's Narcissus according to Jean de Meun's moralizing, after-the-fact interpretation. In a general sense, the argument that the elements of courtly literature originated in Biblical commonplaces mistakes textual similarities (which could result from the independent use of a common source) for a positive indication of filiation (which, requiring much more precise evidence, is considerably harder to prove). More importantly, such a critical vision tacitly assumes that a writer always accepts and perpetuates the ideology of his source materials – a point of view which is at best naïve and ill-conceived.
9 See the pertinent discussion of the Ideal Landscape by Ernst Robert Curtius, *European Literature and the Latin Middle Ages*, trans. Willard R. Trask (New York, 1953), pp. 183–202. Curtius substantiates the nonproper use of the word "paradis" in medieval poetry: "Since Paradise is a garden, a garden can, by transposition, be called a paradise" (p. 200, n. 32). For a further discussion of stereotyped nature description in Guillaume's poem, see Chapter Three, above.

FOUR: NARCISSUS AND THE FOUNTAIN

thought that I was truly in an earthly paradise" [p. 39]); "il ne fet en nul paradis/si bon estre" (638–9) ("there was no paradise where existence was so good" [p. 39]); "il n'est nus graindres paradis/d'avoir amie a son devis" (1297–8) ("there is no greater paradise than to have one's beloved at one's desire" [p. 48]); "graine de paradis novele" (1341) ("fresh grains of paradise" [p. 48]); "or sui cheoiz, ce m'est avis,/de grant enfer en paradis" (3335–6) ("now I have fallen, as I believe, from deepest hell to paradise" [p. 78]). In fact, considering the association between paradise and lovemaking in the third example and the obvious inversion in the last example, one might interpret Guillaume's usage of the word as fundamentally parodic. In a similar vein, the word *Dieu* is used with such variation that one is often unsure whether it is designating the Christian God or the God of Love.[10] In short, even if the garden imagery used by Guillaume participates in, or even originated in, a set of Christian archetypes, their connection in this text is too loose to justify an orthodox theological reading.

Immediately following is the Narrator's account of the Narcissus story. The first-person retrospective narration that had characterized the initial development of the romance gives way abruptly and without transition to the third-person narration which is most common in medieval French romances and lais. The shift is important inasmuch as it is the first break in the Lover's personal experience, foreshadowed by the above-mentioned remark about Amor's covert surveillance. It relates thematically to the distinction between Narcissus as an *exemplum* and the rest of

---

10 Likewise, one could interpret the Narrator/Lover's naïve evaluation of the *carole* dancers as angels (723), reminiscent of Perceval's first encounter with the knights in the forest, as fundamentally ironic. Later in the poem, Guillaume paints a garish portrait of the lascivious "goddess" Venus, only to complete it with the hilarious observation that she was not particularly religious ("n'iert pas de religion" [3413]). This demonstrates even more cogently than the "dieu d'Amors" example the glaring contradictions of a single word (*dieu*) used to designate both pagan deities and the single transcendent Christian God, as was the case in medieval writings. On the assimilation of the pagan gods to Christianity, see Jean Seznec, *The Survival of the Pagan Gods,* trans. Barbara F. Sessions (Princeton, 1953); and Hans Robert Jauss, "Allegorese, Remythisierung und neuer Mythus," in his *Alterität und Modernität der Mittelalterlichen Literatur* (Munich, 1977), pp. 285–307 (French trans.: "Allégorie, 'Remythisation' et nouveau mythe. Réflexions sur la captivité chrétienne de la mythologie au moyen âge," in *Mélanges d'histoire littéraire, de linguistique et de philologie romanes offerts à Charles Rostaing* [Liège, 1974], pp. 469–99).

the personifications: The Lover never meets Narcissus. Our interpretation of the *exemplum* will call for different tools than those required to decipher the personifications.¹¹ A "grammatical" reading will not be possible.

Although considered by some to be inferior or incomplete, Guillaume's version of the myth is structured in an exceptionally artful manner. It actually consists of two stories with a marked separation: that of Echo and that of Narcissus. The episodes can be conveniently divided up in the following fashion:

    I. Introduction/*mise-en-scène*   (1423–36; 14 lines)
   II. Summary of Narcissus's plight   (1437–41; 5 lines)
  III. Drama of Echo   (1442–66; 25 lines)
  IV. Drama of Narcissus   (1467–94; 28 lines)
   V. Brief Summary   (1495–1504; 10 lines)
 VI. Moral Application   (1505–8; 4 lines)

Guillaume's neat symmetrical ordering of the narrative segments highlights the diptych formed by the double crisis (III–IV).

The Narrator introduces Narcissus quite simply as one who was captivated by Amor, making no mention of Echo:

> Narcisus fu uns demoisiaus
> qui Amors tint en ses raisiaus;
> et tant le sot Amors destraindre
> et tant le fist plorer et plaindre
> qu'il li covint a rendre l'ame....   (1437–41)

---

11 We follow the preliminary schematization of Hans Robert Jauss ("Alterität und Modernität der Mittelalterlichen Literatur," in his *Alterität* (pp. 9–47), for whom the *exemplum* distinguishes itself from among the other medieval short genres insofar as it presents a moral lesson by means of an illustrative, historically authentic narrative. According to Jauss, it differs from the other medieval examplary genres (parable, fable and allegory) by its specificity (parable), its exegetical framework (allegory) and its historicity (fable). It might be added that the parable is virtually unknown in medieval literature (pp. 43–4) and that Jauss has some difficulty marking a precise difference between *exemplum* and allegory. In medieval usage (following the classical rhetoricians), the defining quality of an *exemplum* is its historicity (having taken place) and/or its connection to an *auctor*. Cf. Geoffroi de Vinsauf, *Poetria Nova* (ed. Edmond Faral, *Les Arts Poétiques du XIIe et du XIIIe siècle* [Paris, 1924]), lines 1255–7: "Vel cum nomine/Auctoris rem, quam dixit, vel quam prius egit,/Exemplum pono" ("I put forward as an exemplum, with the name of an author, either something which he said or something which he once did"). An allegorical story need not be considered to have any prior or separate existence. For a different typology of the vernacular exemplary short forms (*lai, fabliau, exemplum, legenda,* and so forth), which tends to reduce the differences in favor of a generalized poetics of the short form, see Paul Zumthor, *Essai de poétique médiévale* (Paris, 1972), pp. 391–404.

FOUR: NARCISSUS AND THE FOUNTAIN

> (Narcissus was a young man whom Love caught in his snares. Love knew so well how to torment him, to make him weep and complain, that he had to give up his soul. [p. 50])

The Narrator proceeds to give the ostensible reason why, Echo's curse, by telling *her* side of the story: "car Equo . . . /l'avoit amé. . . ." (1442-3) ("for Echo . . . had loved him" [p. 50]). The story of Echo is recounted almost exclusively from her point of view and she dies alone, of her own grief. It should be emphasized that her death is portrayed purely as a function of feelings which she created within herself:

> Quant ele s'oï escondire,
> si en ot tel duel et tel ire
> et le tint a si grant despit
> qu'ele fu morte sanz respit.   (1451-4)

(When she heard him refuse, her grief and anger were so great and she held him in such great despite that she died without delay. [p. 50])

Although Guillaume omits any precisions about Echo's past, her very name serves to evoke her mythological status (the disembodied voice) insofar as it was a common noun in both medieval Latin and Old French. It is moreover not coincidental that Guillaume expresses each character's feeling of rejection in a manner appropriate to the "sense" for which they became famous: Echo "*s'oï escondire*" ("*heard* that she was refused") whereas Narcissus "*vit* qu'il ne porroit/acomplir . . ." (1495-6) ("*saw* that he could not accomplish" [p. 51]).

The story of Narcissus's torment follows with almost no mention of Echo. It is as if her sorrow were placed aside so that we might view the solitary upset of Narcissus. The well-known fountain scene recounts Narcissus's mistaking of his own reflection ("ses ombres" [1484]) for the face of a beautiful child ("un esfant bel a desmesure" [1486]). Then the fact of his self-love is stated in quite explicit terms: "il ama son ombre demainne" ("he loved his very own reflection") (1492). The two characters, Echo and Narcissus, die in a flourish of mutual destruction that is actually a function of their own solitary condition. The one theme that unites both parts of the story is that of vengeance and punishment; so accentuated is it by the Narrator that it could almost be considered a leitmotif. Fully one half of Echo's story is devoted to her *priere* for revenge (lines 1455–66) and Narcissus's tale is studded with terms referring to Amor's retribution: "venchier" (1487), "guerredoné" (1490), "guerredon" (1504), and "merite" (1504). Curiously, however, the figure of Amor is carefully placed in between the two as mediator (receiving Echo's prayer and inflicting punishment), as if to ensure their complete separation while attenuating Echo's role. Her name, in fact, is mentioned only once in the entire romance and the sole allusion to her revenge within the framework of Narcissus's story refrains from naming her:

> Ensi si out de *la meschine*
> qu'il avoit devant escondite
> son guerredon et sa merite.   (1502–4)

(Thus did he receive his deserved retribution from *the girl* whom he had scorned. [p. 51])

In the other statement of vengeance, Amor seems to be reacting to a personal affront made to himself, without regard to Echo:

> Lors se sot bien Amors venchier
> dou grant orguil et dou dangier
> que Narcisus li ot mené.   (1487–9)

(Then love knew how to avenge himself for the great pride and the resistance that Narcissus had directed toward him. [p. 50])

At the very least, the narrative separation can be interpreted as the crisis of communication that frequently characterizes courtly lyrics and lais, but there is more to be said.

Not only does the account of each character follow a similar narrative pattern, but there are also direct textual parallels associating the two experiences. At the moment of refusal, Echo "ot tel duel et tel *ire*" (1452). Narcissus also "perdi d'*ire* tot le sen" (1500). The result for Echo: "ele *fu morte* sanz respit" (1454). For Narcissus: "*fu morz* en poi de termine" (1501). We might add that Narcissus's death is mentioned no fewer than four times in a space of less than 150 lines (lines 1441, 1493, 1501, and 1572), an instance of rhetorical *amplificatio* as well as of the Narrator's obsessive preoccupation throughout the *Rose*.

This cold and unrelenting portrayal of involvement with the self and isolation — valid for both Narcissus *and* Echo — has none of the sentimental features of the twelfth-century *Lai de Narcisse*, with which it is often compared.[12] In the *Lai,* the female who is in love with Narcissus is called Dané and not Echo. Any hint of the theme of vocal reflection, which complements that of Narcissus's visual reflection, is thereby suppressed. Moreover, in the *Lai* the two stories are not told in isolation as in Guillaume's account, but rather combined in a narrative interlace that doubles the corporeal interlace uniting the two figures at death. Whereas Guillaume's version, by taking place in a nearly atemporal universe, emphasizes the mythical shadowing, the anonymous *Lai* is embroidered with all the trappings common to contemporary romance stylization (localization, clothing, social status, and so on), much in the manner of the "anachronistic" twelfth-century retellings of the Troy and Thebes legends. In any event, we cannot confuse the two versions of the ancient myth: Guillaume's account contains virtually none of these modernizing elements, while following more closely the scheme of Ovid's narrative.

The anonymous *Lai* reassumes the legend, albeit rather bluntly, into the stereotyped scheme that had developed as a basis for a certain number of twelfth-century *lais* and romances (compare Tristan, certain *lais* of Marie de France, Pyramus and Thisbé), those that emphasize the impossibilities or barriers facing love relationships. The message is as follows: True love between two people does exist but cannot maintain itself in the context of modern society. The *Lai de Narcisse* adapts to this pattern primarily through the repentant change in attitude of the central character just before his demise. Narcissus finally realizes the ability to love another, but too late. The two lovers are united in death in a manner reminiscent of Thomas's account of the death of Tristan and Iseult. None of this is part of Ovid's tale (or of Guillaume's, for that matter).[13] When we read Guillaume de Lorris according

---

12 The most recent edition is that of Martine Thiry-Stassin and Madeleine Tyssens, *Narcisse: Conte ovidien français du XIIe siècle*, Bibliothèque de la Faculté de Philosophie et Lettres de l'Université de Liège, Fasc. 211 (Paris, 1976).
13 This is not to imply that Guillaume's tale and that of Ovid (*Metamorphoses*, III, 339–510) are at all identical. A number of central features of Ovid's tale are deleted in the greatly condensed French version: The tale of Tiresias's prophecy and the birth of Narcissus; Narcissus's recognition of his own image in the fountain; the final transformation into a flower (cf. our discussion, below); Echo's own mythological background;

to the *Lai*, we assume a similar narrative patterning in the former.[14] Nothing is more emphasized in Guillaume's tale, however, than the separation, physical *and* spiritual *and* narrative, between the two characters, underscored by the mediating presence of Amor.

Guillaume's tale of Narcissus ends with what we labeled above the "Moral Application," or *sententia:*

> Dames, cest essample aprenez,
> qui vers vos amis mesprenez;
> car se vos les lessiez morir,
> Dex le vos savra bien merir.   (1505–8)

(You ladies who neglect your duties toward your sweethearts, be instructed by this exemplum, for if you let them die, God will know how to repay you well for your fault. [p. 51])

This moral has baffled many critics and at the very least upset a number of likely interpretations. Let us first consider the *sententia* in its context and in relation to the subsequent actions. The Lover has approached the fountain and finds himself in more or less the same spatial situation as Narcissus. As if to emphasize this point, the Narrator informs us that the two fountains are indeed one and the same. The reader is prepared to parallel the two fountain experiences. In other words, the exegete/reader's task appears to be that of figuring out how the Lover and Narcissus are comparable. No, the Narrator says, this tale is meant to point to the ladies in the audience (and thus obliquely to *the* Lady addressed in the prologue) but not to the male lovers. He is, of course, referring to the familiar situation of the haughty, far-off Lady of the lyric tradition, who continually rejects or at least distances the suppliant lover. The above warning could, for instance, have been

---

and Echo's final vocal interplay with the dying Narcissus. The two elements mentioned by Lecoy in his edition of the *Rose* (I, pp. 274–5) as additions made by Guillaume are the attribution of the fatal curse to Echo (in Ovid it was performed by a spurned male lover) and the final moral.

14 For Frederick Goldin (*Mirror*, p. 22), the *Lai de Narcisse* "suggests the meaning of the story of Narcissus for much of the literature of the Middle Ages." His references to the "medieval Narcissus" while discussing Guillaume de Lorris further substantiate his belief in it as a fixed, rigorously codified concept. Moreover, Goldin's adherence to the Augustinian notion of the truth of the mirror and the aspiration of man's soul toward higher truths leads to a denial of anything resembling personal judgment, which is so crucial in the narrative development of the *Rose:* "this concept of personal truth, which denies the validity of the mirror, was not available to medieval man."

directed quite rightly toward the Guenevere of Chrétien's *Chevalier de la Charrete*. Lest the parallel not appear obvious, we should perhaps spell it out. The *sententia* points up a potential misdeed committed toward lovers such that they are allowed to die, and, furthermore, threatens an inevitable vengeance by God which will "reward" this misdeed. Now, in the Narcissus/Echo *exemplum* as recounted in the *Rose,* only one character rebuffs a suitor, allowing that suitor to die, and is punished by a God — Narcissus. Were the Narrator simply asking the ladies to take pity on lovers such as Narcissus, the mention of God's revenge would be a meaningless threat. Furthermore, Echo would have no place therein. And since the tale as told by the Narrator features the dual theme of vengeance and retribution as a leitmotif, its relevance to the moral *sententia* must be considered. In addition, textual echoes accentuate the connection: "merir" (1508) explicitly recalls Narcissus's "merite," mentioned only four lines before (1504). Echo refers to the sorrow of "li loial amant" (1463) — a masculine reference, we note — as being her own, thus projecting to "vos amis" in the *sententia*. And of course, one of the attributes displayed by Narcissus, and almost exclusively associated with the courtly Lady, is "dangier" (1488).

In the present context, then, this quite matter-of-fact assertion forces us to reconsider our first option and select a second one: If Narcissus and his plight serve as a warning to the Lady — if Narcissus can be perceived as a "type" of the lady — then our Lover can be compared to Echo, the hopeless desiring subject. After some thought, we find a number of reasons for accepting this reading. First, and most obvious, both Echo and the courtly Lover pursue an object of desire that in turn rejects or distances them. Echo and the Lover are both victims of Amor and yet, paradoxically, address themselves to him for help. Both live for the most part in isolation. And, finally, both are figurations for the human voice, which addresses but which is eventually a reflection, a disembodied sound. Echo fits this description, since her name personifies her to some extent. The Lover, we remember, is also a poet, whose essential function is to sing — a fact that explains his frequent metaphorical association with birds. The courtly poet's "remains," the body of love poetry, are a written analogue to the ubiquitous verbal echo. The association is doubly important here, insofar as the Narrator is telling/singing his dream to his Lady both as a delightful message and as an erotic invitation.[15]

While some critics have accepted this moral as it is expressed, others have rejected it as patently absurd.[16] This is indeed a crucial moment in the text, for it gives rise to a conflict of interpretation that becomes a part of the text itself. The reader is invited to respond either to the outright moral *sententia* or to the comparison inferred from the logical ordering of the text. This brings the attentive reader, at least momentarily, to question the motives of the Narrator, who is, after all, not only telling the story but also directly implicated therein. Could he be unreliable or possibly trying to trick us? If he meant to indicate that the Lady was a type of Narcissus, why is the Lover alone associated with the fountain? On the other hand, if no comparison between Narcissus and the Lover was intended, why have the Lover experience the rose *through* Narcissus (and not, say, directly)? If Narcissus is to be interpreted as a negative *exemplum,* as many have indicated, why is he *in* the garden instead of painted on the outside wall? The same question could of course be asked of Jalousie, Dangier, and the others, the inimical rose guardians, and does indeed provoke a surprising answer (they are integral components of the love quest), as we saw in Chapter Three. Perhaps a closer look at the Lover's own experience at the fountain will help us to interpret the simultaneous affirmation and denial of his comparison with Narcissus.

Textually speaking, the Lover's experience serves as a repetition of, and possibly a palinode to, that of Narcissus. The Lover approaches the fountain and, after a moment of hesitation caused by his memory of Narcissus's fate, he looks into the water:

> quant je i fui, si m'abessai
> por voair l'eve qui couroit

---

15 The inclusion of Echo might even constitute a real innovation with regard to the courtly use of the Narcissus *exemplum:* Roger Dragonetti (*La Technique poétique des trouvères dans la chanson courtoise* [Bruges, 1960], pp. 202–4) states that early *trouvère* use of Narcissus treats him as the perfect lover in search of an inaccessible love. Only in Richard de Fournival, Dragonetti tells us, will the tale's symbolic density be developed and the figure of Echo brought into play as still another figure of the poet.

16 Nichols, "Rhetoric," p. 117, asserts, "When the author-narrator digresses to tell a story such as the myth of Narcissus, he is careful to make an explicit commentary pointing up the proper conclusion to be drawn in accordance with the tone of the general narrative." Poirion, on the other hand, calls Guillaume's use of the moral a "contre-sens délibéré" ("Narcisse," p. 157).

> et la graveile qui bouloit
> au fonz, plus clere qu'argenz fins.   (1522-5)

(when I was near I lowered myself to the ground to see the running water and the gravel bubbling up at the bottom, clearer than fine silver. [p. 51])

From the outset, descriptive detail, mostly absent from Narcissus's vision, abounds. Moreover, this is not the Lover's first glance into water: We recall, at the beginning of the dream:

> De l'eve clere reluisant
> mon vis refreschi et lavé,
> si vi tot covert et pavé
> le fonz de l'eve de graveile.   (118-21)

(As I washed my face and refreshed myself with the clear, shining water, I saw that the bottom of the stream was all covered and paved with gravel. [p. 32])

The mentions of the gravel and the bottom ("fonz") are overt foreshadowings of the later fountain scene. References to freshness and clarity proliferate strikingly in various contexts throughout the first half of the poem.[17] This is one of numerous examples that demonstrate the poem's idiosyncratic stylistic organization. Its structure is based on a continual reiteration of naturalistic descriptions that, through their new contexts, develop wider and increasingly more figurative meanings. The placement of such remarkable visual impressions in the foreground underscores thematically the repetitive, and yet constantly refined, vision of the Lover. Everything, in fact, that the Lover does at this moment he has done before, just as everything that he sees in the fountain he has "seen" before in his purportedly thorough inspection.

The Lover goes on to perceive, unlike Narcissus who saw "son vis, son nés et sa bouchete" (1482) ("His face, his nose and little mouth" [p. 50]), a pair of conduits, the alleged sources of the fountain (".II. doiz cleres et parfondes" [1530] ["two bright and deep conduits"]), and ".II. pierres de cristal" (1536) ("two crystal stones"), which are to be found at the bottom, "el fonz" (1535).

---

[17] Various mentions of *clarté:* "clere estoit l'eve" (110); "fontaines cleres et vives" (1390); "vit en l'eve clere et nete" (1481). Another frequently occurring notion is that of freshness: "L'eve est tot jorz fresche et novele" (1528); flowers are "fresche et novele" (1402); "l'erbe fresche" (744, 1380).

The question of the crystals has posed problems for nearly all of the poem's critics. The first truly brilliant modern interpretation, that of C. S. Lewis, viewed them as a poetic image for the eyes of the implied Lady, whose person is figured in a different way by the rose.[18] With various purposes in mind, critics since Lewis have provided countless modifications for this basic crystals/eyes symbolism: They are the Lover's own eyes; the Lover's reflection of his own eyes in those of the Lady; or even the Lover's vision or awareness of the Lady's eyes.[19]

However ingenious some of these interpretations might be, most do not take account of a further, more specifically philological, inconsistency. The Narrator begins by talking about two crystals, only to make a shift, seemingly without explanation, to the singular. Félix Lecoy, one of the more recent editors of the poem, admits his difficulties with the passage:[20]

> Qu'il y ait eu "deux pierres de cristal au fond de la fontaine" (1535–6), cela ne fait pas de doute. Il n'en est pas moins vrai que les vers 1541–1568 posent à l'éditeur un problème pratiquement insoluble, aucun des manuscrits jusqu'ici consultés n'ayant une leçon cohérente, sauf quelques-uns de ceux qui ont adopté en principe le singulier pour la tirade (comme c'est le cas du nôtre). Ce singulier peut, à la rigueur, se défendre, si l'on y voit le singulier d'un nom de matière (cf. cependant 1603).

None of the above interpretations accounts for the singular/plural problem either. A careful look at the variation between the two possibilities, however, reveals a heretofore unnoticed pattern. The crystals are referred to in the plural at the very beginning and at the very end of the discussion (lines 1536 and 1603), whereas the middle section consistently uses the singular (lines 1545, 1547,

---

18 C. S. Lewis, *The Allegory of Love: A Study in Medieval Tradition* (London, 1936), pp. 128–9. He actually states that the rose is the "Lady's love" (p. 129).
19 Frappier, "Variations," p. 151: "Très probablement aussi, les 'pierres de cristal' qui, de prime abord, semblent doubler sans utilité le rôle joué par le miroir de l'eau, représentent les yeux de la dame, ou, plus subjectivement, la vision de ces yeux par l'amant." Robertson, *Preface*, p. 95: "These are not the eyes of his beloved, as one romantic account of the poem would have it, but his own eyes. . . ." Köhler, "Narcisse," p. 160: "ce caractère double du reflet de l'oeil dans l'oeil . . . est au fond du mythe de Narcisse." Rychner, "Mythe," p. 43: "Ce ne sont pas les yeux réfléchis et contemplés. Ce sont des yeux regardant."
20 Lecoy, ed., *Roman de la Rose*, I, p. 275.

FOUR: NARCISSUS AND THE FOUNTAIN

1558, and 1568). The switch to the singular at line 1545 coincides with a shift from past to present verb tenses, which is rigorously maintained as the Narrator discusses the general properties of the fountain/crystal:

>1536: *avoit* .II. pierres de cristal
>(there *were* two crystal stones)
>1541–7: Quant li solaus, qui tot *aguiete*,
>   ses rais en la fontaine *giete*
>   et la clarté aval *descent*,
>   lors *perent* colors plus de cent
>   ou cristal, qui par le soleil
>   *devient* inde, jaune et vermeil.
>   Si *est* cil cristaus merveilleus. . . .
>(when the sun, that *sees* all, *throws* its rays into the fountain and when its light *descends* to the bottom, then more than a hundred colors *appear* in the crystals which, on account of the sun, *become* yellow, blue, and red. This crystal *is* so wonderful . . . [p. 51])

The digression on the fountain's properties, termed a "tirade" by Lecoy, is initiated by a passage in the Narrator's direct, commentative voice:

>Mes une chose vos dirai
>qu'a merveille, ce cuit, tendroiz
>maintenant que vos l'entendroiz.   (1538–40)
>(There is one thing I want to tell you which, I think, you will consider a marvel when you hear it. [p. 51])

When we are returned to the past tense of the narrative account (signaled by the transitional "adés"), we find once more the plural "cristaus":

>Adés me *plot* a demorer
>a la fontaine remirer
>et as cristaus, qui me *mostroient* . . .   (1601–3)
>(Just then it *was* my pleasure to remain there gazing at the fountain and the crystals, which *showed* me . . . [p. 52])

Moreover, the word "cristal" (singular) seems to vary freely with "miroër" and "fontaine":

278

> Si est cil *cristaus* merveilleus. . . .
> ausi con li *mireors*. . .
> tot autresi vos di por voir
> que li *cristaus* . . .
> si n'i a si petite chose,
> tant soit reposte ne enclouse,
> dont demontrance ne soit feite
> con s'ele ert ou *cristal* portrete.
> C'est li *miroërs* perilleus,
> ou Narcisus, li orgueilleus,
> mira sa face. . . .   (1547–71)

(The *crystal* is so wonderful. . . . Just as the *mirror* . . . just so, I tell you truly, does the *crystal*. . . . There is nothing so small, however hidden or shut up, that is not shown there in the *crystal* as if it were painted in detail. It is the perilous *mirror* in which proud Narcissus gazed at his face. . . . [pp. 51–2])

We are also reminded that the crystal (singular) is equivalent as well to the fountain of Narcissus. Far from a philological oversight committed by some early scribe (considered by Lecoy as the lack of a "leçon cohérente"), the singular and plural variants of the word "cristal" denote two entirely different concepts. Used in the plural, the word refers to two objects, which, in the dream story, the Lover saw in the bottom of the fountain (temporally fixed and related to a unique experience). In the singular, the word refers to the mirror effect of the water's surface, or even the fountain itself (atemporal and independent of the Lover's experience). The Narrator explicitly separates the two in a passage quoted above: "a la *fontaine* remirer/et as *cristaus*" (1602–3). The ambiguity exists, but it is a functional aspect of the word itself. Recognized as such, this grammatical ambiguity or distortion can be seen to parallel the Lover's own visual distortion. Moreover, to suppress the mention of eyes for the sake of the crystal(s) is a way of transferring our attention from the object of vision to the visual faculty itself, the manner *by which* things are perceived.

In attempting to relate the Lover and Narcissus, we are perhaps wrong in assuming that because the Lover walks away from the fountain he has transcended the level of Narcissus's plight.[21]

---

21 Cf. Köhler, "Narcisse," p. 162.

FOUR: NARCISSUS AND THE FOUNTAIN

When he sets out in pursuit of the rose bush, he is actually after precisely what he saw in the fountain. No change in his sight is alluded to. Some critics contend that the Lover, unlike Narcissus, is spared by Amor; however, the shooting that the Lover undergoes at the hands of Amor could hardly be considered gentle treatment. Indeed, Amor's action seems but to reinforce the effects of the fountain vision. As if in corroboration, Amor tells us later that such treatment is typical for any who serve him (see especially lines 2404–10 and 2583–96). To evaluate the happenings in the garden in terms of our moral notions of good and evil clearly contradicts the oxymoronic code that characterizes Amor's domain. The Narrator himself comes to express regret about the fountain situation much as Narcissus had done:

> Cil miroërs m'a deceü.
> . . . ou laz cheï
> qui maint home a pris et traï.   (1607–12)

(That mirror deceived me . . . I fell into the snare that has captured and betrayed many a man. [p. 52])

Narcissus, we recall, also was held in the "raisiaus" (1438) of Amor, and also lamented that "ses ombres l'avoit *traï*" (1484). Later, at the end of Guillaume's poem, we are made to see not only how the Lover approaches Narcissus's fate ("Ja mes n'iert rien qui me *confort*" [4026] recalling "il ne porroit avoir *confort*" [1498]), but also to what extent he recalls both Narcissus *and* Echo through the use of the key words *ire* and *mort*:

> Par un poi que je ne fons d'*ire* . . .
> si ai poor et desconfort,
> quime donront, ce croi, la *mort*.   (4010–14)

(I almost melt with *anger* . . . And I think that my fear and my pain will bring me my *death*. [p. 88])

Lest we not perceive this important facet of the story which reinforces the connection between the Lover and Narcissus, Guillaume includes a further disclaimer when, in the midst of his discussion of the crystals and their properties, he indicates the existence of still another mystery:

> Mes ja mes n'oroiz mielz descrivre
> la verité de la matere,
> quant j'avré apost le mistere.   (1598–1600)
>
> (but, when I have revealed the mystery, you will never hear the truth of the matter better described. [p. 52])

In the preceding hundred lines, the reader has been given the moral of the Narcissus story and the explanation of the crystal's optic properties. Can there be more to learn? We recall from our discussion in Chapter Two that this is just one in a series of interventions by the Narrator that subtend the dream account. They all in some way refer to the discovery of a hidden meaning, designated by such words as *verité* or *senefiance,* and yet, as Jauss has pointed out, they are all strategically placed at points where we might think we just understood the message.[22] The Narrator's disruptive play with words and meanings, with beginnings and endings – paralleled by the unknowable "jeus d'Amors" – brings the inquisitive reader and his natural desire to find meaning, to "make sense," into the fold of the quest motif. The discovery of the "mistere" of Narcissus, if such discovery is possible, will come neither as easily nor as simply as expected.

In short, most readers interpret Narcissus exclusively as a model for human behavior, a critical enterprise that invariably leads to difficulties. Such a moral/thematic reading requires two basic assumptions prior to its elaboration. First, the two points of the comparison must be determined: With whom is Narcissus comparable? Second, the exemplary value of Narcissus (or the judgment passed on him) must be made explicit, since morality, or teaching, is at the base of any doctrinally oriented exemplary text. As the preceding discussion has shown, both questions are left unanswered and, indeed, barely articulated. As for the first one, both the Lover *and* the courtly Lady can be reasonably compared with Narcissus. Even assuming the first question resolved, an answer to the second is far from self-evident. Treating the ladies as Narcissus, according to the specified moral, forces us to overlook

---

22 Hans Robert Jauss, "La Transformation de la forme allégorique entre 1180 et 1240: d'Alain de Lille à Guillaume de Lorris," in *L'Humanisme médiéval* (note 5), pp. 107–46 (p. 109).

a considerable portion of the text. Such an interpretation, while marginally valid, is largely impractical as an explanation of the text as a whole.

To view the Lover as a "type" of Narcissus requires the imposition of a moral attitude, since none is given in the text. The interpretation of Narcissus as a negative *exemplum* would seem to contradict his very position at the center of the garden. Even to view him as an infantile stage of the Lover's growth into maturation invites contradiction, for it is clear that the Lover's subsequent vision (the Rose) results directly from his gaze into the fountain (that is, his repetition of the primal Narcissistic act) and that his vision undergoes little or no change from that moment on. We should expect the fountain, which supposedly brings death, to be eliminated from the idyllic eternal paradise represented by the garden of Deduit. On the contrary, its central position seems to support the idea that the fatal unrequited passion is an essential part of the courtly love quest. Is the poem, rather, a fundamentally pessimistic statement about the quest for a goal that can never be reached? Such a conclusion would be plausible were it not for the Narrator's apparent assurances of his ultimate success.[23] Moreover, it ignores the self-reflective theme, thereby returning us to an interpretation similar to that of the *Lai de Narcisse*. A further refinement might emphasize the Lover's simultaneous identity as a poet, one for whom poetry and its elaboration become primary and who thereby turns away from the exterior object and toward a concentration on the self. This final interpretation, perhaps the most all-inclusive, nonetheless neglects the curious textual undercuttings, the distinctly unsatisfactory moral explanation of Nar-

---

[23]   mes en ce songe onques riens n'ot
       qui tretot avenu ne soit
       si con li songes recensoit.   (28–30)

(but in this dream was nothing which did not happen just as the dream told it. [p. 31])

          . . . li murs fu levez
       et li chastiaus riches et forz,
       qu'Amors prist puis par ses esforz.   (3484–6)

(the wall was raised and . . . the rich and powerful castle that Love seized later through his efforts. [p. 80])

For an interesting interpretation of the last passage, see Douglas Kelly, "'Li chastiaus . . . Qu'Amors prist puis par ses esforz': The Conclusion of Guillaume de Lorris's *Rose*," in *A Medieval French Miscellany*, ed. Norris J. Lacy (Lawrence, KS, 1972), pp. 61–78.

cissus, and the seeming disclaimer of the various didactic moments, all of which, as we have seen, lend a distinctive hint of duplicity to the poem's texture.

As might be gathered from the preceding discussion, moral interpretations depend to a great extent upon the establishment of a context. Perhaps the Narcissus story in and of itself has a negative moral message, inasmuch as his actions result in death, an eventuality that most human societies greet with fear and aversion. Nonetheless, the context provided by the garden, which excludes reprehensible characters (compare the portraits on the exterior wall) and admits only social desirables (the folk participating in the *carole*), would argue for a positive reading of the myth. In fact, our hope to find a guiding moral context is deliberately confused by the Narrator, and nowhere do we find a better model for his actions than in the God of Love, whose autocratic rule requires blind obedience and a paradoxical pursuit of what one least desires ("les maus d'amer") ("the ills of love"). The respective experiences of Narcissus and the Lover *are* to be associated, but we must not make the mistake of assuming that association to be typological in nature. While basing itself on a certain fixed doctrinal content, the typological interpretation arises from a narrowly mimetic relationship between two events.[24] Neither do the Lover and Narcissus see the same objects in the fountain, nor do the ensuing actions even resemble each other. In order to pursue their relationship any further, we will have to reject our initial reading of the Lover's act as a repetition, and view Narcissus as a broader poetic image – a symbol – with allusive and not predicative value.

ALLEGORICAL FOUNTAIN OR FOUNTAIN OF ALLEGORY?

Although critics usually offer interpretations either of Narcissus's experience or of the Lover's vision of the crystals, rarely do they

---

[24] On typological interpretation in literature, see Erich Auerbach, "Figura," in *Scenes from the Drama of European Literature* (New York, 1959), pp. 11–76; and A. C. Charity, *Events and Their Afterlife: The Dialectics of Christian Typology in the Bible and Dante* (Cambridge, 1966). Auerbach's definition of typological relationships, which he calls *figura*, is of utmost clarity: "*figura* is something real and historical which announces something else that is real and historical. The relation between the two events is revealed by an accord or similarity." (p. 29).

FOUR: NARCISSUS AND THE FOUNTAIN

lay the two experiences side by side in order to extract the similarities and the differences, a normal first step toward the understanding of any metaphorical relationship. In all likelihood Ovid first associated the Narcissus and Echo stories because of their parallel figuration of a reflected sensory perception (visual, and oral/aural, respectively).[25] In fact, Ovid attenuates the revenge motif typically thought of as Echo's *raison d'être* by having one of Narcissus's boyfriends voice the curse that brings his downfall. While Guillaume differs from Ovid through his admission of Echo's role as the one who cries for vengeance, he vitiates the narrative causality in other ways, through his distancing and separation of the two characters, as well as the extended parallelism of their two fates. As described by Guillaume, the two figures double each other in representing the pain and death resulting from an unrequited desire. Whereas the courtly point of view, as exemplified by the *Lai de Narcisse*, tends to establish characters in subject/object relationships, Guillaume's subversive vision reveals an irreducible subjectivity. Perhaps our attention is to be focused not simply on the story as narrated, but rather on the recurrent theme of subjective judgment.

Not only in the Narcissus episode, but throughout Guillaume's tale, a great emphasis is placed on sensory perceptions. The reiteration of terms denoting visual or tactile perceptions (for example, "miroër," "clarté," "cristal," "ieuz") overflows the bounds of pure expressivity. We must not forget, moreover, that the fountain provides the single tangible link between the story of Narcissus and the Lover's experience. Considering that the Lover looked into water previously with virtually no effect and that his first inspection of the garden elicited little more than a neutral reaction, it becomes clear that the fountain functions as a change or refinement in one's vision. Through the special perception afforded by the fountain, the garden is transformed. In a similar way, as we have seen, the transformation from a natural to an allegorical universe is effected by the encounter with the garden. What this suggests is that figurative transformations occur at several levels of the *Rose* text — considerably more complex than the traditional

---

25 Cf. Vinge, *Narcissus Theme*, pp. 11–12, as well as Hermann Fränkel, *Ovid: A Poet between Two Worlds*, Sather Classical Lectures, 18 (Berkeley, 1945), pp. 82–5; and Brooks Otis, *Ovid as an Epic Poet*, 2nd ed. (Cambridge, 1970), pp. 157–8.

univocal view of personification allegory — and that, moreover, each of these transformations is marked by a textual sign. Such is the entry into the garden, such is the gaze into the fountain.

The main reason for rejecting the comparison between Narcissus and the Lover results from the mistaken assumption that the myth can only have a sexual meaning. The mutual interaction of the two fountain experiences, universalizing the import of both, reveals that the Narcissus story treats the broader question of the perceptual relationship between Self and Other. The paradox of Narcissus is not "Why one cannot possess oneself" but rather "Why one needs to go beyond the self." Narcissus *was* self-possessed and content before the Echo episode. In this respect, it is significant that Guillaume suppresses the entire Tiresias episode, which underscores Narcissus's knowing himself, as well as the explicit recognition of his image in the fountain reflection. All he discovers in Guillaume's account is that "il ne porroit/acomplir ce qu'il desiroit" (1495–6) ("he could not accomplish his desire" [p. 51]). Narcissus *was* able to reject society. What brings his downfall — and here, Guillaume tells us, is the symbolic meaning of the fountain — is the alteration in his vision effected by the fountain. The object of his vision could as well be an unattainable exterior object. In spite of the particular irony that so strongly characterizes the reflection motif and constitutes the effectiveness of the myth, it is important to remember that it is *not* the self perceived internally — as Self — that seduces and destroys, but rather the self perceived externally — as the Other and as a creature of fiction.

Already within the Narcissus story, the transformational power is highlighted by the presentation of two distinct Narcissus's: the one before and the one after the fountain experience. The second is actually a reified version of the punishment deserved by the first (according to a precise ethical scheme particular to Amor), and thus functions much as the Dantesque punishments in the *Inferno*, according to the logic of the *contrapasso*. The characters in *Inferno* signify concretely (or exteriorly) what had been interior moral characteristics, and thus need to be "read" or interpreted in order to be understood. In this sense, one might say that they have been typified, or allegorized. In much the same way, the fountain transforms Narcissus from a character into a sign by emblematizing what had been his primary characteristic and making that the tool of his destruction. Narcissus's punishment makes no sense except in its signifying function, that is, its outward display of what had been an invisible, inner quality.

Once we realize that Narcissus saw *both* himself and another, then we have a better insight into the detail of the Lover's vision at the fountain. The latter saw both a pair of crystals and a single crystal ("miroër"). In effect, there is no mix-up in vocabulary or syntax. The true genius of Guillaume's exposition consists in showing that the fountain is much more complex than the mirror. What is too often overlooked is that water is, in addition, limpid and clear — thus admitting a glance that not only pierces the surface but can reach the bottom ("fonz"). The tantalizing aspect of this image is the inextricable mixture of the two "visions," the simultaneous clarity and opacity. We might note here that the word used to characterize Narcissus's reflection is *ombre* (1484), not only a translation of Ovid's *umbra*, but a word with no fewer than three distinct meanings, all of which pertain to this context: "shadow," "reflection," and "soul."[26] The Lover sees both the reflective surface and the revealing profundity, the image and shadow, and it is perhaps this dual projection that brings out the truth of his being, the soul. Following the logic of Narcissus, he sees himself and, at the same time, the Other. The total ambiguity of the situation, accompanied by the obscure allegorical covering, accounts for the scene's force as well as the disturbance that it has elicited among critics. The point of gazing into the fountain is also the point where the self becomes aware of his exterior, his society. It is logical that the Lover's true indoctrination into the courtly world, his evolution from passive observer to active participant, should follow *not* his introduction into the garden, but rather his Narcissistic fountain experience. It is not only irrelevant to ask whether he saw his own eyes or those of his beloved — the question is not to be asked.[27] What the Lover pursues is the result of a double vision that happens also to be the renewed perception afforded by the fountain. The filter, or faculty of perception, and not the object perceived, is the central concern.

26 Cf. Köhler, "Narcisse," p. 159 and Frappier, "Variations," p. 138.
27 Similarly, Narcissus's first vision of himself (lines 1481–2) does not include any mention of his eyes ("son vis, son nés et sa bouchete" [1482]), which resurface in a later formulation (1571). Cf. our discussion of this displacement, below.

We should not delay in seeing that the fountain, as that which alters and/or highlights the individual's perception of the "natural" world, is the image of fiction itself. Much has been said about the medieval *speculum* as the principal access to knowledge of the world and of the secrets lying behind.[28] The mirror tells the truth of the world. At the same time, as partaking in the neo-Platonic view of this world as an imperfect reflection of the eternal realm, the mirror came to take on the sense of that which is false, fictional. Where the fountain image goes one step further is in thematically developing the real/fictional duality into a tactile image. The deceptive double vision of which we have been speaking characterizes the dual essence of the poetic message and, in particular, of allegory. If we remember that the Poet, represented in the text by the Narrator's voice and just as present as the Lover, experiences these happenings through a dream – another image of this real/fictional duality (compare Chapter Two) – then the association of poetic vision and imagination with internal fictionalized images becomes conclusive.[29] The glance into the fountain signals that special perception afforded by the literary imagination – the trigger for figurative speech – which founds the very poem's existence.

The fictional moment does indeed unite the various strands of our discussion. The quintessential motion toward exteriorization that is simultaneously the point of most intimate contact with the self is, of course, that of literary creation. We cannot interpret the courtly lyricist as a Narcissus because he comes to appreciate his lady through a proper understanding of himself, nor because his attention is drawn from his lady back to himself; rather, the poet is narcissistic to the extent that his artistic vision attempts an expression of subjective values through the manufacture of externals, the literary pretext. The poet, in a curious in-between position (and here we recall that the Narrator deliberately situates

---

28 Cf. Goldin's discussion of Augustine's *De Trinitate*, in *Mirror*, pp. 207–51, as well as the more general treatment of Johan Chydenius, *The Theory of Medieval Symbolism* (Helsinki, 1960). Neo-Platonic elaboration on mirror symbolism in a Christian context finds its ultimate justification, of course, in the famous lines of St. Paul, I Corinthians 13:12, "Videmus nunc per speculum in aenigmate: tunc autem facie ad faciem."
29 On the complex relationship between the poetic vision and the dream account in medieval dream poetry, see the unpublished dissertation by Francis X. Newman, "Somnium: Medieval Theories of Dreaming and the Form of Vision Poetry" (Princeton, 1963).

himself at a point after the dream vision and prior to its realization) face to face with the image-making poetic faculty figured by the dream/fountain, becomes the reader of his own experience. As such, the Lover presents through his own endeavors an analogue to the medieval (or modern) reader who must seek to decipher his own experience through that of others.

At this point we are in a position to understand more fully the curious textual enigmas that have created impasses at various moments of our study. We might call Guillaume's inclusion of Echo a narrative lure, the function of which is to make us think that the story is actually about the attempt to reach outward to another person, that is, the stereotyped love story. This is what the author of the *Lai de Narcisse* attempted to do. Viewed in this way, Echo would play a central role in the surface fiction. And yet her part is strictly marginal, or at the very least disconnected. In addition, she is just as much a lonely self-involved person as Narcissus. She is not to be understood narratively (as the superficial plot would indicate) as the cause of Narcissus's death, but rather figuratively, as one of the many examples of a self-destructive passion (comparable to Narcissus, the Lover, and the hypothetical *amant* described by Amor in his lengthy speech). By giving her the name "Echo," and allowing it to dissipate after the first mention, Guillaume is certainly alluding to her reflective vocal properties, thus reminding us of the original Ovidian motivation to associate the two stories. The strict parallelism of the Echo and Narcissus stories — carefully separated — alerts us to the additional fact that the message of Narcissus is of universal, and not strictly masculine, application.

The Narrator's address to the *dames* functions in precisely the same manner. It is an attempt to steer the reader and his fictional expectations in one direction, while the weight of mythic expression continues along another path. Indeed, it is the logical contradiction introduced by such a superficial gesture of narrative incorporation which gives rise to doubt and suspicion. To be sure, a cursory reading of the poem in the context of the courtly love *fabula* will support the similarities between Narcissus's heartless rejection and that of the lady. And yet the mere hint of sexual reversal (Narcissus/ladies; Echo/Lover) calls for a broader application than the courtly model will allow. In a more direct way, the blatantly unsatisfactory moral calls attention to our interpretative powers and defies our use of them. Our search for a content, or doctrine – that is, our unveiling of the allegory – is thwarted by the radical inconsistency of the materials.

In conjunction with these narrative lures the contradictory nature of which suggests a significant textual enigma, the sequence of references to an excess of meaning, the *verité* that will come out at the end, occurring at precisely those moments that are the most revealingly doctrinal, invites us to suspend our final judgment and to await a further interpretative possibility. These announcements are all the more annoying in retrospect since the text has no ending of this kind and certainly no final explanation of the allegory. If we supply an answer, the ultimate meaning of the work, we are in effect searching for that which the text will not, or cannot, give us. It is as if the Narrator were teasing or taunting his reader. Does he or does he not wish to communicate these ideas to which he alludes so frequently? The question is indeed appropriate and, if we have been reading carefully, we should realize that there is no answer to give. The path of reading constitutes a participatory meandering through spaces of mystification and discovery. The task of the narrator (in any narrative) is to captivate the reader, to lure him in such a way that he will follow attentively and not let go. Such captivation is particularly important in a work of which the express purpose, as in the *Rose,* is to seduce or tempt. In a fiction that self-consciously sees itself as fiction, which incorporates the fictional quest into its own texture, an ending cannot be. As a mystery, the text must continually deny its own message, leading the reader astray, and eventually end in irresolution.

The relationship between the fountain image and allegory should here be evident. Allegorical expression maintains within itself a curious tension between a doctrinal message and a clear fictional excess. Does allegory exist *only* for the sake of its message, or does the fictional "cover" command an interest of its own? Going as far back as Saint Augustine's discussions of the desirability of figurative speech, we find a preoccupation with this perhaps unanswerable question.[30] The pleasure of the text, fully

---

30 In his *De Doctrina Christiana* (II, vi, 8), Augustine relates the writer's use of signs and symbols to his more general philosophy of use and enjoyment (wherein the only thing to be enjoyed and not used is God), and thereby comes across the paradox of the doc-

acknowledged but not expressly advocated by Augustine, would be eliminated were an exclusively doctrinal orientation to dictate the conception and reception of the written text. Indeed, the continually reassessed figurative modes that are found in the *Roman de la Rose*, along with such dislocations as the ultimate humanization of Bel Acueil and Dangier, point to the adamant desire of fiction to remain fiction and not reduce itself to mere content.

Ultimately, Guillaume's doubling of the Narcissistic moment, through the account of the myth itself and the Lover's reliving of the mythic adventure, plays on this important conceptual theme in a visual mode – the simultaneous surface reflexivity and penetrating stare of the experiencing subject. Our poet thereby underscores the myth's universal application, its relevance *not* as a description of aberrant personal behavior but as an unavoidable corollary to human modes of perception. Put in another way, Narcissus is certainly not an alternate version of Oiseuse, the personification caught up with the image she sees in her handheld mirror.[31] Guillaume manages to plumb the depths of the mythological image by using his own experiences to flesh out what is left unsaid in Narcissus's stonelike reflection. By means of his treatment of the ancient myth, Guillaume attempts to show us that the creation of poetry occurs at a supreme moment of Narcissism, which is to say at a juncture where fictional projection necessarily adumbrates but never totally replicates a transcendent meaning – the deceptive

---

trinally oriented writer's use of metaphor: "Sed quare suauius videam [truths expressed metaphorically and obscurely], quam si nulla de divinis libris talis similitudo promeretur, cum res eadem sit eademque cognitio, *difficile est dicere et alia quaestio est.* Nunc tamen ambigit et per similitudines libentius quaeque cognosci et cum aliqua difficultate quaesita multo gratius inveniri" (emphasis mine). "But why it [truths expressed metaphorically and obscurely] seems sweeter to me than if no such similitude were offered in the divine books, since the thing perceived is the same, *is difficult to say and is a problem for another discussion*. For the present, however, no one doubts that things are perceived more readily through similitudes and that what is sought with difficulty is discovered with more pleasure" (D. W. Robertson, Jr., trans., *On Christian Doctrine* [Indianapolis, 1958], p. 38; emphasis mine). In sum, Augustine admits to the pleasure of figurative speech while dodging the question of its theological justification. In a recent book on the theory of allegory, Maureen Quilligan (*The Language of Allegory: Defining the Genre* [Ithaca, NY, 1979]) has suggested that the notion of interpretive "levels" traditionally used to treat allegory leads inevitably to a hierarchy of interpretations that eventually privileges the doctrinal message (over and against linguistic or other factors).

31 However, Vinge, *Narcissus Theme*, p. 36, indicates that Narcissus became in the Christian apologetic tradition an illustration of *Vanitas*, "the emptiness of outward, perishable beauty."

surface of fiction whose overwhelming power to fascinate is matched only by its very fragility.

REVERSED PERSPECTIVES

The corpus of mythological tales available to the poet is perhaps his single most important resource. The distanced reverence and traditional authority accorded to myth offer the possibility of telling a story whose ramifications, however wide-reaching, do not entail an express authorial commitment. The convenient alibi that consists of relating a familiar tale absolves the storyteller of any sense of responsibility. In this respect, the inclusion of a moral lesson as an explanation of a given mythological tale, most frequent in the Middle Ages, is itself somewhat of a paradox. On the one hand, it has the effect of turning the essentially undetermined myth into an *exemplum,* and thus satisfies the need for a fixed meaning, which is in fact the antithesis of the uncodified mythic imagination. On the other hand, if the myth needs to be recuperated by moral teaching in order to have any value, why not simply dispense with it? Of course, the paradox is only a paradox in a situation where a doctrinal message is the sole or primary justification for a written work of fiction. The daring move to perpetuate fictional tales in a culture of writing where anything smacking of frivolity exposes itself to the risk of reproof or possible censorship attests to the persistent human need for storytelling in its own right, separated from any pedagogical concern. Truly brilliant authors have always understood and manipulated the tension that arises between the unbridled, potentially subversive power of fiction and the social obligation that bends writers to the dictates of linguistic stability and a firmly fixed meaning. Such a manipulation explains the arrestingly playful nature of Guillaume's opening *sententia,* as well as his seemingly ingenuous treatment of Narcissus as a moral *exemplum.* As we have seen, his introduction of a moral lesson ultimately has a contrary effect, calling attention to this paradox of mythological expression by means of the contrast between its superficially plausible application and its otherwise deeply inadequate explanation of the poetic frame. Guillaume does not stop there, however, and in a second move he amplifies his own story in order further to exploit the possibilities of the

Narcissistic moment, thereby creating a second myth that feeds off the first one. Guillaume's double transformation of the Narcissus figure, from self-involved boy to visual emblem to courtly lover/poet, eliminates any circumstantial aspects of the tale and thus reveals the universality of Narcissus and the fountain as a narrative figure for the creator and his fictional image. Not only does the self-reflexivity of Narcissus, simultaneously active and passive, suggest the mechanisms involved in fictional projection, but it also intimates the unattainability that is in its essence the reader's role. Insofar as it arises from a self-begetting myth, a myth about mythic creation and mythic subversion, the utter figural intangibility of Narcissus, the impossibility of ever comprehending him as more than a fascinating image, explains the reader's paradox, the human need for mystery, for unknowingness — that factor of human fictions that feeds the ongoing quest for knowledge but can never by definition satisfy it. The infinitely fascinated glance, like the mutual reflection of parallel mirrors, figures the never-ending, because never-endable, principle of man's intellectual quest.

Accordingly, Guillaume manages to exploit a positive side of what may otherwise appear to be a myth of atrophy and desolation. The victimization inherent in the Narcissus myth is clearly not unidirectional nor is it totally innocent: The shadowy and deceptive truth of the fountain is also a projection of the subject, an outward application of the individual's own perceptions. If the fascinated glance of Narcissus, in this way parallel to that of the allegorist, focuses upon those obscure images in the world that stand for other things (and not for themselves), it is also a fact that those images are a part of us, in some way projecting from our individual and collective processes of cognition. The tantalizing polysemy of the word *ombre,* oscillating between an accidental physical marking (shadow) and a revealing intimacy (soul), is here most significant. We may by all rights be considered the readers of our own experience, but it might further be suggested that we are also the creators of the very experience of which we subsequently *become* the readers. A sense of subjectivity, in other words, is perhaps itself a fountain illusion, a personal "depth" that we posit in others but which simply ends up being an imposed self-reflection.

It is in this way that the personified landscape as we described it in Chapter Three constitutes the primal Narcissistic achievement of our poet, deconstructing what appears to be a very different quest. The creation of an array of personifications whose figurative goal is to portray a female locus seems feasible initially, but the Narrator's eventual impasse, the incapacity to situate the Lady either mentally or physically (which, in a personification allegory, would amount to the same thing) translates the recognition of what one might term an expressive Narcissism. The radical discontinuity of the narrative, in this manner parallel to the dead-end experience of Narcissus, implies the resistance of the highly objectified courtly world model to this transcendent mythic reality of human perception. By the end, the Narrator's fictional creation vanishes, leaving him with his own isolated vision and a final awareness that he and the Lover persona are one and the same – temporally and experientially. This "end," which might not appear terribly conclusive, finds its ultimate rationale in Narcissus, whose myth demonstrates the inherent unity in an apparently dual focus. The final reversibility of the castle/prison barrier (outside looking in or inside peering out?), underscored by the insertion of the Lover's spectral double, the galant Bel Acueil, unambiguously replicates the Lover/Narrator's own Narcissistic moment. Narcissus could not progress in the fountain experience because he was not *really* involved with the outside. Guillaume's *Rose* starts out as an elaborate development of the Narcissistic image-making faculty in the context of the courtly tradition, a tradition with the express and contrary goal of creating and affirming a separate subjectivity. The principal allusion to the existence of an irreducible meaning, the rose, is of course a part of the poem's title – indeed, its central focus. The rose's immateriality is nevertheless foreseeable from the start, since it is viewed *not* through the crystals at the bottom, but in the surface mirror ("El miroër . . . choisi rosiers chargiez de roses" [1613–14]) – that very mirror which, he tells us, deceived him: "Cil miroërs m'a deceü" (1607). Ultimately, a return to the lyric voice, a disappearance of the rose, both mark a move toward the recognition of the poet's original source of inspiration and imagination.

It might be objected that the "suspension" of Guillaume's end does not resemble the fate of Narcissus, whose story has the privilege of being the only tale told in the *Roman de la Rose* that does conclude in some absolute fashion. However, it is here that we can best view Guillaume's extraordinary subtlety and poetic insight, which allow him to create a version bearing striking contrasts with what tradition had handed down to him. Ovid's tale of Narcissus, the most authoritative and complete version from antiquity, ends with the transformation of Narcissus into a flower (or, more precisely, his substitution, and consequent commemoration, *by* a flower).[32] In the various accounts that follow this version, his death is attributed to excessive sorrow, grief, or a lack of nourishment. The flower conveys a sense of quiet contemplation, while physically resembling in its bent-over fashion Narcissus kneeling at the fountain. A second version, which seems to have originated in the writings of Plotinus, portrays Narcissus plunging into the water, succumbing to death by drowning. This is an interesting variation, for not only does it make the fascinating illusion a direct and violent cause of death, but it also ends with no corporeal trace as in the other version.[33] For Plotinus, as for other neo-Platonic writers, this represents the disastrous confusion between the illusion of reality and the true reality, which cannot be perceived.[34] Death by drowning stresses the desire to unite physically with the immaterial creatures of fiction. The result of such desire is not simply a failure to reach the image, but a physical annihilation directly attributable to the meaningless materiality, the "stuff" of the image. Moreover, Plotinus's version implies that the very existence of the image is jeopardized if we attempt to approach it, that is, to believe in its reality; the only way to preserve the illusion is to view, but not touch, the image. We are further reminded that the

---

32 Cf. ibid., pp. 18–19. The text of Ovid reads as follows: "nusquam corpus erat; croceum pro corpore florem/inveniunt foliis medium cingentibus albis" ("his body was nowhere to be found. In place of his body they find a flower, its yellow centre girt with white petals") (*Metamorphoses*, ed. and trans. Frank Justus Miller [Cambridge, MA, 1971], III, 509–10, pp. 160–1).

33 Whereas there are some versions in which the flower clearly does not appear because of a corporeal transformation but rather as a commemorative marker (for example, Conon, cited by Vinge, *Narcissus Theme*, pp. 19–21), it is significant that the flower motif is not normally associated with the drowning motif. Indeed, the two would appear to be mutually exclusive.

34 The "anonymous mythographer," quoted by ibid. (pp. 38–9), is most instructive: "For he did not drown in the water, but when he saw his own shadow in the stream of matter, that is to say life in the body, which is the ultimate image of the true soul; and when he tried to embrace it as his own, that is to say filled with love for this life, he drowned and sank beneath the water, as if destroying his true soul, that is to say the true life that belonged to him."

image only exists in the measure that the viewer is there to contemplate and be reflected.[35]

Guillaume's treatment of Narcissus's death differs considerably from both of these versions. Most superficially, neither does Narcissus turn into a flower, nor does he end up drowning. The first description of his death gives virtually no reason whatsoever, with the exception of the ambiguous pronoun *en:*

> ... il musa tant en la fontaine
> qu'il ama son ombre demainne,
> si en fu morz a la parclouse,
> c'est la some de ceste chose.   (1491–4)

(he mused so long at the fountain that he fell in love with his own reflection and died because of it in the end. This is the gist of the affair. [pp. 50–1])

He died at the end "because of it" – because of his fascination ("musa"), his love ("ama"), or for some related reason? We have here nothing like Ovid's lengthy analysis of grief and frustration (*Metamorphoses,* III, 425–505). Then, a fuller explanation is provided:

> Car quant il vit qu'il ne porroit
> acomplir ce qu'il desiroit
> et qu'il estoit si pris par fort
> qu'il ne porroit avoir confort
> en nule fin ne en nul sen,
> il perdi d'ire tot le sen
> et fu morz en poi de termine.   (1495–1501)

(For, when he saw that he could not accomplish his desire and that he was captured so inescapably that he could in no way take any comfort, he lost all his reason from anger and died in a short time. [p. 51])

---

35 Ovid finds an even more seductive way of expressing a similar concern. Narcissus's liquid tears, at first only welling on his cheeks, take part in the image and then, when they fall into the fountain, they obscure the image:

> et lacrimis turbavit aquas, obscuraque moto
> reddita forma lacu est; quam cum vidisset abire,
> "quo refugis? remane ..."

His tears ruffled the water, and dimly the image came back from the troubled pool. As he saw it thus depart, he cried: "Oh, whither do you flee? Stay here..." (*Metamorphoses,* III, 475–7)

First of all, it is clear from the syntax of this sentence that Narcissus's madness and death follow directly from his perception ("il vit" – literally "he saw") of two interrelated problems: "quant il vit . . . , il perdi . . . et fu morz." The two problems are delineated as follows: "il ne porroit/acomplir ce qu'il desiroit" ("he could not accomplish his desire"); and "il estoit si pris . . . qu'il ne porroit avoir confort/en nule fin ne en nul sen" ("he could in no way take any comfort"). It is striking that both of these impasses, paralleled by means of the formula "il ne porroit," are expressed in terms of endings or ending metaphors. *Acomplir* comes from the Latin *complere*, which means literally "to fill up" ("plenus" = "full"), and later takes on the figurative sense of "to make complete or perfect, to finish." As for the second impasse reached by Narcissus, "en nule fin" is an expression meaning "in no way," but of course the word "fin" also happens to be the simplest word for "end." The traditional way of translating these lines, which considers "en nule fin" and "en nul sen" to be synonymous ("he could in no way take any comfort"), could be revised in order to maintain the literal value of both words: "he could take consolation in no end and in no meaning."[36] Thus, in both cases, the reason for Narcissus's death is in some way related to an impasse of closure. It might further be noted that the statement in the passage above, that he died "a la parclouse," is ambiguous: It could mean that he "finally" died or, more literally, that he died "at the end," at the absolute closure ("par-clouse"). Which comes first in this expression, the death or the closure? The statement of Narcissus's death in the second passage ("fu morz en poi de termine") relates through the Latin *terminus* to a semantic cluster involving boundaries, limits, and thus endings. If the psychological or physical reasons for his death appear to be obscured in this account, their aesthetic ones are obsessively repeated.

An answer to this uncertainty, a "way out," is perhaps to be found in the final mention of Narcissus's death several lines later,

---

36 For a good overview of recent discussions concerning the meaning of the word *sen* in twelfth-century French texts, see Karl Uitti, *Story, Myth, and Celebration in Old French Narrative Poetry, 1050–1200* (Princeton, 1973), pp. 135–7 (note 6). One would gather from the Tobler-Lommatzsch *Altfranzösisches Wörterbuch* (vol. IX, cols. 428–9) that expressions of the form "en . . . sen" were extremely common: *en autre sen, en maint sen, en nul sen, en tel sen,* and so forth. The example of Guillaume, however, appears to be the only one in which this expression is doubled with another one.

the only recall of the mythological character subsequent to the Lover's vision of the crystals:

> ... Narcisus, li orgueilleus,
> mira sa face et ses ieuz vers,
> dont il jut puis morz toz envers.   (1570–2)
>
> (proud Narcissus gazed at his face and his sparkling eyes, on account of which he afterward lay dead, flat on his back. [p. 52])

As in the previous statement, a specific sense of motivation is obfuscated, this time by the noncommittal *dont,* which could refer to a direct or indirect causality. What is more significant, however, is that Narcissus's eyes are here mentioned for the first time (in the previous account, he saw "son vis, son nés et sa bouchete" [1482] – everything *but* his eyes) and are described as "vers," which, when applied to eyes, can be translated as "sparkling."[37] *Ver,* or more commonly *vair,* comes from the Latin *varium,* meaning "changing, diverse," which is much in keeping with our discussion of the fountain's deceptive visual properties, especially since this quality becomes the focal point in this final description. Then, we are told, Narcissus lay dead on his back "envers," the opposite of "adenz," a word that had been used earlier to describe Narcissus's posture when drinking at the fountain. Now, the word "envers" presents a certain equivoque arising from the liberty of Old French word formation, for it could be split apart and read as "en vers," "in poetic verse," a reading that proves to be surprisingly applicable in the present situation: "He then lay dead totally in poetic verse."[38] The visual rhyme with "vers" in the previous line provides further support for this interpretation. Narcissus of course lies dead in verse each time his story is told, a result of his myth's commemorative linguistic status. But Guillaume further marks the physicality of this transformation by insisting that the fountain is *labeled* as that of Narcissus: "ot ... escrites ... letres petites" ("had written small letters") (1433–4). Whereas Guillaume leaves

---

37 See the discussion by Alice Colby, *The Portrait in Twelfth-Century French Literature* (Geneva, 1965), pp. 41–2, who demonstrates convincingly that *vair* could not designate a specific color.
38 In a somewhat broader context, this possible reading has been pointed out by Dragonetti, "Pygmalion," p. 110.

out the commemorative flower marking Narcissus's passage, he insinuates another marker — a sequence of letters, a text. The existence of a written signpost is later reiterated by the Narrator, so that we not forget: "Quant li escrit m'ot fet savoir" (1509) ("When the inscription had made clear to me" [p. 51]). Narcissus did indeed die, out of a crisis of ending or closure, but he turned himself around ("envers") and opened himself up as a book ("en vers") to be read by all who come across the fountain, including of course the Lover.[39]

Guillaume's own poem is a reply to, and continuation of, this particular reading of Narcissus, the result of which is a new myth of closure and poetic perpetuation. What comes out, what becomes the positive response to a potential aporia or an individual, self-contained musing is the material existence of the poem itself which, in a cyclical path, becomes an object of fascination for the future recipient of the poem, who can place himself in the Narcissistic pose of entranced reader/contemplator, literally "adenz," and ultimately perhaps continue the lineage by himself turning the compliment, committing himself "en vers." This is, I think, the "final word" to Guillaume's text, the reaching out to posterity by means of a seductive, unclosed word necessitating an answer and completion. If some readers' responses are inscribed in certain fictional texts, Guillaume's response is a material result of the scribal fact of textual perpetuation. And it is here that a full circle is drawn, leading back to the discussion of the medieval text and author in Chapter One. Reading and writing were complementary and highly prestigious activities in the Middle Ages, the one necessarily implicating the other. Textual reproduction was largely dependent on reaching and interesting a reading public. Since the *reading* public (as opposed to a listening one, which could equally

---

39 The richness of book metaphors throughout the Christian Middle Ages is documented by Curtius, *European Literature,* esp. pp. 302–32. While metaphors for scribal acts are probably the most common, the mystical religious tradition created several others as, for example, the connection between the red ink of the *rubricator* and human blood. It might be added that the word *vers* attests to a metaphorical development turned back on itself: In the medieval tradition, the scribe's art came to be compared with plowing and the various implements of the former are likened to those of the latter: ploughshare ("volmer") = stylus ("stilus"); to plow ("arare") = to write ("scribere"); thorn-bushes = scribal errors. (Ibid. pp. 313–14). What Curtius does not note, however, is that the Latin *versus* (= a line of writing) is itself a metaphor, the literal sense of the word being "a furrow," that is a *turning round* of the plough (from the verb *verto,* "to turn, turn round or about"). Cf. Lewis and Short, *A Latin Dictionary* (Oxford, 1969), p. 1977.

have been the original audience for which the *Rose* was destined but which would have had much less impact on the chances of the work's survival in written form) of which we are speaking was probably composed largely of clerks (those who could both read and reproduce in writing), a certain veneer, a sense of decorum, had in all likelihood to be maintained. This further explains the text's duplicitous nature, the careful skirting around fundamental and yet unspeakable truths such as the Narcissistic one. Why the poem's "afterlife" should directly concern Guillaume comes as less of a surprise when one considers the text's elaborate and explicit structuring of seductions, the series of actual and potential addresses. We need only come back to a quotation from Marie de France included in our first chapter by way of showing to what extent an author might have occupied him- or herself with the listening, reception, and praise of the work's audience, a preoccupation that goes far beyond the automatism of a rhetorical stereotype:[40]

> Quant uns granz biens est mult oïz,
> Dunc a primes est il fluriz,
> E quant loëz est de plusurs,
> Dunc ad espandues ses flurs.

(When a great good is widely heard of, then, and only then, does it bloom, and when that good is praised by many, it has spread its blossoms.)

While the nature of their stake in communication is similar, Guillaume's purview differs in its material detail from that of Marie, who by her many remarks appears to be concerned primarily with an oral diffusion. Guillaume's is a written text, and the blooming ("fluriz") of which it is capable relates undoubtedly to the act of reading, equivalent to the auditory reception ("oïz") of an orally produced poem; the "spreading of flowers" can be none other than the circulation made possible by the poem's scribal transcription (or poetic continuation?), which would be, ultimately, the most welcome show of praise ("quant *loëz* est de plusurs").

[40] *Les Lais de Marie de France*, ed. Jean Rychner, CFMA 93 (Paris, 1968), Prologue, lines 4–8. English translation by Robert Hanning and Joan Ferrante (New York, 1978), p. 28.

Guillaume's poem is, to be sure, about love, but it shows what is in love a more general problem of personal interaction and intersubjectivity. Dealings with others in erotic or intellectual endeavors are always a function of the tension between outward projections, that surface reflection which takes the form of a preconceived narration, and a sense of profundity or truth. Poetry situates itself in this intermediate space, a fact that explains both the threat that it poses and the satisfaction that it elicits. While it is often difficult not to perceive the projected elements of illusion and fiction that result from our own vision, one must in day-to-day life believe in an objective truth — however blindly — in order for society, and even the individual, to exist. This imperative often extends to our poetic fictions, which should, on the contrary, provide a lucid deconstruction of this perceptual dilemma. Guillaume's subversive personal myth speaks otherwise, however, and reinforced by the tale of Narcissus at the fountain, central focus of the *Rose,* it dissects the fictional/allegorical underpinnings of the fiction in which it is portrayed. The myth's *mise-en-abyme* positioning as an inner reflection of the totality (the dream enclosure) would totally subvert the fictional surface were it not for Guillaume's masterly use of trickery and tantalizing hints at a final meaning, not to mention superficially plausible moral explanations. By playing themselves out in the area between imagination and understanding, allegorical fictions — including those of the reader/critic — naturally desire to reveal themselves, to disclose their inner workings, and yet, were they to do so, they would be destroyed. So, in the blink of an eye, they must reveal and conceal, present a surface opaque *and* transparent. The Lover-as-Narcissus, the reader-as-Narcissus, has but to plunge his fascinated glance, never knowing where truth lies, experiencing a paralysis that is nothing more than the simultaneous joy of discovery and deception.

Postscript

> li faus enquereour
> Font oevre maleüree,
> Engiens de mainte coulour,
> Pour metre joie a tristour.
>   (Le Châtelain de Coucy)
>
> If up until now we have looked at the text as a species of fruit with a kernel . . . , the flesh being the form and the pit being the content, it would be better to see it as an onion, a construction of layers . . . whose body contains, finally, no heart, no kernel, no secret, no irreducible principle, nothing except the infinity of its own envelopes – which envelop nothing other than the unity of its own surfaces.
> (Roland Barthes [trans. Seymour Chatman], "Style and Its Image")

The foregoing analyses raise certain questions about the interpretation process, which I would now like to address briefly. Our point of departure in Chapter One was the historical evaluation of reading and writing practices, involving medieval conceptions of authorship and the literary work, by way of formulating the hypothesis that the first *Roman de la Rose* – that attributed to Guillaume de Lorris – is a finished work as it stands. The following three chapters each measured the likelihood of this possibility through a specific mode of literary interpretation: a grammatically based narratological study in Chapter Two; an intertextual, or generic, study focused on the rhetoric of personification allegory in Chapter Three; and a symbolic reading of the poem's central myth, that of Narcissus and Echo, in Chapter Four. More than just a "new" reading of the *Rose,* the study brings to light the significant interpenetration of two normally distinct domains: literary history (for lack of a better term designating the collective forces that transmit, contextualize, and frame literary works); and interpretation. Even if the establishment of the text must precede interpretation, that very establishment is itself subject to prior types of interpretation in the form of personal experience, as well as beliefs about what literature is and how it signifies. To suggest (or insist) that the *Rose* is a finished work is thus not trivial, for it implies a significant revision of many commonly held aesthetic notions concerning the integrity of literary works, authorial intentionality, and, more specifically, the writing project of courtly literature. It also, of course, calls into question medieval readings or interpretations of the *Rose* text as reflected in the very transmission of the poem. It is quite evident that medieval readers were not interested in such an interpretation and were impelled to see the poem's allegorical framework carried through with an ending: The continuation that Jean de Meun provided admirably suited late-thirteenth-century "literary" tastes and propelled the work to a position of enduring fame.

My hypothetical reading thus admittedly goes against the most common medieval readings of the work. Furthermore, as is quite obvious in the final chapter on Narcissus, the basis of my interpretation can be largely credited to modern theoretical projections, those involving structures of *mise-en-abyme* (fictional internalization of the writing process itself) and, along with that, an inner reflection of the reader in the text. How does a careful medieval contextualizing of the poem square with the obvious imposition of modern critical allegories? What is the status of such an interpretation?

The problem of the justification of any literary interpretation — the very status of the interpretive discourse — is indeed one that cuts across the several discussions contained in this book. At the outset it was suggested that in the medieval context of fictional writing the respective roles of author, reader, and interpreter allow for much more variation and mutual interference than is commonly the case in our modern interpretive communities. From there, it might seem to follow that the literary text (or rather the text treated as literary) is by definition one with an "open," unfixed meaning actualized only by the reader/interpreter. But for anyone who believes that literary language, like language in general, is a communication system involving an agreed-upon code, such "open" readings are profoundly dangerous, leading ultimately to a situation where interpretive discourse would be primary and self-sufficient, with the possibility of reading anything into any text, regardless of literal meaning or even expressed authorial intention(s). The other extreme position adheres to the text's literal meaning as its sole correct and admissible signification. Critical discourses often seem to oscillate between the polarities described by the terms "authorial expression" and "critical interpretation," "objective" and "subjective" readings of texts, without realizing that the argument itself is pointless and in fact misrepresents totally the necessary dynamism of textual interpretation. To begin with, the question is never purely synchronic, but rather, practically speaking, always turns into a diachronic one. Instead of dealing with "what the author said" or "how the critic interprets," the crucial question ought to be "How does the critical discourse confront the text?" or "How does the interpreter restate the text's intentions?" This shift in emphasis provides a way out of the impasse of "right versus wrong" readings insofar as its aim is to study the cultural assimilation, transmission, and transformation of types of discourse. It presupposes that no critical eye is purely removed from the situation of reading, and that it must therefore be situated within a critical moment just as much as the text itself. Interpretation involves an adjustment of two different discourses or voices that are by definition not consistent or coincidental. Were this not the case, we would simply be speaking of one voice, one undifferentiated text. The critical voice is always at a remove, submitting (through quotation or other means) the voice of an other. As Jauss and others have attempted to show, one way of understanding the status of interpretation and its relation to a wealth of interpretive communities can be sought by evaluating the differing filters through which a given text has been read and specifically by measuring the distance (both chronological and conceptual) between various critical discourses and the literary ones they attempt to explicate. At one end of the scale, I might place my own attempt to understand the text that I jotted down yesterday and whose implications (or intentions) I don't see quite so clearly anymore; at the other extreme are my efforts to read a medieval text. It is the unbridgeable gap between my own discourse and the strangeness of the medieval work, its "alterity," which shakes the normally solid foundation of my own vision when confronted with familiar objects. The shock of this alterity acts as a necessary corrective, forcing us (and allowing us) to ask questions that might never even be considered within a unified context of experience.

The debate over the relative primacy of textual expression or critical interpretation is an ongoing, and perhaps insoluble, one. I have clearly opted for a transactive position, one that neither denies the contribution of critical visions nor grants it unlimited powers; one which neither limits itself to what we call the "literal" meaning of a poem, nor neglects the practical concerns of traditional philology. While, methodologically speaking, many positions are possible, there is one area in which literary history itself can be shown to derive from the context created by successive interpretations, and that is the domain of canon formation. The works universally hailed nowadays as the "great" works of the French Middle Ages (for example, Marie de France's *Lais*, the Oxford *Chanson de Roland*, Chrétien de Troyes's romances, the *Tristan* fragments of Béroul and Thomas) were quite likely not seen as such by the majority of medieval readers. It is of course unwise to gauge a medieval work's popularity according to numbers of manuscripts that have come down to us, given the fragility of such testimonies, complicated as they are by the role of chance in determining their survival. Nonetheless, certain reliable conclusions can be drawn based upon *relative* numbers of surviving manuscripts. It is clear, for instance, that the popularity of the *Roman de la Rose* was unrivaled by any of the above texts in the fourteenth and fifteenth centuries. Indeed, it is unlikely that these "classics" of the twelfth century were much read at all past the end of the thirteenth century and, furthermore, we have no reason to believe that the case would have been any different for Guillaume de Lorris's *Rose,* had it not served as the basis for Jean de Meun's popular continuation. We do know that there was an important shift in vernacular manuscript production (both in total numbers and in types of works transcribed) after the mid-thirteenth century that would account for the relative scarcity of popular works transcribed primarily during earlier periods. However, even within one same period we find certain works considered secondary today (for example, Wace's *Brut,* Benoît de Sainte-Maure's *Roman de Troie,* the anonymous *Partonopeu de Blois*) surviving in more manuscripts than any of the above works, with the exception of Chrétien's *Conte du Graal* (which itself received a shot in the arm through a series of mediocre continuations added on over a period of some thirty-five or forty years). On what grounds, then, can we justify the modern glorification of Chrétien de Troyes, when there is only marginal evidence of a similar attitude toward him among his earliest public?

A close examination of the manuscript sources brings to light certain paradoxical aspects related to our perception of the medieval literary scene. While in most cases we cannot tell the motivation behind the transcription of a given manuscript, we can in general assume that it was a function of specific literary and aesthetic tastes; works continued to be transcribed when it was thought that there was a likely readership, or listening public, for them (or, more directly, because of a commission), and works ceased to be transcribed when they no longer interested audiences or when it was felt that existing copies were sufficient for the public that was still seeking out those works. Our own access to these texts is thus profoundly conditioned by the shifts in medieval readership. But further complicating the situation is the fact that the period responsible for the transmission of the bulk of vernacular manuscripts (the two and a half centuries stretching from the mid-thirteenth to the late fifteenth century) was producing works that are themselves little read today. The paradox is stunning, for while medievalists specializing in French literature frequently evoke the authority of typical medieval mentalities in the context of their research, their own corpus tends to be a rarefied, highly selective one that has little in common with what we can infer to be the viewpoint of the "typical" medieval readership. The medieval corpus that we have assembled is largely beholden to modern tastes in fiction and that very arbitrariness is itself significant. Were we to give popular works their due in our survey courses, we would have to include such moralizing fictions as the *Pèlerinage de la vie humaine*, the *Ovide moralisé*, or the miracles of Gautier de Coincy. The medieval works we recognize as masterpieces (and here I am speaking of the French tradition) have attained that status not as based upon a studied archeology of medieval taste, but as a reflection of our own sensibilities. Does it not behove us to ask what is it about modern aesthetics that is drawn to certain types of medieval works but remains indifferent to others? Is it not by understanding our own confrontation with these far-off works that we can hope to gain some understanding about the shifting tides of popularity that are quite apparent in the thirteenth century?

These questions are of course closely connected to a broader one involving the nature of the literary public(s). It is often assumed that the great twelfth-century works appealed to at least as large an audience as the later works mentioned above, whose popularity is more clearly documented — but through oral rather than written transmission. This is very likely true, but then it begs the further question of whether we are justified in using tools developed for the purpose of written textual commentary in the schools (that is, rhetoric and grammar) or in monasteries (techniques of biblical exegesis) in order to explicate them. Had works such as Chrétien de Troyes's romances been read in the context of these speculative works during the medieval period, then they probably would have been considered more appropriate to be written down than they actually were. It is quite possible that the marginal transcription of these earlier, manifestly nondidactic, works betrays a situation of cultural and linguistic heterogeneity. This would account for an astonishing indifference to the content of these early works, which would not have been taken seriously precisely because they were not written in Latin. It also explains why the spread of the vernacular as a written language in the course of the thirteenth century — its increasing acceptance as a vehicle for philosophical, historical, and religious ideas — does not bring along with it a flourishing of the great courtly fictions as they had been conceived in the twelfth century. Instead we find a subordination of such fictions, when they were perpetuated, to ethical and religious concerns. The marginal, unorthodox nature of courtly fiction could only be maintained as long as the vernacular itself was not identified as a worthy instrument for the promulgation of official doctrine.

There is thus an implicit methodological contradiction between certain types of interpretation common to medieval studies as it is practiced today and the likely mode of composition and transmission within a specific cultural milieu that supposedly explains the existence of those texts. Medieval audiences attentive to allegories and moral explanations for fictional behavior were certainly responsible for the great popularity of the prose *Lancelot-Grail,* but they would not have found what they were looking for in any of Chrétien de Troyes's romances, which carefully avoid drawing allegorical or moral conclusions. It is upon these grounds, and not those of poetic form (rhymed octosyllabic couplets versus prose), decreasing intelligibility, or the Arthurian subject matter, that we must understand the dwindling of Chrétien's popularity through the thirteenth century. How then can we justify using allegorical or symbolic methods of a moralizing sort to explicate Chrétien's texts when the methods themselves were cultivated within a social group that was possibly quite distanced, culturally and ethically, from the concerns expressed therein? Any allegorical reading is deeply entrenched in interpretive ideologies, but the weakness of the type usually displayed in the work of modern medievalists is a direct result of the fact that it refuses to recognize its own historical arbitrariness.

Since any claim to "faithfulness" (to text or author) is only a disguised projection of cultural and personal presuppositions (and, further, a notion that would probably not have occurred to most medieval readers), the alternative proposed by "right" or "wrong" interpretation seems less appropriate to literary scholarship than a careful delineation of interpretive criteria that will allow the reader to evaluate the scope and success of any given interpretation. By not recognizing our inherent limitations, we run the risk of perpetuating misleading cultural constructs and hopelessly static polemical arguments. A clear example of just this sort of misunderstood critical claim is available in John Fleming's controversial book on the *Roman de la Rose*. He does not in fact provide an interpretation of the poem, but rather an exposition of a certain facet of late medieval interpretations of the poem as reflected in a sequence of carefully chosen manuscript illuminations and some allegorizing texts (such as the *Echecs amoureux* gloss). In its own context, Fleming's approach has a certain expository validity, but the narrow limitations of his study must be understood. Furthermore, the simple fact that the selected fourteenth- and fifteenth-century moralizations of the text have no more reasonable claim to authority in the matter than do our own interpretations suggests that we ourselves reconsider Fleming's implicit claim to have found the definitive meaning of the poem.

One of the many important insights developed in Pierre-Yves Badel's much more comprehensive study of the history of *Rose* reception in the fourteenth century is the nearly total incongruity between medieval styles of interpretation and those practiced today. In speaking of the same *Echecs amoureux* gloss (which Badel considers, by the way, to have been "abusively" read by Fleming), Badel points up an astonishing lack of interest in poetic structure, in any type of totalizing interpretive vision, or even in the clarification of meaning in specific passages. Badel concludes that for this commentator poems do not themselves merit commentary, but instead commentary — however voluminous or disjointed — confers authority upon a given work. The medieval sense of interpretation that can be gathered from this and other glosses is frequently looser than we would care to imagine, assuming a primacy that traditional philologists would, contrariwise, prefer to deny the discourse of modern readers.

As suggested by the latter observation, not only is our attraction to particular medieval works possibly at odds with medieval sensibilities, but so are the bulk of our most basic critical instincts. To expect in a work a unified structure or a concurrence of poetic means aimed at a common end; to seek inner coherence or systematization at one level, or among levels, of analysis; to perform a "close" reading based upon textual echoes, repetition or linguistic effects; to study the "logic" of poetic images or symbolic modes — these are all methods common to modern readers (so common that they are scarcely questioned) but potentially at variance with, or only marginally espoused in, medieval critical practice. Must we then simply abandon them as anachronistic? Of course not, and here is where we must consider the *necessarily* anachronistic enterprise of reading the medieval text. From whatever direction and at whatever level, the modern reader must be aware of the multiple projections he is imposing on a text even when he makes the most simple or innocent of judgments; a tacit denial of one's own cultural or literary background merely serves to undermine the authenticity of one's very research.

The modern appreciation of courtly literature thus has a lot to do with the sorts of ideas, aesthetic values, and cultural myths we read into those fictions. It is not difficult to enumerate those qualities in courtly poems that appeal to modern literary tastes: ambiguity, frivolity, language play, metaphorical invention, concern with self-expression. Furthermore, in a modern age that has been greatly marked by anti-establishment, nondoctrinal impulses at all levels of society, the appeal of a corpus lying outside the direct restraints of church dogma, and frequently conveying questionable moral standards, becomes easy to understand. From the beginnings of the courtly tradition, a carefully developed association among playfully conceived riddling, linguistic arbitrariness, and erotic relations is readily observable. We might call as witness the *first* Guillaume, ninth Duke of Aquitaine and seventh Count of Poitou. By virtue of his being the "first troubadour" and the grandfather of Eleanor of Aquitaine, whose reputation as foremost promulgator of courtly literature in the Northern courts, however apocryphal, has been widely mythologized, Guillaume IX can be considered the spiritual, literary, *and* biological fountainhead of courtliness. His position remains highly enigmatic as well, for although his are the first courtly vernacular poems that have come down to us in writing, they presuppose a codified network of rhetorical commonplaces, verse forms, and technical vocabulary. His frequently biting irony, coupled with a determined self-consciousness, suggests, moreover, that whatever previous tradition there was — perhaps uniquely oral in conception — is not simply being perpetuated but satirized from the depths of its premises. It is not surprising that Guillaume's small but variegated poetic corpus contains *in nuce* the themes and attitudes that will be elaborated in a host of works through the succeeding decades.

"Farai un vers de dreyt nien" ("I shall make a poem out of absolutely nothing") is the opening of Guillaume's most famous and most opaque poem — basically a *devinalh* (riddle poem), which takes the poetic tradition of erotic expression as the basis for its sequence of nonsense statements and logical contradictions.[1] The first line boldly asserts one primary quandary of expression: a poem without a subject, form adamantly separated from meaning. If the poem turns out eventually to be *about* (literally, "surrounding, in the vicinity of") love and its illusory existence, it is also about the communication of that love, a state of affairs that comes to be the cause of the illusion. Clearly, a Narcissistic hint of provocation and self-projection is much in evidence as of the courtly tradition's first written traces. The poem is *about* nothing other than the logical contradiction of the poet's own discourse, which thus takes on a verbal substance and con-

---

1 *Les Chansons de Guillaume IX*, ed. Alfred Jeanroy, CFMA 9 (Paris, 1972), pp. 6–8.

stitutes its own justification. Guillaume IX becomes the first, but certainly not the last, courtly poet to tell his reader that his lady, prominent in the already traditional poetic discourse, is in some respects a mirage or at least ineffable: "Amigu'ai ieu, no sai qui s'es" (25) ("I have a sweetheart, but I don't know who it is"). Our natural response is to consider the entire poem "nonsense," but I would submit that the famous troubadour is dead serious in his attempt to articulate his own contradictions in a coy and endlessly self-reflecting discourse whose provocative hermetic tactics have bemused and fascinated generations of readers.

In the final stanza, the *envoi,* Guillaume maintains the contradictions of expression by steering the codified address to the listener and its communicative implications into the labyrinth of his self-serving rhetoric:

>   Fag ai lo vers, no say de cuy;
>   E trametrai lo a selhuy
>   Que lo·m trametra per autruy
>   Lay vers Anjau,
>   Que·m tramezes del sieu estuy
>   La contraclau.   (37–42)

(I have made the poem, I know not of what. And I shall send it to that person who will send it for me via someone else over there toward the Anjou, so that [s]he might send me the skeleton key from his/her box.)

The first line contains a careful response to the poem's opening line. The latter, expressed in the future ("Farai") is here converted to the past ("Fag ai"). The task *has* been accomplished, the poem *does* exist, the matter is closed. Again recalling the *incipit,* Guillaume refers to the poem's lack of a subject, but here with an important difference. In the hypothetical opening statement, Guillaume's programmatic announcement, the poem was to be about nothing ("rien"); that nothing to which he alluded laid claim to an existence. In the final statement, the poem is there and the meaninglessness does not result from its containing nothing, but from the ignorance of its author, "no say de cuy." If initially we are told to expect a gap between poem and meaning, here we find a third instance of incompatibility, that which adheres to the poet's subjective vision and his incapacity to understand his own creation. A more simple questioning of authorial intentionality has perhaps never been articulated.

In the succeeding lines, Guillaume plays with the stereotyped poetic closing, the address to the *jongleur* who will carry the poem off and sing it to the ultimate addressee. The *jongleur,* often named, plays an important role in the troubadour tradition as the primary means of communicating a poem destined to be sung and accompanied with instrumental music. Here, not only is the *jongleur* not named, but "his" anonymity and multiplicity is underscored, for Guillaume speaks of a *series* of communicative acts, an anonymous chain of transmitters: "E trametrai lo a *selhuy*/Que lo·m trametra per *autruy*" (38-9). What better way of suggesting the simultaneous openness and closure of the poetic destination, the intertwining of successive reader/listeners? There is, however, a final destination, an implied end to the chain, "Lay vers Anjau" (40). One assumes that the addressee attached to this place name, similar to that of the *Rose* and scores of troubadour and *trouvère* poems, is the lady to whom the love message is addressed. But no sex is indicated, no pronoun given. A place without a person? The purpose of the transmission is given in the final lines and does not appear to have anything to do with erotic persuasion. Rather, the poem is heading to Anjou in order to be deciphered; an unnamed, undesignated person will pull the skeleton key ("contraclau") out of his (her, its) box: "Que·m tramezes del *sieu* estuy/La contraclau" (41-2). Aside from the fact that pulling a key out of one's box evokes certain sexual overtones, not atypical of Guillaume's poetry, the referent of "sieu" is left totally ambiguous. It could be a male or a female addressee, the "box" alluding to some mysterious source of wisdom. But the "estuy" could also be the poem itself – meaning that the unnamed receiver would pull the key out of the hermetically sealed container that is the poem itself. A key that, we remember, is unavailable to the poem's creator. Not simply a key, but a "*contra*clau," *the* "contraclau," a key that literally functions "against" something else, containing within its own designation an answer, a response to what is unopened in another (or its own) structure. The series of transmissions, future and optative (subjunctive) – "trametrai . . . trametra . . . tramezes" – coupled with this mysterious counter-key, places the enigma right where it belongs: in the hands of the poem's receiver who will confront the closed/open hermetic box and discover that his act is itself the unspeakable, unknowable *subject* of the poem.

Seen in this light, our interpretation of Narcissus should appear less as a shockingly modern imposition than as an inward-looking symbolic rendering of a longstanding, highly self-conscious poetic tradition. By remaining resolutely modern, my approach uncovers aspects of Guillaume's poem that could perhaps never have been articulated, or even perceived, by one of the poem's contemporary readers — which is not the same as saying that these aspects are not there to be found. Part of the reason for this resides in a very different critical sensibility; commentary on fiction at that time was much more likely to take the form of fictional rewriting (as was the case for the Grail legend) or of continuation (the *Perceval* continuations or, of course, that of Jean de Meun), or of response (the *Bestiaire d'Amours; Cligés* as fictional reply to *Tristan*). The other important factor, as we discussed in Chapter Three, is the likelihood that the *Rose,* written late in the courtly tradition and at a time when poetic discourses were becoming increasingly diversified, was received by an audience that either had little affinity for the poem or that was simply not in touch with the heavily codified and restrictive courtly paradigm. Especially by this period, the frequently echoed distinction between *courtois* and *vilain* had little to do with actual social affiliation but was probably more evocative of intellectual and aesthetic affinities.

The principal objections to my reading are, as I see it, twofold. First, it might be said that the typical courtly interpretation of the myth limited itself to aspects involving unfulfilled longing and left totally unexploited any facet of the character's self-reflexivity; the second is that moral readings of *exempla* or myths in the Middle Ages are rarely systematic or rigorous and that, consequently, it is unrealistic to read Guillaume's text so closely. There is much truth to the first objection: Treatment of Narcissus in courtly lyric is usually limited to an evocation of his name with little accounting for the entire myth as told by Ovid. The only earlier narrative account, the anonymous *Lai de Narcisse,* turns the hero into a repentant courtly lover at the end, making for a tragic ending more closely related to that of Pyramus and Thisbe. But is an individual author's departure from stereotypical elements not to be accounted for? One of the unfortunate aspects of much medieval criticism today resides in the attempt to reduce discrete works to the level of the most stereotyped forms of expression. And yet it is highly unlikely that such a diversified corpus will present *a* "medieval Narcissus" or a single version of courtly love, or, even worse, *a* "medieval mind." The variety of fictional works produced in the vernacular is astounding and it is our task to account for their multiplicity (and appreciate it), not to reduce it to its least common denominator. What we recognize to be masterpieces in the medieval corpus has in fact a lot to do with their atypicality and innovation within traditional poetic forms. Guillaume de Lorris's version of the Narcissus myth is, quite simply, unlike any other medieval retelling, involving as it does a complex interweaving between the terms of the Ovidian original and certain existential problems of the courtly lover. Not to give this vision credit for its difference is to greatly underestimate it. This leads into the second objection mentioned above, which amounts to a criticism of any close reading of medieval fiction, on the grounds that in medieval practice mythical *exempla* (and, by extension, poems themselves) only admit of very loose scrutiny. Is Narcissus, in this context, vaguely allusive, evocative solely of the most general ideas surrounding unrequited adoration? This is a possibility, but I must confess that I, as a modern reader accustomed to close readings of texts and analysis based upon what I have called in earlier sections a "logical" approach to rhetorical or narrative figures, cannot satisfy myself with interpretations of a vaguely associative nature. Only recently have medieval literary studies disposed of such deeply ingrained notions as poetic *naïveté* and inferiority of detail, as though the works would not stand up to the kind of rigorous analysis used on modern texts. What I have attempted to demonstrate, on the contrary, is the intricacy and allusive power of the text, the way in which it exploits the imagistic density of what has by now become a universal myth of perception and desire. My reading should thus not be seen as a wrenching of the poem from its original context, but rather a recontextualization of the work with the help of modern tools. If such a dual focus does not provide a recapitulation of what the medieval audience said about the poem, it might nonetheless contribute to an explanation for *why* certain works retain a fascination beyond their own limited historical framework while others do not. We are in no uncertain way responsible for the fictions that characterize us, and Narcissus, as a cultural myth, is if anything more "alive" in the twentieth century than ever.

In this sense, the variety of possible interpretations of the *exemplum* of Narcissus is itself exemplary, which is to say instructive of a certain constant in literary interpretation. This constant, which I have termed "Self-Fulfilling Prophecy," hovers over most of the steps of the present study. I have used the term little in the course of the book, for I did not intend it as a simple catchword; rather, it was meant to suggest a universal perceptual disposition in which the results of interpretive hypotheses are very likely to be the generating motivations for the hypotheses themselves. Critical terminology is never disinterested, never lacking the imprint of the results it seeks. This prior determinacy is especially significant in those critical tools and concepts that we question the least. In a certain way, the courtly poet provides a literary paradigm for the generalized idea of the Self-Fulfilling Prophecy, which for him resides in the imaginary creation of an object of desire that inevitably disappears or is deferred by the linguistic mechanisms serving to evoke that image. In the version of Guillaume, the Lover/Poet somewhat fatalistically ends up gazing into the fountain of Narcissus. The visual interplay between viewer and (reflected) image provided by the Narcissus myth is thus a symbolic rendering of the unwitting self-projection inherent in all our relations with the external world. The enticing indeterminacy of the *Rose* construct, its own acting out on a literary level of the impasse of desire, itself serves as a further myth to be read, interpreted, and projected upon. The poetic text comes to displace the desired image in its capacity as a new object of fascination, this time in a context motivated by mechanisms of literary desire. Enter Jean de Meun. When looked at on the level of theme or subject matter, Jean de Meun's continuation can be seen as a historically grounded interpretive gesture inspired by a reaction to courtly fiction that was undoubtedly shared by his contemporaries, as we may gather from the work's immediate and overwhelming popularity. This is not to say that it constituted a *condemnation* of courtliness, but rather a conversion of it to more acceptable literary models of the time, based upon a utilitarian accumulation of knowledge, and the ample dimensions of pseudo-scientific allegorical exposition.

However, the continuation also displays a persistent metacritical interest, resulting in a complex mythologizing of Jean's own interpretive act. Jean's symbolically charged *mise-à-mort* of Guillaume de Lorris (as officiated over by Amor), serving as a justification for reopening a discrete poetic text, invites our interpretation as the necessary pretext to interpretation itself. In a more traditional mythological mode, the replacement of Narcissus by Pygmalion adumbrates a passage from the static, unfulfilled act of poetic creation to a situation characterized by the perfectly externalized expression of poetic vision, which can be said to occur only in the critical discourse. Furthermore, death and life, as metaphors for completion and interpretation, are reminiscent of another, unstated myth, that of the Phoenix: Jean de Meun, we remember, will be adorned with Amor's wings (10607) once he has "arisen" from Guillaume's poetic ashes. In still another figurative context, Jean's obsession with dissemination and a contrary condition, castration (lack of fertility), suggests that the use of language, especially in the interpretive mode, is a basic, indeed quasi-biological, function.

What I have attempted to demonstrate throughout is that the nature of interpretation is frequently determined by metaphorical constructs and that poetic closure is possibly one of these. Nowhere is this more noticeable than in the work of Jean de Meun, who provides a broad interpretive program that consistently subordinates author to continuator, quest to goal, language to meaning, and myth to *sententia*. A myth of authenticity (*pace* Amor) subverts the myth of authorship, just as the continuator's life feeds directly off the author's death. The curious bipartite *Roman de la Rose* reenacts within its poetic fabric the complementary gestures of poetic creation and interpretive realignment, the latter conceived as a "new" creation in its own right. But while detailing his strategy of investing the *Rose* with new meaning, Jean is also making a strong ideological statement, one that denies the solipsism of the courtly ideal and replaces it with an encyclopedic display of knowledge. Divergent readings of Guillaume's poem as fragmentary or complete (including the present one) are thus bound to be determined by personal sympathies or beliefs in reaction with the ideological model provided (or imposed) by Jean. But however much the modern reader is unavoidably induced to read the first *Roman de la Rose* through the eyes of Jean de Meun, let him at least keep in mind the limited status of his own mythical authority.

Name and title index

(Note: For modern authors, first full bibliographical reference and, therafter, only substantive entries, are listed)

Abelard, *see* Peter Abelard
Adam de la Halle, 21*n*, 200*n*, 205*n*
Altercatio Phyllidis et Florae, 191, 199
Amor (God of Love), 134, 171, 212, 265–8, 271, 280, 283; Gui de Mori and, 43, 48–50; personified agency of, 229–34; Reson and, 236–8; speech of in Guillaume de Lorris, 165–8, 176–84; speech of in Jean de Meun, 10–14, 18–25, 78, 86–8, 100–3; Thibaut de Champagne and, 213–17, 220
Andreas Capellanus, 197, 235*n*, 249
Anonymous Mythographer, 294*n*
Aristotle, 3, 17, 118
Auerbach, Erich, 283*n*
Augustine, St., 97*n*, 122–3, 139*n*, 287*n*, 289–90

Badel, Pierre-Yves, 21*n*, 307–8
Barthes, Roland, 167
Bel Acueil, 50, 231–5, 238–45, 246–7, 253, 256, 293
Le Bel Inconnu, *see* Renaut de Beaujeu
Benveniste, Emile, 139*n*, 142–3
Béroul, 20, 304
Le Bestiaire d'Amours, *see* Richard de Fournival
Bonaventure, St., 61*n*
Bossault, Robert, 72*n*
Braet, Herman, 114*n*, 127–8

La Chanson de Roland, 18, 30, 67, 68–9, 304
La Chastelaine de Vergi, 21*n*, 205
Le Châtelain de Coucy, 195–6*n*, 201*n*, 205, 209–10
Chaytor, H. J., 28*n*
Chenu, Marie-Dominique, 61*n*, 62
Chrétien de Troyes, 18*n*, 33*n*, 113, 129*n*, 196, 258; posterity of, 45–6, 304, 306–7; separate works of: *Le Chevalier de la Charrete*, 20*n*, 32, 68, 188, 192, 252–7, 274; *Cligés*, 182–

3*n*; *Le Conte du Graal*, 20*n*, 69–70; *Erec et Enide*, 20*n*, 44*n*; *Yvain*, 44*n*, 46, 117*n*
Cicero, 118–19, 131
Crosby, Ruth, 30*n*
Curtius, Ernst Robert, 11*n*, 267*n*, 298*n*

Dangier, 87, 234–5, 238–43, 274–5; Thibaut de Champagne and, 217, 220
Dante Alighieri, 194*n*, 285
De Arte Honeste Amandi, *see* Andreas Capellanus
Delbouille, Maurice, 29*n*
Dragonetti, Roger, 19*n*, 193*n*, 194*n*, 208–9, 220, 246*n*, 275*n*
Dubois, Jean, 195*n*
Duggan, Joseph J., 30*n*, 68–9*n*

Echecs d'Amour, 56–7; gloss of (*Echecs Amoureux*), 307–8
Echo, 269–71, 272, 274, 280, 284, 288
Eisenstein, Elizabeth L., 26*n*
Eneas, 244*n*

Faral, Edmond, 5, 30*n*, 113*n*
Fleming, John V., 58–9, 75–6, 307
Florance et Blancheflor, 191, 199
Fortune, 49–50, 77, 105–6, 246
Foucault, Michel, 62–3, 90
Foulet, Alfred, 34*n*, 96–7*n*
Foulet, Lucien, 151–2
Frappier, Jean, 196*n*, 197–8, 199, 266*n*, 277*n*

Gallais, Pierre, 30*n*
Gautier de Dargies, 204
Genette, Gérard, 139*n*
Geoffroi de Vinsauf, 269*n*
Gerbert de Montreuil, 52–3*n*, 70, 206
Goldin, Frederick, 266*n*, 273*n*
Gottfried von Strassburg, 91*n*, 183*n*
Gui de Mori, 34–55, 56, 59–60, 63–4
Guiette, Robert, 114*n*, 194*n*, 196*n*

317

NAME AND TITLE INDEX

Guillaume de Dole, see Jean Renart
Guillaume IX, 309–12
Guillon, Félix, 15–16n
Guiot, 33n

Hunt, Tony, 95n, 96–7, 113n, 129n
Huon de Méry, 45–7, 70–1, 126–7n, 190, 212

Imbs, Paul, 130n, 154n

Jameson, Fredric, 187
Jauss, Hans Robert, 71n, 92n, 187n, 188–90, 236n, 268n, 269n, 281, 303
Jean de Meun, 10–14, 16–25, 36–40, 48–55, 56, 58–9, 76, 77, 81, 86–9, 90–1, 109, 207, 260, 264n, 267, 302, 314–16
Jean Renart, 52n, 189, 202–6
Le Jeu de Robin et Marion, see Adam de la Halle
Joufroi de Poitiers, 71, 193
Jung, Marc-René, 34n, 35, 36, 41, 42n, 53, 54–5, 67n, 127n, 189–90, 227n

Kelly, Douglas, 32n, 171n
Köhler, Erich, 201n, 204n, 222n, 235n, 266n, 277n
Kuhn, Alfred, 45n, 74–5, 76

Lai de Narcisse, 264n, 272–3, 282, 284, 288, 312
Langlois, Ernest, 15, 21, 22, 34n, 35, 36, 41, 48, 54–5, 65, 131
Le Gentil, Pierre, 29n
Lecoy, Félix, 16n, 23n, 65–6, 277
Lejeune, Philippe, 139n
Lejeune, Rita, 15n, 194
Lewis, C. S., 99n, 225, 277
Lubac, Henri de, 123n

McCulloch, Florence, 215n
Macrobius, 118–25, 137, 138, 180–1; as authority, 129–31, 133; dream classification of, 119–20; and neo-Platonism, 122–3
Manessier, 70
Marie de France, 20, 31n, 95–7, 244–5n, 272, 299, 304
Melior et Ydoine, 191, 199, 200
Ménard, Philippe, 152
Micha, Alexandre, 65n
Mölk, Ulrich, 11n, 204n
Montaigne, Michel de, 105–6, 109, 132n

Narcissus, 66, 75, 77, 164, 229, 263–300, 312–14; courtly poet and, 287–8, 290, 297–8, 300; moral interpretation of, 273–4, 281–3, 291–2
Nichols, Stephen G., 266n, 275n

Oiseuse, 211n, 221–3, 226, 229, 290
Ollier, Marie-Louise, 113n, 192n
Ong, Walter J., 28n
Ovid, 135, 212, 216, 272–3, 284, 288, 294–5

Partonopeu de Blois, 71, 193, 202, 304
Pépin, Jean, 123n
Peter Abelard, 139n
Philibertus, 57–9
Philostratus, 1–3, 4, 8–9
Pickens, Rupert T., 120n
Pidal, Ramón Menéndez, 18n, 29n, 68n
Plato, 131
Plotinus, 294
Poirion, Daniel, 5–6, 10n, 264n, 275n
Pouillon, Jean, 140
Prose Lancelot, 32, 306
Pyramus and Thisbe, 272, 312

Raoul de Houdenc, 45–6, 190
Renaut de Beaujeu, 71, 192, 196, 202
Reson (Lady Reason), see Amor, Reson and
Richard de Fournival, xiv, 21–2, 43, 71–2, 200n, 205n, 215n, 275n
Riffaterre, Michael, 188
Robertson, D. W., Jr., 120n, 123n, 277n
Le Roman de la Poire, 21, 23n
Le Roman de Renart, 31, 72–3
Le Roman de la Rose, authorship of, 10–17, 39–40, 56–7, 89–91, see also Gui de Mori, Philibertus; manuscripts of, 21–4, 35–6, 45n, 58, 77–89, 178n, 207; reception of, 259–60, 304–8
Le Roman de la Violette, see Gerbert de Montreuil
Rouard, M., 36n, 39n, 50
Rychner, Jean, 28n, 192n, 266n, 277n

Segre, Cesare, 29n, 43n
Smith, Barbara Herrnstein, 107
Spearing, A. C., 109n
Starobinski, Jean, 139n

Thibaut de Champagne, 200n, 213–20, 256–7

318

Thomas, 182, 216, 272, 304
Le Tornoiement d'Antechrist, see Huon de Méry
Tyssens, Madeleine, 72–3n

Venus, 211n, 234–6, 241–2, 265, 268n
Vinaver, Eugène, 27n

Vinge, Louise, 263n, 294n
Virgil, 124–5, 126n
Vitz, E. B., 110n, 138n, 139n

Zink, Michel, 30n, 189n, 194
Zumthor, Paul, 17n, 18n, 28n, 67, 114n, 191, 194n, 195, 204–5, 250n, 269n

Topical index

abstractum agens, 220n
ainz, 130
allegory; Biblical exegesis and, 96–7, 122–3, 190, 266–7; end-oriented nature of, 166–8, 184–5, 289–90; exemplary narrative and, 269n, 285–6, 291, *see also exemplum;* figural interpretation (typology) and, 283; obscurity of, 96–7, 122–5, 289; personification and, 189–90, 211–12, 217–18, 220–7, 244–6, 249–50, 292–3; reader-reception and, 96–7, 167–8; *see also* dreams, prophetic structure of
anonymity, *see* author, naming of
anonymous conclusion, 22–3, 39, 89, 175
auctor, aucteur, 45n, 61–2, 92, 118, 133, 160n; mention of in exemplary narrative, 269n
auctoritas, 62
author; naming of, 14–15, 24, 31–2, 47–9, 51–2, 54–5, 63, 89–92, 102–4; portraits of, 15, 45n, 58, 74–89, 200n
authority, expression of, 43–5, 128, 131–3, 160–9, 180–1, 315–16, *see also* dreams, prophetic structure of
authorship; fictionalization of, 12–14, 16–21, 49–51, 89, 98–101, 205n; historical conception of, 16–21, 24–5, 26–34, 56, 60–2, 100–1, *see also* Foucault, Michel; intentionality and, 74, 91, 94–5, 102, 175; originality and, 29–30, 32–3, 46–7, 63, 94; scribal intervention and, 43, 52, 54–5, 59, 78–81, 91–2, 109
autobiography, narration of, 138–41, 158, 169–70

chanson (lyric), 67, 135, 194–202, 205, 248, 259; expressive register of, 206–7, 267–8; metaphorical expression in, 210–11; nature motifs and, *see Natureingang;* versus romance, 197–8, 210–11; *see also* Thibaut de Champagne
chansons de geste, 29–30, 31, 32, 67, 72–3, 127–8, 260

clercs and *chevaliers,* debate between, 191, 198–200, 257–8, 299
closure; metaphors of, 101, 182–4, 295–6; narrative, 160, 175, 178, 183–5, 293–4; poetic, 25, 100, 103, 105–8, 260–2
compilation, manuscript, 21–2n, 60, 72–4
composition, oral, 27–30, 67, 73; and bilingualism, 28–9
continuation, poetic, 13, 23, 39, 49–50, 53, 54–5, 69–72; visual depiction of, 81f, 83, 86
courtly love, 190, 194–7
cuer, 177, 216–17, 219, 237, 247

discours, narrative register of, 139–40, 142–3, 145t, 147, 156n, 157–8, 160–1, 169; *see also je* (first-person pronoun); *puis* (adverb); verb tense
dreams, 109–74; allegorical exposition and, 168–9, *see also somnium;* doctrinal value of, 163–9; interpretation of, *see* Macrobius; narration of, 111–12, 115–18, 127–9, 142, 158–9, 173–4, *see also* autobiography, narration of; prophetic structure of, 116–17, 125–6, 127–9, 136–8, 141–2, 164, 170–4

edition, critical, of medieval texts, 64–6, 98
énonciation, 195
entention, 35, 44, 188
exemplum, 228, 233, 274, 282, 291, 312–14; personification and, 268–9

fable, fabula, 117, 121; and *narratio fabulosa,* 121–2
fabliau, 31, 243
fragmentariness, *see* closure, poetic

genres, literary, 31, 186–90, 257–60
gradus amoris, 230–3

histoire, narrative register of, 139–40, 142–3, 145t, 157–8, 160, 169

320

insomnium, 119–20, 180
intertextuality, 188–9

je (first-person pronoun), 142–3, 145*t*, 150–1, 159

literacy, 31, 60
livre, 53–4, 165, 182, 184
losangier, 201*n*

manuscripts, production of, 21–2, 304–5; see also compilation, manuscript
matiere, 35, 44
mensonge, 114, 116–18, 180
mythology, uses of, 265, 268–70, 290, 291–3, 314–15

narration, levels of, *see* autobiography, narration of; *discours*; dreams, narration of; *histoire*
Natureingang, 208–11, 248, 266–8

oeuvre, 58–9
ombre, umbra, 270, 280, 286, 292
or, 156*n*
oraculum, 119–20
orality, *see* composition, oral

parfaire, 58–9, 78, 89
pastourelle, 190–1, 208
printing; author-idea and, 26, 64; standardization of texts and, 27, 65–6
prologue, 113–15, 129–37, 163–6, 172; rhetorical use of, 43, 113
puis (adverb), 153–4

quotation, 11, 92, 160*n*, 176, 185

reader; role of, 15, 73–4, 81–2, 97, 108–9, 167–8, 288–9; scribe as, 67–8, 298–9
reception, literary, 92, 95–9, 168, 259–60, 304–5
reverdie, 162, 208, 212
roman, 30–1, 53, 164–5, 182

scribe; reading and interpretation of, 34, 66–8, 109; role of, 33–4, 39, 60–1, 76–7, 298*n*; *see also* reader, role of; authorship, scribal intervention and
senefiance, 131, 163, 166, 169, 171, 281
sens, 32, 68, 96–7, 188
sententia, 129, 133, 273–5, 291
somnium, 119–20, 122*n*, 123
songe, 114, 117–18, 180

trobar clus, 203–4
trouvères, 200*n*, 201*n*, 204, 218

unity, poetic, 59, 63–4, 72–4

verb tense, 142–4, 145*t*; future, 12, 143–5, 177; historical present, 146–50, 152, 154; imperfect, 143–5, 146, 149; passé composé, 142–5, 149, 151–3, 154, 155, 159; passé simple (preterite), 143–5, 146, 149, 155, 156, 158, 159, 171; present, 12, 142–5, 146, 155, 156–8, 159, 171, 195
verité, 97, 133, 163, 169, 171, 281; ending and, 164, 166, 289
vernacular, *see* composition, oral, and bilingualism
vers, 157, 158, 297–8
vidas, 71, 205–6
visio, 119–20
visum, 119–20, 180–1